Jeremy Brett Playing a Part

Maureen Whittaker

First edition published in 2019
© Copyright 2019, 2020
Maureen Whittaker

The right of Maureen Whittaker to be identified as the author of this work has been asserted by her in accordance with the Copyright, Designs and Patents Act 1998.

All rights reserved. No reproduction, copy or transmission of this publication may be made without express prior written permission. No paragraph of this publication may be reproduced, copied or transmitted except with express prior written permission or in accordance with the provisions of the Copyright Act 1956 (as amended). Any person who commits any unauthorised act in relation to this publication may be liable to criminal prosecution and civil claims for damage.

Every effort has been made to ensure the accuracy of the information contained in this book. The opinions expressed herein are those of the author and not of MX Publishing.

Hardcover ISBN 978-1-78705-588-9
Paperback ISBN 978-1-78705-589-6
ePub ISBN 978-1-78705-590-2
PDF ISBN 978-1-78705-591-9

Published by MX Publishing
335 Princess Park Manor, Royal Drive,
London, N11 3GX
www.mxpublishing.com

Cover compilation by Brian Belanger

Special thanks to Richard Ryan, Gretchen Altabef and Steve Emecz for their support in editing and compiling this book.

Contents

Foreword by David Burke	*5*
Introduction	*7*
Beginnings	
- *Berkswell*	*10*
- *Eton*	*21*
- *Central School*	*25*
Film Television & The Stage	*29*
Manchester Library Theatre	*31*
The Old Vic	*39*
Musical Theatre	*45*
Jeremy and Anna	*55*
Television	*80*
Films – 1960s	*95*
The National Theatre 1963	*102*
Hollywood	*106*
Death of Colonel Huggins	*120*
Television	*125*
National Theatre – 1967 – 1971	*142*
A New Decade A New Approach	*177*
Television	*185*
Canada and USA	*211*
Home and Away – 1980s	*245*
Sherlock Holmes	*281*
- *Jeremy and Joan*	*331*
- *The Secret*	*385*
- *Jeremy and Linda*	*425*
Afterword by Linda Pritchard	*455*
Tributes	*459*
Appendix	*461*
Bibliography	*462*

Foreword by David Burke

Arthur Conan Doyle was a man at war with his own genius. Detective fiction, a genre he had virtually created, seemed to him an inferior art form. The public knew better and refused to let matters rest. His Holmes was literally resurrected, after which he achieved a sort of immortality and certainly provided Doyle with the kind of wealth few writers are blessed to enjoy. Again and again in his private correspondence, he complained of the treadmill of the Sherlock Holmes stories, but when Doyle died, his creation was still alive and, so far as I know, is still striding up and down Baker Street today.

Sherlock Holmes has continued to make money for others too. There have been feature films and television films based on the stories. In many cases their authenticity is in serious doubt. Many people identify Holmes with Basil Rathbone's impersonation, but those Hollywood based films bear little connection with the original stories beyond the actor's hawkish profile and deerstalker hat.

I was myself lucky enough to be involved as Dr. Watson in the mammoth Granada TV series which began in 1983 and continued long after I had left it. This series owed a colossal debt to its first producer, Michael Cox. It was he who set it up and was responsible for the inspired casting of Jeremy Brett as the famous detective.

At the time I knew Jeremy Brett only by name. He was chiefly famed for two things: his physical beauty, which even in middle age caused grown women to swoon and for being a little mad. The madness I soon discovered was largely a delightful streak of eccentricity and determination to "celebrate" in spite of almost anything life threw at him. He once entertained a lady friend to lunch in the workaday BBC canteen by covering the plastic formica with a fine linen tablecloth upon which he placed a brass candelabra and some sweet-smelling freesias in a fine china vase.

While at Granada Studios in Manchester, I grew used to Jeremy arriving in the make-up room extolling the beautiful day waiting for us outside. "But, Jeremy," I would protest, "It's pouring with rain!"

"Of course, my dear," he would reply. "But the liquid atmosphere will make us both look wonderful."

Jeremy was generous to a fault in celebrating the people who were working alongside him to create this phenomenal successful series. He would use a Polaroid camera to take snaps of every member of the crew and post these up on a notice board for everyone to see creating a warm family atmosphere among all those talented folk. He was also diligent to the point of obsession in ensuring that what the viewer saw and heard on screen was faithful to the word on the page.

The Collected Stories were his Bible and went everywhere with him, and woe betide the writer or director who did not have a good reason for deviating from the original. He once insisted on a retake because he had worn his deerstalker back to front. No one but Jeremy could know which was the back and which the front of this eminently symmetrical hat. But he was not po-faced about these things and was the first to laugh at himself.

He told me how he once accosted a helmeted police constable on Clapham Common and congratulated him at great length and in the most flowery of language on the increase in the number of bobbies on the beat, recently promised by the Home Secretary. He concluded by saying, "We the public will all be grateful to you splendid fellows that we shall be able to sleep more safely in our beds." The policeman replied, "Why don't you p*** off, sir," and plodded on his way. The irony of the situation was not lost on Jeremy, and he could hardly contain his mirth.

I miss my dear friend's passion and humour, qualities which he brought to his peerless interpretation of the world's greatest detective.

David Burke 2017

Introduction

For many people Jeremy Brett remains the quintessential Sherlock Holmes, featured in the Granada *Sherlock Holmes* series for the Independent Television Network, and indeed some people know of him only through this performance. His outstanding success as the unique genius detective would forever link him with the character much as Basil Rathbone had been fifty years earlier. However, his work encompassed much more than this one portrayal. His career covered thirty years on stage, film and television before he accepted the role which brought him international fame as a great actor.

Jeremy's commanding stage presence at the age of 26 made him a "noble and poetic Hamlet" at the Strand Theatre. His interpretation was proclaimed a critical success for such a young and fresh actor. Just a few years later in 1966, his outstanding portrayal as the dashing, passionate hero D'Artagnan in *The Three Musketeers* for the BBC Sunday serial thrust him into the public spotlight. For those who grew up with the *Play of the Month* on BBC Television on a Sunday evening, Jeremy's appearance as the romantic lead was always welcome. His good looks made him perfect casting for the attractive yet dangerous Lord Byron and as a supremely handsome Captain Jack Absolute in *The Rivals,* he revelled in heroic exploits. In contrast, as the duplicitous Joseph Surface in *A School for Scandal* he explored the role of the anti-hero; *"outwardly a paragon of virtue, but inwardly a miserly fortune hunter."* The classics would become a familiar platform for his rich, modulated tones. He excelled as a haunted Maxim de Winter in *Rebecca*; the tortured, yet morally maimed, Edward Ashburnham in *The Good Soldier*; the fervent Robert Browning and the *'fascinating'* William Pitt – all created with authenticity and passion. Through consistently outstanding performances Jeremy had attracted a loyal and firm fan base.

Visitors to the National Theatre from the years 1967 to 1971 would have seen him in the roles of which he was most proud as he worked with his mentor and "*great God,*" Lord Olivier: playing the romantic suitor Bassanio to Joan Plowright's Portia in *The Merchant of Venice*; Orlando to Ronald Pickup's Rosalind, in the modern day all-male production of *As You Like It* and as the first of Shakespeare's great human beings, Berowne in *Love's Labour's Lost*, a part which he "*adored*" and made his own. His portrayal of Che Guevara was perhaps the most significant role at this time. The critics praised him for a performance "of considerable imagination and power." His career in the United States was also memorable with his introduction to Hollywood in *War and Peace* in 1955 as Audrey Hepburn's youthful, exuberant brother, Nicholas Rostov, and again playing opposite Audrey as Eliza's romantic suitor, the charming Freddie Eynsford Hill in *My Fair Lady*. Later, he would be praised and rewarded for his Broadway *Dracula* and also for his Doctor Watson in *A Crucifer of Blood* with Charlton Heston as Sherlock Holmes which would be helpful a few years on.

With a career of this length which covered such a wide range of roles, it is no surprise that Michael Cox, an executive producer of Granada Television, chose Jeremy for the role of Sherlock Holmes in the new Granada series, *The Adventures of Sherlock Holmes*. He wanted a man with the voice, the bearing and the presence of a classically trained actor; someone who could jump over sofas or pursue a clue like a bloodhound, often on his hands and knees. In Jeremy he found all this and much more. Not only did he become the definitive interpreter of the role, but he also brought a new army of fans who were intrigued by this new Holmes, and for some reason, spellbound by the chemistry that existed between actor and camera.

Many people tell of Sunday evenings kept special for the weekly pilgrimage to Victorian London in the company of Jeremy Brett and David Burke, his first Doctor Watson. The series ran for ten years in which Jeremy "*became*" Sherlock Holmes. When David Burke left the series, Jeremy exchanged his first Watson for Edward Hardwicke. Together they finished the series and wowed a new army of fans at Wyndhams Theatre from 1988-89 when the play Jeremy commissioned, *The Secret of Sherlock Holmes* filled the theatre every night.

As an actor, Jeremy was a perfectionist and set himself the highest standards in his work: his sheer enthusiasm for his art, his professionalism, hard work and commitment would earn him many accolades over the years. When he died in 1995, David Stuart Davies in his book *Bending the Willow*, expressed what many people felt: "Jeremy Brett's sudden death in September 1995 robbed the acting world of one of its incandescent lights and the world of Sherlock Holmes of one of its finest – debatably its greatest – interpreter of that complex creature who dwelt at 221B Baker Street." Many people still feel that this is the case twenty five years after his death. Peter Wyngarde, one of his co-stars in *The Three Gables* an episode of *The Memoirs of Sherlock Holmes* caught the man when he said: "Jeremy's absolute dedication was phenomenal. It was not selfish. It wasn't for him, it wasn't for Jeremy Brett – it was for Sherlock Holmes." Alan Coren who wrote for *The Mail*, said: "Jeremy Brett's performance is still so superlative that no superlatives of mine are adequate to describe it."

In Oscar Wilde's *A Picture of Dorian Gray,* a story that Jeremy played twice, once as Dorian and the other as the artist Basil Hallward who says, *"Any portrait painted with feeling is a portrait of the artist."* Jeremy was a man of great feeling, and this was a major contribution to his success on stage. In his personal life he suffered too much from life's slings and arrows. Until the age of seventeen he was tongue-tied and suffered from dyslexia throughout his life. His rheumatic fever at the age of sixteen, with its legacy of heart trouble, had changed him from the sport-loving, constantly active young man into a human being of great compassion and warmth. The traumatic loss of the two people he loved the most – his mother and his second wife, Joan – both of whom died too soon, brought a great deal of emotional turmoil from which he never really recovered. Consequently, his response to others showed great sensitivity and understanding; he was a man who was universally loved, and yet he displayed the common touch with a willingness and ability to share his experience. He had a strong desire to achieve his dreams even if it took all of his courage to do so. He became an inspiration to fellow sufferers of manic depression as he movingly and eloquently shared his experience of the condition which dogged his final years. Many who worked with Jeremy talk about his joyful spirit, a life lived as if it were a celebration, or "*a festival*". He always loved to sing and although we do not have any record of the remarkable soprano voice of his youth, we can admire his pleasant baritone in his performance as Danilo in *The Merry Widow* which is available on record. Dancing was also a source of great enjoyment for him. His extraordinary generosity and his exuberant welcome were celebrated by all who visited him and those privileged people still hold him in the highest esteem. They remember every detail of their meeting and sincerely wish he had received some recognition for his extraordinary achievements.

During interviews Jeremy was always self-effacing, always praising his colleagues and never taking the credit for himself, even when it was most deserved. His humility showed the Quaker values of hard work and equality, and he became a reflection of his mother, Elizabeth, whom he described as beautiful inside and out and as a light of great warmth. It seems appropriate to approach a record of his work with his words wherever possible. It also gives the essence of the man who was very much part of a team, even when he led it, as he did in the Granada *Sherlock Holmes* series. In this book I wish to honour his privacy and if he didn't give details of his private life then it isn't included here.

A *TV Times* article on 24th February 1973, gave a resume of his life to date: "On the handsome face of it, actor Jeremy Brett would appear to be the man who had everything: looks, talent, security. Then there's his Eton education, fame at 21, a fashionable marriage at 24 (wedding snaps taken by courtesy of Anthony Armstrong-Jones, as he was then), leading ladies of the calibre of Audrey Hepburn, Ingrid Bergman and Deborah Kerr, and a son and heir on whom he dotes and who has just won first place in an all public schools examination to Radley. Could a chap with the plain, no-nonsense name of Huggins ask for more?" (1) Indeed, he appeared to have taken every advantage that his life had offered and his family life seems to have been ideal.

Beginnings

Berkswell Grange - By Courtesy of S. Rubin

"It all started for me on 3rd November 1933. I began life with everything a child could wish for. We had a huge, glorious, country house on the outskirts of Berkswell, near Coventry, with tennis courts, squash courts, horses and dogs, and a wonderful terraced garden created by my artistic mother, Elizabeth. The family was spoiled rotten, for we had three live-in staff, plus four other people who came in to help. We always seemed to be entertaining a houseful of fascinating people; the door was always open." (4)

The Huggins family was a significant part of the delightful Berkswell village in Warwickshire. William and Elizabeth had decided to move to the rambling, attractive Berkswell Grange in 1929 to accommodate a growing family. The three boys, John, Michael and Patrick needed somewhere to play and to ride, so the move from Holly Lodge in Duggins Lane, the home bought for them as a wedding present by the groom's father, was necessary. A large impressive house was chosen in nearby Truggist Lane. The house featured seventeenth century timber framing, and nineteenth century additions, including a tiled roof.

Colonel Henry William Huggins, Bill to his family and friends, was born in King's Norton, Worcestershire and became a distinguished soldier. He was commissioned as 2nd Lieutenant to the Warwickshire Royal Horse Artillery and saw action in all the major battles of World War I, being mentioned in despatches five times, decorated with the DSO and the Military Cross by the end of the First World War. He left the army in 1920 with the rank of major and joined the family business as managing director. *"My father, Colonel Henry William Huggins (Huggins is my real name), a much-decorated hero of the First World War, had a peacetime position with a firm called Tube Investments. In my childhood memory, he seems to me to have spent a lot of time on horseback. Then, after the Second World War broke out, he was away from home running an army training camp in North Wales."* (4)

Berkswell Grange

Jeremy was proud of his father's war record and that was the first detail he gave whenever he was asked. *"My father... was very famous, a great soldier, decorated, honoured... a particularly successful soldier by which I mean he was sufficiently cowardly to be incredibly brave. Trying to prove himself and conquer his cowardice he earned one of the first DSO's of World War One and twice won the M.C."* (2) He told his interviewer on Desert Island Discs: *"I was so proud of him because he had won so many medals... and he once had the grace to tell me as a child that he only won them because he was so frightened."* Jeremy requested the record of *The Tuba Mirum* from Mozart's *Requiem* as it reminded him of his father. *"He used to play the bugle and the beginning notes of the* Mozart Requiem, *this particular part, reminds me of a misty morning with the sun coming across the fields."* (3)

His father was a large, strong-chinned man of twenty eight when he met Jeremy's mother, Elizabeth Edith Butler, in a Quaker meeting house in Birmingham, and fell in love. She was from a wealthy, prominent Quaker family, the great granddaughter of John Cadbury who with his brother Benjamin set up the Bournville Estate in Birmingham as an expression of their belief in social responsibility and social reform to ensure that all human beings should be treated equally. She was a beautiful young girl of nineteen with a traditional Victorian upbringing and he courted her by pushing notes under her bedroom door. They married in 1923. *"I'm told that when they drove away from the wedding, my father said: 'Where shall we go now?' And my mother said: 'I've always dreamed of Paris.' So off they went to Paris and he got chicken pox. It was an improbable marriage of opposites."* (1)

The Grange, where Peter William Jeremy, affectionately named Benjamin by his parents, was born, is a beautiful house with sweet smelling flowering wisteria on the front elevation and nestled in a magical vista of gardens, landscaped by Elizabeth, known as "Bunny", who was the centre of this loving family. New additions included a dovecot, stables, a squash court, tennis courts and the essential air-raid shelter. When he was three years old Jeremy's hand print was placed in the cement of the new exterior wall of the house as the vast nursery which had been constructed in the west wing was reduced in size and eventually became the snooker room. This remains as a permanent reminder of his presence.

Jeremy's handprint - By Courtesy of S. Rubin

Berkswell Grange

Due to its grandeur and welcoming hostess, the Grange was the centre of village events, of Christmas parties, of afternoon teas and of music and entertainment. William's brother, Dr. Leslie Huggins, was *"a doctor of Music and a master of foxhounds, which was an amazing combination. He was music master of Radley School in Stowe – Radley where my son went to school – an amazing man... and we had a huge drawing room with a grand piano at the end and when he arrived, I used to drag him to it and make him play, which I'm happy to say he was happy to do. Yes, my whole home was full of music. I had the most wonderful family life."* (3)

He told one interviewer that he had *"a marvellous youth with every kind of animal under the sun, from ferrets to rabbits to mice to horses, to monkeys even. It was like a paradise, and a gorgeous home."* Horses were a familiar sight at the Grange, and Jeremy was very proud of his own pony Babs whom he taught to climb stairs and frequently teased Nanny Clifford by riding her up to bed. Unfortunately, Babs left behind some unpleasant reminders of her presence which would not have been welcome. The fact that she was unwilling to go down the stairs would have been another unwelcome character trait. Jeremy soon had riding lessons and took his place in the local gymkhanas. He spent a great deal of time at the stables;

practising his riding skills on Balsall Common, or riding across the unhappy neighbours' gardens and at Eton he enjoyed riding across the 5,000 acres of Windsor Great Park. In an interview with Terry Wogan in 1988 he revealed that he wanted to be a cowboy from a very early age. The time spent watching the cowboy films at the cinema on the Common had sparked that interest in him although in the same interview he went on to say that it had really been a dream as his English accent would have been unsuited for the role. Riding was something at which he excelled and he was always at home in the saddle. His relationship with horses is clearly based on mutual respect between a man and his mount: apples and sugar were ready in his pockets if he knew his horse was to be on the Granada film set, and he was bubbling with joy at the prospect of riding again. Jeremy had a very special relationship with all animals. He welcomed dogs as earnestly as he welcomed his friends and often on his knees to greet them, face to face. His own dog, Mr. Binks was a Jack Russell terrier that he affectionately called his *"hound of heaven."* Jeremy's explanation for this treasured relationship was that his brothers were considerably older than he and his speech impediment meant he was often lonely in his youth, so he learnt to speak to anything that was available. *"I had three brothers, being the youngest by five years I was a bit resentful for I got their throw-out clothes and in school holidays they went off on their own whilst I spent the time with nanny. Compared with my brothers I felt so tiddly. I did have my own awful gang of pals, but often I'd be hurled into the company of my cousin Joanna, who was the same age as me. To express my annoyance I'd pull her hair and cut her plaits, which made her very cross. When we were both eighteen and no longer forcibly lumbered with each other, we became good friends and today we see each other often."* (4)

Jeremy reading his Dandy at the door of the Grange

Jeremy astride his horse

Ellen Clifford appears as the traditional nanny, plump, and smiling whilst pushing the young Jeremy in his pram or having afternoon tea on the lawn of the Grange and she was with the family for 53 years, having been Elizabeth's own nanny. Jeremy may have created the mistaken impression that she was all starch and unfeeling in interview where Jeremy explained the inner life he had created in order to get into the character of the emotionally challenged Sherlock Holmes. He said he had imagined a Victorian nanny who *"scrubbed him, but never kissed him. I don't think he probably saw his mother until he was about eight."* (23) He would later correct any misapprehension with his love for his nanny. *"She was a little cottage-loaf shape like Judi Dench and she used to wear straw hats and starched aprons. Basically, nanny and I were like lovers because when I was very small she used to sleep in the same room as me. So I knew all about her fascinating corsets and combinations. I used to help her do them up. In the late 1950s she and my mother went to the local cinema to see me in the film version of 'War and Peace'. It lasted four hours or something. At the end my nanny said. 'No, I'm going to watch it once more for Master Jeremy.' I adored her."* (5)

Pictures of Jeremy at the Grange are always of a smiling, charming boy, well-scrubbed, traditionally dressed and capturing the attention of the viewer, something for which he was renowned in his career. *"As a small child I loved entertaining people. At the age of three, when we held the village party in our grounds, I was put into a wonderful pixie costume and took part in a performance of 'Sing a Song of Sixpence'. On reaching the bit where the blackbirds come out of the pie, I suppose I looked incongruous as a pixie among the blackbirds, but this didn't bother me. I wasn't a bit shy – shyness came later. At around the same age I made my 'cabaret debut' as Little Boy Blue in a concert at Bournville, for my mother was a member of the Cadbury family."* (4)

Colonel Huggins had given all the boys a love for the outdoor life: swimming, tennis and riding to hounds. Jeremy remembered his own first blooding at the age of eight and was proud of his attendance at the North Warwickshire hunts. This is maybe a controversial sport today but it was very much part of the countryside tradition and a regular occasion for the whole family. Archery was another sport at which the four sons excelled. William and Elizabeth were both keen archers so it is no surprise that Jeremy took this seriously and belonged to the Woodmen of Arden, a notable club for the sport. *"You really have to concentrate if you take up archery. My brother John shot two of his teeth out once, simply forgot to take the pipe out of his mouth… Accidents will happen. On another occasion my brother Michael winged someone walking in the woods near the targets. Nunky was the old chap's name and the arrow hit him in the arm. But he couldn't have been nicer about it… The whole family were toxophilites. Actually my mother was a brilliant archer, won many awards. She had a special lightweight bow, and when I was growing up I used her hand-me-downs. Looking back I must have been about four or five when my father gave me my first lesson. The outfit is really glamorous – Lincoln green cut-away tailcoat, buff waistcoat with gold buttons, white slacks, white shoes and a New Zealand style hat that turns up at the side…"* (7)

Archery Week was hosted by the Huggins family at the beginning of August each year and to accompany the competitions on the extensive grounds at the Grange, they featured special balls for about 30 or 40 people for dinner followed by dancing in the ballroom. *"The dancing finished so late that breakfast was often served to the guests before they left for home the following day."* (6) *"Naturally, I'd been practising like mad for the occasion. Firing at 100 yards I nervously let the arrow go. It wobbled in the air and to my astonishment landed smack in the middle of the target. I was made Master Forester on my first day – a title which carries with it sitting at the High Table. Socially, archery can be pretty heavy going. That day the lunch ran to 12 toasts and I remember staggering out afterwards full of venison and summer pudding, cheeks pink from the port and nose still twitching from my first pinch of snuff…"* (7)

Jeremy enjoyed archery throughout his life and in his final home overlooking Clapham Common in South London, he would do early morning archery practice using the large horse chestnut tree facing his apartment; the eighteenth century gatehouse on North Side. His bow would be kept above the bath so that it could remain pliable and ready to use. *"First thing in the morning I slip out of my flat with my bow and arrows and aim at an enormous cushion placed at the foot of a tree. The moment it's light I have only about 10 minutes before people start arriving. Then I have to pack up because it's no longer safe."* (7) His expertise can be seen in the Sherlock Holmes episode *The Problem of Thor Bridge* where Sherlock is challenged by Neil Gibson, played by Jeremy's brother-in-law Daniel Massey although it has been said that he took care not to outshine Gibson.

William Henry Huggins

Elizabeth Edith Huggins

John, Michael, Patrick and Jeremy

Elizabeth Huggins had an enormous effect on the growing Jeremy and some would say that he was very like her in his response to others. *"My mother had this extraordinary way of making us flower. She wasn't just my mother; her name was Elizabeth, and she had open doors and windows in her soul – that's the only way I can put it. Everybody came to my mother. She was a like a light of great warmth."* (8) *"Money to me is a very complicated game and I'm not very good at it. I try very hard, but I regard it merely as a necessary means to an end. I've no idea how to look after it. And my parents had no idea either. My aunt was telling me a story about them recently. It seems the bank manager came to tea and looked rather worried. My mother asked him the reason. 'It's your overdraft,' he said. 'Oh, Lord! How dreadful,' said my mother. 'You mean you want some money? Of course! Now where did I put my cheque book?'"* (1)

Her reputation was always one of kindness to others, especially towards the homeless in the community. Gypsies and vagrants were frequent visitors expecting to be fed, have a wash or receive fresh clothing, and William's shirts or trousers, could often be seen on these visitors leaving the Grange. Coded signs were left behind to show that this was a house where help could be found. One tramp, by the name of John Dixon, showed his love and appreciation for Mrs. Huggins – he was killed in an accident and a note in his pocket left a little bag and all his worldly goods to her. She, apparently, had an arrangement with the bank whereby he could collect half a crown if he needed it. Mrs. Huggins would go out and find Gypsies, taking them back to the Grange – the Colonel would come home from work to find a "Gypsy encampment with a great cauldron in the walled court-yard, and clothes being dried in the saddle-room." As payment they would "pretend to do some gardening" but Jeremy can remember Tom Houghton, the gardener, saying "they're not doing much."(6)

During the Coventry bombing on 14th November 1940, in which more than four thousand homes were destroyed, including the 14th century cathedral, Jeremy's mother, alerted by the sirens, the noise of exploding bombs and the sight of leaping flames across the open countryside, left her family to drive to the nearby town to do what she could to help those who were caught up in the devastation. "The whole city was ringed with leaping flames, bathed in brilliant moonlight and a few searchlights were sweeping the smoke-filled sky." (9) Consequently, one family was taken into the Grange and 42 members of the extended family lived there until alternative accommodations could be found. There was no question in her mind about the decision; it was simply her first and characteristic response to suffering. She also left a special bouquet of flowers on the altar of the ruined cathedral for those who had suffered as a result of the bombing. Jeremy and his brothers did not discover her involvement in this heartfelt gesture until after her death in 1959. *"She was a dazzling woman, half Irish and fully Quaker, and ran our home, a large country house deep in the Black Country outside Coventry, in a sort of Flower Power way, always filling it with people that she'd picked up. I remember her bringing home a whole family called Weston during the war and all of them stayed in our stables."* (5)

Elizabeth was also a proud member of the Cadbury family who had created a whole village community to bring comfort and security to the people of Birmingham, and Jeremy had inherited the same values. There were many stories of how he had personally telephoned to thank those who left him gifts at the Stage Door of Wyndham's Theatre or who wrote to request his assistance with some project. Indeed, the request that Linda Pritchard made for help in publicising her 5,000 mile run around Great Britain in aid of Cancer Research showed just how much he was prepared to become involved. His support was invaluable and in the process Linda and Jeremy became very close and lived together for the last few years of his life.

William became Lord Lieutenant of Warwickshire and served as Master Forrester from 1936 to 1960. With the approaching Second World War he had been promoted to the rank of Lieutenant Colonel and given charge of 600 volunteers who regarded him with admiration and absolute loyalty. He may have been described as "hot-tempered" but he earned enormous respect as a leader of men who led by example. He would never ask his men to do something he himself wouldn't do, as on one occasion he cycled to the top of the hill in treacherous mountain terrain on his motorcycle, saying, "There you are, if I can do it, you bloody well can." In the home Mrs. Huggins was less easily persuaded. When the boys were growing up he was understandably upset by their lack of purposeful occupation, whilst she insisted that they should do nothing foolish or indeed anything that they didn't want to do. *"I remember one time [my father] came back and found four huge men lying in this immense drawing room in the country, all exquisitely dressed in lovely clean white shirts, trying to work out what they were going to do with their lives. I had an amazing mother who used to say to us, 'I don't want you to do anything until you absolutely can't help it, or you're sure you want to do it.' Then, when my father would come home and scream, 'For God's sake, get these boys going!' my mother would answer: 'Not until they know what they want.'"* Jeremy thought they were "desperately unhappy, but stayed together for the children... People didn't get divorced in those days; they stayed together... Looking back, I'm very proud of what my parents did. They *sacrificed a great deal."* (8) In spite of the tensions and differences between them, their four sons were each a credit to them: the eldest John became a clergyman, the second Michael a painter and Patrick was a farmer. Jeremy carved out his own very different path in the theatre. His career of forty years saw him acting with many of the great lights of the theatre, such as Laurence Olivier, John Gielgud, Maggie Smith, Judi Dench, Derek Jacobi and all before his name became synonymous with the familiar incarnation of Sherlock Holmes.

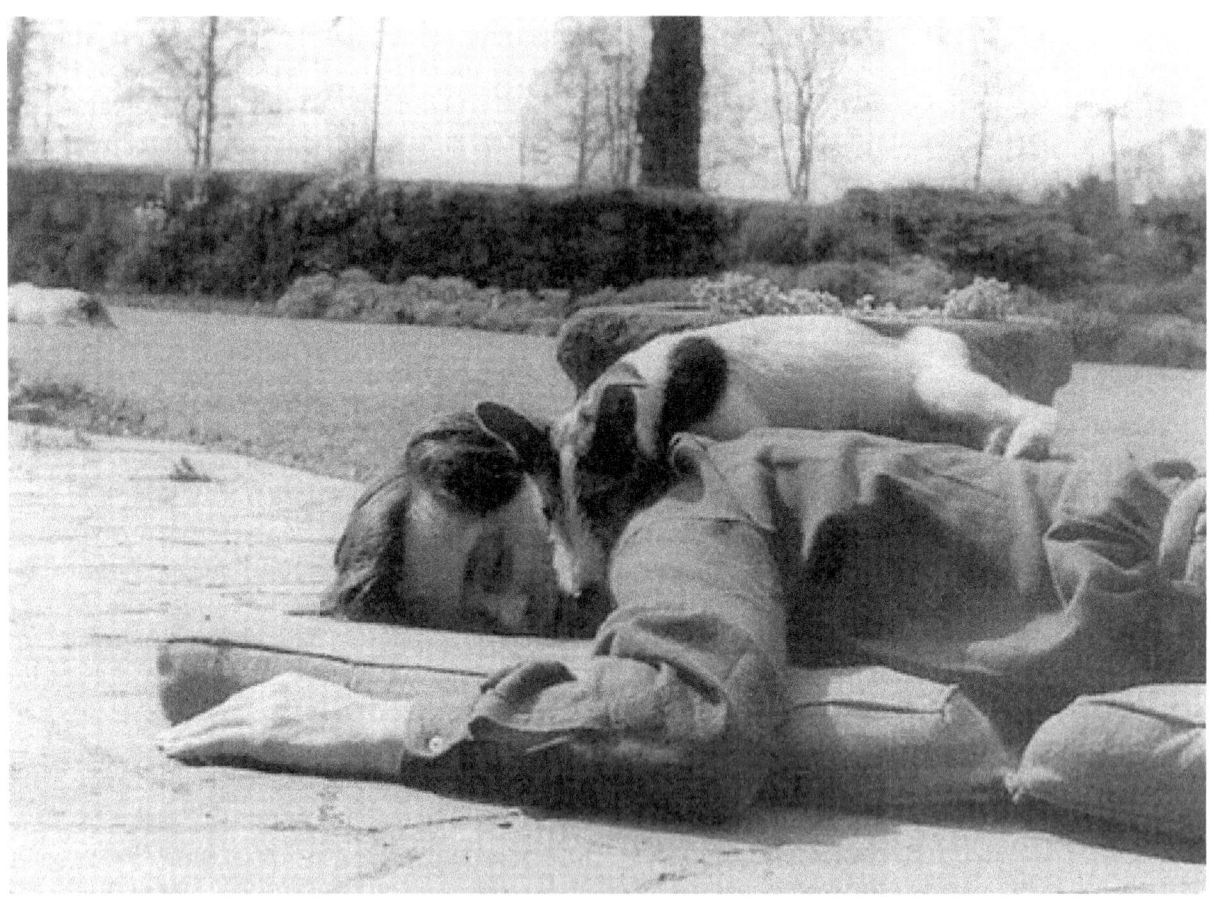

Taking a nap with Mr Binks

Eton

Jeremy's schooling was not a success because he suffered from dyslexia although at that time, knowledge of the disability was relatively unknown and the sufferers were usually identified as "slow learners." His first teacher, Miss Kenderdine who had set up a school at the Grange thought he may have had hearing difficulties, but the tests were negative, although he continued to struggle with his learning. When dyslexia was finally diagnosed, his mother read to him in a concentrated effort to help him catch up with the others. After a time at Abberley Hall prep school, Worcester, where he was Head Boy and their "shining star," at the age of thirteen he was sent to Eton like his brothers before him. He hated it. *"I remember the desolation when Mummy's car left and I was marooned. I found that so frightening. And having my own room made me instantly lonely. I cried the first night because I was alone."* (10) *"I was Jeremy Huggins at Eton where I was also known variously as Buggins, Juggins and Muggins."* (1) He said it was *"a tremendous shock to go to school"* and described his time there as one of *"academic disaster."*

Jeremy in Eton costume

The compensation lay in Jeremy's singing voice which was remarkable and frequently described as like that of Elisabeth Schwarzkopf. It was perfected in the Eton College choir alongside his attraction for the stage. Very soon after his arrival at Eton Jeremy was receiving his first fan letters which represented *"a most consequent mail"*, although his masters were less complimentary or sympathetic as they accused him of having histrionic tendencies and overacting: *"The only way I stood out from the other boys was with an exceptionally good singing voice, which soared like a skylark. After our music master, Dr. Sydney Watson, picked me out to sing the solos in the Eton College Choir, I got fan mail from the other boys' sisters, requesting my autograph – and I even made a record."* (4) *"I was the number one chorister in the boys' choir, so I had all the solos, wonderful things to sing. I used to dramatise them quite dreadfully and get quite emotional."* (9) *"I remember an evensong in the devastatingly beautiful college chapel when a shaft of light came through the window. I'm sorry to say I thought it was for me and moved into it for the* Brahms Requiem*... 'And ye now therefore have sorrow, but I will see you again, and your heart shall rejoice...'"* (11) *"It was an unbelievable sound and I'm ashamed it went to my head a little... I got a sharp ticking off... and I don't think I've let anything go to my head since."* (12)

The boys were attracted by the incredibly beautiful sound he made and flocked to the chapel for Evensong to hear him sing where *"everyone sort of fell over backward."* One boy wrote in his memoir of the crush he and so many other boys had on Jeremy, "For the last three years of my time at Eton, most of the boys, including me, were in love with the same boy. They may have forgotten it now, after busy successful heterosexual lives, but that is the way it was. The boy's name was Jeremy Huggins... He had the most beautiful treble voice you could imagine, and he was remarkably handsome. In his white vestal robe, with his brown hair brushed until it glowed, his eyes gazing heavenward and his mouth open in pure song, he could make his audience swoon away during the psalms." (13) *"Then my voice broke. Quite suddenly I could no longer reach the top note, and I was aware I'd lost something for ever."* (4)

Eton schooling may be helpful for the careers of budding politicians but is not suitable for histrionic drama students. Jeremy certainly struggled in this situation. *"I was crippled by a kind of beauty which was hell for me and I got a lot of wrong responses. I had blondish, long hair, and in a school full of boys that is the nearest thing to a girl you can get. It makes you very self-conscious... The older boys could send junior boys on errands, and I was sent by one of the top members of my house to take a message to a boy in another house. And when I got there, after a few minutes, I was aware that I had been sent for other reasons, and I began to retreat. He said, 'I want a picture of you, that's all.' But I felt threatened by him and frightened by the fact I had been set up by the boy in my house."* Jeremy said it taught him how to grit one's teeth in difficult situations. He remembers that he was beaten by some of the boys and experienced considerable misery. On one particular occasion he received 158 strokes of the cane, *"which now seems unbelievable"* and the effects of the continual punishment were long lasting: *"Sometimes I wasn't quite certain why I was being beaten... that made me very bitter. The experiences haunted me for quite a time after I left. It made me very unsure of my gender, because I was attractive. When girls found me attractive, that was the most enormous relief... Later on, I had my nose smashed, on stage at the National Theatre. I wish I had had it smashed at school, if I was going to have it smashed at all..."* He was justifiably angry at the injustice of his treatment. *"I can't think of Eton except with rage. And for many years I used to have a nightmare that I was back there. But that's gone now. I've had such a wonderful life since..."* (14) The only compensation remained in the opportunity to sing. *"It was very tough,*

As the hostages observed if you can survive an English Public School, you could survive anything. They were very difficult days." He also commented on the black costume the boys had to wear from the age of thirteen, chosen to keep them in mourning for the founder. *"I found it a great strain to be dressed constantly in the uniform of striped trousers and black coat. I felt tremendously lost in a quagmire of little black mourning people... I remember the first morning trying to open my starched collar with a nail file so I could breathe."* (10) *"Etonians don't really belong...they are quite isolated people and I think I am very private. It's being made to feel like an adult at such a young age."* The black costume of frock coat and starched white collar he wore as Sherlock Holmes also reminded him of those nightmare days and probably contributed to his dissatisfaction with the role on occasions.

At the age of sixteen Jeremy contracted rheumatic fever from the dirty water of the River Thames during his preparation for Eton's annual swimming competition which he won. The illness began with boils in his ears, developing into a severe infection which endangered his life. The joints in his feet swelled up and his heart became enlarged to twice its normal size. *"I was completely flattened."* (11)

For eight weeks he was under complete sedation and was bedridden for eight months during which time he grew considerably. At his mother's suggestion, a set of wheels was added to his bed and the boys pushed him along the Berkswell lanes, sometimes joining him on the mattress. *"That bed was my kingdom. I could lie there watching the trees go by. I did exams from there, learned chess. I was the centre of attention. After eight months, I began to enjoy it. So my parents put a motor bike at the foot of the bed as an incentive to me to get well."* (15) His father and brothers bought him a motorcycle with which they struggled up the stairs to place at the bottom of his bed. It was meant as compensation for his time confined to bed, but, in fact, his first ride resulted in his meeting a bus, going over a hedge and in broken toes. So he was back in bed and suffered even more weeks of immobility. *"This changed my life completely. I was sure I was going to die. I turned from someone who had always loved sport into someone less competitive and I began to read a lot of philosophy. I became more thoughtful... aware of a lot of things I'd never noticed before, such as people's kindness. I was so grateful to be alive... everything seemed wonderful. I wanted to know where I was and why I was here. And the habit has stayed with me... Facing death... as I thought I was... changes your priorities. I'm religious and pray regularly."* (16) Jeremy always carried a copy of the *Footprints* poem in his pocket.

He later told Linda Pritchard in their meetings in Tea Time Coffee Shop at the beginning of their relationship, *"Doctors thought I would never recover from the illness. They told me I would never run up stairs and that I would be chair-bound for the rest of my life... Nothing is attributed to the will of the human being, how the human will can surpass physical handicaps and limitations. Anyway, I did manage to run up stairs and have since done a lot with my life, things those very same doctors thought would be impossible."* He went on to comment on the results of his illness, when he was very close to death, *"Knowing that there is more to us than life and death makes one realise that all things are possible..."* (17)

Jeremy the Actor

Jeremy had wanted to become an actor from the age of eight when he enjoyed singing to records in his bedroom and visited the Cameo cinema, originally known as the Balsall Palace, recently opened on Balsall Common. He had cycled there four times a week and fallen in love with the movies especially those of Sir Laurence Olivier playing *Henry V* or Heathcliff in *Wuthering Heights* and decided he wanted to follow his hero's example. "*My brothers went to either Oxford or Cambridge. Two became painters, the third an architect… I took a different path from my brothers after my imagination was caught by Laurence Olivier's performance in the film* Wuthering Heights. *Later, after seeing him on horseback in* Henry V, *I felt I might be qualified to follow his example, because I could ride, too. Thinking back, I should have gone to university, but at seventeen I enrolled at Central School of Speech and Drama in London.*" (4)

Colonel Huggins was opposed to his son becoming an actor. His explanation was that he didn't want the family name brought into disrepute. "*I would like to have been a soldier for a while for my father's sake, but I had rheumatic fever at sixteen and never saw any kind of military service.*" (18) "*My father thought any respectable middle-class boy shouldn't do a thing like that. He thought it was all drinking champagne out of slippers.*" (19) "*I was the last child born in the ninth year of their marriage and, in many ways, the last straw… when I said I wanted to be an actor, it was the end. I was a great disappointment to my father.*" (1) William may also have had another reason, for his youngest son was tongue-tied from birth which gave him a speech impediment, an inability to pronounce his 'r' and 's' sounds, and his father may have wanted to protect him from ridicule. "*Not being able to pronounce the letters 'r' and 's' is not something an actor can get away with. But because of my belief and probably a good dose of stubbornness, I just would not let go of my dream. I knew there had to be a way to overcome the obstacle. There just had to be.*" (17) His speech wasn't put right until he was seventeen when he joined the London Central School for Speech and Drama. "*I had to have my tongue cut, like a crow, to get my tongue moving… I had to learn to speak… all over again. So, I had a tremendous battle with that… a huge fight with my body because I had been in bed for over eight months and I finally got up in a very odd shape.*" (2) "*That really got me involved with words and I had to do a lot of vocal exercises. I still do them every morning.*"(18)

Many a young man in his situation would have decided that a career on the stage was not a suitable choice. But Jeremy's explanation was a spiritual one, "*It is doubt that stops us from achieving our ambitions and aspirations. Never ever let doubt override the power that is within you to make your dreams come true.*" He went on to call it God power, "*if we would only realise that we are not separate from God, but a part of God, then we could achieve anything. I'm a rebel and that's because my mother gave me this freedom and confidence. So I went down to London. I knew I was going to be an actor from about the age of eight. We're talking about the age of about seventeen and one-half that I walked into Tyrone Guthrie, who was doing* Tamerlane the Great *at the Old Vic (1951), and I said, 'I want to be an actor vewy, vewy much.' He was kind of overwhelmed at this idiot. I remember I was wearing my brother's coat to make me look bigger. And he said I could have a walk-on part in* Tamerlane. *'Or,' he said, 'you should go with that 'r' sound to Central School.' So I had my tongue cut, went to the Central School of Speech and Drama, and gave it my best effort. And it worked. About ten (six) years later I worked with him on Broadway when I played Troilus for him. 'Trroilus! As true as Troilus,' I had to say.*" His mother also helped bring his father around to accepting the decision. *"My mother... made up her mind long before I was born that she wanted something like an actor."* (8)

Central School of Speech and Drama

"I went to Central School, of Speech and Drama... That was a difficult time, working very hard, not only to get rid of the impediment, but also training... Eton had frightened me so completely, that I gritted my mouth tight. I had to learn how to open my jaw; I should not have been an actor at all. It was hopeless from the beginning!" In spite of his difficulties he must have made a considerable impression because he won two prestigious awards whilst studying there and earned sufficient self-confidence to take the next step into repertory. Amongst his fellow students were Wendy Craig and Mary Ure, for whom Jeremy developed a passion which was to last until her death at the early age of 42. *"My first great love was Mary Ure, who later married John Osborne... We met at drama school and we adored each other."* (5)

When he arrived in London, all he had was a place to stay. *"When I came to London from Warwickshire I was 17, and God, I was frightened. I had a razor, but I hadn't used it often and I hadn't told my father I wanted to be an actor. He would have loved me to follow him into the Army. He was bewildered about my choice of career – I think he was terrified that I would fail... At first I stayed in Maida Vale with friends of my mother's but during my time at the Central Drama School, I lived in a different area every term. I once lived in a mews just off Kensington High Street, which cost £2.10s a week, including breakfast. The morning after I left to go on holiday to Scotland the roof fell in, landing on my bed."* (21)

Central School was the prestigious place attended by some of the biggest names of the Theatre, including Peggy Ashcroft and Laurence Olivier both of whom left in 1925, sharing a Gold Medal for their performances as Portia and Shylock in *Merchant of Venice*. Their careers would dominate and define the stage for the next sixty years. John Gielgud and Alec Guinness acted as the teachers and amongst the alumni the names of Edith Evans, Sybil Thorndyke, Robert Helpmann, Virginia McKenna, Claire Bloom, Vanessa Redgrave and Judi Dench would be instantly recognisable. The school was set up by Elsie Fogerty in 1869 as a school for Speaking Therapy, Movement and Dramatic Art. She had no dramatic experience herself as it was not the proper activity for girls to go on the stage in Victorian Britain. However, she believed that each person must recognise the unique contributions he or she can make and co-operate with others to achieve them. Her life reflected that belief.

"The Speech Therapy Department was always small in comparison to the rest of Central, but what fun and how much we achieved... we had the best foundation in normal voice and speech, something now sadly lacking... It was not unusual to find ex students who were on the brink of glittering careers, such as Claire Bloom and Virginia McKenna popping in, or to find Hermione Gingold holding court in the student canteen, having come to see Stephen Joseph, who was on the staff. Every term the key question was who had been back in the holidays to receive voice coaching from Gwynneth: 'Oh! My dear, haven't you heard? It was Larry!'" (Cynthia (Harries) Young in The Central Book)

A Point of Departure

Jeremy appeared in a "catastrophic production" of Purcell's *King Arthur* directed by Stephen Joseph, with "a stellar cast" that included Wendy Craig and Harry Landis (later President of Equity). Paul Schofield and Hermione Gingold were in the audience to see the banners carried by the procession of proud actors become entangled with an extra bank of lights, thereby catching fire. This was made even more dangerous by the actors tumbling over each other "into a smouldering pile." Lumps of newspaper snow thrown from above thudded onto the cut out waves amongst which the audience could clearly see Antonia Grimaldi as Britannia crawling to her position upstage; and through all the chaos, everyone agreed that Jeremy's performance as an iceberg "was memorable." But it was Craig who brought the house down when she appeared in baggy tights to cry, "I've left all right behind!" at which everyone collapsed into uncontrolled laughter. Schofield laughingly admitted that it had been "one of the most enjoyable afternoons" he had spent in the theatre. (Taken from The Central Book by Lolly Susi)

One student who entered the School in 1954 said, "I was just 17 when I entered Door 9 of the Albert Hall to start at Central. C Stage was the lowest class and those in A Stage and in their final year were our gods! Jeremy Brett – too gorgeous to look at directly – Mary Ure, Wendy Craig, Heather Sears, Benny Arnesson... They were a world away from us chubby teenagers and I was terrified. The teachers were even more alarming. Determined to break us of any preconceived ideas or fancies, they set about removing any vestige of confidence that we might have had – and I had precious little to begin with." (Jennie Goosens in The Central Book by Lolly Susi)

Perhaps the most surprising is Jeremy's lack of self-confidence in himself as an attractive young man. He had a poor image of his appearance and of his attraction to women. *"The only women we saw at school were the housemaids who were 70 and had scurf. But suddenly at drama school there were all these girls. One day a friend and I were walking along the street, and there were two girls we knew behind us. One of them said to the other, 'Hasn't Benny got an attractive neck?' And the other said, 'And so has Jeremy.' I remember running back to my digs to have a look at my neck and wondering what made it attractive..."* (5)

The Central School Matinee was Jeremy's opportunity to show the skills he had achieved and his natural talent for his chosen profession. *The Stage* magazine reported on the final performance and the two prestigious awards given to him. "The annual matinee by students of the Central School of Speech and Drama is always worth watching, and the performances... once again introduced two or three young actors whom one would like, and rather expects to see again. Of the hero and heroine of the afternoon there was no doubt whatever. The scene from *The Misanthrope*... had not been under way five minutes before it was plain that the brilliant bickering of Celimene and Alceste proceeded from a mutual affection as deep as it was differently expressed. It is not impossible to drill young actors into stylish performances, but when the characters begin to show between the lines, as Miss Wendy Craig and Mr. Jeremy Brett discovered Celimene and Alceste to yesterday's audience, we may be sure that it is the work only of strong natural talent. Since even good actors are better in some parts than in others, and may be quite bad in parts which do not suit them, it is the sensible custom of these matinees to show most of the performers in more than one role. Mr. Brett was fortunate in having, in the part of the disappointed host in the second act of *The Liars*, a part that suited him, and it must be said that the second act of *The Liars* was fortunate in having him..." (The Stage 1954) At the end of the performance the judges awarded Jeremy two prizes: the Elsie Fogerty Prize and the William Poel Memorial Prize. (20)

Jeremy Huggins became Jeremy Brett to accommodate his father's wishes. *"My father wouldn't let me use the name Huggins when I decided to act, although it would have been a good balance."* (18) The new name was chosen from the label on the inside of Jeremy's first, green tweed suit, *"My father had my first suit made for me - actually two – by a tailor called Brett of Warwick. So I took the name from that, and it pleased my father, so that was good enough."* (3) His father didn't see him act until four years later when Jeremy wrote to his mother to ask if he could borrow Bill's cavalry boots for the role of soldier in a play he was appearing in at Manchester Library Theatre.

"The great day when he came to see me, I was doing Bruno (Hurst) in John Whiting's Marching Song. *I'd written to my mother to say could she sneak me his cavalry boots, because I thought they'd be great to have under the suit."* The boots arrived buffed and gleaming, personally addressed by his father, and Jeremy was alerted to his father's visit by a phone call from his mother to say he was coming to Manchester. *"He was sitting in the second row, but he didn't recognise me when I came on because I didn't speak for a bit, but he recognised the squeak of his boots, and I remember vividly the angle of his head changing."* (22) *"I saw him at once, he had this great military chin. He was a magnificent man."* Jeremy was upset at the end of the performance when his father hadn't waited for him, but later was delighted to find him sitting on the steps of his flat above the Astoria Ballroom with a bottle of champagne and two glasses, but above all by the shout. *"You were a triumph, dear boy."* (Wogan Interview 1988) *"And funnily enough, when I played* Hamlet, *he then gave me permission to change my name back to Huggins, and I said, 'Oh Dad, it's too late. I've established it.'"* (22)

An article in *Arts and Entertainment* recorded his first professional appearance at the age of nineteen, possibly *A Point of Departure,* and Jeremy recalled the event with a smile: *"It was a marvellous little old-fashioned play, and I was the juvenile. (Gosh was I the juvenile!) And I remember I missed my entrance and someone said, 'You're off' and I ran and leaped in through the window. But the window was meant to be the second floor. So I'd leaped up thirty feet, and the audience howled at this sort of India-rubber nineteen-year-old who jumped thirty feet through the girl's bedroom window. I very nearly got sacked for that."*

Film, Television and The Stage - 1950s

On leaving the Central School of Speech and Drama in 1954 with two prestigious awards Jeremy simultaneously appeared in three different media. He was to take the juvenile role in the film *Svengali;* to join the cast in a recording of the play *Mrs. Dot* for BBC television and also to win a regular place on the stage in repertory in Manchester at the Library Theatre. Jeremy's career was beginning at a time when mass media in Great Britain was in its infancy, but with the developing popularity of television the whole spectrum of acting would change. High definition television began broadcasting from Alexandra Palace in 1936 and although the war had interrupted its development, the Queen's coronation in 1953 brought the new media into many households. At the beginning of the decade television was a luxury item and present in only 350,000 households but by the end of the decade three quarters of the population had a television.

Repertory Theatre offered opportunities for local writers to have their work performed and presented a training ground for young actors to gain important experience. It had begun in the 1930s, but by 1954 there was a huge expansion for repertory theatre and this was where company theatre had its beginnings. Jeremy would also appear in musical theatre and seemed to fit into this genre effortlessly. His joyful experience of singing in the Eton choir and in many of the country's cathedrals stayed with him so that his early career showed him on stage combining his love for both musical and classical theatre.

Three very different disciplines would contribute to Jeremy's success in his chosen profession. They offered continued employment for him in a usually unstable field of work. It is the actor's lot to be unemployed and searching for work after every play, show or film. He became known for his versatility, his classical aristocratic speaking voice, his keen intelligence and his balletic movement across the stage, "surprising for such a big man." (Jeremy Paul) His talent, his determination to overcome all obstacles to success and his enthusiasm made him an attractive casting choice.

Svengali 1954 - Film

Svengali released 1954 in "gorgeous colour" was Jeremy's first film role in the small part of the student **Pierre**. He appears in just two scenes with a couple of lines which he delivers with youthful enthusiasm. The film starred Donald Wolfit in the title role of the sinister hypnotist/mesmerist who hypnotises the lovely artist's model, Trilby, played by Hildegarde Neff and transforms her into a world-famous singer. "Svengali is a masterful and menacing hypnotist, bearded and unkempt, who draws a young woman, Trilby, into his lair. She has worked as a nude model for many artists and now, cajoled by Svengali's manipulative gift, she leaves behind her family in order to pursue a singing career on the concert circuit. What Trilby does not know, however, is that she can perform only upon the hypnotist's command. Svengali and Trilby are pursued by a young artist who, like Svengali, is madly in love with Trilby." (2011 remastered dvd cover)

Mrs Dot 1954 – Television

Jeremy's first appearance for the developing media was on 1st August 1954, in the play **Mrs. Dot** for **BBC** Television, a farce in the Edwardian style in three parts by W. Somerset Maugham. **Freddie Perkins**, "played by Jeremy Brett, who is fresh from a drama school where he has won awards and high honours at the school's public shows" is described in the text as *"a vivacious boy of two and twenty,"* (Mrs Dot) the penniless, handsome nephew and secretary to Mrs. Dot (Mrs Worthley). It tells the story of a wealthy widow played by Sonia Dresdel who is in love and plans to marry Gerald Halstane (Jack Watling), a fashionable bachelor on the verge of bankruptcy due to his extravagant lifestyle. The prospective marriage could solve his problems, in spite of the origins of her wealth being a brewery (left to her by her husband Mr. Worthley) but the snag of a previous engagement to Lady Sellenger's daughter Nellie (June Thorburn) looks as if it will stop the proceedings. If Nellie wishes to marry her fiancée the plans of Mrs Dot will come to nothing and Gerald is too honourable to jilt her for the woman he has fallen in love with, especially as the accidental death of the last remaining relative, Lord Hollington, a soldier in India, means he will inherit the peerage, seven thousand a year and be a good catch after all. As each member of the play reassesses their expectations in the light of this startling news it is Freddie who will "whisper nonsense" in Nellie's ear and run away with her, which shows how unpredictable farces can be. Jeremy said it was *"a walk-on part"* but Freddie appears throughout this very funny play, and by falling in love with Nellie he is used by Mrs. Dot to achieve her own ambitions of marrying Gerald Haldane.

Manchester Library Theatre - The Stage

Bird in Hand - By Courtesy of Manchester Libraries and Archives

Amphitryon 38 - By Courtesy of Manchester Libraries and Archives

Jeremy began his career on the stage in repertory at the Library Theatre in Manchester in 1954. The Library Theatre had opened in 1952 in the basement of Manchester Central Reference Library, built in 1934 with its columned rotunda design often compared to the Pantheon in Rome. Jeremy arrived in the provinces with huge enthusiasm and youthful good looks so that he seemed perfect for the leading romantic role. He told the story of how he interrupted a rehearsal with *"outrageous arrogance and foolhardiness"* to announce to the bemused director, Peter Lambert, that he was going to be the juvenile lead for the next season. During a break for lunch he was given the audition he had been promised and made such an impression that by 2:30 p.m. the same day he had a contract for two years at £7 a week. Robert Stephens described Lambert as a good director, "highly strung and brooding" and David Scase who would later take over from Peter Lambert as "an even better director and a much nicer man," so Jeremy had made a good choice of theatre in which to make his debut and learn his trade, especially as Manchester was to be a successful repertory theatre. The company was given three weeks to rehearse instead of the usual week adopted by most repertory companies which ensured that the performances were always better and "you learned more."(Robert) "There was also a high level of production and 42 weeks continuous employment for theatre personnel." (History of Repertory Theatre D. Colley 1956)

Jeremy's arrival was proudly announced: "Members of last season's company who will again be joining the resident group are Joan Heath, Bernard Warwick, Ralph Nossek, and Joan Saunders. Newcomers will include Mary Steele, a 20 year-old player from the Bristol Old Vic and Jeremy Brett, a prize winner from the Central School of Drama." (The Stage 19th August 1954) His first role in repertory would be **Gerald Arnwood** in *Bird in Hand* 13th September 1954 in a comedy by John Drinkwater which the producer, Peter Lambert, hoped "should prove as delightful and charming a beginning to a season as anyone could wish." The *Manchester Guardian* summed up the action, "a heavy father who thunders like Lear because he has caught his daughter sheltering from the rain in a summer house with a young man – a youth so proper that any spirited curate might be thought dangerous by comparison." (N.S. 22nd September 1954) *The Stage* thought it was a good start to the season, "It is some time since this light-hearted but by no means pointless piece was given a professional airing in the North – long enough in fact, for the beholder to realise how much the world has changed since it was first presented in 1927. Peter Lambert who directs has wisely chosen to garb his players in the clothes of the early 1920s and gives the whole thing much more point thereby. He also treats it on broad lines and helps things along by some nice tricks of production… Jeremy Brett and Mary Steele are the young lovers…" (The Stage 30th September 1954)

It is at the Library Theatre that Jeremy met his lifelong friend, Robert Stephens. A more unlikely friendship couldn't be imagined. Jeremy was from a middle-class public-school background with a patrician manner which was very different from Robert's working-class background; a shipbuilder's son with a huge chip on his shoulder. "I had a terrible childhood, with no money, no love and no prospects." (Robert) "Jeremy was my oldest friend. We first met at the Library Theatre in Manchester where we shared a flat. He was just 21, an extremely beautiful and athletic young man. Coming from the working classes as I did, he was the first true gentleman I ever met." (The Guardian 14th September 1995) "I had never before met anyone so elegant so charming, so Etonian" of impeccable military background and "terribly good-looking" for which he suffered considerably: he was frequently approached by unsuitable men who found him attractive, and Robert was the one who took on the role of protector by sitting in between them. They shared the two-room apartment above the last A of the Astoria

Ballroom in Plymouth Grove which had been opened as "a huge, tastefully decorated" Irish Dance Hall in 1949. They lived as many young men do, drinking, smoking, enjoying a chicken or a prawn vindaloo once a week at the local curry house. Tarn Bassett, Robert's girlfriend who would become his wife in 1956, made up the three "inseparable best friends" living a lifestyle which was anything but glamorous "but we were always screaming with laughter." Robert explained his philosophy, "It is impossible to be a dull man and an actor... I love to live in the moment as well as in the spotlight." And Jeremy agreed, *"My great best friend Robert Stephens, the acclaimed Shakespearean actor and I, when we started our careers, used to press our noses against the window and say one day we'd stay here (The Midland Hotel). So I am living a dream. It was a great, dusty womb where many wonderful people met, discussed life and found their talents."* (To Andrew Duncan in The Radio Times 19th March 1994)

During the next eighteen months at the Library Theatre Jeremy appeared in a variety of roles including **Bruno Hurst** in ***Marching Song,*** a provocative yet contemporary play by John Whiting opening on 12th October 1954. It is the story of an Army leader in a defeated country, "a general who lost his last battle and with it... his honour" and for which he was imprisoned for seven years during the enemy occupation. On his release he was threatened with a public trial to appease the people, as a scapegoat for their humiliation, but "by killing himself before it opened, he spared his near-ruined country the further shame that would come from the muckraking of the evidence. The situation, in an age addicted to political ritual murder, it is sufficiently credible; the thirty-six hours during which the general comes to his decision divide themselves almost spontaneously into the three acts of a play. The general himself, taking his pride intact to the grave..." (N.M.R. in Manchester Guardian 13th October 1954)

In a totally different part, he would play the God **Mercury** in ***Amphitryon 38*** opening on 23rd November 1954, in a story of the intrusion of the God Jupiter and his son Mercury into the affairs of men. Pictured amongst the clouds, Jupiter and Mercury make plans for the divine seduction of the beautiful yet virtuous Alkmena, and in order to remove Amphitryon from his wife's side, Mercury suggests that Jupiter have the Athenians declare war on Thebes. As general of the Theban army, Amphitryon will hurry to defeat the enemy. Mercury in the guise of a servant will tell Alkmena that her husband will momentarily desert the battle and return to her bed that night. Alkmena may swear fidelity to her vows and refuse to admit a false lover, but Jupiter changes form and successfully impersonates her husband in her bed whilst Mercury holds back the dawn. The play received the faintly comic headline *"Jove in Pink Socks".* (The Stage 2nd December 1954) The farce element emerges when Amphitryon returns from the wars with accusations of his wife's adultery whilst Jupiter is still present, attended by Mercury, both in disguise. It was called "a scintillating play". The production was described as a drawing room comedy, "inane" but "delightful," "a mad frolic this, a heavenly farce turned conjugal comedy of manners and a perfect vehicle for one of the witty, graceful productions at which Peter Lambert excels." Jeremy was judged "a mobile Mercury." *The Manchester Guardian* also approved: "The framework is a little obscured at Manchester during the first act, with some of the actors hardly audible in their straining for the appropriate style, but the production by Peter Lambert mellows admirably as it goes along... Jeremy Brett as the procurer Mercury and Doris Speed as Queen Leda are the quickest of the cast to find their places..." (The Manchester Guardian 24th November 1954)

A new version of ***Puss in Boots*** by Nicholas Stuart Gray took the pantomime season eight-week spot starting 14th December 1954. Directed by both Peter Lambert and David Scase with Lambert in the role of Puss with a clever mask, a feline approach accompanied by a mix of "purring unctuousness and an easily offended dignity" clearly relishing his triumph in the battle of wills with the Ogre. "The story is well told and the tasteful production by David Scase fully exploits the fun, the noble sentiment and the thunder. You should just see how the cat braves the ogre's castle, saves the master and ends up with the ogre-mouse delicately imprisoned in a golden cage... "I could see it over and over again," said the 13-year-old who came with me to see *Puss in Boots* at the Library Theatre ... we both liked everybody..." (Fred Isaac Evening Chronicle 15th December 1954) "It is always the larger than life that impresses children in the theatre, and last night Peter Lambert, whose Puss had a neat, feline astringency, and John Saunders as a comic military commander earned the most vociferous and consistent encouragement from the audience." (Manchester Guardian 15th December 1954) "Jeremy Brett plays effectively as **Gerard**, owner of the cat which brings him fame." (The Stage 31st December 1954)

Saint Joan began its run of four weeks on 8th February 1955. It was Peter Lambert's most successful production and he called it a tragedy and not melodrama as there were no villains in the piece. Joan is a human being of enormous strength, the young girl who is convinced she is chosen by God to become the commander of the French army, yet she achieves greatness and sainthood as she is judged a heretic and executed by her accusers, Jessie Evans earned the headline "*Saint Joan with a Welsh Accent*" and received praise for making a simple, sturdy, peasant girl believable. She was physically small but her quality of "simple obstinacy" mixed with a deep spirituality created a "notable performance" with "telling flashes of dramatic power." As she was tried and forfeited her life "she played with an undeniable power and sincerity. It was a moving and unforgettable performance." (Alan Bendle in Manchester Evening News 5th February 1955) "Art and even artifice had their part in her triumph." All the supporting roles were described as "excellent" and Jeremy was deemed "noble" and "ably doubles the parts of **Gilles de Rais** and **Brother Ladvenu.**" Robert said the experience *of Saint Joan* "convinced me that the best company of actors is the happiest company of actors, bound in a common purpose with democratic, shared objectives... made me so happy that I thought, on the last night... that my heart was going to burst... One really felt one was in the presence of greatness..."(Knight Errant) Both Jeremy and Robert would appear again in the Shaw's *Saint Joan* in 1963 at the Chichester Festival with Laurence Olivier directing Joan Plowright in the leading role. Once more this outstanding play would earn the two friends considerable praise.

Richard II had its opening night on 8th March 1955, and starred Peter Lambert as Richard II and Jeremy as the **Duke of Aumerle**. The producer explained his necessary cuts to the long play, "I have tried, however, to keep in at least the bare essentials of the so-called 'Aumerle sub-plot' which it is now fashionable to excise entirely – a fashion which can harm the play as a whole and Bolingbroke's character in particular" so Jeremy's role would be preserved. Richard may be a King ordained by God to rule but he is weak and ineffective and his vanity threatens to divide the great houses of England, York and Lancaster, in a civil war which would last 100 years. *The Manchester Guardian* thought it was "a play of glitter and gloom; of treason, conventional violence and a well-nigh unutterable weariness that manages nevertheless to get itself incomparably uttered... All the same, Peter Lambert's Richard has substantial virtues. His appearance – dressed most effectively, as is the rest of the cast... is full of elegance and pride. He preserves, in short, the king's dignity. Though gazing so wanly into the glass of his self-pity, cultivating the death-wish centuries before its official time, hugging his griefs like comforts... his most passionate complaints are well tuned..." (N.S.

Manchester Guardian 9th March 1955) Alan Bendle in the *Manchester Evening News* said, "Peter Lambert makes of Richard a moving figure, tragic yet noble... Notable among supporting performances are Jean Bloor's Queen and Jeremy Brett's Aumerle. Sally Jay's settings achieved wonders with the utmost economy."

The role of **Dick Tassell** the assistant master at Hilary Hall would take Jeremy back to his schooldays at Eton in *The Happiest Days of Your Life* on 5th April 1955. The play was described by the producer as "possibly one of the best written and constructed farces of recent year" with "a laugh on every line" promising to be a most successful comedy. Set in the English private school it featured an invasion by the "doughty girls" of St. Swithins, clearly bent on destruction in an orchestrated battle of "brilliantly swung hockey sticks. But here it comes up again, surprisingly fresh and lively, thanks to a production which keeps wisely short of caricature, making the farcical look absurdly real... and to some first-rate casting which has fitted out the company with just the right mortar-boards and gym-slips in this violent academy; a place where the boys are backward and the girls are forward." (R.S. Manchester Guardian 6th April 1955) The comedy hangs on the sharing of the limited resources and in spite of the efforts of the respective masters and mistresses to display separate establishments to the visiting parents, the true situation is inevitably revealed. It is no surprise that Jeremy's Dick Tasssell becomes close to Joyce Harper an assistant mistress of St Swithins played by Jean Bloor.

It is perhaps *The Have-a-cigarette Othello* 22nd November for four weeks in which **Cassio**, played by Jeremy, suddenly offered Robert's Iago a cigarette, which became one of the most memorable highlights, "a moment fraught with dangerous anachronism." (Robert) The director had suggested that the character smoke a cheroot, a square-cut cigar and Jeremy said, "*We hadn't time to rehearse it, so during the performance I offered my Iago a cheroot – I thought it was only fair. But of course he was talking so much he wouldn't take it. So eventually in desperation I said, 'Have a cigarette, Iago.' You should have heard the audience. And in the paper the next day, the heading was,* Have a cigarette, Othello." *The Stage* magazine commented that "Iago, in Peaked Cap Smokes Cigarettes and draws a pistol" but added an appreciation of the acting: "Robert Stephens adds considerably to his growing stature as a player by his work as a cynical, sneering Iago." The tone of the Shakespearean tragedy had not been lost as each of the major roles, Othello, Iago and Cassio received good notices, Jeremy received the commendation, "The production is marked by the return to the company of Jeremy Brett, a gay and handsome Cassio in a sky blue uniform..." (F.W.F Manchester Guardian 22nd November 1955) Othello was played by the Welsh actor Brendon Barry who rather struggled with the role exacerbated by the first night's incidents which sent him into floods of tears: Cassio forgot to make his entrance whilst Brendan was lying on stage in his epileptic fit. When Robert left the stage in search of Jeremy, poor Othello remained alone, just lying there. In one schools' matinee all the actors stopped in the middle of their performance whilst Brendan told all the children to be quiet, "to shut the hell up" which they did for a short time and then began again. It is no surprise Brendan was on edge throughout the play. In spite of these difficulties, *The Stage* concluded, "The Shakespearean magic begins to work, and the whole thing takes on more, rather than less life." *The Guardian* thought "the acting as a whole was excellent" and commended Othello for his, "flamboyant rage admirably controlled." This production is also memorable for the appearance of Rosalie Williams as "a sadly-sweet Desdemona" who would marry the new director David Scase. Rosalie was to remember this part when she was approached by Michael Cox, who had also been a member of the Theatre, to join the team at *Granada Studios,* and she readily accepted the role of Mrs. Hudson to work alongside Jeremy's Sherlock Holmes. Their special relationship had obviously begun thirty years before in Manchester.

Julius Caesar on 4th February 1956 would be Jeremy's last production for the Company and the critics praised his performance as **Mark Antony** in "A Memorable Caesar." It was the most successful play of the season and almost 11,000 people came to see it. Brendan Barry's Caesar was "electric: a neurotic blaze of a man, lit with a perilous head of power and ready at any moment... to consume himself and all of us in a blue flash. Certainly a remarkable piece of acting though the following scene, in spite of some powerful histrionics from Jeremy Brett as Antony, shouts itself down and nearly out." Jeremy made "a good-looking Antony" and played him "with a hint of earnestness." Another critic thought the funeral oration was "excellently done." One article for The Manchester Evening News titled *"We'll Keep our Eyes on this Trio"* celebrated the contributions made by Robert, Jeremy and Brendan whilst announcing their departure. "That happy hunting ground for producers in search of talented young players, the Manchester Library Theatre, has been invaded again. Three of the company's best actors – Robert Stephens, Jeremy Brett, and Brendan Barry – have accepted contracts that bring them nearer to a famous future. They are leaving Manchester after the four weeks' run of *Julius Caesar*... 22 year old Jeremy Brett has been signed up by the Old Vic... This last year has been a hectic one for Jeremy, who was whisked away to Rome to find himself playing opposite Audrey Hepburn in the shortly to be released film *War & Peace*. He went back recently to complete the job. An early appearance of Mercury in *Amphitryon 38* was infinitely promising and perhaps his Brother Martin in *Saint Joan* was as significant. He makes his bow as Mark Antony. Watching *Julius Caesar* will, then, have two added interests – taking a last look at those who go forth to conquer elsewhere." Whilst Jeremy left for London to work with Tyrone Guthrie, Robert would join the English Stage Company, later renamed the Royal Court in Sloane Square, led by George Devine and Tony Richardson and work with John Osborne.

Mark Antony in Julius Caesar

War and Peace 1955 - Film

War and Peace

Jeremy's time in Manchester was cut short by the fact that his picture had been seen in the actor's Who's Who magazine, *Spotlight*, by King Vidor, who was making a new version of **War and Peace** and had whisked him off to the Cinecitta Studios in Rome to appear as Audrey Hepburn's brother, **Nicholas Rostov,** in the Hollywood version of the epic novel. The filmmaker had appreciated Jeremy's physical similarity to Audrey and when seen together they represent a perfect match of youthful exuberance, talent and striking good looks. *"I still have a bit of a chip on my shoulder about my looks, largely because I suspect they got me some of my early parts. The most striking example of this was soon after I had crashed my way into repertory at Manchester and someone who saw my picture in the stage directory picked me out of the blue for the part of Audrey Hepburn's brother in the film of* War and Peace *simply because I looked like her."* (Magazine 1967) Audrey and her husband Mel Ferrer, who were playing Natasha Rostov and Prince Andrei in the film, had gone to Rome to occupy the house in Albano, where they had spent their honeymoon, with its ornate swimming pool and featuring a huge marble head from which the water gushed. An early visitor was Jeremy, *"When I arrived at their house, Mel met me and under his right arm popped a little girl with no makeup who looked about sixteen years old – an exquisitely delicate, porcelain doll. I was spellbound. I remember swimming with them and banging my head on the side of the pool because I was so busy looking at her... I almost drowned in the pool because of the beauty of her."* (Jeremy in Audrey Hepburn by Barry Paris) However, swimming became a rare pastime as filming schedules meant ten-hour days with late evenings and because it was August the Italian heat was extremely tiring. The winter clothing of velvets and furs created their own difficulties and the snow scenes were created by the use of wind machines which blew cornflakes coated in gypsum, fabricated by the big Italian chemical firm, Montecatini. Movie trivia has recorded the fact that Jeremy was the only member of the cast who rode his horse in the hunting scenes. Everyone else can be seen on a mechanical horse, including Audrey, Mel, Henry Fonda, Barry Jones and May Britt.

The six months which Jeremy spent filming in Rome at the Cinecitta Studios were made much more bearable by the presence of his friends, Robert and Tarn, whom he had requested to join him. Robert had left a letter of farewell in a book he gave his friend to read on the plane and he was so moved by the sentiments he found there that he promised he would pay all their expenses for a holiday if they could raise the money for their tickets. As a result they spent an enjoyable three weeks in an apartment with Robert Graves' daughter, Diana, all at Jeremy's expense. "Jeremy, bless his heart, gave us pocket money from his own salary." He also persuaded the director to give Robert a part in the production. Unfortunately, his one line ended up on the cutting room floor amongst the thousands of feet of discarded film, although he had been well paid for the experience.

In spite of the popularity of the Tolstoy story, the reputation of the director and its stars, the film *War and Peace* did not fulfil the promise as a box office hit. The monumental novel was too long and needed pruning but Tolstoy oversimplified resulted in a loss of atmosphere and power. The sheer scale of the production meant that it took almost two years to film at a cost of 6 million dollars and "boasts spectacular battle scenes and magnificent photography." Almost the entire Italian army of 15,000 soldiers were engaged to don French uniforms for the battles of Borodino and Austerlitz, with 10,000 appearing in just one scene: 8,000 horses and 3,000 canons were engaged on the battlefield which resulted in far too many accidents so that 64 doctors were needed to carry out the necessary first aid. Jeremy would need a doctor in an incident that happened on his first day's filming. When a group of the actors from the Manchester Library Theatre visited the Mayor of Manchester during their rehearsals for *Othello*, the Lady Mayoress was amused to hear of Jeremy's experiences of filming in Italy, *"Just my luck - I twisted an ankle on the set and you should have seen the fuss. They sent me home in an ambulance and five doctors came to see my ankle."* (Manchester Evening Chronicle 8th November 1955)

Jeremy's and Audrey's faces appeared on the front of *Life Magazine* and other Italian publications but in Hollywood there is the need to keep proving yourself in order to make a reputation and in spite of the promises Jeremy was not given that opportunity. *"I was whisked off from Manchester to Rome and lived in a fantasy world for six months. At the end of the film there was talk of taking me to Hollywood to groom me into a star."* (Television Sherlock Holmes)

Troilus and Cressida 1956 - Old Vic Company

Jeremy as Troilus and Rosemary Harris as Cressida

In spite of the excitement of filming in Rome Jeremy's heart would remain in the theatre with the thrill of a live audience, and he spoke to the *Evening Chronicle* on his return to Manchester. He said that filming was not going to keep him away from the theatre. *"You need at least four years' theatre work to learn how really to be anyone else but yourself on the screen,"* he said. In weeks he was signed up to the **Old Vic Company** by Tyrone Guthrie, the theatrical director who had encouraged him to attend the Central School of Drama in 1951. His first appearance was as **Patrocles** in ***Troilus and Cressida*** with Charles Gray in the role of Achilles at the Old Vic Theatre. *"It was my first job in London, and it was a very small part... Patrocles had about 36 lines... but I think I realised how important it was to be working with Guthrie. I was coming back on the train – I used to go on weekends to the country to visit my parents... and I suddenly had this idea that I might play it one way, like a little boy lost in the battlefield... This idea caught Guthrie's imagination. It isn't often that little Patrocles gets first mention in the critics, but basically it did because it was something that was absolutely created, because Guthrie was there saying, 'Yes! YES!' He had the whole of the Trojan army coming off downstage and facing upstage to me, who only had two lines... He said, 'I think it's more interesting actually to listen to Jeremy listening to you than watching you talk.' He could change an entire production around if he believed in something."* (Sunday 2nd July 1972 Green Bay Press-Gazette)

Jeremy's keen eye on production would be appreciated so when the company transferred to the Winter Garden in New York he took over the main role of **Troilus** from John Neville. Guthrie presented an ambitious and "strikingly original production" of the play and by choosing the First World War period he had aroused considerable intrigue. *Troilus* is a difficult play to stage but the setting gave some relevance to the murky elements of politics and war. The critics were unsure how to respond. The New York press hailed the Old Vic's *Troilus* as a success and the company a "gifted group" who provided "a thoughtful and often brilliant repertory of the Bard." There was approval of the present "spoofery" of transposing the action to the Edwardian era, "the characters are permitted a freedom of expression and behaviour which would ill become the cloak and sandal adornments in which it was originally laid." (New York: (NANA)

To another critic, "the director's triumph is that he has gotten it on the stage and, with theatrical trickery, can make people listen to it. Further, the Old Vic company is giving corking performances, highly individual, zestful, spicy, uproarious and immeasurably pitiable." He judged Jeremy and Rosemary excellent as the "title's pretty young lovers" and went on to say "the playing makes one marvel how expert are the English in making fun of the English." (Richard L Coe Guthrie Pulls A Major Trick) "Jeremy Brett is handsome and a necessarily straightforward Troilus and Rosemary Harris is a most beguiling Cressida. She has great good looks and transmits a large load of the physical decibels without which the play would flounder. Other notable performances are offered by Charles Gray..." (Calgary Herald January 4th 1957) To help those who were unfamiliar with the play Guthrie was prepared to lead the audience to an understanding rather than following the purist route. He told Jeremy and Rosemary: "This is where Shakespeare needs a little help." Brooks Atkinson called it "Mr. Guthrie's practical joke." However, he praised Jeremy's performance: "Jeremy Brett's youthful, eager Troilus, who can hardly believe Cressida's treachery, is... a first-rate bit of straightforward acting."

Troilus and Cressida

But even the best productions can have accidents and this had an incident in the duel scene, *"I'm hardly likely to forget* Troilus and Cressida *because I was very nearly seriously hurt during one of the performances. Towards the end of the play, there is the duel scene with Diomedes and it was all arranged that Diomedes should have a blunted sword and I the sharp one because he was to slash at my eye during the duel, though even a blunted sword can be painful. When we snatched up our swords on the stage, I could tell by its weight that I had got the wrong one. I shouted out that we should change swords, and we did, even though it wasn't exactly what Shakespeare had in mind when he wrote the play. It was either that or being blinded."* (Star Quality: Jeremy Brett Plays and Players by William Foster)

Jeremy loved Broadway and seemed overwhelmed by everything and everybody he saw. He was always *"wildly enthusiastic"* about things so that when he attended a party in New York with his co-star Rosemary Harris, he was thrilled to see so many stars gathered together in one place, which included Edward G Robinson, Charles Laughton, Humphrey Bogart, Lauren Bacall, the Gish Sisters, Judy Garland and Stanley Holloway, and he told his companion that he wanted to lock himself into the kitchen or he felt he might faint. Making his debut on Broadway was a magical experience for him as it must be for any actor and he was also receiving crucial publicity. His image and that of his co-stars in *Troilus* were caricatured by cartoonist Al Hirshfield for the *New York Times 23rd December 1956*. At 23 years of age he was playing Troilus in the Guthrie production of *Troilus and Cressida* on Broadway. And across the street his name was set in lights on the front of the cinema where *War and Peace* was playing. He thought he had really made it big. *"I was big-headed. I think it may have stopped the drive a bit. I thought I was better than I really was. I was able to choose my own roles and that's a heady thing for a young man."* (The Black Box Interview)

A sound recording of ***Troilus and Cressida*** was made by **The Shakespeare Recording Society,** released by Caedmon in 1962, directed by Howard Sackler, with Jeremy in the role of Troilus, Diane Cilento as Cressida and Alan Howard as Paris.

Old Vic Company - Romeo and Juliet 1957

Jeremy toured America with the Old Vic Company, first to Chicago and Baltimore then to Canada, repeating the Shakespearean roles he had played in England. His debut on American television was in a colourcast for NBC Producer's Showcase on 4th March 1957, as **Paris** in ***Romeo and Juliet***. John Neville played Romeo and Jeremy acted as understudy although he never played the role himself. Other members of the cast were Claire Bloom as Juliet and Paul Rogers as Mercutio with Charles Gray as the Prince of Verona. When the plays had originally appeared in London at the Old Vic *The Stage* magazine also showed some reservations and was not encouraging in its comments which suggested that more conviction and depth of feeling was needed in interpreting Shakespeare's poetry and although it was "charmingly decorated by Loudon Sainthill, they are animated by players who have not yet reached the point of making the story burst into life and take on the dramatic progression poetry and magic that must be there if we are to be drawn into the lives of the star-crossed lovers. Often the acting of the leading parts is so uninspired, not to say pedestrian…" Neville who played Romeo was the only actor who brought some passion into his encounters, although he too lacked real fire in his declaration of love. "His Romeo suggests more a sober man than a lover with his heart afire." There was praise for Jeremy and Charles Gray, "There is a dignified Escalus by Charles Gray and a noble-looking Paris by Jeremy Brett." (The Stage 14th June 1956) *The Illustrated London News* would be more encouraging as it highlighted Jeremy as the one character showing emotion. "In one part, Romeo, John Neville shows how verse should be spoken. In this play we must have the sound and with Neville we have both the sound and the heart of the matter, the rapture and the grief, the lyric tragedy unhazed. Claire Bloom's Juliet, though her technical equipment is thorough and her reading is lucid, stays coldly outside the part, and elsewhere – except in Jeremy Brett's Paris – there is little feeling for the verse. Paul Rogers, with Mercutio's fire, has nothing of the man's fantasy: the Queen Mab aria lacks its gleam…" (ILN 30th June 1956)

A production of ***Edward II*** by Christopher Marlowe took place at Ludlow Castle as part of the Ludlow Festival in 1956. Edward Petherbridge took the role of Gaveston and the play also starred Graham Crowden, Charles Kay, Paul Curran, Jeremy Brett, John Stride, Leonard Pearce, Robert Lang and Geraldine McEwan. This edition of the play is featured on the Edward Petherbridge website with the comment: "Jeremy Brett, my favourite Sherlock, played the King's brother **Earl of Kent**. Imagine Sherlock Holmes and Lord Peter Wimsey on the same stage!" (Edwardpethebridgefansite.yolasite.com) In this season Jeremy would also reprise the role of the **Duke of Aumerle** in *Richard II,* a one-man play, "dominated" by John Neville who gave "a compelling" performance in the title role at the Winter Garden Theatre, New York City, touring with the Old Vic Company. Directed by Michael Benthall with Leslie Hurry responsible for the sets, costumes and props.

Richard II

Whilst at the Old Vic Jeremy would take the part of **Malcolm** in a production of ***Macbeth*** and he would appear in the play several times in his career, eventually playing the title role in 1981. One critic said he made a very attractive Malcolm and "an actor to mark". *The Illustrated London News* commented on this production, "Distinguished now by Coral Browne's first appearance as Lady Macbeth, a firm, urgent performance… Michael Benthall's production is, in effect, that of last season, with an important difference: it is quieter, and we have not to disentangle the tragedy from the noise. Coral Browne is an exceptionally good Lady Macbeth, strong and baleful…Warmly I think of Jack Gwillim's honest Banquo. Jeremy Brett, as Malcolm, is an actor to mark…" (ILN 2nd June 1956) Patrick Newley writing a summary of his career after his death wrote, "As an actor Brett was capable of fire and passion on stage, his style was old-fashioned but electrifying to watch. He tackled major roles such as Malcolm, Paris, Aumerle and Troilus…" (The Stage 20th September 2001)

Macbeth 1960 - Hallmark Film

Jeremy as Malcolm

The film version of **Macbeth** was scheduled for NBC-TV and released by *Hallmark* in 1960. The filming took place at Hermitage Castle and Glamis Castle in the Scottish Highlands to create authenticity and also at Elstree Studios with Jeremy reprising the role of **Malcolm** starring Maurice Evans as Macbeth and Judith Anderson as Lady Macbeth with a supporting cast of Michael Hordern, Felix Aylmer and Megs Jenkins.

One reviewer offered praise for the performances but not for the final release of the film. "If George Scaefer's purpose in filming *Macbeth* had been simply to preserve the performances that Maurice Evans and Judith Anderson had already given on stage, he would have done well to adopt the stylised approach. Instead he seems to have been attempting a form that would suit colour television in the United States and cinemas elsewhere in the world, while permitting his two stars to act in a convention that is strictly theatrical. The result is not filmed theatre, but a cumbersome compromise in which unfilmic acting dominates some tentative stabs at film technique... the screenplay is right enough but the realisation of it falls short..." (Gordon Gow in Films and Filming 1961) Jeremy recalled that Maurice Evans, *"had the most lovely voice – marvellous, marvellous voice"* and Anderson, *"looked extraordinary – fierce with blazing red hair – like the wicked queen in* Snow White and the Seven Dwarfs *with red hair."* He also remembered that when he was required to ride into a castle on horseback as the crowd cheers with his naturally straight hair, *"I had to be curly haired in the next scene and in this moment of impetuousness, I just raised up my helmet and all these pink rollers were revealed on the young king's head."* (Arts &Entertainment 1992) An *IMDb* review points to the high quality of the production, the settings, lighting, soundtrack and the excellent staging of the battle scenes which would remind the viewer of the film *Braveheart*. It also says, "Watch for a breathtakingly handsome 27 year old Jeremy Brett as Prince Malcolm." Broadcast on the Hallmark Channel on 20th November 1960.

Jeremy was gaining both in experience and expertise working at the Old Vic simply by the quality of the acting within the company. When you work with the best you have to raise your game. In 1957 he was named by *The Stage* magazine as one of those with "promise and eager for the part that would put them right up with the leaders... Jeremy Brett, who gained many supporters in *Troilus and Cressida*." The prize was "Stardom – and perhaps, eventually, the mantle of Sir John or Sir Laurence, leading the company at our long hoped-for National Theatre." (The Stage 4th July 1957) Some of the other names mentioned were John Neville, Paul Schofield, Paul Rogers, Richard Burton at the top of the list with Laurence Harvey and Denholm Elliott, Keith Michell and Michael Gough.

Meet Me by Moonlight 1957 - Musical Theatre

Jeremy as Roderick Dashe

Alongside his development through classic theatre Jeremy appeared in a singing role as **Roderick Dashe** in London's West End at the Aldwych Theatre in *Meet Me By Moonlight* August 1957, written by Anton Lesser, with Michael Denison and Dulcie Gray. This was a Victorian comedy set in Henry Mansfield's house in the country in 1884, partially rewritten with music of the period and told of a Victorian father and his match-making sister, Aunt Tabitha. Henry Mansfield (Ellis Irving) firmly believed the eldest, Mary Ellen (Sonia Graham) should be married before her two younger sisters and he had designs on a young lawyer Charles Cuttinghame played by Michael Denison as a suitable match. She had already chosen the handsome Roderick after a clandestine romance, but in spite of herself, was intrigued by Mr. Cuttinghame. She neglected to keep her usual rendezvous with Roderick who was swiftly identified by Aunt Tabitha as a possible suitor for Sarah played by Stephanie Voss. A mystery surrounded Roderick's identity and he was banned from the house, but when the truth was revealed the happy ending for both daughters was assured. The *Cambridge Daily News* described him as "a young man, played in a very bronzed and personable way by Jeremy Brett who is so Byronic and romantic that he nightly leaps a ten-foot garden wall and presents the object of his elevated desires with a rose from her own father's garden, when all the house is asleep." This was also a musical and therefore not seen as particularly mainstream theatrical material but it did have "oodles of charm and some delightful songs of the period, with Jeremy Brett as the young romantic interest." (British Musical Theatre) With the headline of "*Victorian Charm, Music and Husband-trapping,*" *The Stage* magazine called it a simple story and pleasantly told. "Into the elegant drawing-room in which the little story is unfolded, comes, first, Roderick, a young man of mystery who sings in the moonlight with Mary Ellen, and, secondly, Charles Cuttinghame, a bachelor lawyer of forty with a large measure of seriousness."

Roderick and Mary Ellen

One article in *The Stage* written by Kenneth Smart was less enthusiastic about the show and about Jeremy's singing voice. "So I ask myself: Why do really fine artists agree to accept amateur status in a field other than their own? Why should Jeremy Brett, fresh from Shakespearean triumphs, risk his growing reputation by accepting a leading musical role in the West End, when he must know that his singing voice falls between the two piano stools of bleating baritone and husky crooner? Is the answer 'versatility'? The true artist's desire for a 'change of pace'? This thought occurred to me listening to Mr. Brett singing one of his numbers and watching him desperately falling back upon his considerable acting ability to get through it…" (Speaking Frankly. Actors Should Stick to Acting in The Stage 15th August 1957) Maybe it was articles like this which would cause Jeremy to call a halt to his singing and concentrate on acting.

"I really wanted to be a singer more than anything else…an opera singer. And I had the most… marvellous soprano voice… singing things like 'Ye Are Now Sorrowful' *from the* Brahms Requiem. *I was in every major cathedral in England… I went to Rome to make a film of* War and Peace *and I was there nine months and I met a wonderful singing teacher, and she said, 'You have a wonderful tenor voice. Now, are you going to take this seriously which means really, you should stop acting (and) dedicate your life to this.' And I made some noises in her room which nearly excited me as much as my soprano voice, but the trouble was that my soprano voice was completely and utterly natural… My tenor voice was work… But what is so sad about our profession is the fact that if you sing, you are not taken seriously as an actor…."* (Jeremy 1991) *"I had to stop singing because I realised that no one would employ me. It's a terribly sad thing. If you're a Singing Actor, you're not an Actor. And I wanted to be an Actor's Actor."* (Arts &Entertainment 1992)

Marigold

Marigold 1959 - Musical Theatre

Sally Smith as Marigold and Jeremy as Archie Forsyth

Jeremy would accept only two more roles in musical theatre before he would call a halt. First he would play **Archie Forsyth** in ***Marigold***, and then a priest in ***Johnny the Priest*** which was to be his last musical for a while. *Marigold* was a musical romance in two acts and Jeremy starred opposite Jean Kent as Madame Marly, a famous French actress, who lived in a Highland manse, caring for her secret' daughter, Marigold, who had grown up believing she was an orphan. When she went to see Queen Victoria in Edinburgh, on a visit to the Scottish town she saw the handsome Captain Archie Forsyth, played by Jeremy and fell in love. This play also featured a comic Scottish aunt, Mrs Pringle, a text-quoting divinity student, Peter Gloag and James Payton, a turnip loving suitor. There was a scene where Archie leads his fellow officers in drinking the health to Her Majesty and became more and more drunk in the process and the presence of a Scottish reel with its attendant fun continued the party atmosphere. It appeared at the Savoy Theatre in May 1959 and ran for seventy-seven performances. The action was set in Peebleshire in 1842, described as a "gentle, tartan pastiche" with a good deal of emotion and nostalgia reminiscent of the US musicals, "Sally Smith is an enchanting heroine (as Marigold). Her daisy-fresh singing... captivates us as effortlessly as it did the handsome, dashing Archie Forsyth of Jeremy Brett." (Marigold album)

"Could there have been a more handsome leading man than Jeremy Brett, fine of voice and confident in song? He brings a welcome dash of masculinity to proceedings that are dominated by the female stars." (Flops of the 1950s: Marigold) Another critic was more specific in his criticism, "I couldn't get excited about *Marigold*... It's just tedious and dull. Marigold's wish to escape a conventional marriage to a farmer in exchange for the stage exemplified in Madam Marly, but the discovery that the actress is her mother causes her to run off to Edinburgh where she meets the dashing Archie... young Jeremy Brett is a debonair Archie and is in good voice too if you can forgive his odd wavering note." *The Stage* reported, "In the title role is Sally Smith who gives a refreshing and vibrant performance. Jeremy Brett who took over Captain Archie Forsyth at very short notice made an excellent job of the part." (The Stage 14th May 1959)

Johnny the Priest 1960 – Musical Theatre

Rev. Richard Highfield

Johnny the Priest

The second of these performances was as the vicar, **Rev. Richard Highfield** in ***Johnny the Priest*** based on R.C. Sherriff's *The Telescope* by Peter Powell, which premiered on 19th April 1960 and ran for fourteen performances at the Princes Theatre, and then transferred to the Shaftesbury. The play was set in Maybury in the East End Dockland area of London and dealt with the problems amongst the dingy atmosphere for the youth of the day. This was the period when the effects of the war were being replaced by a new hope and when teenagers were beginning to be seen as something more than children waiting to grow up. Jeremy played an upright and caring vicar who attempted to win over the teenagers and wayward youth of his parish by providing worthwhile activities for them with a friendly smile and a readiness to understand. This became his crusade and the amount of energy he put into the young people caused concern to the church council, but not to his wife who supported him. Unfortunately, his methods did not work for all the boys and a young delinquent named

Johnny (Bunny May) for whom Highfield had secured a placement in the Navy, was found guilty of stealing a telescope. As the vicar was unable to compromise and provide him with an alibi the boy is left facing jail. The seriousness of the topic and the dramatic edge was softened by the songs showing that they were not hymns but sympathetic personal exchanges and at the heart of the production faith could be seen as still having an impact on personal lives.

The Stage criticised the story as "ridiculously naïve and lacking in originality and insight. The characterisation is stock and the attitude of reform through boy-scout methods is extremely antiquated." However, "Jeremy Brett deserves high praise for making the dull priggish priest bearable, even likeable, and for adroitly avoiding the laughter that a less dominating performance might provoke." Another critic was sympathetic; "One couldn't help feeling sorry for Jeremy Brett and Stephanie Voss for being made to sing such maudlin stuff. Jeremy Brett is to be congratulated on his performance as the noble, clean-limbed, young Vicar who tries to fight boredom in the young with old volumes of Punch, ping-pong and boxing gloves. One shudders to think what the part would have been like in less capable hands. As it is, he managed to retain sympathy and was even touching in his final dilemma and defeat." (Theatre World May 1960

Jeremy was also recognised for his ability, to create a sympathetic character which would be a skill that he would take into so many different spheres over the coming years. "Jeremy Brett, in particular, deserves credit for his presentation of Highfield. The danger in acting a man who will not tell a lie to save a friend is manifest; one touch of priggishness and the sympathy of the audience is lost. Mr. Brett gives him the honourable simplicity which convinces us that for him only one course of action is possible. Also, and this is a surprise to me at least, he sings acceptably." (Daily Telegraph 26th April 1960

Jeremy and Stephanie Voss

He regretted his decision to make these his last two appearances in musicals, especially as he enjoyed singing so much. Although it may have seemed the right decision, others have said that the musical stage suffered a significant loss, because Jeremy was a handsome romantic lead with a confident singing voice, a stage presence and therefore ideal for the genre. "But he was a real loss to the British musical theatre, one of the most handsome, confidently voiced, masculine and attractive actor-singers." He would return on occasions to a singing role for television in *The Merry Widow* in 1969 and in the theatre in 1977 in *Robert and Elizabeth*, but for the time being the difficult decision had been made.

Variation on a Theme 1958 – The Globe Theatre

Variation on a Theme

There was always a concern in the theatre that an actor could be too handsome and Jeremy suffered considerably for his tall, dark and handsome appearance. His face and figure were becoming his problem rather than his asset. In **Variation on a Theme** opening 8th May 1958, Jeremy played **Ron**, a handsome ballet dancer with a French accent, a man who "has no hips and no morals." This new play written by Terence Rattigan, and directed by John Gielgud at the Globe Theatre saw him once more in the traditional romantic role although this time based on fact. Rattigan had taken the idea for the play from the tempestuous love affair between Margaret Leighton and her younger lover, Laurence Harvey, with the hope that Margaret would accept the role of Rose Fish and Laurence that of Ron Vale. Margaret had accepted but Laurence refused. After another actor played the part in the provinces, both Gielgud and Rattigan decided he was not what the role needed and Jeremy was chosen to play the young ballet dancer just two weeks before the London opening. John Gielgud wrote, "Margaret Leighton gives a heavenly performance... The provincial press has not been good, and there is trouble over the leading young man (Tim Seeley), who may have to be changed before London." As Seeley's replacement, Jeremy was rewarded with praise from The Master, Noel Coward in his diary, "Young Jeremy Brett was excellent." The audiences responded enthusiastically and it was labelled a success. The New Statesman called it, "Mr Rattigan's best play so far... passionate, raw and truthful."

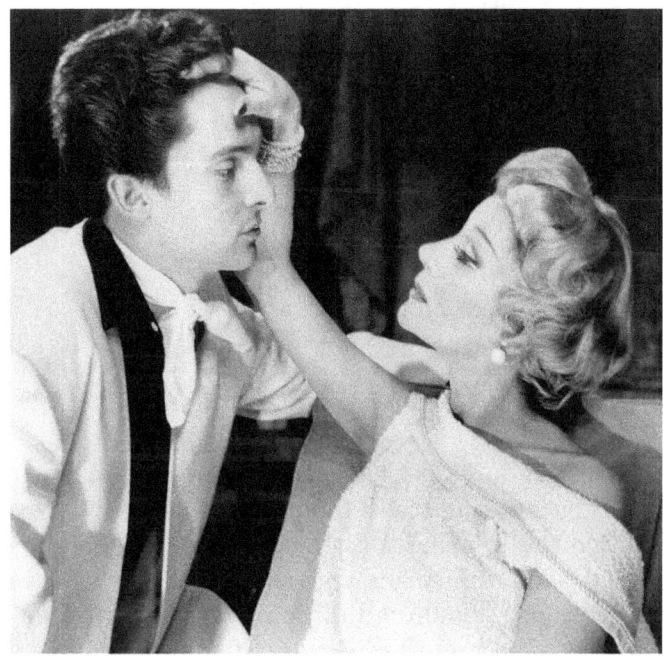

Jeremy as Ron Vale and Margaret Leighton as Rose Fish

The love affair was a modern telling of the Dumas' *La Dame aux Camélias* set against the glamorous and exotic social scene of the 1950s French Riviera. Rose, a beautiful and wealthy socialite in her mid thirties, has been through four marriages and looking forward to her next, but tragically is suffering from "consumption". When Ron, a twenty-six year old bisexual ballet dancer comes into her life, she sees him as an adventurer but really he prefers older women and his simple expression of love captures her heart. But as she is persuaded to sacrifice her own happiness and let him return to ballet dancing, Ron is heartbroken, unable to face life without her. They recognise there is no escape for them and at last, realising she has not very long to live she cancels her visit to the sanatorium to enjoy a few final months of happiness. Rattigan wrote about the relationship between Rose and Ron: "Two self-sufficient people meet and find they need each other. He needs her materially, at first, later maternally – possibly sexually. She needs him first cold-bloodedly for fun. Then more warmly for a pet, finally because of his need for her." (Terence Rattigan by Geoffrey Wansell) "As Ron, the most completely satisfactory character, Jeremy Brett gives an extremely clever understanding interpretation." (The Stage 15th May 1958) *The Times* said, "Mr Jeremy Brett gives a good unsentimental account of the lover whose self-pity is his chief stock-in-trade." (The Times 9th May 1958)

Variation on a Theme

John Gielgud could be a very challenging director as he had come from an age of theatre where styles were very different, almost old-fashioned. An interview with Alec Guinness for Gielgud's biography elicited the information that he could reduce an actor to tears with his attention to the smallest details of just one speech. Jeremy's predecessor in the role of Ron had received an hour of his time, "teaching him to be flamboyant, how to don an opera cloak and make an exit. When he asked him the next day if he had practised overnight, the young man said he'd preferred to go out and forget all about it." (Jean Anderson who played Hettie) Gielgud was heart broken; "the boy is hopelessly inexperienced and has broken my heart with his lack of discipline and stupidity. I really shan't care if he is thrown out, and I am pretty sure it is essential he should be." (Gielgud's Letters) He could seriously damage the confidence of those who were sensitive, simply because he was repelled when actors made a hash of it, but Jeremy later told a reporter how much he thought he had learned from working under his directorship, *"I was fearfully arrogant and complacent… I went into Terence Rattigan's* Variation on a Theme *at the Globe and John Gielgud, who was directing, gave me my first long lesson in how to act. After that, I was much humbler."* (Homes and Gardens 1967) The play did not relate to the new wave of playwrights, John Osborne or Harold Pinter and Jeremy's Ron was clearly a romantic but a more recent production called the play a "hidden gem" that was "gripping and heart-wrenching."

Jeremy and Anna

Jeremy and Anna

Jeremy and Anna at Princess Margaret's wedding

Jeremy and David

Jeremy met Anna Massey in 1957 when he was appearing in *Troilus and Cressida* on Broadway with the Old Vic. and she also had a role in *The Debutante*. "Jeremy Brett was playing Troilus and like most of the young girls who came into contact with him, I fell under his spell. At this stage I didn't get to know him well, but his charm and enthusiasm were very powerful attributes... During the run I did meet up with the dashing Jeremy again. He came to a party that Mother gave at The Grove. I met him the following day and out of the blue he said, 'You must find somewhere to live where you are not under your mother's dominance.' I was amazed. No one had ever spoken to me on this subject before, but Jeremy had seen the situation clearly in the course of the evening, and had dared to speak out. He was quite right... Jeremy was the most complex of men. He was eccentric and often embarrassing in his outspokenness." (Anna Massey in Telling Some Tales) Anna followed his advice and moved into an apartment and her romance with Jeremy blossomed.

They married on 24th May 1958 at St. Michael's Church. It was "a big showy wedding" with Anthony Armstrong Jones as the photographer, he was to marry Princess Margaret in 1960. "Wilton's Anna Massey gave her nuptials to actor Jeremy Brett in England yesterday, a charming note when she had as her attendants several diminutive misses, all under six... The wedding took place outside London, in a small church in Highgate Village... the Bishop of Coventry, a relative of the bridegroom... officiated. Jeremy and Anna had intended to spend the summer with her father and his wife, Dorothy Whitney, at their home in Honeyhill Rd. Wilton, but there's a complete change in their stage commitments... Instead of coming over to New York to replace Richard Burton as co-star of Helen Hayes in "Time Remembered," Jeremy will continue in the leading role opposite Margaret Leighton in the London production of *Variation on a Theme*... Honeymoon plans are being held in abeyance, Jeremy even having two shows in which to appear yesterday, his wedding day... Besides he has been signed up for film work in London." (Sunday Herald 25th May 1958) Robert Stephens was the best man.

In the evening Jeremy left for his performance in *Variation on a Theme* at The Globe Theatre and thus his wedding night would be delayed until after the performance. On advice from his friend Moss Hart, a suite at the Savoy Hotel was booked and Anna commented that the weekend passed very happily. In her biography *Telling Some Tales*, Anna records some of the enjoyable social gatherings they were invited to which included the wedding of Princess Margaret to Anthony Armstrong Jones and afterwards to the ball at Buckingham Palace attended by the whole of the Royal Family, with Queen Elizabeth the Queen Mother dancing the night away. They mixed with Cary Grant, Judy Garland and Buddy Greco who gave them personal dance lessons at his nightclub in Soho. A press article recorded their life as happy, but busy, decorating their new £12,000 home in Chelsea where Anna was expecting her first baby in August: "We're living in the kitchen and one bedroom. There's months of work to do – two nurseries, a study, a games room, two more bedrooms, sun-lounge and two bathrooms to be decorated. But I'm thrilled with our first real home... so much better than Jeremy's little flat..." The reporter left them having a cold chicken lunch at the kitchen table with Anna declaring: "We feel like two tiny peas in this large pod of a house until the baby comes along. Jeremy is going to be a wonderful help with the decorating, aren't you darling..." and ended with the comment, "Ah, young love."

David Huggins

"Anna Massey (Mrs Jeremy Brett) gave birth to a son, David, at Queen Charlotte's Hospital, Friday last.' (The Stage 20th August 1959) Their son David Raymond William Huggins was born on 14thAugust 1959, and they celebrated their honeymoon in Paris; delayed so long because they were both working. They didn't take David with them, but "placed pictures of him around their hotel bedroom..." An article in the *Daily Express* declared Jeremy the perfect father, "HE is lyrical about 10-week-old David. HE *can give David a bottle, wind him and mop him up as though he had been 50 years a nannie. HE insists on pushing the pram. HE carries him confidently round the house, with none of those worries as to whether his head will wobble off which mark the amateur.*" When David was three months old, Jeremy's mother Elizabeth was killed tragically in a car accident on a mountain road in Wales; on her way to visit the Bishop her car had come off the road. Jeremy was devastated and seemed to lose his equilibrium. When speaking about the loss of his second wife, Joan, he said how much the loss of his mother had affected him. *"I have got used to people saying I will get over it. You never do get over it. But I am not very good at losing people I love. I lost my mother, she was killed in a car accident, and it threw me for a loop."* Jeremy's appearance in *Hamlet* a couple of years later caused one critic to comment on the excessive cruelty he showed towards the Prince's mother, Gertrude, which was probably a symptom of his inability to cope with the loss. Also, his relationship with Anna was not a happy one. They were very different personalities; she was "cerebral, cautious, organised," a very private person whilst Jeremy was "intuitive and impulsive..." loud, extravagant and restless. They may have been hopelessly in love in the first stages of marriage but the realities of living together became a strain. "We realised we were really ill-suited partners" and Anna admitted that she didn't know how to help him deal with the death of his mother. *"David was born three days after my twenty-second birthday. No one could have had a more perfect gift. We were thrilled with him. But when... Jeremy's mother was tragically killed in a car crash in the Welsh mountains, it was the most enormous shock for Jeremy, and from this time on, our marriage suffered greatly. I was filming Peeping Tom and was not around to give him essential support. But looking back, I doubt that I would have been of much help. His mother's death released Jeremy from past restraints. He changed, and our relationship never really recovered."*

The couple parted several times, each time trying to save the marriage but eventually he found another partner so Anna and he divorced in 1962. "He was a kind man but always in flight, and so, to my enormous relief he took flight once more." Luckily Anna's career had taken a good step forward; she was able to be independent. They would negotiate amicably with each other so that Jeremy saw his son regularly. "I can still hear them battling out their differences in my head: my father urging me to take risks; my mother advising me to think things through." (David in The Guardian) In an interview Jeremy said he was proud of her and wished they had "*stayed together long enough to become real friends.*" But on another occasion he said that although they had fallen "*wildly in love,*" he thought their relationship never stood a chance as they were too young. *"Anna was 20, I was 24. You think you can do anything at that age. We had a fairly wild three years – more like a wrestling match. I don't regret it... After the divorce, we decided our son would come first and we'd come second. That's the way we've tried to do it and it's mainly due to Anna that it's worked. I'm proud of her as an actress and as a person. I think she's a smashing mother and a great ex-wife. I'm hoping very much that she'll marry again."* (The Real Jeremy Brett TV Times)

Candida 1958 - Oxford Playhouse

Jeremy as Eugene Marchbanks

Jeremy moved from the boy idol of Rattigan's play into the tortured young poet of **Candida** 1958 by George Bernard Shaw which was staged at the Oxford Playhouse and directed by Frank Hauser who would direct Jeremy in *Hamlet* three years later. Essentially, it is a comedy with a Victorian view of what women want in their marriage partners. Written in 1894 and set in London's East End during the Victorian era as a response to the changing roles of women in society, *Candida* is about the domestic turmoil that ensues when an impetuous young poet comes between a progressive-minded clergyman and his charismatic wife. As a classic romantic triangle, the questions about love, fidelity and the artistic temperament are as enduring as ever and made more relevant by Bernard Shaw's wit and argument. Jeremy at twenty five was playing **Eugene Marchbanks**, the shy youth of eighteen, a slight, effeminate poet with a tormented expression in the now familiar romantic role and desperately in love. *"We all go about longing for love: it is the first need of our natures, the first prayer of our hearts; but we dare not utter our longing: we are too shy."* (Eugene) Candida, played by Dulcie Grey, was the object of his affection. She had the double charm of youth and motherhood and was married to an older, complacent husband, a Church of England minister, played by her real husband Michael Denison,

As Eugene is invited into the family Candida will have to choose between them and decide whether she wants youth and romance or age and stability. "Both men adore her, in quite different ways and for quite different reasons, and she is attracted to each of them for their different qualities. They both forget she is her own woman." Shaw is a master of the debate allowing his characters to take different idealistic stances; Candida as the name suggests is candid, and gives a frank expression of her beliefs. Jeremy's Marchbanks is given the passionate appeal of the youthful poet who considers her to be divine and their love eternal, whilst Michael Denison as the Reverend James Morrell, "a vigorous, genial, popular man of forty, robust and good-looking," is the more mature man of commitment, yet more dependent on his wife whom he sees as not only his wife but also as his mother and his sisters; *the sum of all loving care.*"

Candida, with a strong appreciation of their different qualities, is in love with them both: she deeply loves her husband but she is also taken with the naive sensitive poet and decides her only way to choose between them is to choose the one who needs her most, her husband. The younger man shows the extremity of his distress but leaves with *"a better secret in my heart"* and doesn't share that secret with either of them. In 1989 *The Stage* magazine critic Eric Braun had remembered Jeremy's performance sufficiently to make a comparison between Nicholas Cannon who played the teenage son in the Tabard play *Pavanne* with "such moving intensity and just the right vulnerability" and Jeremy in this role of the poet, "I can't recall a more telling depiction of adolescent traumas since the young Jeremy Brett's Marchbanks to Dulcie Gray's Candida several moons ago." (The Stage 6th April 1989)

Candida

Mr Fox of Venice 1959 - Lyceum Edinburgh/Piccadilly Theatre London

Jeremy as William McFly with Julie Somers

Jeremy would play **William McFly** in *Mr. Fox of Venice* by Frederick Knott, first at the Lyceum, Edinburgh on 16th March and then at The Piccadilly Theatre, London during April until 2nd May 1959, directed by Denis Carey. It was an adaptation of the novel *The Evil of the Day* by Thomas Sterling with its origins in Ben Jonson's *Volpone*. As a gigolo and as the new secretary, McFly (Mosca in Italian) was responsible for the care of the visitors to the home of his employer, Cecil Fox, a twentieth-century millionaire and the wealthiest man in Venice, living in the splendour of a 17th-century palazzo. Like Volpone, Fox pretends he is dying and invites three friends to his deathbed, one of whom is his ex-wife as they are all wealthy. They arrive bearing priceless gifts, yet are greedy for their inheritance, thus McFly has a crucial role to play as major domo. What begins as a comedy, turns into a story of murder as Mrs. Sheridan is found dead from an overdose of sleeping pills, and her nurse/companion suspects McFly of the murder. The humour continued with many shock revelations until the unveiling of the "joke" brings the final shocking truth about Cecil Fox, but only after his death.

The opening, the luxurious set and the references to *Volpone,* were all full of promise, although the thriller element was judged as "not very exciting thrillerdom." For this reason, *Theatre World* didn't particularly recommend the play and saw it as "a third rate farce" but went on to say, "Jeremy Brett as McFly, along with the rest of the cast, brings distinction to the part." And *The Times* agreed. "There is this to be said: those who do the fooling go about their work with an enjoyment which it is perhaps easy for those who can follow the plot to share. Mr. Rogers follows every whim that occurs to him and bullies his secretary when anything goes awry with the ferocity to which great wealth lends grace. Mr. Jeremy Brett is spry enough and does what he can to conceal from us the real purpose of his scheming." (The Times 16th April 1959)

The Stage said, "Paul Rogers gives an excellent performance as Mr Fox... Jeremy Brett strikes the right note as McFly", then went on to commend the whole production. Another *Stage* review thought Jeremy's characterisation showed him as a "somewhat empty, expressionless, young man... the kind of fellow with static good looks who often appears in American college films... Julie Somers offers the interest of her individual personality and the force of sincerity as the conventionally drawn young woman who naturally finds her way into McFly's arms." (The Stage 23rd April 1959) The conclusion was that this was an "another rewarding role: an unusual sort of major-domo with most unexpected duties in unpredictable situations. But he [Brett] is, of course, even in this early stage of his career, a young actor with a quite varied experience and a particular flair for the nonchalance essential for this type of part."

A film version titled *The Honey Pot,* based on the play, was released in 1967 starring Rex Harrison as the "supremely wealthy" Cecil Fox with Cliff Robertson as William McFly.

The Edwardians 1959 - Saville Theatre

Jeremy as Sebastian and Helen Cherry as Sylvia in The Edwardians

It is clear that aristocratic leading men continued to be on offer which was a little passé in the new style of Cockney lads who were gradually taking over the stage and screen. John Osborne's *Look Back in Anger* meant that the mood was changing and Jeremy felt he was too English and too traditional in his appearance to fit into this new movement, *"I've been incredibly lucky. I came in before the Angry Young Men Brigade at the Royal Court. When that happened, my career was over."* (Gary Hopkins: Black Box Interview)

An article in the *TV Times* in the 1980s which looked back at his career commented on the phenomenon, "It is intriguing to note that most of Jeremy Brett's roles have been period ones. Perhaps his aristocratic good looks and precise diction mark him down as a man more at ease in top hats, tailcoats and cravats. Whatever the reason, he has now become the definitive *Sherlock Holmes*. These days it's almost a shock to see him in modern dress..." (TV Times 1988) This concern was emphasised in his next appearance on the stage in **The Edwardians** at the Saville Theatre 1959 where Jeremy played **Sebastian the 12th Duke of Chevron**. Based on the novel by Vita Sackville-West in which she described the fiercely traditional, feudal, yet lavish life that she had enjoyed at her childhood home, Knole, the details are as she remembered them and in her author's note she wrote "no character in this book is wholly fictitious." She described her family as "a race too prodigious, too amorous, too weak, too indolent and too melancholy." In short, "a rotten lot and nearly all stark staring mad." (Robert Sackville-West in Inheritance) Playing the handsome, moody "dark romantic boy" of nineteen and heir to the estate which was like a small town, Jeremy finally realised he was not cut out to be one of the new angry young men who were beginning to dominate the theatre. *"I was *playing a young Duke in* The Edwardians *at the Saville, and I suddenly realised as Ernest Thesinger put the coronet on my head that I'd taken a far greater weight on than just the coronet. I was upstairs and out."* (Jeremy Brett: a new confidence) He envied Albert Finney's success as the factory worker Arthur Seaton in *Saturday Night and Sunday Morning* who was helping his married girlfriend deal with the consequences of an unwanted pregnancy whilst he was playing the love struck young Duke Sebastian, also in love with a married woman but destined for a completely different future. As Duke, his notorious liaison was with the professional beauty, Lady Roehampton played by Helen Cherry, an intimate friend of his mother, who was amused by the thought that Sylvia would teach him much and keep him from more disagreeable entanglements, especially as a young man in his position to have such an affair was quite *de rigueur*. However, Birth and Dignity were the rules they must live by and the scandal of divorce must be avoided at all costs. The intervention by his grandmother, the Dowager Duchess (Athene Saylor) meant a shocked Lord Roehampton received an anonymous letter telling him of the affair, from which unhappy decisions were made. In the novel the husband received the incriminating love letters by post but the repercussions were the same. A deep sense of tradition binds Sebastian to his inheritance and he clearly loves the enormous country estate but discovers he can't have the love of Lady Roehampton too. The influence of the adventurer and explorer Leonard Anquetil will cause Sebastian and his free-spirited sister Viola to question their destiny and right to freedom, in a life which has been ordained since birth. But he must follow his destiny first, even if it means he must marry the perfect girl for his position.

J.C.Trewin enjoyed the production. "Several of the performances in a production by Alan Bridges will linger: Athene Seylor as the Victorian dowager in the wheel-chair... who moves out upon the Chevron terrace like a conquering Tamburlaine... Ambrosine Phillpotts in proud full sail; and Ernest Thesiger's butler, who more clearly than any Duke is heir of all the ages. Jeremy Brett and Helen Cherry as the luckless lovers do all that can be done. I shall certainly remember *The Edwardians*, 'to lead your own life is worse than running away with someone': it has necessarily to be imperfect, but, whatever may happen to it, I shall think of it without facile cynicism." (The Stage 31st October 1959) "When they are found out we get the strongest scene of the evening. Lady Roehampton has been so foolish as to encourage an affair that is inconveniently real. She feels grief, but the creed by which she lives forces her to bear it rather than face extrusion from society. The Duke is left forlornly facing marriage with an entirely suitable girl. In the novel he escapes; in the play he remains a prisoner; but the ending carries no conviction because it has no dramatic force... Mr. Jeremy Brett plays him sympathetically but can do no more than suggest a duke who is rather exasperatingly eccentric. We cannot feel that his gilded shackles really gall him: he is too intent on seducing Lady Roehampton." (Adaptation of Edwardians The Times 16th October 1959)

All Good Children – Bromley Little Theatre - 1960s

All Good Children, at Bromley Little Theatre 1st November 1960, was performed by Company 101 a new professional company. Jeremy played a thirty-five-year-old merchant seaman, described by the author as suntanned "rugged and good looking" called **Maurice Bowers**. Prunella Scales played Anna Bowers, his sister, thirty-one years old and single, and Clifford the younger son, a thirty-three year old biochemist was played by David Korda. The head of this loveless family was the cold and unaffectionate father the Rev. Jacob Bowers a

Methodist minister, played by Robert Eddison, who was to retire after twenty-five years' service and leave his parish. He had called the family together for his last Sunday in the church but it is not the sentimental occasion he planned. He celebrates the fact that one of his sons has succeeded in life by becoming a scientist whilst the other had run away to sea at the age of fifteen and ironically helped fund his younger brother's education

The Stage introduced the play under the headline *Vicar's Guilt-Complex* and called it a "rather cruel story" in which Rev. Bowers' personal anguish has "driven him to instil a wretched discipline on his family." Although the religious symbolism and irony was too overt and the author had tried to achieve too much, "the acting throughout is extremely powerful." The critic applauded Prunella Scales for "a most sensitive and delightful performance of the young daughter." And as her father Robert Eddison, "is inflexible even when his sea-loving son (Jeremy) discharges a tremendous broadside of contempt and condemnation on his father's hypocrisy." Betty Pritchard as the devoted wife gives an "unexpected and impressive confession to her son of his father's lapse, is a fine piece of work. Jeremy Brett as the roving son presents the strength, romanticism and affection for his family admirably." (The Stage 3rd November 1960)

The Changeling 1961 – Royal Court Theatre

Mary Ure as Beatrice-Joanna and Jeremy as Alsemero

The Changeling

Jeremy's decision to forego his singing aspirations meant that his career next moved into the classics of *The Changeling* and *Hamlet*. He mentioned in an interview that it was his appearance in *All Good Children* which was responsible for his being offered the part of Alsemero in *The Changeling*. *The Stage* reported that "Jeremy Brett who stars in ABC-TV's Armchair Theatre presentation, *The Picture of Dorian Gray* has been given his biggest THEATRE break to date." (The Stage 19th January 1961)

Playing **Alsemero** in ***The Changeling*** brought him together with Mary Ure as Beatrice-Joanna, the talented actress with whom he had fallen in love when they first met at the *Central School of Speech and Drama*. The play opened at the Royal Court Theatre, with Robert Shaw co-starring as De Flores and the real-life romance between the two main players, Mary and Robert, would add to the box office receipts. The Middleton and Rowley play was described as the greatest tragedy besides Shakespeare with a story, which mixes the tragic and grotesque in an ugly tale of lust and murder. It also features the madness of a lunatic asylum as it gradually descends into moral degradation and death, before the "terrible workings of Divine justice could bring an end to the mayhem."

As a classic Jacobean revenge drama set in Catholic Spain, its tension is between sexual desire and family responsibilities. The central question of "What would one do for love?" is explored in the intelligent and romantic Beatrice-Joanna who is prepared to risk everything for the opportunity to marry the man she loves instead of the eligible young bachelor chosen by her father. "The crime is Beatrice's capricious bribing of a servant, whose ferocious looks repel her, to murder the man whom her father would have her marry. Although she does not know it, being herself passionately in love with Alsemero, this De Flores lusts after her and willingly accepts the commission. The murder done, he claims his reward. She offers him more money, only to learn that it is herself he single-mindedly desires. A proud, aristocratic woman has then to learn in a magnificently planned scene that the servant she imagined she could easily control is setting himself up as her master." (The Times 22nd February 1961)

The Stage Magazine described the production as "a somewhat workaday, economical unspectacular production" which missed the "grandeur" of the text. "It also demands a cast of Shakespearean quality. Mary Ure can look grave and distressed, and can break gloom with snatches of gaiety, but she does not succeed in making Beatrice-Joanna a moving figure, or even one in which one can take much interest." Robert Shaw earned some praise as "a more convincing figure" and "Jeremy Brett as Beatrice's lover, does well enough with a conventional character, but too often robs us of words with a dropping voice." (The Stage 23rd February 1961)

"The all-important part of Beatrice-Joanna is entrusted to Mary Ure and I can not honestly say I thought that the trust was this time quite justified. She acts with intelligence and looks very pretty. But the finer shades are wanting, especially in the voice, and there is a tendency to modern mincing, to floating about the stage in a dollish way... All the same the play pleases; and among others Jeremy Brett as the final husband... make their mark." (Too little care for the words? Philip Hope-Wallace in The Guardian 22nd February

Richard II - Audio Recording

Jeremy would work with John Gielgud again in a sound recording of **Richard II,** 1961. It is described as "a wonderful classic recording with some of the greatest actors performing Shakespeare." John Gielgud had the reputation of giving the very best performance as Richard II, having played the weak, neurotic king many times, including 492 performances in the play *Richard of Bordeaux* in 1936. At the beginning of the play he is sitting in state as Monarch dealing with a private dispute between **Thomas Mowbray, Duke of Norfolk** (Jeremy Brett) and Henry Bolingbroke later Henry IV (Keith Michell), Richard's cousin. The accusation is that Mowbray has squandered money given by Richard for his soldiers. He is also accused of complicity in the murder of the Duke of Gloucester, although Richard's brother and father believe the murderer is Richard himself. The two warring nobles refuse to be reconciled but Richard will not allow the duel and sends them into exile: Bolingbroke for ten years and Mowbray for life. When John of Gaunt dies Richard seizes his property, thereby denying Bolingbroke his inheritance which angers him further against his king. Richard foolishly leaves England to pursue a war against Ireland appointing his other uncle, York, to govern in his absence so that an uprising takes place with Bolingbroke at its head. All his troops defect and Richard is deposed, imprisoned and killed by an assassin in Pomfret Castle. Edward Hardwicke also features in the cast.

In *Plays and Players* in 1966 Jeremy explained how his approach to acting had changed during this time, of his decision to stop playing *"glossy young men"* and find where his true talent lay. *"I was fearfully arrogant and complacent, getting signed up for a musical that was never produced and auditioning for a Peter Brook production of* Time Remembered *that he finally never directed."* But it was John Gielgud who gave him the essential guidance on how to develop his career. He *"gave me my first long lesson in how to act..."* And since then he had *"changed tack"* making different choices and an extraordinary number of parts had come his way; from the Yorkshire seaman Maurice Bowers in *All Good Children* to "an outstanding part of the neurotic Marchbanks in *Candida* starring with Michael Denison and Dulcie Gray." In considering the part played by The Method and Stanislavsky in his development, he said, *"It's true I used to study Stanislavsky's book* An Actor Prepares, *but everything moves so fast these days, especially in the film world, that traditional methods of training are not necessarily the right ones."* He would refer again to Stanislavsky and his own method of *"becoming"* the part in his approach to Sherlock Holmes and the terms he would use suggest it had not been a comfortable experience, even if it earned him the very best of critical acclaim.

Hamlet 1961 – Oxford Playhouse/The Strand Theatre London

Jeremy as Hamlet and Helen Cherry as Gertrude

Jeremy's appearance in **Hamlet** was the result of a chance meeting with Frank Hauser who asked him if he wanted to play the role and the enthusiastic "*Yes*" meant that he was only 26 years old when he took on the mantle of the most famous and the most challenging of Shakespeare's male protagonists and joined all those actors who wanted to earn a reputation on the stage. Hauser was the innovative and much respected artistic director of the Oxford Playhouse from 1956-1973 and also freelance director for the West End theatres. During this period he presented a large number of world premieres featuring many leading actors of the time, so that Jeremy was in the very best of company at this early stage of his career. There is evidence that Tyrone Guthrie was also anxious to produce a modern-dress version of *Hamlet* with Jeremy in the title role but it didn't appear, maybe due to lack of funding so Hauser's version was a very welcome one.

Hamlet is a revenge play concerned with the nature of evil and death with its introspective central character, sweet and noble, yet seemingly mad. The story of the young, indecisive Prince of Denmark expected to take action against his uncle Claudius who has married Queen Gertrude, Hamlet's mother, and taken the throne after the death of his father is as familiar as that of *Romeo and Juliet*. When the Ghost of the dead King makes his dreadful demand to avenge his "*foul and most unnatural murder*" it goes against everything Hamlet feels is right and the four hours on stage are full of his horrible imaginings and play-acting as he tests the veracity of the Ghost's story. The delay in carrying out his revenge brings accidental death and eventual justice, although the final scene has the four principal characters each meeting their deaths on stage, including Hamlet himself. It is the tragic fatal flaw of *delay* in Hamlet's personality which fascinates the audience as he is swept between grief for his "*two months dead*" father, his mother's "*o'er hasty marriage*" and his attempt to pursue the course of action required of him. The unnatural murder of a king has unleashed a deadly infection and disease into the state of Denmark: "*The time is out of joint. O cursed spite that ever I was born to set it right!*" The *Oedipus* complex also plays a part and there is great drama and pathos in his determined efforts to bring himself to his destiny.

Jeremy said, *"I was asked to play* Hamlet *when I was 26 by Frank Hauser. It was intended just to tour the country, but there had been a quite bad one at Stratford that year, so when we came into London, I cleaned up. The poster of me as Hamlet is pretty well the only piece of theatre memorabilia I keep around my home. It is behind glass, and it is going a bit beige now."* (Hello Magazine 1984) As he reported later, he thought he was very young and handsome, even Byronic: *"I think I got away with it though the only thing I had on my side was youth. I had an enormous sense of identity with Hamlet, though I never understood fully a scene like the Ghost scene, which is why I would dearly like to play the part again. Of course, that's the frustrating thing about these marvellous Shakespearean parts which you must play in your twenties and early thirties, though you're not really fitted to act them properly until you're in your fifties. Just imagine what understanding and warmth Peggy Ashcroft could bring to Juliet, if she was to play her now."* (Homes and Gardens 1967)

On his appearance at the Oxford Playhouse the critics made complimentary comments both to his suitability for the part, his youth, his looks, his intelligence, his princely demeanour and for the delivery of the lines, all of which pointed to a critical success: "The text received full consideration and was delivered with good sense by every speaker, but as to acting, Jeremy Brett as Hamlet was alone remarkable... Here, everyone was in black or dun, and it testified to Jeremy Brett's fitness for the part of the Prince of Denmark that he did not seem to require greatly the usual sable sartorial distinction. He was manifestly a prince among players. His voice was pleasant and pliable... Somewhat taller than most, he was princely in looks, manner, speech, and authority, and had an easy transition of mood." (HGM Theatre World) *Plays and Players* also commented on his delivery of the language which was fine and musical; "*Hamlet* was directed with all Frank Hauser's customary refreshingly direct approach to Shakespeare, with its insistence on clear and musical speech so that the sound and sense are indivisible, as, ideally, they should be. The Hamlet of Jeremy Brett came like a fresh cooling draught... youthful, princely, embittered, passionate in his vengeance-seeking... a man who in voice and mien suggested a royal personage. Mr Brett's speaking of the language had a consistently fine and expressive musicality. I do not think in recent years I have heard the soliloquy "*How all occasions do inform against me'* spoken with such a range of nuance and such flexibility of rhythm." (Frank Dibb in Plays and Players) Another critic saw him as "a very young Hamlet, essentially a student revelling in his own verbal brilliance, delighting in his practical jokes, bursting with energy, capable at times of the passion and violence of the mature man, at others behaving like an overgrown schoolboy." The consensus seems to have been that this was a fine and expressive Hamlet delivered with "courage, high intelligence, simplicity and power and with youth and good looks on his side." (The Guardian)

When the play transferred to The Strand Theatre in London the critics were a little harsher but still highlighted the fact that Jeremy inhabited the role with ease and suitability for the part. "Mr. Jeremy Brett's performance compromises competently between the prince who has undertaken a burden he finds hard to bear and the youth whose busy, hedonistic, characteristically Renaissance temperament asserts itself triumphantly again and again to react against uncongenial circumstance. The result is a lively, sometimes sportive and sometimes over-emphatic reflection of Hamlet's external life. It is never a reflection in depth, and there is hardly any suggestion that the working of a fine intellect is bedevilled by a mistrust of his own intuitions of goodness and truth. The actor speaks clearly, looks well and cuts a sympathetic figure. Alas, we can only guess at what goes on in his mind..." (Man Without A Man Within. The Times 21st June 1961)

Kenneth Tynan who would be invited by Olivier to become the press officer for the National Theatre picked out Jeremy's weak 's' sounds; "When Hamlet appeared, he made straight for the traditional Hamlet chair, a wasp-waist in wood, and took up the traditional Hamlet posture, with one leg bent at the knee and the other out-thrust. Jeremy Brett, the actor in question, looks handsomely overweening and delivers the lines with forthright lucidity, despite a tendency to fizz the sibilants and a weakness for the Gielgud tremolo: what blights his performance is its total failure to enlist our sympathy... it is sound, intelligent and undeserving of jeers." (K. Tynan in The Observer 25th June 1961) And *The Stage* commented on its "positive virtues – clarity and firmness in the production, the play being allowed to speak for itself without unnecessary or over-elaborate outside aids... a touchingly sincere Hamlet in Jeremy Brett... appears to use up all his resources by the time he is half-way through the play, so that a very creditable interpretation that had some depth and meaning becomes shallow and methodical..." (The Stage 27th June 1961)

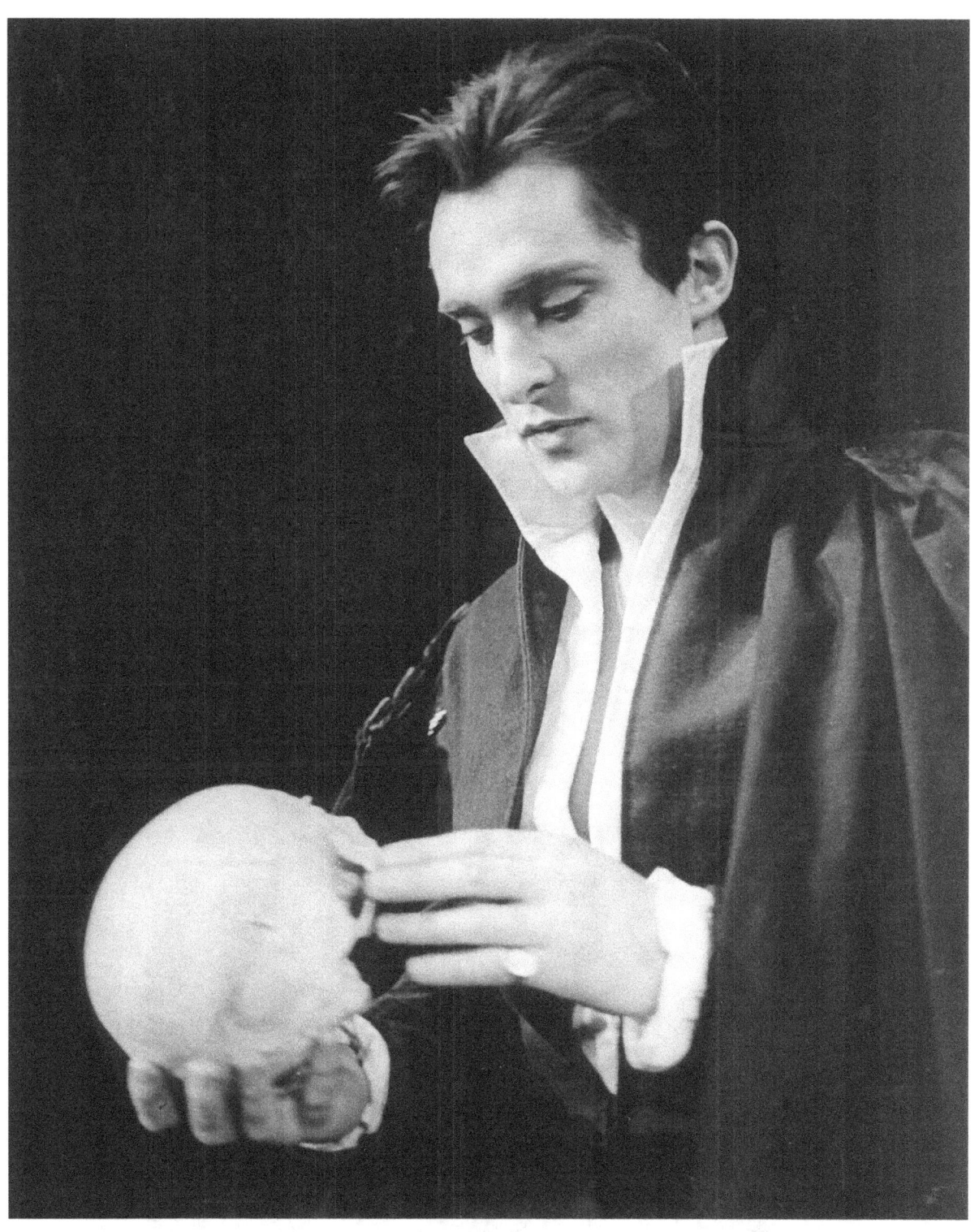

Hamlet

Bamber Gascoigne gave perhaps one of the most effective tributes, "Jeremy Brett's Hamlet is as intelligent and straightforward as the production. He plays those qualities which a modern reader finds in Hamlet – his probing student intelligence, his taste for gloom, his bouts of ineffectual self-criticism, his exhibitionism, his talent for sudden and unexpected bursts of affection and, above all, his exuberance. If the typical nineteenth century Hamlet was a pale romantic, the twentieth century is a manic depressive, plunging from his hectic baiting of the court to the dejection of the soliloquies and then soaring back again... Jeremy Brett catches perfectly this creature. Where greater actors have given us their Hamlet, Brett presents ours….." (The Spectator 30th June 1961) Harold Hobson, the critic of *The Sunday Times,* did highlight one of Jeremy's innovations which he admitted later was a personal response to the devastating death of his mother in an accident. "I have never seen Hamlet so brutal to Ophelia and Polonius as Mr. Brett is. But this seems to be Mr. Hauser's only innovation. The brutality must be deliberate, for it clearly is not part of Mr. Brett's own character or his stage presence. He is a slim and graceful actor, courteous in bearing, and he treats everyone in the play with careful consideration, except for Ophelia and her family. It would appear that this Hamlet's idea of marriage and love has been polluted by his mother and his uncle, and that, after learning of their treachery, he cannot bear, to see anything that might remind him of normal relationships between men and women." (Harold Hobson in The Sunday Times)

Playing the Dane

Jeremy revealed the emotional upset his mother's death had caused him in a documentary named *Playing the Dane* for BBC2 in 1994 in which he thought his treatment of Gertrude was particularly rough; *"I think it was Hobson who said the incestuous bed was at the centre of my performance. I couldn't believe the circumstances. I thought it was so monstrous and I was very rough on my mother... physically rough. I was angry at that time. My mother had been killed savagely in a car accident in 1959 and I was very angry about that because my son, when she was killed, was only three months old... I felt cheated. I felt my mother had been cheated. But the rage of that I think came through... I don't think I was very good at Hamlet! I was too young: I was too young intellectually; I was too young philosophically; I was Byronic; I was very handsome, but I would much rather have seen other people's (Hamlet). I wasn't convinced by me."* Another comment made during this documentary gave an interesting insight from some of the actors prepared to take on the role. "Hamlet remains the most notoriously troubled youth in literature. He is a mercurial observer, at once wise and innocent among the swirl of adult corruption going on around him. The role presents a young actor with a central paradox, as Jeremy Brett, a 1961 Hamlet, observes. *'You're never ready to play Hamlet. When you're ready to play him you're too old."* Christopher Plummer agreed with this comment, "How can you play a part that has so many thousands of colours and experiences until you are old enough to understand those feelings?'" (The Observer 9th October 1994)

A book titled *Five and Eighty Hamlets* by J.C. Trewin (Hutchinson 1987) reviewed in *The Stage* said "Jeremy Brett had height, appearance, and a deep flexible voice. What he did not have was any splendour of personality." Peter O'Toole (National Theatre) and Richard Burton (directed by Gielgud) were dispatched with similar economy, and a host of lesser actors were also dismissed.

And then there was the humour of the loss of the sword in the battle between Hamlet and Laertes in the final Act. Hamlet's sword had *"flashed through the air and landed in the lap of a girl sitting in the front row."* The actors had instinctively frozen in the middle of their battle unable to proceed; *"I knelt down and peered over the footlights and she kindly passed the sword over to me, which I needed rather badly in order to stab Laertes."* Luckily the young lady reacted smartly by *"graciously"* handing back his sword so that the fight might continue.

Hamlet is on stage for almost three hours and has 1,100 lines to deliver so it is no surprise Jeremy said in interview: *"That was challenging simply because it wasn't in repertory. I had to do about two hundred performances, straight through, appearing eight times a week. It wore me out."* (Secrets 1987) However, he explained his fascination for the role in another interview, *"Why every actor loves playing Hamlet is that you can never get it right... It's like trying to run up Everest – you know you're going to be defeated, but what a wonderful way to go! I had a marvellous director who encouraged me when I played it, and I absolutely flew! Got myself exhausted because it's a long, long haul, but there are moments in that play when you suddenly get one or two things right... and you find you're choking back tears because something has come to you, and you long to go back and do it again."* (Green Bay Press-Gazette Sunday 2nd July 1972)

The Kitchen 1961 - Royal Court Theatre

Jeremy as Peter in The Kitchen

The Stage Magazine announced his next appearance in the headline *Hamlet in The Kitchen* and illustrated just how much status had been gained by his success in the coveted classic role. "Jeremy Brett who recently played *Hamlet* at the Strand is one of the new names to join the cast of *The Kitchen*, the Arnold Wesker play which returns to the Royal Court on Monday next for a three-week run..." (The Stage 17th August 1961) The same critic praised the production, "...*The Kitchen*, like *Look Back in Anger*, is proving to be one of the most popular plays presented by the English Stage Company. (The Stage 14th September 1961) *"Really it was kind of a miracle because I'd just played Hamlet at the Strand and I'd followed that through... with* **Peter** *in* **The Kitchen** *at the Royal Court, which was all thanks to John Dexter, who got me out of a very difficult period, because I was a gentleman playing gentlemen, when suddenly 'angry young men' came into the world, which was brilliant at the Royal Court."* (Stagestruck)

"It was Robert Stephens who inspired me to tackle a really different part at the Royal Court, *that of the crazy fanatical cook in Arnold Wesker's* The Kitchen." (Jeremy in 1967 interview) The director agreed so long as he put on two stones in weight and cut his hair, which he was happy to do especially as it was going to change his "pretty boy" romantic image. The story centres on the demands of a kitchen in a high-class London restaurant with its microcosm of workers from different backgrounds and nations. Peter, a lively, highly charged chef, falls in love with a married waitress, Monique, and he goes berserk when she will not leave her husband for him. The chaos of the kitchen as the staff struggles to keep up with the frenzied demands of the situation ends in fights, breakages and heartache. Lasting only one hour and twenty minutes it featured a quick series of thumbnail sketches, amongst the chopping boards, knives, plates, no food, and the developing relationships between the cook and the waitresses coming and going. The love story between Peter and the married waitress was meticulously choreographed with speed and intensity, "you couldn't delve too deeply into Peter's love affair... it was on the move, flying." (Robert in Knight Errant)

The critics recognised Jeremy's performance as intelligent, sincere and pivotal to the production: "Wesker shows us the kitchen through the eyes of Peter, a German chef (very well portrayed by Jeremy Brett) who bullies, jokes and quarrels with his fellow-workers. A highly strung, excitable person, Peter is suspicious of those around him: in a leisure moment he impulsively builds a castle of pots and pans and invites the other chefs to tell him their dreams. One dreams of a shed full of tools, another of money, another of women, and another of friendship. '*I ask for dreams and you give me nightmares,*' groans Peter; for he dreams of destroying all kitchens before they destroy all those who work in them..." (The Montreal Gazette) "Arnold Wesker's *The Kitchen* returned to the Royal Court on Monday last with several changes to the cast. Chief among these was Jeremy Brett, whose exuberant playing of the German cook, Peter, was fired by an inner nervous energy that made this enigmatic character the real pivot of the play. The alternative moods of childish foolery and brooding intensity were equally believable aspects of his character, and the final scene of attempted suicide was carried off without a tinge of jarring unreality." (Return of the Kitchen. The Stage 21st August 1961) "It still catches all the author's moods with great fidelity and builds up its two greatest crescendo finales with exciting, controlled vigour, carrying the play firmly along... The principal newcomers are Jeremy Brett whose tragic Peter is played with an intelligence and sincerity that override his hardly consistent search for a German accent and Miss Sandra Caron whose chilly demanding Monique effectively provides the motive power for his final explosion." (Still Cooking in The Times 22nd August 1961)

Television

Jeremy

Jeremy would create a considerable reputation on television starting as early as 1954 with *Mrs. Dot*. His career had begun at the birth of the new Independent Television and he would appear frequently in the weekly plays on both BBC and ITV. Some of these early performances leave little evidence.

Myself When Young 1958 - ITV Play of the Week

The first Independent Television company to begin broadcasting was the London based Associated Rediffusion on 22nd September 1955. ITV was a network of independently owned regional companies starting with four companies operating in three regions which would gradually expand to fourteen regions over the next seven years. For the first ten years of ITV there was always a single play to be found in the top British programmes of the year, usually taken from TV Playhouse, Armchair Theatre or Play of the Week. Jeremy's first appearance on Independent Television was in The Play of the Week on Wednesday 26th February 1958 at 9pm in the play **Myself When Young** billed as a comedy. This was an adaptation for television of the play *Paul and Constantine* by Dario Bellini in which Jeremy took the role of **Paul Chase**, the young Constantine, and Dennis Price played the more unpleasant older man. "Paul Constantine Chase was a romantic, dreamy and lovable young man - but success has made him selfish, calculating and mean. Engaged in an illicit romance, he is confronted by himself when young. The battle for control between Chase, past and present, is the enthralling situation of the play." (Kaleidoscope Database) The cast included Zena Walker as Lucienne and Maxine Audley as Leonora.

Eden End 1958 - BBC Sunday Night Theatre

In spite of the instant popularity of ITV, the home of quality drama would remain with the BBC and its Sunday night play often starred the new faces of theatre land. This would make them more recognisable and encourage the public to join the audiences in the West End. The J.B. Priestley play **Eden End** was broadcast on Easter Sunday **6th April 1958** in Sunday Night Theatre on BBC, produced by Stephen Harrison and starring Dennis Price, Maxine Audley and James Hayter with Gwen Watford and Jeremy Brett. It was described as a drawing room drama with recognisable personal dilemmas and one of Priestley's most famous and for some, his finest. The action takes place in Dr Kirby's house in the Fells village of Eden End, during the Autumn of 1902. Stella Kirby, played by Maxine Audley, spent eight years running away; leaving home to find her freedom on the stage as an actress, first all over England, then out East and in Australia. In spite of touring and working hard, she felt unfulfilled and a failure, "I've disappointed myself." She is also tired of the "dirty provincial towns" with the stuffy dressing rooms, the cheap places to stay and tea rooms of London. "No space, no fresh air." Now she has decided that the only role left to play is the prodigal daughter as she returns to her widowed country doctor father, played by James Hayter, hoping to discover herself in the familiar surroundings of her childhood home.

Jeremy would need no special make-up, just a moustache to play **Wilfred Kirby** Stella's younger brother, aged twenty four years, "sunburned and in possession of a small moustache, he looks young, unsophisticated." (Eden End) He works abroad, in Nigeria, for the British West African Development Company and is successful. He plays the piano and even sings a little. Stella, as the returning elder daughter is the successful actress, genuinely attempting to recapture some meaning in her life. An old flame Geoffrey Farran (John Stone) appears to be one way of doing so, but Act II is interrupted by the unexpected arrival of Stella's husband, Charlie Appleby (Dennis Price), also an actor and from then on the outcome becomes uncertain. "Priestley's rather Chekhovian study of frustration in 1912, *Eden End*, makes good TV material, because it concentrates on a handful of well-drawn and contrasted characters... In an excellent team Dennis Price gave a performance of such masterly ease as Stella's actor husband that one anticipated his every entry with relish. That old familiar stand by, the drunk scene, was anything but a convenient padding when enacted with such comic, yet not overdone brilliance by Mr Price and Jeremy Brett, as the futilely commonplace young son on leave from West Africa..." (The Stage 10th April 1958)

The Guinea Pig 1960 – BBC Saturday Playhouse

A BBC television performance for Jeremy which also leaves little evidence is a Saturday Playhouse presentation of **The Guinea Pig** a play by Warren Chetham-Strode, produced by Terence Dudley on Saturday 4th June 1960. However, a filmed version starring Richard Attenborough as Read does exist. The story is about the public school system set at the end of the war when public schools were coming under scrutiny and takes place at Saintbury School. Jeremy played **Nigel Lorraine**, the house tutor, and Michael Crawford played the boy, Read. As a working class boy whose father was a poor tobacconist, he enters an exclusive school by winning a scholarship and neither he nor his teachers knew how he could adapt. His house master Mr Lloyd Hartley (Barry Jones) resented his presence at the school but Lorraine, an ex-soldier who had just received a new artificial leg befriended Read. As they were both new in the school with its ancient system of rituals, sport, fags and beatings they established a sympathetic relationship which helped the boy to deal with the challenges.

Tess of the d'Urbervilles 1960 - ITV

Angel Clare in Tess

Jeremy's role of **Angel Clare** in Thomas Hardy's ***Tess of the d'Urbervilles*** for ITV 5th July 1960 would have presented a challenge as the perception of the idealistic, intractable husband, unable to forgive the revelations of the ill-fated Tess is not that of the romantic hero. But Jeremy gave an impressive performance. The tragic story of a simple country girl, who is sent by her father to claim kinship with the aristocratic d'Urbervilles in order to save the family from penury is full of unhappy accidents. The dissolute son Alec is the real villain who welcomes Tess, seduces her and abandons her to care for her baby alone. At Tarbuoys farm she imagines she has finally found happiness when she falls in love with the seemingly upright Angel but as she confesses to her past on their wedding night, his rejection leaves her in hardship and forces her to return to Alec with tragic consequences.

The Times approved, "Actually, in spite of its unpromising opening and the impossibly heavy dialect Miss Geraldine McEwan was forced to adopt in the title role, Mr Ronald Gow's free adaptation proved on the whole surprisingly faithful. It plunged boldly in with Tess's marriage and sped forward combining the events of a sprawling novel into a neatly carpentered piece of television drama. The weaknesses of the play were the weaknesses of the book though a tendency to unconscious self-parody noticeable in the book was naturally accentuated by the very embodiment of the characters in flesh and blood actors. Angel begins as one of the most insufferable characters in fiction, and all Mr Jeremy Brett's efforts could not dissuade us from feeling that he had forfeited all claims on our sympathy... while Tess's awkward, shining honesty remained a little too good to be true..." (The Times 6th July 1960)

This production had used authentic locations for filming and the final scene was set at the two stones connected with human sacrifice – the Altar Stone and the Slaughter Stone at Stonehenge in Wiltshire. "Tess is a murderess, and it is on the open plain at Stonehenge that the law catches up with her. Her husband, Angel pleads with her to move before she is exposed by daylight. But Tess seems to be in no hurry. She feels that it time for justice, and her doom..." The cast and crew were waiting for the sun to rise around seven o'clock before the challenging scene of justice for the guilty Tess could begin. "With an *ITV* film unit, I was waiting for dawn to see the filming of the tragic last scene of *Tess*... Cheerful jazz music helped to dispel the sinister atmosphere. It was drifting over from a car, where Geraldine McEwan, who plays Tess, and co-star Jeremy Brett were resting... Geraldine McEwan giggled. 'We are an odd looking lot,' she said. Jeremy was trying his best to look bright and cheerful, but was feeling quite the opposite as the night before he had been in Bristol recording a television play until about eleven o'clock, giving him only *'about a half-hour's doze'* before starting work on *Tess*. "Just after seven a.m. ... the sun appeared and it was possible to start filming. At seven-ten, the camera started to roll. Tess lay asleep on the altar-stone, while Angel stretched, yawned and strolled forward to scan the horizon..." (David Griffiths in TV Times 3rd July 1960) Unfortunately, filming had to be stopped briefly to remove the modern watch Jeremy was wearing, which was not in keeping with the correct apparel for a Victorian hero. *The Guardian* was impressed by the performances of the stars but had some reservations about the production; 'The Associated-Rediffusion production last night of *Tess* in Ronald Gow's free interpretation was fair enough to the main lines of the plot, but it was a telescoped affair... some impression of the passionate strength of love was certainly given by the acting of Jeremy Brett as Angel Clare, an impressive performance, and by Geraldine McEwan as Tess..." (The Guardian 6th July 1960)

Beauty and the Beast 1960 – BBC Christmas

Beauty and the Beast was a BBC production in two parts by Nicholas Stuart Gray broadcast on 27th December 1960 at 5 p.m. with Part 2 the following Sunday 8th January. It starred Jeremy as **The Prince** and **The Beast** with Jennifer Daniel as Beauty. It was a first-class production and was praised for the costumes, settings, dance routines, the "wonderful shots" and overall presentation which created a most enjoyable contribution to the seasonal programming. One viewer wrote, "I sat entranced throughout *Beauty and The Beast*. What a lovely production." (BBC Archives)

Patricia Garwood who played the other daughter Jonquiline would marry Jeremy Paul which would establish the relationship between them. Jeremy Paul commented on how successful it was. "Jeremy played the Prince and the Beast and was wonderful. Pat and Jeremy struck up a kind of friendship and he came back to our house and played ping-pong late into the night on a number of occasions. We became friends before we worked together. Then I adapted an H.E. Bates story, *An Aspidistra in Babylon* for a Granada series called *Country Matters* and Jeremy played the lead... Working on this production secured our friendship, I guess." (Jeremy Paul in Bending the Willow by David Stuart Davies) Jeremy Paul would write the scripts for several of the Sherlock Holmes episodes and also write the stage play from Jeremy's extensive notes for *The Secret of Sherlock Holmes* as a centennial tribute to Conan Doyle.

The Picture of Dorian Gray 1961 - ITV Armchair Theatre

Jeremy as Dorian Gray

Jeremy appeared in ***The Picture of Dorian Gray*** twice, the second time in 1976 as the painter, Basil Hallward, a more demanding role and some would say more satisfying than the young man of the title. However, in this appearance for *Armchair Theatre* he was obviously chosen for the part of **Dorian** for his looks. It is the story of a cultured, wealthy and impossibly beautiful young man, with a "face like ivory and rose leaves," who like Faust sells his soul to the Devil, here for the gift of immortal beauty and, in spite of his selfish pursuit of pleasure and an increasingly scandalous life style, he remains physically unchanged. The picture hidden in the attic takes on the hideous appearance of Dorian's personal debauchery. The murder of both Basil Hallward (John Bailey) and finally Dorian himself is the outcome of such a dreadful pact. Dennis Price in the Satanic role of Lord Henry Wotton and Jill Ireland as Sybil Vane, the young actress that Dorian falls in love with, but then heartlessly rejects, would be inspired casting. Just three prints of stills remain of this performance although it is on record that Jeremy won the Daily Mirror Award of 1961 for the Most Promising Actor on Television for his role.

The producer of the play had removed a great deal of the wickedness and perversion in the deeds of the central character to make it more palatable to the television audience and to some it appeared rather tame. Overall, the critics were impressed with the performances and the period atmosphere of the production. "Jeremy Brett gave a realistic portrayal of the non-hero of the piece... The portrait itself changed with lurid flourishes that tipped the scales towards the comic – but forceful direction put the balance right in the end. Teleplay: John Bethune, Director: Charles Jarrott, Designer: George Haslam." (The Stage and Television Today 26th January 1961) Dennis Price was praised for the stylish delivery of his "finer flights of wit" and also for his influence on Dorian. "One felt his influence gradually stealing over Mr. Jeremy Brett whose Dorian became less prone to flick away his lines with modern off-handedness as the play proceeded." (A Compressed Dorian Gray. The Times (London, England) 23rd January 1961)

The critic in *The Observer* was more consistent in his praise, "The acting was very nice. Dennis Price's Lord Henry... kept it cool and was unflustered by the docking... of some of his best epigrams such as: 'Crime is the art of the lower classes.'... Jeremy Brett's Dorian was little the worse for a dash of the South American gigolo..." (Maurice Richardson. The Everlasting Oscar. The Observer 29th January 1961) In an interview in 1982 Jeremy thought this appearance was not particularly helpful in the progress of his career because, *"People assume if you're chosen for* Dorian Gray *you must be good-looking – that's not a terribly popular requirement in the British theatre."*

A link can be found between Oscar Wilde and the creator of Sherlock Holmes, Arthur Conan Doyle, who met at a dinner at the Langham Hotel on 30th August 1889, provided by J.M. Stoddart, the managing director of Lippincott's Monthly Magazine of Philadelphia, who was looking for new material for his publication. As a result *The Picture of Dorian Gray* and *The Sign of (the) Four* were both purchased and each author received £100 in payment for magazine serial rights helping them to achieve transatlantic fame. (The Teller of Tales, the Life of Arthur Conan Doyle by Daniel Stashower) Many people believe that Conan Doyle was so impressed by Wilde and his creation *Dorian Gray* that he added some of Wilde's dramatic flair into his characterisation of Sherlock Holmes.

A Kind of Strength 1961 - BBC Sunday Night Play

Jeremy would appear in the role of **Julian Bennett** in The Sunday Night Play ***A Kind of Strength*** for BBC television on 29th January 1961. *A Kind of Strength* was written by the prolific playwright N.J. Crisp, and the setting was the world of business, a world he knew well, The chief characters in the play are Leslie Palmer, a man who had given up a career in teaching for the greater material rewards of employment at a large machine accounting company; and Julian Bennett, an ex-doctor who had joined the same firm for the same reasons. Palmer and Bennett come immediately into conflict with each other, and their mutual dislike was not helped by the fact that the latter falls in love with Palmer's daughter Susan, who worked in the company as a secretary.

Julian Bennett had the added spur of his father's expectations and Palmer could earn twice the salary of a schoolteacher, but both were forced to make a choice as they felt trapped by the world of commerce, and struggled to be free. "In facing the truth about themselves, the decisions they have to make needs a rare kind of strength." *The Stage* put it as "Before Palmer's vocational penny drops, we are treated to a romantic side-plot concerning his daughter, who happens to be the secretary for interloper Brett. A chummy little scene at Palmer's home shows his wife – and the viewers – a drop of Pythagoras to indicate he doesn't want the sordid world of commerce, and would feel much more at home back at school." (The Stage 2nd February 1961) "Last night's play, *A Kind of Strength* by N.J. Crisp, could not be faulted on the ground of violence. It was irreproachably harmless and dealt with nothing stronger than the harshness of the business world, the unfairness of nepotism and the importance of a man doing a job he loved rather than an unloved job for more money. There was sense and truth in the character of Leslie Palmer, the teacher turned manager, who lost his job to the boss's nephew and found he was delighted to return to teaching. This part was intelligently played by Michael Gwynn. The smart young man who took his job and then began to learn that smartness is not enough was dashingly played by the versatile Jeremy Brett, whom we have so recently seen as Dorian Gray... Altogether, this was a fresh play with an unashamed view of the value of integrity..." (Mary Crozier in The Guardian)

The Ghost Sonata 1961 - BBC Television

Jeremy as the Student with the Milkmaid

Jeremy appeared as **The Student** in *The Ghost Sonata,* a surreal play by August Strindberg, translated from the Swedish by Michael Meyer, produced by Stuart Burge and directed by Ingmar Bergman, which appeared on BBC on 16th March 1961, with Robert Helpmann as, "an old man in a wheelchair (who) offers his patronage to a young student on one condition that he goes to a performance of *The Valkerie* and asks no questions." The thirsty Student has been helping to rescue the victims of a collapsing house and the Milkmaid, in reality a ghost, gives him a drink and bathes his eyes at the fountain. "The opening act – mostly a continuous dialogue between Jeremy Brett and Robert Helpmann – establishes both characters firmly: one is a *Sunday Child* with the soul of a poet, (a person in Swedish myth who can see what others can't) while the other is a manipulative user of people who can be charming enough if it is to his advantage."

Robert Helpmann as the Old Man and Jeremy as the Student

"All three principal actors are simply tremendous in this production – they are given great characters to play by adapter Michael Meyer and do not disappoint." They give "wonderful performances, Brett capitalising on his ability to play fey characters and Helpmann almost (but not quite) over-acting with his eye-rolling and Shylockian mannerisms… (they) must behave true to themselves. Anything else invites ridicule and this compelling and intriguing play certainly does not do that." (The Illustrated Gazette) *The Times* agreed that the acting was tremendous. "Mr Jeremy Brett, too, had his moments as the gushing, hyperaesthetic Student who wanders innocently into this nightmare household. But somehow, whether because of the sluggish pace of the production or its lack-lustre lighting, the haunted atmosphere which would have bound all these elements into a coherent whole never made itself felt." (The Times 17th March 1962)

In an episode of the *South Bank Show* which featured the extensive career of Helpmann as a singer and producer in which his fellow stars of opera and film called him *"a wonderful man"*, Jeremy recorded his personal experience of acting alongside him, *"If he knew he had a power over you he could immediately do a Svengali on you. He was powerful. I was scared of him. I was scared."* (BBC Tales of Helpmann)

Dinner with the Family 1962 - BBC Television

Jeremy as Jacques Angela Brown as Barbara and Stephen Moore as Georges Delachaume

The play **Dinner with the Family** by Jean Anouilh, translated by Edward Owen Marsh, was transmitted on 30th March 1962, on BBC television and was described as a charming, fanciful comedy about a handsome young Parisian called Georges Delachaume, played by Stephen Moore. He had been unhappily married for four years to a hysterical millionairess, Christine, and is surrounded by his parents, his sponging friend, **Jacques** (Jeremy) with his wife Barbara who prey on him, living a life of luxury at his expense. Georges may say "I'd gladly give my life for my friend Jacques and he would his for me." But in reality, Jacques is a false friend and his wife as Georges' mistress, will eventually admit to playing the villains in his life as they take whatever money they can before they are cast out.

Georges may have been charming however he was without scruples, so that when he met the young unsophisticated Isabelle (Jacqueline Ellis) and fell in love, he was unable to tell her the truth about himself. Instead he invented the story of a perfect family, filled with the people he would prefer to live with and invited her to dine with them. All he wanted was to pretend he had a normal childhood, which he had not. "A young man in love and for the young lady the ordeal of the first dinner with his family…" No expense was spared as he hired a house, servants and actors to create his alternative reality but unfortunately his real family turned up to spoil the fantasy. His wife threatened him with a gun and mayhem broke out. Georges thought he had lost both his wife and his new love, but the fantasy continued as all the hangers on disappeared and Isabelle left Paris with him to begin a new life together.

The Stage magazine pointed out that Anouilh's works were "highly sought after because they are such admirable vehicles for acting talent" and then gave an example from the television production *Dinner with the Family*. "In his first exposure, Stephen Moore, said to have outstanding promise, was a great disappointment. On the strength of his monotonous portrayal of Georges, he has much to learn before he qualifies as a TV actor. Angela Browne's Barbara was perfectly matched with the parasitical Jacques played by Jeremy Brett, whose performance was flawless. He really is a fine actor and it would have been stimulating to see him as Georges." (The Stage April 3rd 1962) Mary Crozier in *The Guardian* agreed that "Stephen Moore seems curiously cast as Georges. Perhaps the uncertainty of his accent… was an indicator of an uncertain temperament. Jeremy Brett was brilliant as the unpleasant Jacques."

The Bacchae 1962 – BBC for Sixth Forms

The Euripides play **The Bacchae** specifically for Sixth Forms was shown on BBC television on Mondays 15th and 22nd October 1962, with an introduction, produced by Ronald Eyre, broadcast on 8th October. The translation by Neil Curry of the 5th century Greek Tragedy starred Jeremy as the young god, **Dionysus**, and also featured John Carson as Pentheus, Cyril Luckham as Cadmus and Margot van den Burgh. Also known as Bacchus, Dionysus was the last god to take his place amongst the Olympians and he is extremely angry at the insult to his birthright; he had not been granted his full honour as a deity and is bent on revenge. He was the son of Zeus and Semele created with a flash of lightning but the goddess Hera, jealous of her husband's affair with the beautiful mortal retaliated by spitefully tricking her rival into requesting a revelation by her lover, causing her to be burned to death by lightning.

Her unborn son was rescued and hidden in his divine father's thigh but since his birth Dionysus had been hounded by Hera. On achieving his true status as a powerful god he has travelled throughout Asia teaching his rites to man as a bringer of mirth and joy in the essential life force, but when he is denied he becomes an appalling terror. Now he has arrived in Greece heralded by his revelling followers and seeking vengeance for the slight inflicted on both himself and his mother in the lies told by Semele's father Cadmus, the King of Thebes about her marriage to a mortal lover. Although Jeremy's Dionysus appears in Thebes in human form permitting Pentheus to bind him, imprison him and even cut his divine curls he would prove himself to be a god most terrible and bring a dreadful retribution on those responsible for his humiliation. "The brutality of Dionysus' revenge is so horrific, that at the end of the play, our sympathy is firmly on the side of the victims."

Jeremy as the God Dionysus

The Typewriter 1962 – ITV Play of the Week

The Stage and Television Today announced the play **The Typewriter** with the information that Gemma Jones, daughter of Griffith Jones, was to appear in the ITV Play of the Week by Jean Cocteau on 20th November 1962, with Jeremy Brett, Margaret Johnston and Patrick Wymark. Gemma would play the Postmistress Monique Martinez the capital M of the Typewriter's letters. *The Typewriter* by Jean Cocteau was a comedy written in the style of a British drawing room detective drama about twin brothers, **Pascal** and **Maxim,** each with very different personalities and both played by Jeremy. Maxim describes his similarity to his brother as *"absolute twins. No one can tell the difference between him and me."* In truth they are very different. He is an ex-criminal who suffers brainstorms, is terribly vain and self-dramatising, excitable, weak – but charming. The delicate and self-obsessed Pascal, is so good, so predictable and the complete opposite of his physically rough brother

The story centres on a series of poison pen letters which have upset the small French community, especially as they highlight the smugness, the hypocrisies and infidelities of individuals who appear respectable members of the community. The Typewriter chooses families with guilty secrets and as several of them turn to suicide to escape the consequences of the revelations, the police make extensive investigations. There are no murders to investigate only four suicides. As Maxim makes his confession to being the Typewriter he adds his name to the seven others, plus Margot, who have claimed the reputation and says, *"This town is vile, and this world's worse. I paid for that knowledge. I'm a worthless scoundrel."* He wants to enjoy some of the notoriety that the title offers him. Jeremy worked extremely hard, with his customary dedication until he found the two different characters so that the critics praised his performance. One said: "Jeremy Brett portrayed both parts with singular ambidexterity. The greatest triumph was his." And another: "This play was notable for the fine performance of Jeremy Brett, a young actor who has already appeared in a number of television dramas."

All's Well That Ends Well 1962 – Living Shakespeare – Audio Recording

In 1962 Jeremy appears as **Bertram the Count of Rossillion** in a sound recording of Shakespeare's ***All's Well That Ends Well*** for the Living Shakespeare Collection. The Count is desperate to prove himself on the battlefield in Tuscany in the service of his guardian, the King of France, in an attempt to avoid marriage to Helena (Vanessa Redgrave) the Court Physician's daughter. She has been given the choice of suitors in return for her successful cure of the King but, considering Helena beneath him, Bertram leaves immediately after the ceremony declaring she will never be a real wife until she wears his ring and carries his child. Dame Edith Evans, Bertram's mother sympathises with her plight and helps to bring them together.

"The Living Shakespeare recordings of abridged versions of the great Shakespearean plays were made in the early 1960s with world-famous actors and actresses in the lead roles. Not only do they allow the listener to savour Shakespeare's incomparable prose and poetry, these unique recordings also serve as brilliant testimonies to some of the greatest acting talent the world has ever known." (Cover of audio cassette) It certainly has a dream cast and in his anti-heroic role of the spoilt Bertram, Jeremy shows all the wildness and passion that the character requires.

Films 1960s

The Wild and the Willing 1962 - Box/Thomas Film

Even though Jeremy was approaching the age of thirty, he still felt the need to take part in a Modernist film and playing the part of a modern University student in **The Wild and the Willing** was his attempt to do that. The Betty Box/Ralph Thomas production, was filmed in the town of Lincoln and at Pinewood Studios, and had the producer's familiar touch, seen in class and gender issues in a story of the underdog trying to make his way in the intellectual life of University. Ian McShane's Harry Brown was seen as the new symbol of working class Britain. He was a brilliant student who attracted his tutor's notice, but from a poor working-class background and unwilling to cooperate with the teaching staff, or to forego his roistering group activities in the pubs and on the football pitch. Jeremy's **Andrew Gilby** was an upper class snob, at home in a university, who was enjoying the favours of the professor's wife, played by Virginia Maskell, and he bullied the other working class students, usually for making too much noise after drinking, and even informing the authorities on the dangerous

Rag Day stunt. It was an unsympathetic part for Jeremy to play which brought him no plaudits in spite of his success in creating a believable antagonist.

"As a plot, *The Wild and the Willing* is dated and a bit forced, but the interest these days is in the cast... Jeremy Brett (probably the screen's best Sherlock Holmes). So the film is watchable and has interest because of its cast... if you like the usual story of shenanigans at university with a macabre twist, then you'll probably like this..." (letterboxd.com)

Andrew Gilby in The Wild and the Willing

The call from Laurence Olivier to join the Chichester Festival came too late for Jeremy in 1962. He had made his commitment to this film, and he took his commitments seriously. However, the creation of a National Theatre had been awaited for several decades and Jeremy must have realised that Chichester and the rehearsal for the National Theatre was a lost opportunity to make his reputation by joining the company in its original stages and taking on the great challenges of playing under Olivier. He would have to wait until the following year and the second season at Chichester but thankfully his new boss would wait. And he had a couple more films to play first.

The Very Edge 1963 - Cyril Frankel Film

Jeremy as Mullen

The Very Edge gave Jeremy another chance of joining the modern era but unfortunately in the role of a stalker. *The Very Edge* was billed as a tense thriller with a predator stalking a young mother-to-be, waiting for her husband to return home from the office. The *Radio Times* described it as an attempt to lure audiences into the cinema with sensationalist stories of obsession. The stalker in this case was **Mullen**, played by Jeremy dressed in motorcycle leathers, who had developed an obsessive passion for the pregnant Tracey (Anne Heywood) and moved from harassment to assault as he broke into the house, with the result that she lost the baby she was expecting. He had remembered her previous career as a cover girl model and assumed she was available. And although the police insisted that they should handle the case, her husband, Geoff, played by Richard Todd, distracted by an affair with his new secretary ruined the trap laid for Mullen. This decision allowed the deluded young man to find her and continue his harassment on the rooftops of London, but eventually help arrived just in time to confront him as he gracefully plummeted to his death.

An interesting tribute appeared at the time of Jeremy's death in September 1995 in which one reviewer comments on his role in *The Very Edge* and where the sympathy really lay for the audience. "Among my favourite not-so-guilty pleasures is watching the early films of television's most iconographic heroes… the late Jeremy Brett was the most monastic of Victorian sleuths. Not even a marginal hint of attraction to the opposite sex crept into his interpretation. Like a chess master at the top of his form, he was rather dry, brittle, precise, obsessed. What a surprise, then, to discover *The Very Edge,* a dark little British film from the year 1963 in which Brett, then 27, played a full-fledged sexual psychopath, terrorising gorgeous Tracey Lawrence played by Anne Heywood… Brett was riveting as the tortured psycho and his character was developed in such a way that I actually ached when I watched his inevitable swan dive into eternity. Your real hisses were reserved for Todd and the so-called normal life to which Heywood must return…" (Movie Magazine International Review 20th September 1995 by Monica Sullivan)

This was a successful film outing for Jeremy and he was praised by the critics for the authenticity and intensity of his performance. His father must also have seen the film as Bill rang his son and asked if he was about to make any more such films he should make sure they did not appear in their village. The advertising which showed his yellow shot eyes had upset him. *"I remember playing a sex maniac in a British film called* The Very Edge *back in 1963. I had yellow eyes and a green skin. My appearance so shocked my father that he said to me. 'If you're going to do such terrible films, will you make sure they don't come to the village.'"*

Screen Test for 007 James Bond

Sherlock Holmes as 007

When he later tested for the role of James Bond as a replacement was needed for Sean Connery who wanted to move on to other things, his father said, *"It's the sort of role you cannot afford to turn down."* Unfortunately, he was not chosen for part in the film *On Her Majesty's Secret Service* which went to George Lazenby who wore ruffled shirts with a kilt. He was a more passive and unpopular Bond, reputedly a model rather than an actor and much less physical than Connery, but some thought him better than people gave him credit for, creating a touching final scene.

Jeremy thought, *"It would have spoiled my life,"* and told one reporter, *"I thought being 007 was not really me in the end. He's too smooth."* The story is a little more complex than that, as another article revealed that in the audition he had accidentally punched a stuntman. *"I had to go to Pinewood for a screen test. But I decided that since I had time, I'd join some friends for lunch. Unfortunately, I had a few too many glasses of port, and even though I wasn't drunk, or anything, I did get a bit carried away in a fight scene and ended up actually hitting the stuntman who was working with me. For some reason I didn't get the part. But to be honest with you, I don't think I'd have liked the kind of lifestyle that goes with being Bond. It's not me."* A recent programme on the actors who played Bond revealed that the reason George Lazenby was chosen for the role was that he broke the stuntman's nose which suggests Jeremy should have been even more strenuous and physical in his audition.

The Girl in the Headlines 1963 - British Lion Films (Bryanston Films)

Jeremy as Jordan Barker

The Girl in the Headlines is a film of murder and detection. Jeremy was once more seen in a donkey jacket and playing a modern young man, this time as a suspected murderer but in reality someone who was in love with the victim. The stars of this sleazy whodunit were Ian Hendry as the Inspector Birkett and Ronald Fraser as his laid back assistant, Sergeant Saunders, with the only clues to help them solve the murder of a top model being a hidden gun in the toilet cistern and a ball point pen with its hidden message. In their investigations they discover that the girl led a chequered lifestyle, a party girl with a liberal approach to sex and drugs. With drug pushers amongst her acquaintances the enquiry opens up. The Barker family are implicated with Perlita Barker (Natasha Parry) an ex-school friend and model and her domineering husband Hammond Barker, Jordan's brother (Peter Arne) both clearly involved. Jeremy in his role as **Jordan Barker** was finally revealed as the unwitting carrier of drugs in his motor launch; however, he was in love with Ursula and was not her murderer. He does tell the investigators about an incriminating audio tape which was being used to blackmail her and implicated the famous television personality played by James Villiers, but his murder in a gay bar, here called a "jazz bar," brought further confusion to an already difficult case.

"The plot parallels the lives of several people who were involved with a murdered girl: an artist, a shipping-magnet, television actor, nightclub owner and a retired opera singer. The cast list is very impressive with some major stars of the times and some wonderful actors who would later become household names. The appearance of a very young Jeremy Brett is somewhat difficult to spot unless you are looking out for him as his persona of Sherlock Holmes is now so overpowering that we cannot imagine him playing a young love-sick sailor."
(Girl in the Headlines cover by Alan Byron and John Cohen May 2007)

An Act of Reprisal - Wilbur Stark Film 1964

Harvey Freeman

Jeremy would appear in another harrowing tale of troubled times in **An Act of Reprisal** (*Antekdhikissi*) filmed in 1964 although it was not released immediately; an underrated and moving film about the Cypriot uprisings of 1958 which has seldom been seen. It is a polemic of the different demands of the local groups as they tried to carve out a better future in the struggle for independence from British colonial rule and unite the island with Greece. The locals were *"a warm and friendly lot"* but then things changed as they began to seek freedom from their colonial masters and hatred swept over the island. With every act of violence and reprisal, each group, the Greek, the Turk and the British were all caught up in it. Nobody wanted the violence to happen but nobody had the will to stop it or to halt the bloodshed.

The *Romeo and Juliet* story of **Harvey Freeman** and Eleni is set against the EOKA campaign characterised by bombings, kidnappings, and violence. The idealistic yet naive British Commissioner, played by Jeremy, is taken hostage by the insurgents and falls in love with Eleni (Ina Balin), one of his captors, the sister of a 16 year old boy he's had imprisoned for a recent bombing. "The star-crossed couple's progress from city to mountains and back to the city, pursued by British police, turns into a compressed socio-historical pilgrimage involving a fiery partisan leader, brawling guerrillas, a rebel Greek priest, Eleni's madly jealous lover and a chattering Turkish wayfarer... what redeems it is a certain lustiness and clarity in its storytelling. The film may not deserve too much praise, but it certainly didn't merit eclipse." (LA Times 13th September 1991)

"It is basically an anti-war film in that these people who have ethnic and historic hates for each other, discover that this hatred is dissipated as they are brought together in a time of stress." (Wilbur Stark)

Laurence Oliver - The National Theatre and Chichester

The idea of creating a National Theatre in which the works of Shakespeare could be performed was first put forward in 1903 by Harley Granville Barker and William Archer, both leading figures in the English Stage Society. Almost fifty years later, in 1951 the Queen laid the Foundation Stone for the project and it was another twelve years before Laurence Olivier was appointed as Founder Director of the Royal National Theatre at the Old Vic Theatre in Waterloo until it found its permanent home on the South Bank in 1976.

In 1962 Olivier had been made founding Artistic Director of the Chichester Festival Theatre, a hexagonal structure with a 1,400 seat thrust stage auditorium in Oaklands Park which was to become a rehearsal for the National Theatre. Olivier was working to establish an elite group of actors with whom he could present both the classics and the avant-garde plays with which he had been involved in the English Stage Company and he brought together forty actors, "the renowned" and the "to be renowned" to present two 17th century English plays of Ford and Fletcher. Jeremy and his good friend Charles Kay were both invited to appear in the prestigious opening production of *The Chances* (1623) by Beaumont and Fletcher, a play found by accident in the British Museum by Olivier. Described as "a very endearing and pleasant little romp," and "a splendid opening to the theatre itself", but they were contracted to "a not very good film" (The Wild and the Willing - Charles Kay) and would have to wait until the following year when they would take their part in the new company. Their parts were taken by John Neville and Keith Michell alongside Rosemary Harris and Joan Plowright.

St Joan 1963 - Chichester Festival

Jeremy was invited back for the second Chichester Festival in 1963 which featured a revival of *Uncle Vanya* and two new productions, *Saint Joan* and *The Workhouse Donkey*. His first role was as **Dunois in Saint Joan**. He had appeared in the roles of Brother Martin and Ladvenu, at the *Manchester Library Theatre* in 1954. On this occasion, as the character of Dunois, he is the responsible and courageous young commander of Joan's army, good looking and good-natured who believes that she is a good leader and commander, and proves to be one of the few people that Joan can rely upon. As the illegitimate cousin of the Duke of Orleans he was known as *The Bastard*.

The review in *The Stage* continued to praise the whole production "it is the entire *Saint Joan* that fills the theatre with a glory I shall not forget." He went on to list the supporting players, Max Adrian as The Inquisitor, Robert Stephens as the Dauphin, Jeremy Brett as Dunois, Anthony Nicholls as Warwick, Frank Finlay as de Stogumber, Robert Lang as Peter Cauchon and Derek Jacobi as Brother Martin are also outstanding, each creating a full-size character and contributing individually and together to the values of the production." (The Stage 27th June 1963)

In 1966 a four-record sound recording of *Saint Joan* would be made by Caedmon to recreate the production. Instead of Joan Plowright the role of Joan was taken by Siobhan McKenna and Robert Stephens retains his role of The Dauphin and Jeremy his as Dunois.

The Workhouse Donkey 1963 - Chichester Festival

Both *St Joan* and **The Workhouse Donkey** were challenging plays and, as **Maurice Sweetman** in the latter, Jeremy was well aware of the lack of real public interest in the new offering, especially as Joan Plowright was attracting all the interest in St Joan. *"The Arden play,* (The Workhouse Donkey) *was a fine piece of work. It was a good, serious, profound play, and it kept the customers away in droves, while Joanie (Plowright) in St. Joan packed them in."* (Jeremy in Chichester 10) The play by John Arden, was about political corruption in a West Yorkshire industrial town based on the author's home town of Barnsley; a complex offering which could be described as drama, as comedy, as melodrama and also as a musical. It certainly held all these elements. Arden is a moralist who tells a stark morality tale with scrupulous precision and with theatrical effect. Jeremy played the part of Maurice Sweetman, the son of a Tory Alderman. It was a Jonsonian type of classical comedy featuring 'a contemporary theme with social comment' and a fantastic conclusion. John Arden commented on the inclusion of musical accompaniment to create a sense of melodrama.

The playgoer's Bible *Plays and Players* suggested that it was a hopeless case and maybe that would account for the fact that the audiences did not come. "… the plot is so hopelessly involved, and there is so much of it, that we are clearly not intended to take it in detail by detail… a general impression of little people scurrying backwards and forwards, grouping and regrouping like ants… Jeremy's Maurice Sweetman is the son of Tory Alderman Sir Harold Sweetman, who also secretly owns the tawdry Copacabana Club. Young Sweetman ends up drunk with a hostess bunny on his lap while Labour Alderman Butterthwaite is visiting the club. Butterthwaite has the Copacabana shut down on moral grounds." (Plays and Players September 1963)

Terence Rattigan would recall his responses to the production: "I remember sitting in a half empty theatre, this time at a Chichester matinee and feeling I'd never seen anything before quite like John Arden's self-described 'vulgar melodrama'… showing us Napoleon politicians, bent coppers, tawdry showgirls and dubious art collectors. On stage, it made a Dionysiac spectacle that, simply because of its sheer cast-size, is hard to reproduce in today's straitened times…" (Terence Rattigan. Five Theatre flops that deserve a revival. The Guardian 2014) Robert Stephens presented the actor's comment on this new play as one of the "best ever" and an "extremely amusing musical play" but added that further work would have helped it reach its true potential.

In one interview Jeremy laughed as he remembered his father's reactions to the play, *"He slept through* The Workhouse Donkey *at Chichester where there were many more people on stage than in the audience. He did come back afterwards and said, 'Absolute triumph. Rotten play but you were wonderful'"* (Holmes Rule! in Video Today) However, it was his performance in this little attended new play which would attract the attention of Olivier so that Jeremy was offered the part of Juvenile for the National Theatre, which by the next season had left out the Old Vic from its title.

In *Chichester 10 Portrait of a Decade* 1972, a publication which celebrated ten years of the Chichester Festival, some of the principal actors were interviewed and presented alongside a pencil portrait of them. Jeremy's contribution to this publication focused on his friend Robert Stephens who was experiencing difficulties sitting still whilst his portrait was being drawn. Jeremy had sung folk songs to him, with the aid of his guitar, some of which were remembered from his recent travels in South America, in order to keep his friend from boredom. *"I don't mind sitting still. I'm used to it. I have a brother who's a painter, but some people find it tedious to sit still for two minutes. I think I sang every song I could remember. At least it kept him quiet."*

The National Theatre - Laurence Olivier

"The most august institution of world-class theatre in the English language was managed from a row of Nissen huts." Pending the construction of the new National Theatre, the Old Vic with a row of ex-army issue Nissen huts became the company's home. Situated on a bombed-out courtyard, where bolted together the huts formed the offices to house 18 full time staff, a Board Room, a canteen and a rehearsal room constructed from another cluster of huts knocked through into a single space. In these prefabricated constructions the staff froze in winter and roasted in summer, and any rainfall on the tin roofs made telephone conversations inaudible. Beneath the rehearsal room lived "an enormous family of feral cats." The lavatories were very basic and some redecoration was carried out of the Ladies, paid for personally by Olivier. (The National Theatre Story by Daniel Rosenthal) It was in this inauspicious setting that Olivier's vision of a National Theatre was created. He wanted his company peopled by the best actors in the world, performing the best plays in the world, but this could only be achieved by talent, skill and hard work. He wanted actors who could play the central roles of the Shakespearean Canon as well as he had, and still did. He demanded that they be the cream of the new talent who would become the leading actors of the future. However, they had to prove they could work as an ensemble and not disappear into the scenery, or outshine everyone else on stage, "like a spotlit sore thumb". He described the breed of actor he wished to employ at the National as "Versatile ones; people with their hearts in the right place; unlazy ones, deeply enthusiastic, courageous." And he also chose those who would make good company members. Olivier's vision became a reality as the young people learned from the master and many excellent performances of *Richard, Othello* or *Lear* in future years could be traced back to the first National Theatre Company. He must have felt a glow of satisfaction at the outcome of his training as he looked back on the successes of those who had been in his original ensemble. Among them were Michael Gambon, Maggie Smith, Robert Stephens, Lynn Redgrave, Derek Jacobi, Michael York, Frank Finlay and Anthony Hopkins. They would bring an exciting talent to the stage by their "reality, inventiveness and spontaneity" which would have a lasting effect on the company.

Alongside these advantages other changes were taking place in society, the new sound of Liverpool bands with its attendant images would have an enormous effect on Jeremy as Olivier thought that any actor with a public school background, with an upper-class accent, was going to suffer in the years to come. In spite of Olivier's comments, Jeremy, with his *"public school background"* and *"upper class accent,"* had been chosen to be part of this exciting new group, *"When I was a young actor, it was the era of the* Angry Young Man*, so as an ex-Eton schoolboy I was definitely out. Larry (Olivier) saved me by taking me on at the National."* He would be an excellent teacher challenging him to the end of his capabilities. One day, Olivier shouted: "I want your trumpet!" When Jeremy replied that he didn't have one, he said, "Get a trumpet. I expect every actor to have a full orchestra!" It was a strange request for anyone and especially for an actor, but Jeremy explained Olivier's meaning in an interview in 1988 with Terry Wogan where he said his great mentor in the business (of acting) gave him a lot of courage: *"I expect every actor who works with me to have the body of a God* *and the voice of a full orchestra. And there he was doing it. That was what was so sensational, that you had the example before you. He was the greatest actor who ever lived."* (Wogan Interview 1988)

Olivier also insisted he perfect his enunciation of the words; to trill the 'r' sounds and to correct his 's' sounds which Jeremy still needed to work at; it would be advice he would remember and practice for the rest of his career. It is no surprise that he would call Olivier his *"Great God."* Kate Fleming, a voice coach was employed to develop the orchestral voice and a gymnasium was provided in the basement to train their bodies for the greatest roles. "Acting is the projection of certain images that come into your mind through your physical being, which means not only your voice, but all of your body, from your top to your toe." Olivier's body was his instrument. "If you put your arms around Larry you could feel his ribs like an enormous cage. His body was his professional life." (Robert in Knight Errant) One other piece of advice given to each one of his actors was to create a living person with a full biography: the role he was playing in the family, a background and a past: with each person believing wholeheartedly in his own character, his contribution would be believable and the play as a whole would be pushed in the right direction. Providing a personal history and every detail of his private life, from family problems to responsibilities such as a new baby or the loss of a job or his wife, would create "a complete three-dimensional figure and not a cardboard cut-out. To transport an audience, they must see life and not paste." (Olivier in On Acting). Jeremy would remember this technique of finding a character and "becoming" the part as he described examples of his own invention on several occasions over the years. However, Olivier could display a selfish approach to the choice of roles, and would show a "paranoid jealousy" of those who he considered to be "a rival." (Robert Stephens) Jeremy would comment on this character trait in his playing of the part of Berowne in *Love's Labour's Lost* in 1967 when he had returned from Hollywood to work once more under Olivier. He said he found great difficulty in keeping hold of the script as his director suddenly realised how attractive the part was especially as it was one he had never played.

When the call came from Hollywood for *My Fair Lady* Jeremy accepted it immediately: firstly, because the money was most attractive and secondly, as the part he had been offered by Olivier was the supporting role of Laertes in *Hamlet*, when the main role had not yet been decided. As the opening production of the new National Theatre it needed a star name and Peter O'Toole would take the role, but Jeremy's hurt reaction to the situation was understandable as he had appeared as Hamlet in the West End just two years previously. Joan Plowright supported Jeremy's decision, and laughingly said she would have gone with him if Eliza Doolittle had had a sister. Olivier was upset, but later admitted that the £10,000 fee Hollywood had paid for Jeremy's release from his contract, cleared the Company's debts for the previous year. In 1994 Jeremy told Andrew Duncan in the *Radio Times*, *"He wanted me to play the parts that needed sensitivity and virility. I said, 'You mean the underwritten ones?' I thought he just wanted me for a pretty face. When I balked, cheekily, and went off to make the film of* My Fair Lady, *he was furious. Luckily he forgave me and said, 'You'd better come back.' I was so excited I leapt into his arms and nearly knocked him over."* (Radio Times 19th March 1994)

Ian McKellen commented on the wealth of young talent who were working at the National in 1963-5 and why he too felt he had to leave if he was to gain more experience: "The National was jam-packed with us juveniles, from Derek (Jacobi) to John Stride to Gambon, Ted Petherbridge, Jeremy Brett, many, many others… It is astonishing who was there.

Astonishing!" In reality Olivier was building for the future and trying to maintain "a permanent ensemble" in order to "keep the standard consistently on a high fire." Jeremy's decision was a blessing for some of the cast of *Hamlet*. The 25-year-old Derek Jacobi commented on his amazing luck as he had been employed as understudy for Jeremy in the role of Laertes. "Apart from playing Brother Martin in *Saint Joan* I was supposed to be understudying all the Jeremy Brett parts in the season when luck again, he was wanted by Warners for the film of *My Fair Lady* so they bought him out of his National contract and I got the parts…" (The Times 28th May 1977) "You could say I owed my career to Jeremy Brett." He went on to say that Jeremy was celebrated for his "marvellous and famous Sherlock Holmes, but people hardly remember that he was a very fine actor."

My Fair Lady 1964 – Lerner and Lowe Film Hollywood

In 1963 Jeremy left England for Hollywood to appear in **My Fair Lady**. His strong performance as Malcolm in the 1960 film of *Macbeth* had attracted the attention of the director George Cukor who brought him back to America. In his audition Jeremy had beaten forty other hopeful, *"shiny young Englishmen"* for the role of **Freddie**. Not many people think of Jeremy in relation to this box office hit as his singing role doesn't fit into expectations of *Sherlock Holmes*. He was delighted for the opportunity to appear once more with Audrey Hepburn after his experience in *War and Peace* where he had been so happy. But later Jeremy would say it was a mistake as *"I let a few people down through going... and I feel a bit rotten about it. In a roundabout way it was worth it."* (Star-Struck) And he could recognise the implications. *"I realised when I was there that I had made an extraordinarily dangerous decision to leave the English theatre and the National Theatre of England at its conception under Olivier... The line of parts I'd been offered at the National I didn't like. But I felt I might have made the mistake of my life."* (Arts & Entertainment 1992)

The Lerner and Lowe adaptation of the *Pygmalion* play by Shaw, starring Julie Andrews and Rex Harrison, had been a familiar feature on Broadway in 2,717 performances since its opening in March 1956. It had become a momentous hit, so the film version was long awaited. The story of a Cockney flower girl who was taken in by the eminent linguist Professor Higgins, in order to pass her off as a lady was well known and her transformation from a guttersnipe to a goddess was a twentieth century fairy tale. Audrey had controversially taken over the role of Eliza and was not terribly convincing even to herself, as the flower girl. She had been cast primarily for the transformation, and she executed it deftly. "From *I Could Have Danced All Night* she takes off. No one can touch her from there." (Jeremy in Audrey Hepburn)

The critical reviews were rather mixed for Freddie Eynsford Hill and Jeremy was made to feel like an extra. Even George Bernard Shaw in his play *Pygmalion*, on which the film was based, was uncertain about the role the young man was playing in the drama. Jeremy made a romantic and charming Freddie but, without an opportunity to develop before an audience, he would remain a supporting character. Even the spelling of his character's name differs as the critics disagree on his role in Eliza's story. "The story is well-known. Only poor, love-struck Freddy (Jeremy Brett) doesn't have a brain in his head. Shaw, impatient with romantic plotting, sticks him in when he needs him and then drops him without another word." (Roger Ebert) The original *Pygmalion* myth ended with the marriage of the sculptor with his ideal creation the living Galatea, but the play had an ambiguous ending cemented by Higgins' last line in the film script, *"Nonsense – she's going to marry Freddie. Ha ha ha!"* In the Afterword, Shaw left no doubt that Eliza did indeed marry Freddie and together they managed a flower shop, with some success after their initial difficulties.

"Jeremy Brett plays Freddie Eynsford Hill who can be rather a dithery character. When it is necessary for him to be awkward and fall over things, he does it very well. This is surprising because in his song *On the Street Where You Live,* he has strength and appeal, which is quite different but still acceptable." (The Leader – Post) "The collision between Freddy and Eliza in the opening scene when he bumps into her in Covent Garden in the rain and scatters her flowers had to be repeated for more than two hours before the director George Cukor was satisfied." (New York Times) One event, the assassination of John F. Kennedy, couldn't be prepared for and the two actors and would-be lovers reacted characteristically with tears. Jeremy was always sensitive and cried easily. *"We were filming the part where Eliza returns to Covent Garden with Freddy, when suddenly someone rushed up with word that President*

John F. Kennedy had been murdered. We sat in the carriage with the blinds down, holding each other and crying, on stage seven at Warner Brothers." (Jeremy in Audrey Hepburn by Barry Paris)

One reviewer Edward Howard found Jeremy alone rehearsing his song, *On The Street Where You Live* on the Wimpole Street set practising his movements for his interactions with Eliza for the *Show Me* number. He explained his first reactions to America and his preparations for the coming performance. *"Forty-eight hours after they bought me out of* St. Joan, *I was standing in front of St Paul's in the pouring rain trying to hail a cab—only I was here in California. It was as if I'd never left home."* He told one critic about how nervous he felt, *"I'm getting in as much rehearsal as I can, though it's a bit difficult without Audrey. Of course, she has done film musicals and doesn't need as much rehearsal as I do."* (Tough Job Trying To See the "Lady" by Edwin Howard in the Memphis Press - Scimitary)

Unfortunately, the song, *On the Street Where You Live* had already been recorded when he arrived on the set. Bill Shirley sang for Freddie and Marnie Nixon sang for Eliza, which was disappointing as Jeremy had received good reviews for his singing roles and Audrey was determined to perform her own songs. "She has the courage to do it, do it wretchedly at first, but do it." (Cukor) Her "musky mezzo" voice was charming but not quite good enough. "It was the musical film of the decade... you wanted it to be perfect." (Andre Previn) In his interview with Wogan, Jeremy said that he also sang *On the Street Where You Live,* "all, except the top notes." However, his narration of the newly remastered film, *More Luverly Than Ever* presented the opportunity to reveal the 30 year secret of the dubbing of both his and Audrey's singing voices and play the actual recording of Audrey's singing of her "Wouldn't it be luverly?" which was surprisingly good. He said, *"I know exactly how Audrey felt because the same thing happened to me. When I arrived on the set, I found to my horror that someone else had sung my song. What Audrey really had to contend with was the ghost of Julie Andrews."* (Jeremy in More Luverley Than Ever) If Julie Andrews had played Eliza it is quite likely Jeremy would have been allowed to sing too. For the Gala Première of the re-mastered movie in New York held on 19th September 1994, Jeremy was one of the few surviving stars in attendance. He commented, *"I got better notices for Freddie this time around than I did before."*

On arriving in America Jeremy was shocked at the huge distances he was expected to travel. He told another interviewer that his favourite school subject was geography, but when he landed in New York from England, he was shocked to learn that he needed to board a second plane to complete his journey: *"And I said, 'Oh, another plane?' I thought, That's rather strange. I'm in America, I'm here. I said, 'Another plane? I'm sure I could take a car.' And they said, 'No, Mr. Brett, you'll need a plane.' I'd done my geography at school, but I had no idea! So we flew the same distance again."* He was in a complete daze after two long flights when he landed in Los Angeles. He got into a hire car: *"I was so excited and I set off and put my foot on what I thought was the clutch and what turned out to be the brake, because it was automatic, and nearly went through the windscreen. And I got down Sunset a little way, so excited to be there, turned onto the freeway, and nearly ended up in San Diego."* The hierarchy of stars, from the A Listers to the newcomers also brought its frustrations as Jeremy was clearly one of the latter group. He reported, *"Worst decision I ever made! It was eight months of frustration. Yet, it seemed so good at first. I was told they were building up the juvenile lead for the younger audiences, as Rex Harrison was the more mature star. But it didn't work out that way."* However, Jeremy was befriended by two of the other Britons in the cast, Gladys Cooper, who played Mrs. Higgins; and Mona Washbourne as Mrs. Pierce, the housekeeper.

And he very much enjoyed the glamour of the studios, *"It was a marvellous time to go because, although things were changing and the studios were closing, I still got a whiff of the old glamour. I had tea with Mary Pickford and lunch with Dorothy Parker, who was so fragile-looking with exquisite skin, as delicate as a bird"* and had two dinners with Cole Porter. Porter was *"terribly funny, terribly enthusiastic, telling us all sorts of reminiscences and stories and everything. Absolutely wonderful."*

His relationship with Rex wasn't going to be an easy one as Jeremy explained, *"I arrived with a streaming cold, a pale and wan complexion, a beacon-red nose. And, there was Rex, tanned, fit and handsome. The moment he saw me, he said, 'Perfect! Needs no make-up.' I rather guessed how things would turn out from then on... He was so pre-occupied with making absolutely sure that he stole the film that he was impossible to be around."* There was a dispute over Jeremy's use of the street for the singing of his song, *"Rex said, 'Jeremy can't sing* On the Street Where You Live, *'cause I need it for* I've Grown Accustomed to her Face.' *So I looked at Rex and said, 'Does it turn out that we're going to sing it in a coal shed now? Where am I going to sing the song if I can't sing it in the street? I'm talking about* the street. *Am I going to climb up a drain pipe and sing it on the roof? Where am I going to do it, in the basement?'"* He may have been concerned about his own performance but another cause of Rex's ill grace was that he discovered he'd been hired on only a quarter of the salary that Audrey received and, incensed at the inequity, he was prepared to make everyone suffer. As a result, a second Wimpole Street was built and on this occasion Rex didn't get his own way.

Jeremy also recalled that Cecil Beaton, the film's costume and set designer, had problems of his own. Beaton draped sylph-like European extras in his graceful gowns, however, to reduce the cost of accommodating supporting players the film studio insisted that beauty queens from Central Casting were to be used instead. Beaton was not amused: *"[He] stood at the door and ripped the clothes off of them as they walked on the set! We couldn't shoot. With all these enormous you-know-what's popping out of these elegant gowns. It was impossible! Garish lipstick. You know what I mean! Terribly funny time."* Despite the occasional tiffs, Jeremy wistfully remembered the filming of *My Fair Lady* as *"the end of an era."* *My Fair Lady* was one of the last old-fashioned Hollywood musicals and it would remain one of the best remembered and lavishly produced of them all, winning eight Oscars including the best actor award for Rex Harrison. (Taken from: Jeremy Brett Says: Holmes is Where His Heart Is. A & E Magazine, June 1992, and Hope I Made Sense, Says Swashbuckler Brett. Woman Magazine, 18th February 1967)

Freddie

My Fair Lady attracted the reviewers and the personal columns too, so that Jeremy was picked out for an in-depth article with the title *Meet Jeremy Brett*. It introduced him as green-eyed, enough to melt any woman's heart, six feet tall, and "fascinating." His intelligence and sense of humour also impressed the interviewer. He told Carol Ardman he loved the American food, tried weight-lifting as a means of keeping fit and admitted that although he seemed to be extremely energetic, he could sometimes be lazy, *"I guess the only way I get things done is to do a lot of them! When I'm going at break-neck speed, I seem to get much more accomplished. I'm not a very physical person, really. I used to think it would do me a great deal of good to lift weights, but I gave it up when my neck started getting bigger than my head. But food; I adore it! And I find American hamburgers absolutely delightful. I could simply eat my way through the day on them."* When asked if he had been on any dates since his arrival in Hollywood, he replied, *"No,"* and added that he would need to know the girl and like her before going on a date. There would be no blind dates for him.

The article calls him "a fine actor and a stimulating man" but stressed his approach to acting which was altruistic. "Personal integrity and honesty in his dealings with others characterize Jeremy's passionate desire to succeed on his own merits. He refuses to be in any play or movie in which he doesn't believe." His attitude to success is realistic and some may say, ideal, *"I want to fulfil myself in my way. Fame is great, but I want it to flow naturally, if at all, from my day-to-day work. If I have what is required it will out, in time. If not, well… One must be a consummate realist at all times."* (Meet Jeremy Brett) Realism would also be applied to his personal life. *Actors are impossible to live with; I don't know how women put up with us. Actually, arranged marriages are probably best. It's being in love that destroys you, not being without it."* (Jeremy to Margaret Hinxman)

Audrey Hepburn

Jeremy told Carol Ardman that working opposite Audrey *"was a joy"* and that she had *"a special magic about her."* He would very much like to have kissed her in their love scene but a white fence formed a barrier throughout their song, *"Our faces were only a quarter of an inch apart… Audrey really is a darling. There's something wonderful about her that no man can explain but every man can feel."* In an earlier interview after the making of *War and Peace* he spoke about the magic of working with Audrey, *"I had never really known what a star was, or what star qualities were before I worked with Audrey."* (rareaudreyhepburn.com)

After *My Fair Lady*, Jeremy rejected roles in several musicals, including the London stage production of *Hair* and the film version of *The Great Waltz*. He told an interviewer, *"I don't like myself in them. First, I don't think my voice is good enough, and second, if you do musicals in this country, you're not taken seriously as an actor."*

The Deputy 1964 - Atkinson Theater Broadway

Father Riccardo Fontana

Jeremy's next leading role was one full of controversy and of challenging circumstances. This performance would result in his losing fourteen pounds in weight as *"his digestion had gone awry,"* and almost his life, as a passer-by attempted to pull him under a car. ***The Deputy***, sometimes called ***The Representative***, is described as a controversial drama with the proposal that Pope Pius XII (Emlyn Williams) knew about Hitler's extermination of the Jews but kept silent about it. Playing the role of the deputy, who became a martyr because his faith and compassion would not let him be silent, meant that Jeremy was the butt of personal attacks by people who were unable to separate the actor from the role or were incensed by the suggestion of papal involvement in such a scandal and who wished to add their voices to the protests.

Father Riccardo Fontana played by Jeremy was a Jesuit priest serving in Berlin with the papal nuncio when he is informed of the death camps of Treblinka and Belzec by an SS lieutenant who is agitated and incensed by the horrors he has seen. When the troubled priest is finally admitted to see Pius he is told that he knows of the situation and is unable to denounce Hitler openly but can act only with 'discretion'. The angry young priest deliberately pins on the yellow Star of David and goes to his death in the gas chambers. The author had based the character on a real German soldier Lt. Kurt Gerstein who had joined the SS to find evidence of mass murder in the death camps of Poland, in Treblinka and Belzec, and had consequently joined the fight against Hitler.

The reviews of the critics were universally excellent, though they only provided a glimpse of the anguish that Jeremy experienced. One article entitled *Every Night is Terror for Jeremy Brett* highlighted the personal cost of continuing with his nightly performances and described his degree of involvement "*as blistering.*" He told the reporter, "*Each performance is a personal experience. I'm in a state of total absorption. There are moments when I get almost hysterical... A good many people have told me to be more objective. Well, try and do it.*" Jeremy expressed a justifiable righteous anger at the atrocities he was experiencing nightly. "*I'm a rather idealistic person who would rather not believe human nature could sink so low. I was most vulnerable to what the play recalls – and I can't get used to it. At the same time, even though it may hurt like hell, and be hard to do, if the theatre is to survive, such topics must be aired... In the scene each night with the Pope, I sometimes feel as if the roof of the altar was crashing in. I wish Pius was alive to speak for himself. You can't blame one person for these things that happened just yesterday almost...*" (Jeremy to William Glover New York)

Jeremy was always noted for his dedication to authenticity and accurate creation of reality whenever it could be achieved, so it is no surprise that he disagreed with the director Herman Shumlin on whether he should eat the food brought to the priest in the opening scene. Shumlin thought he should shun all food, and explained it was really dog biscuits, which had been glued to the tray. In spite of this warning Jeremy felt he couldn't cheat the audience and "*tore the dog biscuits loose and ate them – without ill-effect.*" The critic of the *New York Times* recognised his level of dedication: "Jeremy Brett brings fire and dedication to the role of Father Fontana." (New York Times)

"*The Deputy* is one of the greatest morality plays the 20th century can produce... a cry against the apathy that exists in all of us. Brilliantly staged, beautifully acted, the play holds the audience for all of its three hours. Brett, a young British actor, turns in a heart-wrenching performance as the young Jesuit... who is attached to the papal legation in Berlin in the early 1940s. He hears from SS Lt. Kurt Gerstein (Thomas A. Carlin) who has been attached to Auschwitz, a plea for papal intervention, but the papal nuncio in Berlin is helpless. He returns later to Gerstein's apartment and gives his cassock and diplomatic passport to Jacobson, a Jew who has been hiding in the apartment. In return, he receives the yellow Star of David which marked all Jews in German occupied countries. From that time on, Brett becomes the master of the play, although not of his own destiny. A tall, frail man, he glows with ascetic cause... Father Fontana's final meeting with the pope where he pins the Star of David and joins the Italian Jews leaving Rome is electric." (San Mateo Times 30th April 1964 Internet Broadway Database) "More than 100 uniform policemen were on hand Wednesday night to insure orderly picketing. At least 10 plain-clothes-men were seated among the audience. There was one minor incident. The 1090 seat playhouse was filled to capacity. Inside the theatre, Jack Gaver, UPI's drama critic said the audience was one 'of the most attentive I have ever seen on a first night... there was tremendous and prolonged applause near the end of the 'big scene' when the young priest learns that the pope definitely will not protest. It came at the priest's exit line, after he has pinned a yellow Jewish star on his cassock and indicates he is going along with deported Italian Jews since "God must not destroy the church because a pope hid when he was summoned." (Gary Gates in The Windsor Star) "Still, as in any production of this drama, the subject overwhelms the details. We find ourselves listening intensely to the facts that the characters recite, confronting the enormity of the historical events, but being less attentive to the tale of the priest and the Pope... Jeremy Brett's priest appeared stronger by contrast, and perhaps he needed that contrast." (The Times 16th March 1964)

The fact that so many people took the play far too seriously, affected Jeremy personally. *"It was really too soon for it to be shown in the States. We had a terrible time. I even had to have police protection because there were great complications. On the first night there were Germans demonstrating, Jews demonstrating and Catholics demonstrating. We had bomb threats..."* (Jeremy Brett: Britain's 2nd TV Ambassador) They sent him threatening letters and abusive phone calls, which meant that Jeremy had to have his telephone number changed whilst the play was being staged. One person even made a chilling personal attack on him. *"One day, I was walking along a street when a man came up and asked me if I was Jeremy Brett. Well, you're always glad to meet a fan, so I reached over to take his outstretched hand. Instead of a shake, however, I was pulled past him at the curb. It was unexpected, and I went sprawling in front of a car that stopped just in time."* Jeremy went on to tell a reporter, *"I hope all my work won't be of equal importance to* The Deputy *because I'd be worn out by 40."*

The Deputy

Three Roads Lead to Rome – The Rest Cure 1963 - ITV Play of the Week

Tonino with Tarwin and Miranda in The Rest Cure

Plinio and Kay McCone in Something to Declare

Three Roads lead to Rome: The Rest Cure an ITV Play of the Week, broadcast on 30th December 1963 was a story about love in an Italian setting. Three stories from three different periods but with the same setting appeared in a 90 minute slot at 9.10pm. It was conceived as a vehicle for Deborah Kerr to show her versatility in the various moods of comedy, ironic triumph and romantic wistfulness. Jeremy appeared in the third play as ***Tonino***, an Italian innkeeper, in love with the wealthy but naive English girl Miranda on a rest cure in Italy; he was clearly becoming the first choice for the romantic male lead at this time. The young handsome Tonino would attract the attentions of the romantic Miranda by his exceptional good manners and gallantry, but he would be in competition with Allan Cuthbertson who played her jealous fiancé Tarwin. In order to avoid a stuffy marriage to the Englishman, Miranda runs off to the country the day Tarwin is due in Rome but the rivalry causes him to devise a plot to defeat the Italian by spreading lies about his dishonesty. In spite of the attempt to blacken his reputation, the love with Tonino survives and Miranda's rest cure becomes a permanent one.

The critic in *The Times* found each of the plays enjoyable in spite of the "high sugar content of *The Rest Cure*": "Huxley's story of the genteel English girl who preferred the simplicity of a young Italian innkeeper to the pomposity of her English fiancé, lacked astringency and became no more than the story of the triumph of Miss Kerr and Mr Jeremy Brett's Innkeeper over Mr Allan Cuthbertson's inefficiently Machiavellian plot to discredit him. Any conversion of the story into naive romance was not, however, the result of Miss Kerr's being invincibly herself but of an adaptation which wished to balance the earlier episodes with something simply happy." (Three moods of Miss Kerr in The Times 1st January 1964)

Something to Declare 1964 - *ITV/ABC Armchair Theatre*

At the start of ITV, the minor companies found it quicker and easier to affiliate with a major company for the supply of both network and optional programming. Instead of searching amongst the different stations and regions they could purchase the entire output of a large company and thereby save time and money. Westward Television, a south-western broadcasting company would include ABC productions. The following play was advertised as "Enjoy Sylvia Sims and Jeremy Brett chewing the scenery in *Armchair Theatre's* 'Something to Declare' at 10.05pm – it's your only chance. The recording is long since lost."

Something to Declare, directed by Toby Robertson, was part of the ABC Armchair Theatre and broadcast on 4th October 1964. In this play Jeremy played ***Plinio Ceccho*** who falls in love with Sylvia Sims as Kay McCone, an American magician in a random meeting in a customs shed on the French/Italian border where she has been detained for further investigation by customs officials and he is intrigued. The television magazine listing summarised the action: "A customs post on the Riviera... a glamorous blonde detained without explanation... a handsome and amorous stranger with an alarmingly intimate knowledge of her private life... and Kay McCone has a date in Nice with another handsome man and an engagement ring... Another lightsome and frothy piece to keep the twinkle in the eye of the new Armchair Theatre season." It was an unlikely and unexplained bringing together of characters, a pretty girl and a stranger, "a wealthy Italian publisher, who lays siege to the lady's heart in the finest continental tradition. Jeremy Brett – impeccably the young English aristocrat – plays him. And Sylvia Sims, an English rose if there ever was one..." (Anthony Shields Look Westward TV Times)

By coincidence, Jeremy's recent role of the Italian Tonino opposite Deborah Kerr in *Three Roads to Rome* would have given him the opportunity to perfect his Italian accent. This play, a welcome debut, was described by the caption writers as a "high class romantic comedy... of the kind that cinema does so well... and takes an American (William Marchant) to write the crackling sophisticated and laconic dialogue that such subjects need. Top of the bill for this production was Sylvia Sims, who had been a contract film star for Associated British Pictures for eight years, making her first appearance in Armchair Theatre. Co-star Jeremy Brett was no stranger to ABC Television drama, but he had just returned from the USA after filming *My Fair Lady* and being on Broadway. A very strong duo in the leads. Audiences like it. The teleplay rated No 5 for the week, drawing 7 million viewers." (Armchair Theatre: The Lost Years) *The Stage* revealed that Kay McCone was "an innocent opium smuggler, the unwitting agent of her fiancé" and thought, "Jeremy Brett was the perfect Italian wooer. The mystery about him was what had this matter to do with Plinio anyway? I never did find out whether he interested himself because he loved the lovely Kay, whether he was after a story for his newspaper, or whether it was pure love of justice... (and) why in a moment of happy lunacy, he sent his stars riding round the waiting room on bicycles." (The Stage 8th October 1964)

A Measure of Cruelty 1965 - Birmingham Repertory Theatre

On his return to Great Britain Jeremy had taken over the caring role for his father whose health was failing. To be near him, living alone in the family home in Berkswell and suffering from heart failure, Jeremy took the role of **Gilbert** (Gideon) in the British premiere of ***A Measure of Cruelty*** at the Birmingham Repertory Theatre. The play opened on 9th February 1965, and ran for four weeks until 6th March. It was a light, macabre comedy described as *A Taming of the Shrew* in reverse. He played Gilbert Courtefigue, described as a "very handsome, very intelligent, very agreeable" young man who was being kept by a wealthy middle aged spinster, Elizabeth Fontanelle around twenty years older than he, and prepared to pay for his affections. On their wedding day, their future happiness is endangered by a visit from Gilbert's former mistress, Anne-Marie with whom he is still in love and the new bride threatens him with death if he attempts to leave her, reminding him of the high price she has paid for his financial stability. "You have the choice between two solutions: to continue to be my spouse or die. If I were in your place, I would choose the second solution right away." And later she would give him a stark warning, "I owe you a measure of cruelty that I shall take a long time to pay off." (Elizabeth)

J.C. Trewin in *Illustrated London News* reported, "In Birmingham now the new version has Wendy Hiller: so moving that I cannot be repelled by the woman's device. A middle-aged spinster in a French provincial town, she looks urgently for a husband. The chance comes when the doctor's son is in danger of imprisonment for debt incurred as a guarantor. In paying the debt she buys him as a husband; when, after the wedding, he repels her bitterly, she holds him prisoner... I find little comedy, and for me the young man (though played with loyalty and address by Jeremy Brett) is intolerable, fit for a ring of jackals. The drama holds me because of the theatrical cruelty of the situation, and in particular because Wendy Hiller, in her emotional resolve and sharp agony (no one can weep as she does) seizes sympathy and keeps it." (Illustrated London News 20th January 1965) Jeremy received a pleasing mention from *The Times of London*: "Mr. Jeremy Brett especially puts a stylish gloss on the bought young man and his consequent marriage of hatred... As it stands, the production veers unsatisfactorily between taking Mr. Passeur's text as a lacerating hymn of hatred and, on the other hand, of making fun of its novelettish plot. A measure more of artificiality would do no harm." (The Times 10th February 1965)

Gilbert and Elizabeth with Anne-Marie in A Measure of Cruelty

Death of William Huggins

Lych Gate

Dedication

William Huggins died on 22nd April 1965, and the family gathered for the funeral and the internment of his ashes in the graveyard of St. John the Baptist Church at Berkswell. The Lych Gate was later dedicated to both Elizabeth and William and a plaque mounted in the wall; the ceremony in April 1979 was officiated at by the Bishop of Coventry. (This Lych Gate was dedicated to the glory of God in memory of William and Elizabeth Huggins on June 24th 1979, by the Lord Bishop of Coventry) The family's close relationship with the church can be seen in a screen mounted in the Lady Chapel of the church dedicated to Elizabeth and placed there by William and the four boys: John, Patrick, Michael and Jeremy. (Text: In Loving Memory of Elizabeth Edith Cadbury Huggins devoted wife of Lt. Col. H.W. Huggins and Mother of John Michael Patrick and Jeremy. Born 1903 Died 1959 In sure and certain hope of the Resurrection) The family home, Berkswell Grange was sold. In an interview some years later he paid tribute to his parents. *"My parents were wonderful. They're both dead now, but I remember them with the most glorious love. I was their youngest child, and I'm sure I was very spoiled, as youngest children usually are. I've always been spoiled, I think, and as one of the few actors in this country who seems to be employed at the moment, I'm still very spoiled. I believe I was an incredibly naughty child. I have a feeling I was allowed to get away with murder. But my brothers could probably answer that better than I can!"* (Secret of Success by Christine Palmer 17th January 1987)

St John's Church Interior   *Huggins Plaque*

Jeremy and his father Colonel Huggins 1960s – By Courtesy of Joyce Jakeman (Sally Cowie)

Berkswell Fete (signed)

PROGRAMME

2.30 p.m. **OFFICIAL OPENING** by Mr. Jeremy Brett

3.00 p.m. **DISPLAY OF DANCING** by the Berkswell School Children

3.30 p.m. **TEAS** will be available provided by the Berkswell Mother's Union.

4.30 p.m. **CHILDREN'S SPORTS**

5.30 p.m. **ANNOUNCEMENT OF COMPETITION WINNERS**

During the afternoon the Scouts will cook and sell Hot Dogs.

If you have to leave early please pin tickets and programmes, clearly marked with your address, on the board provided near the gate

---

Red Cross tent available in case of accident.

DO BE SURE TO VISIT:

THE LADIES WORKING PARTY STALL for Handmade Goods of all kinds.

THE PRODUCE STALL for a wide selection of Local Produce.

THE PLANT STALL for Flowers and Bedding Plants.

THE BOTTLE STALL — Bottles of everything.

THE CAKE STALL for all Homemade Cakes and Scones and other "Goodies".

WHITE ELEPHANT STALL.

THE TOMBOLA STALL — win a First Class Prize.

DISPLAY OF MODEL AEROPLANES (weather permitting)

GAMES. Try your luck at:— "BOWLING FOR A HAM", "FISHING", "CLOCK GOLF" and "HOOP-LA"
Try to beat the World Record for "GUM BOOT THROWING".

THERE WILL BE
PONY RIDES DURING THE AFTERNOON

Berkswell Fete

Family at the sale of the Grange

The photo of Jeremy and the Colonel was taken at one of the fetes held each year at the Grange. Jeremy officially opened the proceedings in 1975. The days of the Country Fete were very exciting for everyone with many stalls and sideshows. Sally writes, "My job was to keep the dogs occupied (Mr. Binks, Mr. Punch and Miss Trixie) and help the stall holders set up if they asked me." Her mother, Joyce Jakeman was the Huggins' housekeeper for many years and she was very close to him, almost his "adopted" mum. Sally also mentions Jeremy's sense of fun. What he had described as *"incredibly naughty"* was a determination to enjoy life and celebrate every occasion. On one instance he turned up at the Grange in his new TR7 sports car and took her mother and herself for a ride around the village, and "with a twinkle in his eye" and a wink for Sally he sped over the humped back bridge on Hodgetts Lane to lift them out of their seats so that Joyce hit her head on the soft top of the car. "Jeremy and I laughed so much but Mum told him off for driving so fast – wonderful days. I had a lot of fun with him and must admit we did get up to a lot of mischief. I wish he could have been here for Mum – she loved him so much and told him many times to stop playing Holmes – she felt the character was too dark and was affecting him too much. He kept telling her he would do soon but of course never did." (Sally Cowie)

Knock on Any Door - Close Season 1965 – ITV Armchair Theatre

The Television dramas broadcast on ABC and ATV were becoming an important part of the schedules. *The Stage* magazine featured an article called "New groupings will bring a sense of occasion," says Lloyd. "The screening of single plays over the different channels was being replaced by groups of plays. The commitment to drama, especially in the case of Armchair Theatre whose aim was to stimulate authors to write specifically for the weekend programme was to continue. However, groups of plays, for example, *Knock on Any Door* and the Victorian mystery thrillers of *Mystery and Imagination* series, produced by Jonathan Alwyn, with Terence Feely as story editor, would feature in the schedules. "Among the stars already cast are Jack Hawkins, Virginia McKenna, Susannah York, Denholm Elliott, Jeremy Brett, Robert Hardy, Ann Bell and Mary Miller." (The Stage 30th September 1965)

An appearance for ITV television followed in the **Knock on any Door** series. The twenty-part series ran from 1965 to 1966 and each week the story was introduced by Ted Willis, the creator of the series, as Himself before the door was opened onto the action. Jeremy appeared as **David** in Part Five on 30th October 1965, at 10.05 which was entitled ***Close Season*** by Arden Winch and Produced by Pieter Rogers. Eileen Atkins played Ruth, Megs Jenkins played Marion Weiss and Mervyn Johns, Mr Purbright. The listing asked the question, "What made David and Ruth come to stay at the Hillcrest Residential Hotel in the close season?"

The *TV Times* described it as a thriller with a strong cast, "*Close Season* has a strong cast of well-known stage actors. It opens with David and Ruth knocking at the hotel door. They are a young brother and sister, played by Jeremy Brett and Eileen Atkins. They are Jewish, apparently of foreign extraction, taciturn and uncommunicative. Their reserve irritates the other guests. The newcomers are not on holiday; there is a menacing air of purpose about them. And then Purbright reports that David has a gun..." (TV Times 30th October 1965)

A feature article appeared in the same copy of the *TV Times* titled, *"Even at school Jeremy was known as a natural actor."* Jeremy told the magazine how he first got into the profession. "Unexpected things spur young people to becoming actors. In the case of 29-year-old Jeremy Brett, who has the leading role in Saturday night's KNOCK ON ANY DOOR Play *Close Season*, it was the caustic comments of a choirmaster helped by an outsize duffel coat and a flamboyant bow tie. *"I had a good singing voice as a boy,"* Jeremy explained, *"so I was in the school choir (the famous Eton one). But apparently I had, to quote my choirmaster, 'histrionic tendencies' which he thought were quite out of place."* Jeremy told the interviewer how hard he found it to control this natural acting ability and the difficulties it created for him at school. Luckily he was able to put these talents to good use when he left. *"That's where the duffel coat and tie comes in,"* he explained how he wore his brother's coat to his audition at the Central School of Drama. *"I put them on to bolster my ego, and imagine I looked a sight because they belonged to my elder brother (Michael) – he is an artist – and the coat was much too big."* He described all his brothers as *"eccentric. But all talented and all successful, too, Patrick, an architect, designed the new chapel for Gordonstoun School. Michael, who is an artist and lives in Majorca, is well-known in America, and John is an authority on veteran cars. They all went to Eton. But in these days of red-brick realism that's not the best background for an actor,"* said Jeremy. *"I've had to live it down.'* He made his debut at the Manchester Library Theatre in 1954 and *"stayed for a year, playing a variety of parts"* but his time was cut short by an amazing stroke of luck. *"Someone thought I looked like Audrey Hepburn,"* he grins, *"and gave me a contract to play her brother Nicholas in* War and Peace. He hasn't looked back since..." (TV Times 30th October 1965) In another interview with Margaret Hinxman at this time he would say that his Warwickshire family was far removed from show business. *"I suspect they're still waiting for me to give up this acting nonsense and get a steady job."*

Jeremy and Audrey in War and Peace

A Month in the Country 1965 - Guildford/Cambridge Theatre London

Ingrid as Natalya and Jeremy as Beliaev in A Month in the Country

In 1965 he was to take on a classic role on stage under the direction of Michael Redgrave, another Lord of the Theatre. Turgenev's ***A Month in the Country***, written by Emlyn Williams from the Russian, had relocated from the Yvonne Arnaud Theatre Guildford to the Cambridge Theatre in London and it is there that Jeremy took over the role of **Beliaev** from his brother-in-law, Daniel Massey, and played the tutor to critical acclaim. A comedy in three acts, it describes how after a month in the country Beliaev had returned to Moscow to discover he had unwittingly prompted love in the hearts of two ladies. The married Natalya (Ingrid Bergman) bored with her life, welcomed the attentions of Mikhail Rakitin (Michael Redgrave), although their relationship was to remain platonic, but the arrival of the handsome Aleksei Beliaev as tutor to her son Kolya upset that and offered romance. Thereafter she became a rival with her young ward Vera who was planning to marry a man 30 years her senior, but joined the fight for the young man's affections. Misunderstandings and suspicions mean that both Rakitin and Beliaev were obliged to leave. Natalya's life reverted to its original state of boredom.

Jeremy had worked extremely hard to achieve the intricacies of the Russian pronunciation and had clearly been able to make a significant impression and earn praise from the critics, who picked him out from a prestigious group of actors including Ingrid Bergman, Michael Redgrave and Emlyn Williams. *The Financial Times* critic, John Higgins, gave his approval of the performance: "But perhaps most impressive of the newcomers is Jeremy Brett as Beliaev. In a production notable for the way in which each of the actors slides into his role like a hand slipping into a well-fitting glove, Mr. Brett is still outstanding. His tutor is still basically a student, even a peasant, as the *muzhik* costume suggests; yet he, like Vera becomes aware of his sexuality for the first time, his power to move others when they want to stand still. Here is Beliaev, gauche and shy, yet with a quick smile of those who are charming by nature rather than adoption, and here was the perfect leave-taking – sad, surprised, yet totally courteous." Another critic, Martin Esslin, observed that, "Jeremy Brett's tutor Beliaev is very remarkable… it is not often that one sees a young man on the London stage whose virile attractiveness is such that it fully motivates the leading lady's uncontrollable infatuation." And a review in the *Chicago Tribune* said, "There's no mistaking the potent charm of Jeremy Brett as the young tutor whose shy smile blows the roof off a dull country house." Jeremy had been given the opportunity to display his personal charm in this production and charm was becoming his keynote characteristic even when he was playing with some of the stage and screen's greatest stars. After his initial worries about playing with the great Ingrid Bergman they *"became very close friends."*

The Stage welcomed it. "The beauty, charm, delicate humour and pathos of Michael Redgrave's production of *A Month in the Country*, which was the first delight at the new Yvonne Arnaud at Guildford, now cast an ever greater spell at the Cambridge, where the play opened on Thursday last. Still somewhat slow in the first act… the drama of Natalia Petrovna's realisation of love through Beliaev, the young tutor, gradually becomes stronger in its grip, while the scenes of Russian country life more than a hundred years ago, weaves their magic with increasing power… Jeremy Brett, replacing Daniel Massey, is extremely good as the tutor…" (The Stage 30th September 1965) "Mr Emlyn Williams' Doctor is a fine figure of seedy provincial dignity, and Mr Jeremy Brett gives a virtuoso account of a thankless role." (The Times 24th September 1965) What was meant to be a six week production had two extensions and turned into eight months and unsurprisingly it stretched the stars to their limits.

As a schoolboy at Eton, Jeremy had become a fan of Ingrid Bergman when he saw her face on the cinema screen. He told a reporter how he felt playing a delicate love scene with her, *"I felt quite a chap and I like that feeling. I was shy but keen when I first heard the news I was to play opposite her. I am star-struck which to start with inhibits me a little bit in rehearsals. I suppose really it's because Ingrid is Ingrid and that's something special. But I soon found that she has a fantastic gift of making one relax."* (Evening News 19th October 1965)

The Queen and the Welshman 1966 - BBC Theatre

The Queen and the Welshman immediately followed the stage production of *A Month in the Country* and saw Jeremy still in costume drama but not in the role of romantic hero; instead, he was playing the saturnine political spy **Villiers**. The period of history was also very different as the fifteenth century and the House of Plantagenet became the focus. As part of the **Theatre 625** series on BBC2, produced by Cedric Messina this play was broadcast on 10th April 1966. An adaptation of the romantic novel by Rosemary Anne Sisson, and set against the battle of Agincourt it told the story of how the victorious Henry V had wooed and won the French princess Katherine to unite the Kingdoms of England and France. However, his tragic death in 1422 at the early age of thirty-five would leave her a young unprotected widow at a foreign court. The fate of the twenty-one year old Queen Katherine became a political challenge for the English advisors who didn't know what to do with her. It was masterminded by the Duke of Gloucester as Lord Protector and his chief concern appears to have been the possibility that she would re-marry and complicate the line of succession by producing more children.

A BFI reviewer called it a romantic footnote to Shakespeare's *Henry V* and highlighted Katherine's situation, "against the wishes of the Court, Catherine conducts a clandestine relationship with Sir Owen Tudor – a Welshman who served at Agincourt" living in seclusion at Hatfield for the next nine years, producing four more children in secret with her Clerk. Eventually, their children would create the new Tudor dynasty with Henry VII and change the course of English history. As Gloucester's undercover agent Villiers would watch over his charge and Jeremy appeared to relish his role as the spiteful guardian of his royal charge: "It is a shame that Jeremy Brett as Gloucester's spy, Villiers, is so long in the shadows and only has a chance to shine in the film in the final gaol scene with Sir Owen." As a cynic and spoiled gentleman, he was played with a perpetual sneer. (BFI Mediatheque webpage) "Jeremy Brett depicted the barrenness of the human soul in the person of Villiers, a man who wed himself to the evils of spying and betrayal. It was to Mr. Brett's credit... that his justifications for his behaviour, as offering some certitude in a world where much could be lost and many hurt, did not appear to be simple villainy." (New York Times 26th April 1969) His lack of compassion lay in the betrayal of a wife who had abandoned his only son leaving him to die in the care of the nurse whilst she left with his best friend. To add insult to injury they had ransacked the house and taken all the gold with them leaving him penniless. *"So much for domestic love and loyalty!... I had slept through a dream of illusion, and now I am awake. I'd been betrayed by men, betrayed by a woman – the experience was invaluable."* (The Queen and the Welshman)

The Lost Stradivarius - ITV Mystery and Imagination 1966

Sir John Maltravers in The Lost Stradivarius

His voice and his demeanour meant that the classics were always present but the growth of commercial television brought a move into other genres, such as the *Mystery and Imagination* series for ITV where Jeremy was chosen for the role of **Sir John Maltravers** in *The Lost Stradivarius* in the first episode of the series. The programme, based on the beautifully constructed ghost story by John Meade Faulkner, tells how a Victorian student musician discovers that playing a certain air on his violin brings an invisible guest to his room. The ghostly visits become more frequent and more sinister, until he eventually sees the figure of a man sitting and listening to his playing. The discovery of a valuable old Stradivarius violin hidden in a secret cupboard in his room brings a change in his character. As his performance on the violin improves it becomes an obsession; he is drawn away from his old values, towards more dangerous interests and finally he succumbs to the restless spirit of the eighteenth century necromancer.

Set in Oxford and Naples in the 1840s it is a story of occult possession by a violin and by a piece of seventeenth-century music, a *Gagliarda*. A feature article had the title *Sold – to the Devil* and Jeremy told the interviewer that he sincerely believed in the power of evil, *"Black magic is a dangerous thing to play around well, and I am sure that if a susceptible person played an evil character long enough, he would be influenced by the role."* He also admitted to feeling rather scared at the use of a pagan crown in his costume for the production and the ritual of black magic had really upset him.

One critic thought the presentation of black magic rituals, the tension, the period atmosphere and fear were difficult to achieve on television. "Mr. Owen Holder's adaptation of *The Lost Stradivarius* had chilling moments in its first two acts; where the ill-fated hero reached Naples and devoted himself to the Black Arts its grip slackened, the atmosphere of tension was dissipated, and it became easy to notice contrivances of direction and inconsistencies of playing. The moments of fear were produced by Mr. Bill Bain's direction with exactitudes of timing and smooth if traditional trick photography. Mr. Buck and Mr. Jeremy Brett, the haunted violinist, only intermittently achieved the stylisation of manner and speech at which they aimed, dropping too often into modern off-handedness. The evil rites were too lucid and too well lit; there was not a large enough space left for the adequate functioning of the imagination." (Supernatural Too Much for TV The Times 31st January 1966) "To present a story such as this with maximum effect, one needs particularly to swathe it in convincing period atmosphere. The more accurate the minute details are the more likely one is to accept the story's improbable basis... The main acting burden fell on Jeremy Brett, who subtly presented the various stages of the hero's disintegration. When he said, after the black magic sequence, '*I saw what Cain and Judas saw,*' it was possible to believe it from his stricken countenance." (The Stage 3rd February 1966) The *TV Times* announced the evil fascination in, *"He fills me with such horror – as if his face is the face of wickedness itself."* "Taking the audience by the hand as story teller during the series – seven stories will be seen now and six more a little later – and frequently as central character, will be David Buck, as a romantic young Victorian to whom strange things happen. In the first story, *The Lost Stradivarius* an eerie tale by J. Meade Faulkner, he will be seen as the faithful friend of an aristocratic young man who falls disastrously under the evil fascination of an old violin. To play the central role, Jeremy Brett had to master the intricate finger movements of an accomplished violinist. Brett so staggered his tutor by the uncanny ease and accuracy with which he took to the violin that one began to wonder, uneasily, if life were, perhaps, going to imitate fiction. His performance is so compelling that one is still not quite sure..." (TV Times 29th January 1966)

Jeremy's playing of the violin would be admired again in his performance as Sherlock Holmes in which he made such an impression that one critic reported that Jeremy had played the violin as a child until the age of eight, suggesting he had some experience. However, Jeremy explained; *"I can't play (the violin), in fact I have got pretty skilful at bowing the instrument. Mind you, to give the impression that I know what I'm doing, I do listen to the music for hours beforehand so that I have the feel of it."*

The Lost Stradivarius

Chopin and George Sand The Creative Years 1966 - BBC Television

On 5th May 1966, Jeremy appeared in **Chopin and George Sand –The Creative Years**, in which he played the pianist. "How antipathetic this Sand woman is! Is she really a woman at all? I am inclined to doubt it." In spite of this unpromising first impression when he met her in Paris in 1836, Chopin was to develop a strong relationship with her, a liaison which was to last ten years. He was a man of elegance, sensitive and reserved, but in his music he was passionate and a widely held genius. George Sand was a novelist who became notorious for wearing men's clothing and smoking cigars with the strong belief that she should have complete liberty and recognition as a woman. She became not only Chopin's mistress, but also took on the role of mother as she nursed him through his illness.

A review in *The Times* reported, "The two earlier programmes in its series have claimed to set music in its historical context. Mr. Hal Burton's piece last night wisely substituted the word 'biographical' for 'historical' in its description, and entirely justified its claim, making it clear that his association with the novelist influenced the composer by creating the situation in which he could compose more, not any specific type of music. Chopin's letters were read by Mr. Jeremy Brett, and George Sand's by Miss Margaret Rawlings; Mr. Burton provided only the necessary links between them. Mr Eric Heidsieck provided the musical illustrations." (The Times 6th May 1966)

The Three Musketeers - BBC Television 1966

Jeremy's appearance as **D'Artagnan** in *The Three Musketeers* would give him the opportunity to match his passionate energy to the classic historical adventure novel written by Alexandre Dumas based on the seventeenth century French court under Louis XIII. As the naive, hot-headed, young man, desperate for adventure he would join the famous swashbuckling heroes the Musketeers as they sought to protect the name and throne of the King from the machinations of Cardinal Richelieu and the treacherous Milady de Winter. Covering the period 1625 to 1628 it also included war with England so fighting and double agents were central to the action. As D'Artagnan travels from Gascony to Paris to become one of the celebrated Musketeers like his father he will be caught up in intrigue surrounding the Queen and the Duke of Buckingham led by the Cardinal, romance with Constance Bonacieux as she seeks to help her mistress and relentless action-packed adventure on horseback and always with his sword in hand ready for battle against all comers alongside Athos, Porthos and Aramis.

It was set in a turbulent time in French history, beset by civil and religious attack from the enemies abroad and within the country itself. The power lies in the intrigues of Cardinal Richelieu. Even King Louis XIII was manipulated by him but the Musketeers are their monarch's courageous and passionate supporters with pride, passion and much swordplay. *"There is so much in the story: it's swashbuckling on one hand and a bitter, real story on the other... a story of lost ideals, youth and innocence, of decay."* (Jeremy) It had an imposing cast with a brave and sensitive hero D'Artagnan, Richard Pasco as the evil Richelieu, and Mary Peach as the terrible scheming Milady de Winter. Jeremy explained to Margaret Hinxman for the *Woman* Magazine the challenges of playing in half hour episodes, *"Hope I made sense. A tense TV serial isn't only a cliff-hanger for viewers, it's the same for us, too. In effect, you're giving a five-hour performance. But you're playing it out in little bits hoping audiences understand that how you act this week will make sense next week!"* Jeremy needn't have worried. Audiences caught on extremely quickly. *The Three Musketeers* had been dramatised on a number of occasions, before and since, but it was felt that there never was a more attractive and physical young man in the role of the seventeenth-century French hero. Jeremy seemed to fit the part like a glove. Although he was in fact thirty-three years old, he was playing a young man of twenty from a proud Gascon family.

D'Artagnan

This appearance brought him a significant number of new fans and his fan mail increased considerably. Schoolgirls fell in love with him. One fan even wrote to say how much she liked his curly eyebrows. But many viewers sent serious critical appraisals of Jeremy's approach to Dumas' classic hero, for it was far different from the traditional swashbuckler. *"Director Peter Hammond and I wanted to portray D'Artagnan as he appeared in the book: a gauche country boy at first: later very bitter. I also think it's useful to be true to the period: to let people realise that in a swordfight you seldom kill a man with one thrust – you're more likely to let him live on horribly injured. Being in love in those days wasn't easy either. If your lady lived twenty miles away, you couldn't just drive over. You had to saddle up, ride hard, arriving bow-legged and sore-bottomed. Only a very ardent love could survive."* "Every scene has a concentrated vigour; every shot counts; every second of screen time is made to work, and work hard." The critic went on to applaud the actors who played *The Three Musketeers* and praised Jeremy as "a subtle, intelligent D'Artagnan and it was he who dominated Sunday's episode… but the most winning aspect of it all, for my licence fee, were the fight sequences." (The Stage 15th December 1966)

Jeremy had suddenly been thrust into the public domain and was interviewed by a number of newspapers and for the feature in the fangirl magazines, all trying to get a personal slant on the new romantic hero. His replies to questions on the swashbuckling hero or on his personal life were, as always, revealing. He told *Plays and Players* that his fan mail had increased considerably. And he chose D'Artagnan as his favourite part. He said, *"What a relief it was, after the straitjacket of modern neurosis in the theatre, suddenly to play a full-blooded character who reacts strongly, intensively and spontaneously. But Dumas provides the actor with such a huge canvas that it's difficult to work in detail and I'm not at all sure he isn't better read than acted. After that series, my fan letters rose dramatically from about ten a week to two hundred, which just shows you what a power in our lives television has become."* However, it was the response from the audience that he most appreciated. *"I'm an actor… I appreciate it, as any actor does, when people see and like what we're trying to do. Dumas was a wonderful writer. We've got just twenty-four-and-a-half minutes each week to put on the screen this wonderful canvas, the bitterness and the true-life parable that he told. I hope people see D'Artagnan for what he was. An innocent, like all of us at twenty, gradually changing under the influence of the other three and the French Court."* (Jeremy in Radio Times 29th December 1966) *"Peter Hammond, the director, helped me to see so much in the character of D'Artagnan and the three musketeers that I've become completely immersed in the production."* It is interesting to note that Peter Hammond would also help Jeremy in his interpretation of Sherlock Holmes where he would immerse himself in Holmes as he did in the character D'Artagnan so that the critics were unable to separate the actor from the character.

"The cast is comprised of outstanding British actors… But most of all, we get to experience a D'Artagnan who is disarmingly portrayed by Jeremy Brett. D'Artagnan, in Brett's hands, is earnest, noble, spiritedly idealistic, and fiercely brave. This is a very fine performance by Mr Brett, who displays the intensity and class arrogance he would later hone to perfection as Sherlock Holmes. But back in 1966, he was young enough (33 years old) that he was able to bring zest and youthful energy into his iconic role. When his father advises him to '*never fear quarrels, but seek adventures*' and to '*fight on all occasions,*' we know Brett is up to the challenge. Showcasing ferocious, energetic sword fights, ensemble acting done with panache and conviction, and a serious commitment to do right by Dumas's greatest work, BBC's *The Three Musketeers* is an honest and true adaptation." (Amazon.com)

Jeremy had achieved television stardom with this role. And as a result the girl's magazine *Jackie* featured an interview with him. He had said that he frequently regretted his matinee idol looks as people in the business did not have high expectations of his talents. *"I still have a bit of a chip on my shoulder about my looks, largely because I suspect they got me some of my early parts."* (Plays and Players) However, in the case of *The Three Musketeers*, his looks were perfect for the passionate, heroic D'Artagnan. *Jackie*'s columnist "caught up with Jeremy Brett kicking last year's leaves into neat piles in Hyde Park. His casual jacket and slacks were very different from the elegant finery he used to wear in the BBC series *The Three Musketeers*. He described his experience of playing the part: *'It was another jumping about trying to have a good sword fight wearing all that heavy gear; and I felt such a nit anyway.'* After the first episode, the fan letters started flooding in, four hundred in the first week. *'I was overwhelmed at first,'* Jeremy told me. *'I had never had proper fan letters before. D'Artagnan, the adventurer I played in the series, was only supposed to be eighteen, and I was that many years ago.'"*

D'Artagnan

One incident that happened during filming was amusing, "*We all knew how to fence, but we weren't much good at parrying with precision. We knocked off each other's hats, neatly ripped and ruined countless silk jackets and lace ruffles, and I even made a whopping great hole in Porthos's best pair of silk hose. As long as we didn't get scratched and slashed, though, nothing else mattered. At the end of the week with no fatal accidents, we thought ourselves very clever chaps. The following Monday, the full cast arrived at the studio for the grand start, and I had my first duel. About five minutes before this momentous moment, I decided to have a quick swing and pulled at the sword fixed in my scabbard – but nothing happened. The producer screamed, 'Jeremy – where are you? En garde, ready for action. NOW!' In a frenzy, I tugged like a superman – and, SMACK, sword, scabbard and chain broke off and belted me in the eye. What a cavalier!*" On the topic of girls and the kind of girl he found attractive. "*I like a girl who looks you straight in the eye, especially when you're talking to her. Girls who give sidelong glances or look around the room the whole time, are no pals of mine. I also think the shape of a mouth tells a lot about a girl's character – and I'm not deceived by make-up, either.*" Perhaps the most telling question that was asked was What sort of person he would like to be? and his reply is what we would most expect of the man that he was. "*I'd like to be the kind of person whom people enjoy being around.*"

The Baron: The Seven Eyes of Night 1967 - ABC Television

Jeff Walker in The Baron

A modern role followed as he was chosen to play **Jeff Walker**, the role of an audacious thief in ***The Baron: The Seven Eyes of Night*** for ABC Televison broadcast on 28th January 1967, and Jeremy's performance was convincing with sufficient menace and bravado. *The Baron,* based on the *John Creasey* novels, was a popular series from the British ITC Studios, starring Steve Forrest as John Mannering, a Texas rancher and international antiques dealer also working undercover for British Intelligence. Much in *The Saint* vein of thrillers it featured exciting car chases, and shoot-outs with thieves and murderers in the midst of ambitious and unlikely frauds. Written by Terry Nation the Dalek creator, *The Seven Eyes of Night* was an intelligent double cross by a gang of thieves in which Jeff Walker, played by Jeremy, had stolen a precious necklace with the help of an insider Nancy Cummins (Hilary Tindall) and, although she thought they would escape together, he had other plans. Mannering was the wrong person on whom to try such a double cross and with his jokey assistant Cordelia Winfield (Sue Lloyd) they tracked down and overcame the gang. Jeremy had created a menace on screen which was hidden by his charm as the attractive womaniser, however, in spite of his vicious crimes he never loses the support of the audience. He said it was easier and ultimately far less satisfying to create a baddie than someone good. "*Villains are very, very boring to do. They're much easier than heroes.*"

Quite an Ordinary Knife - ABC Television 1967

Sergio and Giulia in Quite an Ordinary Knife

Quite an Ordinary Knife was part of the ITV Armchair Theatre series in which Jeremy appeared as **Sergio Rovino** with Judy Parfitt and T.P.McKenna as Giulia and Meno Donelli. Broadcast on Saturday 15th July 1967 it was billed as a suspense thriller with a strong hint of violence and death which neatly fits into "the new issues of the day" that the series was highlighting. Jordan Lawrence set his play in the sweltering suburbs of Milan where Giulia Donelli (Judy Parfitt) is waiting for her husband to return home for the meal she is preparing. Paolo Bracchiana (William Squire) is the stranger who comes asking about her husband. The *TV Times* introduced it with the headline, "The stranger is disturbing." And explained, "For Giulia it is incredible that such a case is building up against her husband Meno. They are devoted. Can the stranger know more about her husband than she does?" (TV Times 15th July 1967)

Tension is created as more and more of Giulia's illusions about her life, her husband, and their friend are challenged by the stranger's questions until very little remains. Meno, a man of routine, should have returned home but as the stranger Paolo comes in to wait for him she will grow more agitated and concerned. "Nor is she much relieved by the unexpected arrival of Meno's workmate, their special friend, Sergio (Jeremy Brett)." (TV Times 15th July 1967) Ann Purser in *Stage and Television Today* found it "contrived and too melodramatic... A girl of bad character has been murdered, the stranger is the Inspector and Meno is the killer. A small red herring in the person of Sergio (Jeremy Brett) fails to fool the Inspector, and Giulia, loyal to the last, quickly knifes her husband before he can be taken away to stand trial." (20th July 1967)

Kenilworth 1967 - BBC Television

Tressilian

After this brief appearance in a modern play Jeremy returned to the familiar costume drama set in the Elizabethan court in **Kenilworth** as **Edmund Tressilian** who was the tragic lover of Amy Robsart, in the Tudor drama of intrigue - a four-part series for BBC2 beginning on 22nd July 1967, with the titles: *The Sparrow's Lure, The Black Arts, The Tide Changes, The Wrath of Lions.* It was based on Sir Walter Scott's *Kenilworth,* the romantic novel in which the long term relationship between Queen Elizabeth and Robert Dudley, Earl of Leicester, is carried out before the whole court making the accidental death of Amy Robsart, Leicester's secret wife appear suspicious. As the Queen's favourite constantly at her side, he has betrayed her expectation of complete devotion but he will show only ruthless ambition and attempt to keep both Amy and the Queen. Selfless love is found in the noble Tressilian, quickly and firmly established as the hero. He had been engaged to marry the beautiful innocent Amy and a more perfect match couldn't be imagined until the Earl of Leicester developed a passion for her and married her. Jeremy reported in interview that *"I had my hand run through when I was playing Tressilian in the film* Kenilworth." His experience with a sword would have been considerable after the swashbuckling exploits of *The Musketeers* but was insufficient protection when faced with a desperate and vengeful Leicester in a duel.

As Tressilian Jeremy had exchanged his more familiar flamboyant character for the serious steadfast lover who would be left heartbroken holding the dying Amy in his arms. The director had written to him asking him to look at the part of Leicester and Tressilian saying that although he appeared an "obvious Leicester" he preferred him as Tressilian. As a result he earned considerable praise for his interpretation, "Jeremy Brett, whose television acting grows more subtle, showed a melancholy profile as the constant lover."

The original script adapted by Anthony Steven avoided much of Sir Walter Scott's rhetoric succeeding in combining history with romance "a pageant of Elizabethan England". "The immortal Amy is sweetly embodied in Prunella Ransome, whose gentle innocence is in sharp contrast to the strong self-will and sharp intelligence of Gemma Jones's young Elizabeth. Graham Lines plays ambitious Leicester, whose wayward passion for Amy drives him to jeopardise his career at court... while Jeremy Brett, honourable and devoted Tressilian again redresses the balance, for this is a tale of good and evil with one character always the foil for another, combatants engaged in the eternal romantic struggle." (The Stage 27th July 1967)

Casanova - BBC Television 1967

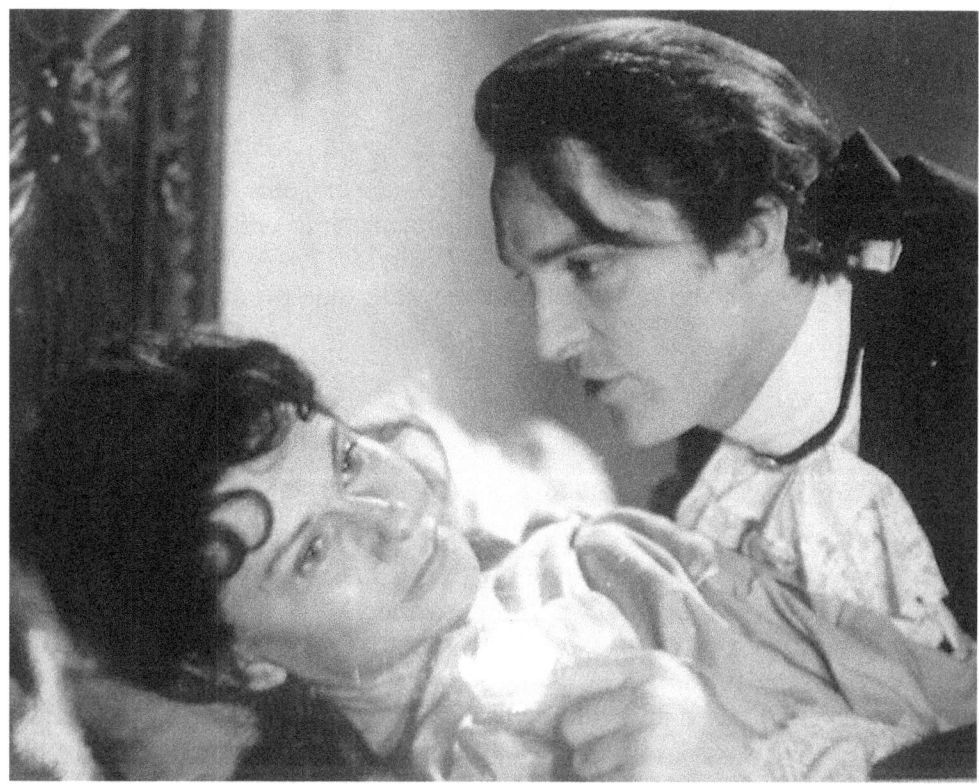

Casanova

The idea that **Casanova** was a magician is an unlikely suggestion but in the BBC trilogy ***The Magicians: The Incantation of Casanova*** 22nd October 1967, this was the implication. The three separate plays explored the idea that magic and spiritualism was very much part of these three contemporary figures. "Ken Taylor has written a trilogy called *Men and Magic* which is about men dabbling with the unknown and unseen. *The Incantation of Casanova* was the second of the series, directed by Herbert Wise, starring Jeremy Brett, Jacqueline Pearce, and Daphne Anderson." (The Stage 24th August 1967) Casanova had a reputation for seducing women and his name has become synonymous with *"womaniser"* yet he was an amateur magician as well as an amorist. Casanova claimed he had the gift of mystical powers, thereby enhancing his notoriety, but it was the use of his scientific knowledge which enabled him to create the unexpected outcome. In one case, a very young and innocent Marquise with a significant fortune would be convinced she could be reborn as a man and paid a great deal for this *"knowledge"* although the outcome remains a mystery.

With the promise of treasure on a local farmer's land, the "magician" offered to summon spirits to discover the hoard for a significant fee. As the farmer's daughter is an attractive sixteen year old virgin, he is pleased to include her in his magic rites with the hope that she will form part of his reward. The ceremony is halted by the intervention of a violent thunderstorm which he recognises as an act of God, persuading him to leave the treasure and the lady unharmed. *The Times*, said: "Casanova's expert use of mumbo-jumbo to add charm and interest to what might otherwise have been the routine but difficult seduction of a 16-year-old girl was comically Rabelaisian… One of the hallmarks of a good play is the quality of the work it demands from its actors. Jeremy Brett, television's favourite romantic actor, was given, and accepted, ample opportunity to glitter with conscious wit by the Casanova of the second play." Stanley Reynolds in *The Guardian* thought it was "a bawdy, blasphemous farce about a legendary lover, played by Jeremy Brett, who passes himself off as a magician in order to seduce a 16-year-old girl." Jeremy was "marvellous as the swashbuckling Casanova, rolling out stylish lines like '*some men are clever, some have wisdom, but only girls have magic."* (Reynolds Stanley in The Guardian 23rd October 1967) "Playing the most famous lover of all time is Jeremy Brett, seen recently on BBC TV in *The Three Musketeers* and now giving a performance as Orlando in the National Theatre's all male production of *As You Like It*."

National Theatre

Any Just Cause 1967 – Adeline Genee Theatre East Grinstead

The year 1967 was to be a significant one for Jeremy's career; his return to the National Theatre was something he would cherish and describe as *"the happiest period of my career."* However, another performance on stage would come first which was also noteworthy for the excellent reviews. His performance as **Ronnie** was described as *"an outstanding piece of characterisation"* in this little-known play which appeared as the second play at the Adeline Genee Theatre, East Grinstead. **Any Just Cause** featured a domestic break-up which had enormous effects on each member of the family. It ran from 21st February to 11th March 1967. This was the first play written by George Pensotti, himself a RADA trained actor, whose great admiration for the Russian playwright Chekhov had led him to write a play about Chekhov's life titled *To Moscow, to Moscow* and also to write several plays of his own in the same style. In the first performance of *Any Just Cause* Jeremy played the elder son and Michael York, the younger, Stephen, who threw away his ambitions to enter Oxford, distracted by the situation at home. Ronnie also changed due to these challenging circumstances and became a different person. The production starred Phyllis Calvert with Philip Grout as Director and Michael Young as Designer.

The *London Times* critic pointed out that the title of the play was based on the words of the marriage ceremony and said the fable was one of "prolonged family witch-hunting." As the curtain rose, the father, Victor, was preparing to leave home; his wife, Alice, was progressively getting more drunk as they discussed the thorny issue of alimony and both boys were trying not to be noticed. Seven years later Victor was married again but the disagreeable wrangling between Victor and Alice had continued in letter form and it had affected both of the sons. "What makes the play worth seeing is its rendering of domestic claustrophobia. Philip Grout's production rises to these moments with great feeling. Its centre-piece is a glowing performance by Phyllis Calvert as Alice: genteel and vulgar, stupid and intuitive in turn. As her elder son Ronnie, Jeremy Brett achieves an outstanding piece of characterisation as he changes from a dull provincial drifter into a suburban miser." (Family Witch-hunt in New Play The Times 28th February 1967)

The Stage found the production "disturbing" and "candid" in its presentation of "the effects of divorce on a pair of grown up brothers... the theme of George Pensotti's tragic-comedy *Any Just Cause* which had its première at the Adeline Genee, East Grinstead. As it depicts the wrangling and fighting of the parents breaking up a family, *Any Just Cause* is witty, disturbing and candid. Phyllis Calvert was not far short of brilliant as Alice, the wife who resorts to drink to control her frayed nerves, while her husband, Victor, smoothly portrayed by Derek Farr, runs off with another woman. As Ronnie, Jeremy Brett grew in stature and gave a striking exhibition of indignation turning to wrath when his own wife – sick of his parents' incompatible behaviour – leaves him...." (The Effects of Divorce The Stage 9th March 1967)

Jeremy was pleased to be back in the theatre. An interview which he gave at this time hinted at some of the frustration he had experienced in filming over the last couple of years. "If you think that making a film is all fun... Actor Jeremy Brett –one of the nicest and most modest actors I've ever met – doesn't think so. *"I've not been pleased with any film I've ever done,"* Jeremy told me. *"There's too much excitement and frenzy over a film. Every time I think I'm doing film – marvellous, I get all excited and worked up about it; then it's done and it's just another... quiet and dreary film... it's mainly hanging about...."*

Fortunately, he was soon to come under the tutelage of Olivier and the classic theatre which would perfect his technique in the most intensive manner. But Jeremy was always a free spirit and reluctant to become tied to the regime of twelve hour days and learning three roles at once. Robert expressed his own concerns about the pressures of working in the new theatre, "We all worked like absolute donkeys. You were either rehearsing or performing all the time." Jeremy added another perspective: *"This is partly because the Theatre is still in the process of formation and one actor very often has to do the work of three. It's all right, I suppose being worked very hard, provided you can have six weeks' holiday a year... I think one needs an awareness of life beyond the theatre, even if one doesn't have time to lead it. That's where doing films come in useful – it gives one a chance to see places that one wouldn't get to otherwise.'* However, the stage remained his preferred home. *'The difference between the theatre and film is to me the difference between tennis and squash. I prefer the theatre because I do like to be able to rehearse a part properly. When you work in a film, the sequences are all worked out like a graph and you feel they are nothing to do with you. My attitude to the theatre is that I want it to go on being part of me for years and years. I still want to have a crack at playing* Coriolanus *some time and, if I can get away from costume parts, I would love to appear as the haunted character, Harry Moncherry, in T.S. Eliot's* The Family Reunion.*'* (Plays and Players 1966)

As You Like It 1967 - The National Theatre

Jeremy and Ronald in As You Like It

Jeremy's attitude towards the National Theatre changed quite dramatically when Laurence Olivier invited him to the dress rehearsal of *Much Ado About Nothing*. After his departure for Hollywood to play Freddie in *My Fair Lady* he thought he would never again be employed by The National Theatre. But the opportunity, mixed with a realisation that he was not part of this special group of players, encouraged him to go into a dressing room and cut his hair into a large fringe, "*bangs*." His desire to be considered for the role of **Orlando** in the upcoming production of ***As You Like It*** was granted when Olivier asked him to take on the part. He had clearly seen that the prodigal had had a change of heart and welcomed him with open arms. "*Then one night in 1967, I was invited to see the dress rehearsal of Joan Plowright taking over for Maggie Smith in* Much Ado. *It was only then I realised that there's a certain amount of gamesmanship. You have to take the opportunities as they come. I knew that the part of Orlando hadn't been cast in the all-male* As You Like It, *and I remember standing in front of my mirror and I just took the scissors and cut a fringe. I thought, 'That's more*

Orlando.' At the end of the show I was in Joan's dressing room and Larry suddenly said, 'Aaahh. Come with me.' And he took me across to his dressing room and said, 'Will you play Orlando for me?' I leapt at him and practically knocked him over with a huge bear hug. That started about the happiest period of my career, because Larry has a tremendous amount to offer any actor. As You Like It was a joy to do and I was allowed to go on and develop." (Jeremy Brett to Ronald Hayman in The Times 1973)

In his contribution to the *Royal National* book and the Omnibus programme for BBC after his death in 1989, in which colleagues and actors paid tribute to their mentor, Jeremy said: *"He was a worker, and could spot someone who wasn't working across a room. He was very tough as a leader, you had to 'take it on.' He would make sure that all his equipment as an actor was ready, because then he could bounce off it. We had to run very quickly to keep up. You could watch him on stage almost literally change width and height. The most important thing when you're working with greatness is to learn from it, not to challenge it. He was an animal of the theatre, which many directors were not. He also never forgot anyone who hurt him. Which I love him for – why get hurt twice?"* (Olivier at Work)

"The casting of Jeremy as Orlando was still unknown when Ronald Pickup met him on the escalator at Waterloo Station: 'I had been cast as Rosalind in the forthcoming all-male *As You Like It* at the time quite a big public talking point. So about a month before rehearsals began I had no idea who was to play Orlando. One late afternoon I was on the packed escalator at Waterloo tube going up – and coming down was a very dashing, Byronic figure, familiar of course, who suddenly yelled across at me. 'Oh! My beautiful Rosalind!' It was, of course, our Jeremy who had just been cast as Orlando. I had never met him, so this meeting had a very un-English lack of inhibition which marked the beginning of a wonderful, joyous working relationship, driven by Jeremy's huge generosity of spirit, on stage and in friendship. His time at the National, like so much in his extraordinary life, was for him 'a Festival' – his favourite word – a word which describes the part he played in all of our lives." (Ronald Pickup 2015)

The concept of an all male *As You Like It* 1967 was inspired by an essay *Bitter Arcadia* by Jan Kott, a Polish critic who saw the changing roles as an interesting opportunity for such a play. The Shakespearean tradition of boys playing the female roles demanded by the Elizabethan mores of the theatre, offered such interpretations but in 1967 a boy playing Rosalind, Celia, Phoebe or Audrey presented a different viewpoint for the twentieth century audience and a story of love at first sight could have been interpreted differently by a modern audience. The National Theatre was already committed to the idea of an all-male cast before Clifford Williams was asked to direct it. He told *The Times*, "The designer Ralph Koltai, and I went through all sorts of absurd ideas like prisoner-of-war camps in Japan, and we said, "We can't do it." Months later Ralph had a sort of idea and I sparked on it. It was a great joy all the way through. Jeremy Brett and Ronnie Pickup worked so well together and Charlie Kay never found anything funny or outré about these two men going through this type of situation together. He just gave it his full regard, and they felt great confidence." (Clifford Williams: A Question of Identity. The Times 8th December 1973)

As You Like It

Olivier would have liked the production to have had shock value, "He came in splashing his usual energy all over the place and galvanising everyone" creating women with lipstick and padded breasts but this was rejected. The decision to dress them in the sixties' fashion of ski boots with large gaudy earrings made them look ridiculous. "We said to them, 'You look marvellous', when they were terrible and they knew it. So they went away and designed their own costumes. Charlie appearing in a mini-skirt, Ron in a trouser suit – and both now did look wonderful." (Derek Jacobi) *The Stage* magazine saw the all-male production as completely justified. "One believes entirely in Ronald Pickup's Rosalind in every phase of the character's progress, and the ardour of Rosalind and Orlando is no less convincing… Rosalind really seems fathoms deep in love. Mr Pickup has a light touch made strong by an underlying gravity that has its own richly moving quality. This is a memorable performance, human and poetic, by a very fine actor. Jeremy Brett's Orlando is on a relatively subdued note and lacks the fire of poetry, yet is still an excellent piece of work, particularly effective in the scenes of mock lovemaking with Rosalind." (The Stage 5th October 1967) *The Times* agreed. "Mr Pickup's Rosalind, a beaky long-legged figure in a yachting suit, does conform to Kott's specification of the boy-girl – except that it is completely non-erotic. It begins demurely with a few well observed feminine gestures, and takes on character only during the Ganymede scenes. It is a blank that comes to life under the stress of intense platonic feeling; and there is real excitement in seeing this Rosalind and Jeremy Brett's very masculine Orlando being taken unawares by serious emotion in the midst of their game." (Irving Wardle in Comic Result when Men Take Over from Actresses. The Times)

Jeremy was playing the very masculine Orlando, so no compromises were needed for his performance, but his challenge was a different one. He came to the conclusion that he might be a little too old to be playing the juvenile leads. *"I accepted myself suddenly one night. I discovered I was an actor and not just a Black Country boy who'd come up to town. I was a very old twenty and a very insecure one. I felt like mutton dressed up as lamb until then, truly... And suddenly it dawned on me, playing Orlando when I was deep in my thirties, that juvenile parts were character parts. I thought, 'I'll accept that I've got something to offer and I'll try to put the right price on my own head.' Before that, I tried too hard, and that meant I wasn't sure. I felt inadequate."* (Jeremy Brett: A New Confidence. The Times 17th November 1973)

The Stage magazine reported on his responses to the casting: "For Jeremy Brett, the production means the beginning of a new chapter in his career. The handsome Old Etonian, whose real name is Peter Huggins was captured from television by Sir Laurence Olivier and he could not be more pleased. We talked this week in the shabby Nissen huts that stand in for the offices of the National Theatre. Brett, 32, has recently been seen on television as D'Artagnan of *The Three Musketeers* and has just completed another three part series for BBC-TV in which he plays the role of the lover Casanova. Of the new *As You Like It* he said: *'Of course, it thrills me because when Rosalind is played by a woman pretending to be a boy, Orlando is not supposed to recognize her.'"*

One sequence of the play called for a wrestling match between Orlando and Charles the Wrestler. The Producer Clifford Williams who wished to preserve the reality spent long hours rehearsing Jeremy and his rival Charles, played by John Flint, with the aid of a professional wrestler. *"We're just praying that nothing snaps in the falls. We've learnt a couple of TV tricks - a couple of falls accompanied by those awful grunts where no one gets really hurt. You can cheat to a certain extent."* Unfortunately, Jeremy had his nose broken during these rehearsals; it was "split open", but after a short pause to strap it up, the rehearsal continued. *"My nose was smashed, centre stage at the National, when I was playing Orlando in* As You Like It *and I had to have it stitched up."* Olivier paid to have it fixed and afterwards Jeremy thought his appearance was more suited to character parts than his previous *pretty boy* image. "As You Like It *was a joy to do, and I was allowed to go on and develop."* (A New Confidence in The Times)

Orlando

Jeremy's close friend Sue Locke commented on the challenges that faced Jeremy in performing Shakespeare. "His Shakespeare roles were always the greatest challenge and at the same time brought the greatest rewards. The problem with dyslexia was ever present and we would spend hours rehearsing together. I believe he was at his peak at this time and with Larry's encouragement he did some wonderful work for the National. His Orlando in *As You Like It* was superb. I must have seen it two dozen times. If he knew I was in the audience he would do it slightly different so that I would not get bored." (Letter to T. Manners)

As You Like It

Much Ado About Nothing 1967 – The National Theatre

Claudio and Hero in Much Ado About Nothing

The next role onstage at the National Theatre was that of **Claudio** in the romantic comedy ***Much Ado About Nothing*** 1967. As the partner to his Hero their "love at first sight" idealised romance was to present the foil to the more cynical Beatrice and Benedick who loved each other but were unable to reach an understanding until the final curtain. Claudio's repressed violence in the malicious defamation of the chaste Hero at the altar, in belief of her infidelity, is instrumental in bringing the two warring lovers together to ensure a happy ending. Joan Plowright had taken over from Maggie Smith as Beatrice, and Robert Stephens remained in the role of Benedick from the original production which also featured Albert Finney as Don Pedro.

By setting the play in the small town of Messina in Florence where Shakespeare had laid it, Franco Zeffirelli had created a new slant on the familiar story of the two lovers who were unable to admit that they loved the other with its underlying themes of honour, shame and court politics. The carnival atmosphere meant that the church scene began comically which made Claudio's base cruelty intensely shocking and the savage force of "Kill Claudio" stunned the audience. In this setting the heavy Mafia overtones amongst the splendour and squalor of the Mediterranean brought Claudio's accusation credibility. To add further drama Benedict's loyal response to male honour "Ha, not for the wide world!" was whispered.

Tartuffe 1968- The National Theatre

Valere in Tartuffe

Jeremy played **Valere**, a minor role in **Tartuffe** by Moliere 1669 which is a very funny play of misrepresentation and fraud. In a new approach to his career at that time he had accepted that he *"had to play my small parts"*. Robert Stephens played the role of Tartuffe with John Gielgud as Orgon. The two lovers Valere (Jeremy) and Mariane (Louise Purnell) were split up when her father the rich bourgeois Orgon was taken in by a wily opportunist, a parasite adopting pretence of sanctity. The deceiver has been established as an honoured guest by the household. Tartuffe has plans to marry Mariane in order to gain control of the family finances and property and he is almost successful until the King's moral insight brings about his final undoing. When Orgon orders his daughter to "Marry Tartuffe, and mortify your flesh!" he is agreeing to Tartuffe's aims, thereby becoming his instrument and sharing the blame. Martin Esslin in *Plays and Players* gave an enthusiastic response to the "splendid production" and said: "Jeremy Brett and Louise Purnell turn the usually insipid lovers into delightfully observed comic portraits."

The Drama critic from the *Glasgow Herald* was uncertain about the interpretation but praised Jeremy and Joan for their excellent performances as Valere and Dorine; "...the vehicle is rendered the more awkward by Richard Wilbur's translation with overtones, for me at least, quite inseparable from pantomime. They raise an occasional giggle on their own account, but more often get in between the words and their meaning to a degree that undermines Mr. Guthrie's whole approach. The result is epitomised in John Gielgud's Orgon: grey, uncertainly hovering between wisdom and stupidity and rare fun, really not very entertaining. Robert Stephens presents Tartuffe as a shrewd yokel – which allows him to show rigid rhythms of the text into interesting incantatory patterns but never somehow creates a total personality. Jeremy Brett displays great vigour and cutting edge as Valere, and Joan Plowright is excellent as Dorine, the comic maidservant, traditional repository of common sense and proper values." (Glasgow Herald 25th November 1967)

The Director gave his approval of the attitude of the players and their preparation for the new challenge: "*Tartuffe* was directed by Tyrone Guthrie who was 'very impressed' with the *esprit de corps* on a poorly received production." (The National Theatre Daniel Rosenthal) In spite of the kind words, Robert Stephens as Tartuffe found this almost as difficult to play as he had found Benedick in *Much Ado About Nothing*. The National Theatre was challenging people's interpretations by introducing a new approach to classical literature and the actors were at the forefront of the development. Jeremy had little to say about this probably because he had begun his career under Guthrie's advice and later under his directorship of *Troilus and Cressida*, but Robert and others expressed their disquiet as they approached their parts.

Edward II 1968 – National Theatre

Another of Jeremy's smaller roles was as **Kent** in the play ***Edward II***, in Bertolt Brecht's version of Marlowe's historical drama. In translation from the original play Brecht had written a very different account where Edward's passion for the court favourite Gaveston became the central theme and thus brought about his downfall and death. What had been the minor theme of the original was now centre stage and could no longer be ignored.

Jeremy highlighted the quality of the advice that Olivier was giving to his actors which displayed his ability to pinpoint any crucial errors in interpretation, *"When I played John Stride's small, weak brother, Kent in Brecht's* Edward II, *Larry came to a rehearsal and said, 'I've never known an actor who's claimed the limp, the stutter, the glasses and the sway because he isn't quite sure about the size of his role. Don't you think we could do with just two?'"* (Jeremy in A New Confidence)

Love's Labour's Lost 1968 – The National Theatre

The role of **Berowne** in *Love's Labour's Lost* 1968 was his prize and one which he almost lost, or never really managed to secure from Larry, who Jeremy discovered, had very much wanted to play him: He had read that this character was one of the first authentic human beings created by Shakespeare. This was also one of Jeremy's favourite roles, having performed it several times before, so he was anxious to keep it from his director. *"For two weeks, I could hardly get on the stage. I think if the truth were out, if Olivier could have broken my leg or had an excuse to get rid of me, he would have. Instead, Olivier gave me the most brilliant notes on the performance."* The note given on the first night was full of essential advice and one which Jeremy would frame and display in his Clapham apartment, "on his desk there is a treasured first night good luck note from Laurence Olivier." (Holmes Front)

Do's: Do think. Keep your neck back. Think. Be frank. Think.

Perceive. Think. Listen. Think. Be in love with Joan. Blaze.

Don'ts: Don't be Ingratiating. Soft. Adorable. Glamorous.

Earnest. Polite. Gobblesome.

On the reverse: *Love wishes. Love gratitude. Love admiration.*

Love from Larry

The story of the King of Navarre's aim to create *"a little academe"* in the Royal Park of Navarre where the nobles forego eating, sleeping and the company of all women for three long years in order to study without any distractions is not only an unrealistic aim, but also a foolish one. High comedy follows with the arrival of the Princess of France and her ladies in waiting who very quickly entrance the King and each one of his courtiers, so that the necessary adjustments have to be made to the oath that they had all signed in the opening scene of the play. Jeremy in the role of Berowne, renowned for his wit, and his challenging stance, even with the King, had initially denounced the proposal and it is he who leads them through their dilemma. Each member of the court will find a corresponding romance amongst the visiting ladies and their happiness seems assured until the intervention of Boyet spoils the progress of their wooing by carrying overheard conversations to the Princess and just when the relationships are recovering from the humiliation they each receive, another more serious development intervenes with the death of the Princess's father.

A review in *Plays and Players* highlighted Jeremy's suitability for the part of Berowne and also on his relationship with Joan which was a benefit to both. It also mentioned how much Jeremy had developed under Olivier's tutelage at the National "Jeremy Brett, an actor whose talents have really blossomed at the National, (as in an ideal state) is quite splendid as Berowne. He brings to the part the almost mocking strength of the student court's most mature member, and delighted surprise at the depth of his love. As Rosaline, Joan Plowright is bustling and bubbling, her wit irrepressibly darting. Rosaline and Berowne, Joan Plowright and Jeremy Brett, are made for each other and hopefully, it's a partnership which will be seen again soon." Jeremy recognised the quality of Olivier's advice. *"Larry taught me how to dare. He challenged me when I was playing Berowne in his production of* Love's Labour's Lost. *Berowne's the first of the great human beings that Shakespeare wrote, and I remember that one day I went into Joan's dressing room when Larry was there and he said 'Joanie and I have decided that you've done it.' Fortunately my confusion was covered by my wig and my make-up. I said, 'Thank you, Sir.' Then he said 'How?' 'Because you challenged me.' Then he exploded. He went 'Hkloupp!' And he picked me up – and I'm not light.'"* (Jeremy Brett in A new Confidence: Ronald Hayman 1973)

The Times added its praise for a splendid production. "Goodness, how splendid it is to encounter once more a Shakespeare comedy produced unselfconsciously, without gimmicks, beautifully but conventionally dressed and designed, and spoken throughout with poetry and understanding... the nobles of France and Navarre turn from rich dolls from the aristocracy of Hamley's into live lords and ladies whose ideas of wit may be fairly elementary but never fails to be elegant. Here Jeremy Brett can do proper justice to Berowne (and how excellently he speaks those gorgeous lines that end with the russet ayes and honest kersey noes)." (B.A. Young Financial Times)

Ronald Bryden in *The Observer* was full of praise for *"the lushest grown-up pantomime in town"* in which "as Rosaline, Joan Plowright shows a black-eyed impishness more delicate than her Beatrice in *Much Ado*. And as Berowne, Jeremy Brett dominates his scenes with a wryly curling nostril and deep-eyed strength which suggests that, when Sir Laurence comes to divide his kingdom, he would make as natural an heir to his heroic roles – Romeo. Hotspur and Coriolanus – as Robert Stephens to the character parts." (The Observer 22nd December 1968)

The actors who were part of the National Theatre at that time all tell of the outstanding camaraderie and support, something which had been established by Olivier in his company approach to theatre. Jeremy told especially of the fun that was had in rehearsal, *"I remember when I was playing Berowne in* Love's Labour's Lost, *I had this huge Plantagenet costume made by a designer called Carl Toms. It was very beautiful, but, unfortunately, it was just a little too big for me. When we had the dress parade, I tried sitting down, and my head disappeared inside the costume, so that I looked like a tortoise. Thank goodness it wasn't a performance, but my colleagues screamed with laughter."* (Secrets of Success. 17th January 1987)

Caedmon records released an **audio** version with Jeremy still in the role of **Berowne** and Derek Jacobi as Ferdinand but with Geraldine McEwan as the Princess and Judy Parfitt as Rosaline. The description reads: Formal and scholarly, rich in wordplay and poetic invention, ***Love's Labour's Lost*** is perhaps the most demanding of Shakespeare's comedies, but on this recording Sir Derek Jacobi, Jeremy Brett and Geraldine McEwan lead a distinguished cast in a lively performance.

In an interview with *Woman and Home* in 1984 Jeremy was asked, of all the characters he'd portrayed, which one he identified most strongly with. "Without a pause to think, he replies, 'Berowne in Shakespeare's *Love's Labour's Lost. I've played him four times, at drama school, at the National and twice on record and adored being him. He's bright and dazzling, with a brilliant brain. He's such fun, yet cool and mischievous.'"* The reporter makes the comment that Jeremy "has these bright dazzling qualities himself" which was probably a sign of Jeremy's willingness to share his passion for acting with anyone who asked. In another interview he would share the delight he experienced acting at the *National Theatre*, *"The National is kind of the dream situation. For example, I was playing, in one week, Orlando in* As You Like It, *Berowne in* Love's Labour's Lost *and Che in* Che Guevara... *and maybe a couple of nights off. That was my idea of paradise."* (Sunday 2nd July 1972 Green Bay Press-Gazette)

Television

Television appearances would be slotted into Jeremy's busy timetable at the National Theatre and for the most part they continued to cast him in the traditional costume roles of the Restoration or Victorian gentleman. Just occasionally he would come up to date and give a performance as a contemporary young man and his next appearance for London Weekend Television where he was dressed in a bright yellow shirt, trendy suit and colourful tie was one of these rare opportunities. It would be the first time we would see him in full colour although there is no recording of the play in existence, just a number of production photographs on Rex Features. It was also a very funny play and Jeremy loved to laugh.

For Amusement Only: Time for the Funny Walk 1968 - ITV London Weekend

Henry Raynor in Time for the Funny Walk

An opportunity for Jeremy to play a comedy role was offered in the play, **Time for the Funny Walk** in the series *For Amusement Only* broadcast on 25th August 1968 for London Weekend Television. Inspired by an actual television interview with a famous, wildly raucous Irish writer some years before, it documented the efforts of the unfortunate **Henry**, an interviewer on the programme *Late Night Omnibus*, to keep the Irish-Liverpudlian Mulcathy known as "the people's poet," out of mischief for a day. Jeremy in the role of Henry was given the task of caring for the interviewee who was loud and drunk, bawdy and quarrelsome and in need of restraint, if he were to appear at the studio in one piece for the late night interview. "The adventures of the unfortunate Henry would have been heartrending if it were not for the fact that he had a magnificent day and he would melt splendidly from uprightness to sinful enjoyment during the time he spent in this man's company."

Henry and Mulcathy in Time for the Funny Walk

The Stage had the headline *No Bore But Not Much Else* and said, "The interviewer, played by Jeremy Brett has the unenviable task of spending the day with the hard-drinking, hard-playing poet, to make sure he does not wreak too much damage, and turns up in the studio, sober and on time. The play was chiefly concerned with chronicling the various troubles which beset the group… the adventures also smacked of Beatlemania – a visit to an extremely posh restaurant, where all the inevitable things happen, an exchange with an establishment-type poet in a Soho pub – but the play as a whole lacked the impact of the film, chiefly because it also lacked its sense of fun…" (The Stage 12th September 1968) However, others disagreed. Henry Raynor in *The Times* called it "the most riotously funny play we have seen on television for quite a time."

The Merry Widow 1968 – BBC Television

Danilo and Anna Glawari in The Merry Widow

Jeremy's next appearance as **Count Danilo** Danilovitsch would provide an opportunity to escape from the National Theatre and take him back into musical theatre. He was thrilled to accept the role and would bring his friends from the Old Vic to watch him in rehearsal as the fun-loving Attaché at the Pontevedrian Embassy in Paris whose favourite evening entertainment was drinking champagne at Maxim's the home of the can-can. Franz Lehar's ***The Merry Widow*** (*Die Lustige Witwe*) first broadcast on 25th December 1968 is a love story with the conventional happy ending and an opportunity to sing probably one of the best known parts in the best loved operetta. The lavish production also starred Mary Costa, the glamorous star of the Metropolitan Opera as the recently widowed millionairess Anna Glawari. Danilo is commissioned to woo her for her vast wealth which would be vital to the small kingdom of Pontevedro whilst she is hoping to rekindle her lost romance amongst the glamour and gaiety of the embassy ball.

With its tuneful music, glamorous settings and costumes the production was a perfect celebration for the Christmas season which earned special praise for the two principals and the critics commented on Jeremy's charm which enhanced his abilities as a singer. The *Radio Times* said, "As Count Danilo, a young secretary at the Pontevedrian Embassy, Jeremy Brett breaks new ground by singing as well as acting. Theatregoers have seen him in many Shakespearean roles, while TV viewers know him as D'Artagnan in *The Three Musketeers*." And the *Stage* was "hooked," "Franz Lehar is not my cup of tea either, but Cedric Messina's production of *The Merry Widow* was so disciplined and firm, and Jeremy Brett so handsome and romantic, that I found myself hooked and waiting anxiously for the happy ending." (The Stage and Television Today 2nd January 1969)

Jeremy's friend Sue Locke commented on the preparation that Jeremy made for this performance, "on this occasion he sang every note, much to his great joy. He was so serious about it and had many singing lessons in preparation. It was my proudest moment when he took me to the preview at the BBC. I knew all the songs backwards and of course he had sung them to me many times." Robert Stephens mentioned Jeremy's performance in his autobiography. "I have never been professionally jealous of anyone, not Brando, not Larry, not Robert de Niro. Except once: of Jeremy Brett. Jeremy is my oldest pal, and when he was playing Danilo in *The Merry Widow* on television with Mary Costa, the opera singer, he looked fantastic and he sang beautifully – after a three month crash course – and he drove me crazy with jealousy." (Knight Errant)

An audio version of *The Merry Widow Highlights* from the production was also released in 1968 with a different cast, starring June Bronhill, David Hughes and Ann Howard but with Jeremy still in the role of Danilo. A review in *Gramophone* welcomed the English version and said, "I have been most impressed on hearing this version for the first time. Christopher Hassell's remarkably good lyrics come across well, and the work is excellently produced with original scoring and full regard for the style of the work... I have heard many worse performances of Danilo's set numbers than these and few performers can have put the role across with such charm and allure... so that anyone speaking an English version should be very well satisfied to find anything as well performed and recorded as this." (Lehar The Merry Widow Excerpts A.M.L. Gramophone January 1977)

Jeremy and June Bronhill in The Merry Widow Highlights

An Ideal Husband 1969 - Oscar Wilde BBC Play of the Month

Lord Arthur Goring and Mabel Chiltern in An Ideal Husband

Jeremy's next appearance was as **Lord Goring** in Oscar Wilde's extremely witty play *An Ideal Husband*, broadcast as a BBC One Play of the Month on 11th May 1969, a sumptuous interpretation, directed by Rudolph Cartier. It was a similar role to Danilo in *The Merry Widow* with a wide audience appeal and seemed to fit Jeremy like a glove. Aided by Wilde's peerless wordplay he sparkled from the opening scene until the last, in this sophisticated romantic comedy displaying his natural exuberance and flair. Lord Arthur Goring professes to be *"the idlest man in London"* but he proves to be a worthy opponent by successfully outwitting the scheming of an old flame in her plans to blackmail his best friend, Robert Chiltern. Robert may be an honest politician but Mrs Cheveley has revealed a past error of judgement, of money for information. Her price for keeping her lips sealed was a speech before the House of Commons in which a fraudulent investment scheme would now be promoted. Without Lord Goring's intervention the politician would have lost both his wife and his reputation as the "Ideal Husband" of the title.

The star of the production was Margaret Leighton as Mrs Cheveley but Jeremy was ideally cast as a Wildean hero, with his good looks and elegance of style, perfectly tuned to Lord Goring's witty remarks which stole the limelight. "Jeremy Brett as Lord Goring opened the *Play of the Month* production last night with a flood of *bon mots* delivered with an elegance and gaiety as good as anything out of *The Importance of Being Earnest*. And really, Goring, the typical Wilde dandy, is the hero and not the honest and dull statesman and ideal husband..." This scene with its mix of style and humour set the tone for the rest of the play with its underlying melodrama of a scheming woman attempting to blackmail an admirable politician.

A more recent showing on the large screen at the *British Film Institute* in June 2014 brought the play once more into focus where it was again praised for the "impeccable casting" and gained a special mention, "Jeremy Brett's is the other stand-out performance in the second lead role of Viscount Goring, faithful friend to Chiltern and the architect of Mrs Cheveley's defeat, for which he is rewarded with the hand of Chiltern's sister Mabel." (screenplaystv.wordpress.com)

Jeremy and Susan Hampshire

The National Theatre Company

Laurence Olivier would give Jeremy the opportunity to play a modern-day hero in his next performance for the National Theatre. The critics would applaud him for his sensitivity and for his ability to convey the legendary cult hero Che Guevara. He looked nothing like the man he was playing but with the help of the make-up department and his joie de vivre, he filled the stage with his presence.

MacRune's Guevara 1969 - The Jeannetta Cochrane Theatre

MacRune's Guevara written by John Spurling appeared at the Jeannetta Cochrane Theatre in February 1969 and it was a very different outing to the Shakespeare Jeremy had been heavily involved in since his return to the National Theatre but he would be "a memorable Guevara". The MacRune of the title is a Scottish painter (Paul Curran), a recluse and an unorthodox Marxist, who has covered the walls of his room with drawings of his idol, **Guevara** (Jeremy). When he dies, his room is let to Edward Hotel (Derek Jacobi), who though his political sympathies are very different from MacRune's, recognises in the murals what he considers an original artistic talent and determines to realise each separate drawing in a dramatised form. "Thus Che is seen at third, and sometimes at fourth, hand, through Hotel's interpretations of MacRune's fantasies or... fantasies about the reactions of the guerrilleros to their leader... the effect of this kind of theatre is immediately stimulating, witty and imaginative."

This was the first performance of the play written whilst Guevara was still alive in the Bolivian jungle but he had been captured and executed by the Bolivian Army by the time it was finished. Although the 39 year old guerrilla leader is portrayed as a gangster, responsible for the shedding of innocent blood, he would become a Latin American Robin Hood, a martyr for the cause and achieve heroic status. Containing the myths and known facts about the man, it became a complex study of a revolutionary with high ideals shown from shifting points of view and Spurling explained, "my play was not really aimed at Guevara at all – indeed was ultimately partly in sympathy with him – but only against those who made use of Che for dubious purposes of their own." (johnspurling.com)

The Observer said everyone provided a magnificent performance: "Derek Jacobi teases the maximum wit out of Hotel's clichés, Paul Curran is ringingly profane as MacRune, and Jeremy Brett balances skilfully their comic and heroic visions of the bearded guerrilla.... But is it sentimental of me to feel that neither version is as interesting as the man himself – fanatic, generous, struggling with asthma, fever, carbuncular feet and diarrhoea through the high American rainforest in a cause at once hopeless, ruthless and magnificent – whom Brett's performance is strong enough to suggest he could have played?" (Ronald Bryden in The Observer 1st June 1969)

In this new phase of confidence and experience Jeremy was becoming worthy of the extravagant praise and indeed some would go on to say this was his best role to date. Che Guevara was an unexpected role for a man of his looks and stature, especially as he didn't look at all like the revolutionary. But Jeremy used his now familiar approach of steeping himself in the character and becoming the person he was presenting. R.B. Marriott in *The Stage* thought Jeremy's performance was outstanding, "I have never seen Jeremy Brett so good. Previously, he has seemed to me to be an ordinarily, competent, sometimes sensitive but rather stiff actor. As Che in *MacRune's Guevara*, he gave a performance of considerable imagination and power, revealing himself as an actor of much finer talent than one had ever imagined." (The Stage 6th March 1969)

Jeremy was so absorbed in Che's story that when he was released from his responsibilities at the National in December 1970 he set out on a six-month journey hitchhiking across South America, to follow in the footsteps of Che in his travels from Argentina, through Peru, Columbia, Chile and Brazil. *"I was very intrigued by Guevara's exploits over there, so I decided to go and follow his route. Actually, this was a rather sad thing to do because, of course, everything ended for him in Bolivia..."* (Jeremy to Yvonne Wyatt-Rees in My Weekly 4th July 1979)

'It was a hazardous and *"hair-raising experience"* which he would not talk about because *"it's too private to me"*, but it became an essential part of preparation for the next chapter in his career. Guevara's daughter wrote in the introduction to her father's book *The Motorcycle Diaries*, "If you ever have the opportunity to follow his footsteps in reality you will discover with sadness that many things remain unchanged, or are even worse..." (Aleida Guevara March)

Charles Kay and Jeremy in Macrune's Guevara

Oedipus 1970 - The Young Vic

Frank Dunlop, a founder of the Pop Theatre in Edinburgh, wanted to create "a new kind of theatre for a new generation – one that was unconventional, classless, open, circus-like and cheap. He was inspired by influential French actor and director Jean Vilac, who claimed that theatre should be as indispensable to life as bread and wine. The Young Vic was conceived as a "paperback" theatre where high quality work would be made available to all at a low cost. With council funding and a subsidy from the parent company the theatre was opened 12th August 1970 by Sybil Thorndike with Moliere in modern dress and followed by Yeats's version of Sophocles' **Oedipus** with Ronald Pickup in the title role with Jeremy playing **Creon**. They loved playing Oedipus for a much younger more volatile audience in front of a full house with queues of people waiting for returns and to be able to bounce between the Old Vic and the Young Vic and back again was exciting.

The Merchant of Venice 1970 - The National Theatre

Bassanio and Portia in The Merchant of Venice

The headline of *The Stage* magazine of 18th June 1970 informed its readers that the "National would have the largest repertoire ever in 1970-71. Olivier announces new productions: *Guys and Dolls, Cato Street."* The new theatre under construction on the Southbank was still not completed so the sixteen productions were scheduled for two theatres, the Old Vic and the Cambridge. The season was to be a time of building the repertory in preparation for the move to the new premises. *Hedda Gabler* was to open the season at the Cambridge Theatre with Maggie Smith in the title role, Jeremy as Tesman and Robert Stephens as Loevborg. *The Merchant of Venice* with Sir Laurence as Shylock, Joan Plowright as Portia and Jeremy as **Bassanio** would follow. *Love's Labour's Lost* would continue to feature in the season's programme at the Old Vic Theatre.

Olivier's Shylock in **The Merchant of Venice** 1970 was heralded as "One of the most powerful dramatic performances of our time!" And "a tragic character, forced to exact retribution upon a cruel society." (New York Times) His interpretation of Shylock would expose the Christian community as "truly vile, heartless, money grubbing monsters" guilty of deadly Venetian prejudice. As a highly respectable orthodox Jewish father who had lost his daughter to a Christian, she would have died for him. What appeared to be light-hearted fun to them was a profound tragedy to Shylock and with the opportunity to gain personal vengeance on his oppressors it would become his duty as a grieving father to take it.

"Jeremy Brett is the handsome attractive Bassanio, revealing fully the weaknesses of the character which are the often overlooked motivation for the whole plot…" (The Stage 7th May 1970) His Bassanio was an opportunist and his need for funding for his quest of the fair Portia had put his friend Antonio within Shylock's grasp. His first reference to Portia as "a lady richly left" suggests his friendship for Antonio is built on a financial base and only through the horror of the trial is he able to reveal his much deeper instincts. Jeremy and Joan had become a formidable partnership which the critics had noticed on several occasions and in her diary Joan thought that although Portia was aware of Bassanio's reasons for coming to Belmont she had already met him and fallen in love with him. "Portia can send up the first two suitors and deliberately engage the two wicked singing ladies to relieve her own boredom but… she takes Bassanio's scene in deadly earnest, for she is deliriously in love for the first time in her life." (And That's Not All) J.C Trewin of ILN thought "She will get in the Bassanio of Jeremy Brett a rather arrogant young husband whom she can control with ease." "The comedy otherwise is in very fine shape, with its deliciously funny-silly casket scenes, and excellent playing from such people as Derek Jacobi as Gratiano and Jeremy Brett as Bassanio…" (Philip Hope-Wallace. The Guardian 9th November 1970) "A fine piece of work, marvellous acting… Larry, Joan, Jeremy Brett, Anthony Nicholls, Derek Jacobi. It seemed all the top actors in Britain were on that stage." (Trevor Nunn)

Oliver would receive well-earned extravagant praise from the critics, but Jeremy also received a pleasing recognition for his Bassanio. "I liked Jeremy Brett as Bassanio. He has energy. A rare moment of inspiration in this production occurs after Shylock has been publicly humiliated and forced to convert to Christianity. Bassanio looks positively nauseous. He is just human enough to find the trial that strips Shylock of his livelihood and Jewish faith a travesty. Interesting choice and very effective." (Bardolatry.com)

Olivier's cry of rage and shame at the close of the trial scene brought sympathy, but so powerful has his justification proved that it is hard to remember that he is a villain who deserves his punishment. Bernard Levin wrote in the TV guide, "So tremendous is Olivier's acting that he can dominate a stage or screen even when he's not in it; listen to the cry of anguish he gives after Shylock has stumbled from the courtroom, and watch the way in which the camera jumps from one face to the next, as the realisation of what they've done to him sinks in.... These are no longer actors and actresses... they are really Portia and her maid, Nerissa, Antonio and Bassanio, Lorenzo, and Shylock's daughter, Jessica." Great acting is difficult to explain but when it is seen at that moment, it is both exciting and magical. When Olivier achieved the mountaintops in one of his great roles it was like watching a force of nature happening before the eyes.

Jeremy with Laurence Olivier in The Merchant of Venice

The filming for television of **The Merchant of Venice** was carried out at Elstree Studios, in July 1973, with the outside scenes recorded at West Wycombe Park, a National Trust property belonging to the Dashwood family in Buckinghamshire, a house which also appears in the *Downton Abbey* series and others because of its beautiful porticoed frontage and Italianate appearance. The interiors were copied from the *Caffe Florian* in St Marks Square, Venice, with its stylish mirrored opulence. Thus the 1880s moneyed business backgrounds were established for the Christians in the play.

An **audio** version of *The Merchant of Venice* was recorded for Collins Caedmon in 1963 with Jeremy in the role of **Bassanio** and Hugh Griffiths as Shylock. "The Merchant of Venice is the 1963 Shakespeare Recording Society discs superbly transferred to (two) cassettes. Hugh Griffiths one of our best Lears, was also one of our best Shylocks. He does not chew the scenery, only gnaws at it like a rat. And what a supporting cast! Everybody who was anybody in the 1960s is in it, from Dorothy Tutin, Ian Holm, Harry Andrews and Jeremy Brett to some who would soon be somebody (Ronnie Barker, Stephen Moore and Roy Marsden)." (Observer)

Hedda Gabler 1970 – The National Theatre

Tesman in Hedda Gabler

"*Hedda* in London was not a good production. All the rehearsals were plagued. I despise London." (Ingmar Bergman. www.ingmarbergman) Olivier considered it one of his greatest achievements to have persuaded the famous Ingmar Bergman to do a production of Ibsen's ***Hedda Gabler*** in 1970 in London, "a place he clearly detested," especially as it would be his first play outside Sweden. Maggie Smith described Olivier's methods of persuasion as "coercion" and said Bergman disparagingly referred to Olivier as "the Lord". He was hoping it would be a near replica of the 1964 *Royal Dramatic Theatre* production in Stockholm which he had much admired. There was a brilliant cast prepared and waiting for him with Maggie as Hedda and Robert Stephens and Jeremy in the supporting roles but they had learned their lines by the first rehearsal and worked much faster than he was used to. They did so well that after just one week Bergman told Olivier that "he had done all the work that was needed and that now the company could get on perfectly by themselves" which they did for the next month working with the masses of notes he had left for them.

Olivier had been persuaded to switch the roles so that Jeremy would play the sincere, dull husband **George Tesman** with Robert taking the role of Loevborg who had designs on his new wife. Tesman is a scholar and historian, absorbed in his work but his new wife would test his patience and tolerance. Jeremy described Bergman's advice on how to play him: "*We worked... without a break. It was total concentration. He (Bergman) said, 'I know exactly how you should play Tesman – as Winnie the Pooh.' It was impossible to know how he got that idea. He gets right at the root. It's not comforting to work under him. It's like being raw. You're under pressure all the time, but he's incredibly loving to his actors. Once I forgot my script. Maggie Smith (Hedda) who has a temper like lightning, snapped away. Bergman said, 'Jeremy, everybody's very angry with you, but I'm not. See how much you remember.' I remembered it all. That's the gentleness of the man.*" And the result was pleasing as Jeremy presented "a wonderfully quiet and watchful Tesman..." (Robert Stephens)

Maggie Smith would receive a Best Actress Award for her performance as Hedda, the badly spoiled daughter of an aristocratic general, who has just returned home from her six months honeymoon with her husband George Tesman the young, aspiring, and too reliable academic. She is bored already with the prospect of their lives together and she feels trapped, possibly pregnant, and determined to be free. Hedda is narcissistic, wilful and manipulative, caring for no one and she amuses herself with Loevborg, a past lover, undermining his newly acquired sobriety. As she tries to control everyone around her we see her own world unravel.

Ronald Bryden in *The Observer* described Hedda as "a caged animal living in a bare, red cage of imprisoned passion, a windowless chamber... where she dreams of sex, power and violence she dares not act in life... it becomes the inner sanctum to which Hedda retires to brood and punish her piano, from which she emerges like a tigress raiding sheep... pacing and snarling to herself at their genteel inanities... Hedda's trap is not sex or the denial of it, but society. Society, embodied in her husband's drawing room is the battlefield on to which she stalks, like a wild beast in captivity... Jeremy Brett excels himself as Tesman, babyish, fumbling, betraying the panic behind the handsome facade." (The Observer 5th July 1970)

"Where the Swedish production represented the inside of Tesman's house almost as a dungeon in the Troll King's palace swarming with the dwarfish gaolers of Hedda's imagination, the British cast do more individual justice to the household. For all his clumsiness and foolish toothy smile, Jeremy Brett's Tesman is allowed the self-respect of a scholar: and the character undergoes a real development in the reconstruction of Loevborg's manuscript. Robert Stephens's Loevborg is more half-reformed drunk than nascent genius: a shock-headed hell-raiser, who hardly bothers to conceal his contempt for Tesman and makes a grab for Hedda's groin over the snapshots of the Dolomites." (Irving Wardle in The Times 30th June 1970)

Olivier may have wanted Jeremy to play Loevborg, the dashing lover and writer and he agreed it suited his personality. *"I'm rather an obvious Eilert. I'm built for it... But I told him, 'I can see it in my head, and I'm bored by it. I took a chance on it and got away with it. That's what I think is interesting, especially about repertory. You don't actually present the same thing all the time.*" His obituary in the *Daily Telegraph* in 1995 recorded this as one of his finest performances: "One of Brett's best performances was his masterly portrayal of feeble devotion to Maggie Smith's Hedda Gabler under Ingmar Bergman's direction. He created a wholly credible character, not the usual bungling fool but a very presentable, handsome young man who just happens to be too dull, too scholarly and too conventional for his wife." Jeremy told a critic his time at the National had been the "*happiest period in my career, because Olivier had a tremendous amount to offer any actor.*" He admitted that he had not credited himself as an actor until that time, lacking the experience and determination to succeed.

Tesman in Hedda Gabler

Jeremy and Maggie Smith in Hedda Gabler

The Champions 1969 – ITV Television

Sharron Macready and The Bey in The Champions

Moving effortlessly between the two disciplines of stage and television Jeremy would appear in a modern adventure alongside his familiar performances as the heroes of classical fiction. The first of these was the series **The Champions** which was a huge success in the 1960s influenced by the American programmes that were gathering so many viewers on ITV. The group Nemesis is an international intelligence organisation. On their first mission to Communist China they became victims of a plane crash in a remote area of the Himalayas where they received superhuman powers from their rescuers. Thereafter, they would display exceptional hearing, strength, telepathy and perception amongst other powers which were needed to protect governments or individuals.

Jeremy played **The Bey** in episode 25 called ***Desert Journey.*** It was broadcast on 19th March 1969, and with the aid of a Middle Eastern accent he was very believable as the disenfranchised and reluctant potentate. He was abducted, drugged, and carried on a journey across the desert in first a plane and then by truck; he was understandably uncooperative and angry with his rescuers as he had enjoyed being a playboy far too much with his advisor, Said's money, that taking responsibility for a war torn country was not his choice. The *TV Times* described the episode as, "Danger in the desert faces the Champions when they escort a reluctant Bey to his strife-torn North African state." The critics would say it was simply fun and not to be taken seriously but the stories were made believable with true life situations, often based on world events. They were also well-produced with realistic settings and for that reason popular. Jeremy gave another convincing performance. It also represented a brief escape into adventure in the modern world, of good in the face of evil, and leaving behind the lives of fictional heroes.

Solo - Byron 1970 - BBC2 Television

Jeremy as Byron

In his next production for television Jeremy would appear as the poet George Gordon, **Lord Byron**, one of the most infamous writers of English literature; he was a genius obsessed by image, sexually irresistible to both men and women, a nineteenth century super star who was fated to live fast and die young. Ladies were mesmerised by him and the wild, impulsive Lady Caroline Lamb, the wife of the future Lord Melbourne, famously labelled Byron, "Mad, bad and dangerous to know." The scandals that surrounded him would shock the whole of society and consequently the personal memoirs discovered after his death were burned by his friends as publishing them would have condemned him to even greater infamy.

The whole series of *Solo* performances is reportedly lost. There are only a couple of photographs of Jeremy's appearance in the series which features personalities who had gained world recognition by their contribution to literature and the arts. They revealed more about themselves, their lives and their work, in the form of a monologue using the character's own words. Some of the other plays in the series included Tom Courtney as *D.H. Lawrence*; Ian McKellan as *John Keats*; Janet Suzman as *Charlotte Bronte*; Michael Jayston as *Wilfred Owen* and Eric Porter as *Leo Tolstoy*.

Jeremy would take the role of **Byron** again four years later in **Second House** broadcast on BBC Two on 20th April 1974. The original programme broadcast may have provided some of the same source material; however, it was a fresh attempt to honour one of the greatest British poets, a leading figure of the Romantic movement on the 150th anniversary of his death. Introduced by Melvyn Bragg, it featured a profile of the man and his work. Jeremy read extracts from Byron's letters and poems and Melvyn Bragg talked to one of Byron's biographers, Doris Langley Moore, and film director Midge MacKenzie about the Byron legend. BBC4 Radio again featured **Byron** in **The Years of Exile** on the following Tuesday.

The Rivals 1970 - Sheridan BBC Play of the Month

Captain Jack Absolute in The Rivals

Captain Jack Absolute/Beverley in *The Rivals* is a comedy part which seems especially made for Jeremy whose appearance in the Army Officer's red coat and breeches suggest a gentleman and whose *savoir faire* fits the grace and manners of the time; in spite of the grey wig. Broadcast on 17th May 1970 as part of BBC Play of the Month it enabled Jeremy to show his natural gift for comedy with face to camera in a conspiratorial manner to invite the audience into his dressing room or into the middle of his relationship with Lydia. This comedy of manners satirises the affectations amongst the upper classes in the romantic helter-skelter of the aristocratic Captain Jack Absolute adopting the cover of Ensign Beverley, a simple army officer, in order to win his love Lydia Languish who is determined to marry for love and poverty. We share his dismay when his father offers him the hand of the heiress he has chosen for him, which Jack first rejects, until he discovers she is his Lydia the girl he truly loves, bringing delight and then mayhem. Evasive action must take place, his father must think him a dutiful son or he risks disinheritance, and his love must accept that he is not who she thought he was. Lydia's aunt the pretentious Mrs Malaprop must also be won over before she can withhold her niece's fortune. Jeremy displays all his charm and earnest expression in the convincing portrait of a man in love, staying resolute and determined to fight for the girl of his choice. But this is the playful Jeremy too as Captain Jack expertly manages each of the characters according to the part they play in his future happiness.

The Rivals was a play of artifice and deception where marriage was one of convenience, of benefit to one or both parties, whilst the threat of falling in love with the wrong partner meant being cast out of polite society. The romantic novels which fill Lydia's head with the affairs of those prepared to seek love over duty at first inspire her wish for an elopement, but only the threat to Jack's life in twin duels will make her realise how much she loves him. "A spirited and deft production of the witty Richard Brinsley Sheridan's 1775 class play about amour and honour. Jeremy Brett is simply a delight as Captain Absolute, wooing or conniving." (The Evening Independent 6th November 1975)

The Rivals was later shown as part of *Classic Theatre* on PBS in 1975. It was at this meeting that Jeremy would meet his future wife, Joan Sullivan Wilson; they would fall in love and marry in November 1977. Joan was the second executive producer of *Masterpiece Theatre*, which after the success of *The Forsyte Saga* had reached the conclusion that British television programmes were the best for the *Public Broadcasting Station*. Jeremy was acting as a presenter of *Masterpiece Theatre* and was involved in filming an introduction to Sheridan, at the writer's final home on Saville Row, London. "Jeremy Brett, who stars in *The Rivals*... recounts playwright Richard Brinsley Sheridan's successes and tribulations and personally conducts a tour of Sheridan's home. Prof. William Appleton of Columbia University gives background notes and historical perspective about the play and its milieu." He introduced the American audience to Sheridan, and provided essential background to the play. Jeremy was interviewed by Joan for the programme about his role in *The Rivals*. The time onscreen was cut to just four minutes but the interview lasted for more than two and a half hours as the chemistry between them was clear to see. She told him later that she had been in the audience at a performance of *Design for Living* in 1973, and said, *"That's the man for me. She organised the meeting and we married in 1976 (1977). We had a decade together... I loved her dearly, she was so beautiful and gutsy."*

The Rivals

Jeremy - Man of Fashion

Man of Fashion

In the press at the time Jeremy was making a name for his style and appearance as much as for his acting ability. The Palm Beach Post in 1970 with the headline *"New Heartthrob"* welcomed Jeremy as a new rising star with a sense of style. It reported that Sir Laurence Olivier had picked him out as *"the younger generation's next screen idol."* The article went on to say, Brett 33, but looking much younger, goes with swinging young dress designer Susan Locke who runs a boutique on the Kings Road in London. He had also agreed to be part of a new male line in models for shop windows in the coming year. *"I did it originally because a girlfriend with a boutique in the King's Road was told she'd have to wait six months for a dummy to dress her window. I jumped into a car and went to see Adel Rootstein. She offered me a dummy... immediately, provided that I would agree to be part of her male line in models the next year."*

Jeremy was developing a reputation as a trendsetter as there were several features in the glossy magazines calling him a *Man of Fashion*. *Vogue Magazine* and *Queen Magazine* both featured him wearing the latest style. *The Four Men in Vogue* 1967 showed him in silk dressing gown holding embroidered tapestry slippers with a JB monogram and also pictured him wearing a fedora hat. The photographs for the *Queen Magazine* featured more colourful check jackets and dark, moody images with thespian style scarves.

Audio Recordings

Richard III - Audio Recording

Jeremy would also make several audio recordings of Shakespeare and other classical plays during his time at the National Theatre. Starring some of the theatre's greatest actors they would become highly regarded. One of these was **Richard III** for the Shakespeare Recording Society. The complete play in five acts starred Robert Stephens as Richard III, Dame Peggy Ashcroft as Queen Margaret, Glenda Jackson as Lady Anne, and Jeremy in the role of **George Duke of Clarence**. As Richard's elder brother George, Clarence should have acceded to the throne before his brother but he was prompted to rebel against his brother King Edward IV and his rebellion would result in his death in a butt of malmsey wine. "Good school investment with a top notch cast."

The Infernal Machine - Audio Recording

A recording of the Greek Tragedy *Oedipus Rex* in **The Infernal Machine** for Caedmon was released on vinyl and cassette in 1967, written by Jean Cocteau in 1936, translated by Carl Wildman and directed by Howard Sackler. Jeremy played the ill-fated **Oedipus** and Margaret Leighton his wife and mother Jocasta in the tragic story of a prince who will kill his father and marry his mother, and although carefully avoided by his well-meaning parents, it is circumvented by the gods who bring about the impossible. Cocteau had brought the stylised tragedy up to date by a more colloquial use of language and a fuller characterisation; he had removed the gods from their pedestals and humanised them. Jeremy moves effortlessly from the idealistic youth of the young prince to the intensely tragic King who is forced to recognise his marriage as evil. Margaret Leighton gives an excellent performance too as his mother Jocasta in a production of dramatic intensity.

Sophocles' Antigone - Audio Recording

Sophocles' **Antigone** again released on Caedmon would follow, starring Dorothy Tutin as Antigone with Max Adrian as Creon and Jeremy as his son **Haemon**. Antigone and Ismene had remained with their father Oedipus at the close of the previous play in the trilogy. However, Oedipus's sons Polynices and Eteocles fell out about who should rule Thebes and as they could not agree on how to share power, they fought each other and were both killed. The body of Polynices was left unburied with only the dogs and carrion to deal with it. Creon (Jocasta's brother) as the new King of Thebes has issued a decree that it must remain so and only Antigone is prepared to attempt his burial.

The Duchess of Malfi - Audio Recording

Another sound recording was made in 1968 in which Jeremy and Robert starred together in John Webster's **The Duchess of Malfi** for *The Theatre Recording Society* and issued by Caedmon Records on vinyl and cassette. As a Revenge Tragedy this is a macabre story of the Duchess (Barbara Jefford) who is caught up in the machinations of her two brothers vying for power in a corrupt court. She is not the wanton widow here but displays her virtue, her purity and dedication to her family and especially to her chosen husband, her noble major-domo, **Antonio Bologna** (Jeremy) with whom she had fallen passionately in love and secretly married. Jeremy is once more very effective in the role of passionate lover and husband. The play was based on the true story of Giovanna d'Aragona, the widowed Duchess of Almalfi whose secret marriage to the master of her household, Antonio Bologna lasted for eleven years before it was discovered.

I Love Alas - Elizabethan Music with Poetry

A recording of Elizabethan music with Jeremy reading a selection of poems was released in 1969. The collection called *I Love, Alas,* an anthology of madrigals, poetry and pieces for lute was described as a "pleasing collection of Elizabethan romantic music and songs, with the Purcell Consort of Voices, interspersed with Jeremy Brett reading some of Philip Sydney poems."

Flowers of Cities All 1972 - City of London Festival

A *Times* article gives evidence to another appearance which doesn't feature in any of the biographical lists. Jeremy made a contribution to a recital at the Fishmongers' Hall for the *City of London Festival* on 11th July 1972. The programme covered the accession of Queen Elizabeth I to the execution of Charles I in a series of contemporary spoken pieces with sung interludes accompanied by the lute from Robert Spencer and Barbara Jefford as Queen Elizabeth. The list of events includes a mention of Jeremy reading a schoolboy's recollection of the queen "delivered in a breathless adolescent orgasm of excitement which seemed to stir in her a regal pity".

A New Decade with a new approach - 1970s

A Voyage Round My Father 1971 - Haymarket Theatre

Jeremy with Alec Guinness in A Voyage Round My Father

On leaving the National, Jeremy also left England to follow in the footsteps of Che Guevara and live off his wits for six months backpacking around South America. *"They told me I'd never work again if I did this amazing journey,"* Jeremy said. But after his arrival home, *"The phone rang and it was John Mortimer. He said, 'Jeremy, we're casting the story of my father's life,* **A Voyage Round My Father** *with Alec Guinness. Do you want to play me?' And I said 'Yes.' He said, 'Where have you been?' I said, 'Away.' He said, 'Oh! Have you had a cold?' I said, 'Yes.' And we started rehearsals the following Monday... and it ran for eight months at the Haymarket in 1971."* (Jeremy in Desert Island Discs) Jeremy was to take on the role of the **Son** in this play, specially written by John Mortimer "as an undisguised family memoir" about his relationship with his father who had gone blind in middle age. He would continue his life and his practice as a brilliant barrister as though nothing had happened using his devoted wife or his son as his eyes and although John had become a success in his own right as a lawyer and playwright, a novelist and screenwriter he had never been credited at home by the person who mattered most, his father.

A Voyage Round My Father was written with Mortimer's characteristic flair, using sensitive memoirs, amusing anecdotes and hilarious flashbacks. A review in *Plays and Players* admired the whole production; the writing, the adaptation and the direction. Jeremy was given particular praise for the characterisation. "As the son, Jeremy Brett deserves more praise than he's had for creating a plausibly gauche, angular figure out of fairly slender materials..." The journey to earn his father's respect is carried out with humour and respect as he shares the evening pursuits in the potting shed, the crossword puzzles and the nightly purges on earwigs and even the embarrassing behaviour with family and guests are all presented with love. "Mr Mortimer confines himself rigorously to the realm of comedy, which makes the play all the more moving. Only at the very end does the Son register the sense of loss, a loss fully understood and shared by the audience. The sensitive, modestly inhibited son is played with suitably crumpled charm by Jeremy Brett. Leveen McGrath is the patient mother, and Nicola Paget lends her feline beauty and sharp claws to the tough, unsentimental daughter-in-law. The cast is uniformly excellent. The play stands or falls with Father and Sir Alec Guinness is superlative." (London Telegraph)

Jeremy said, *"He builds his parts like a mosaic, a polished mosaic..." (Desert Island Discs)* *"I learned from Alec Guinness how disciplined you have to be to sustain a role... He's also very human. He does not like the audience. If someone coughs, he sends his man with cough drops to Row J, Seat 5. Once, on a rare hot day, someone in the front row was using the programme as a fan. Guinness knocked it out of his hand with a cane. Totally destroyed the illusion of blindness."* (1991 interview)

Although Jeremy enjoyed the success of the play he was also worried by it. *"When I heard that this show was a success I thought, 'Oh, my God! I'm trapped!' There's always that element in my nature... I don't run for it. I stick around, but there's always that element of wanting to get out."* And after eight months, *"I love the fact that I'm finishing this play on Saturday, and I haven't a clue what I'm going to do next. That's absolutely thrilling because it means you don't get stuck... I could be working in Australia... in New York... in Canada... I adore travelling. I have a terrible wanderlust which doesn't help very much when you're in the theatre or in films."* (Britain's Jeremy Brett: Dreamer, Traveler, Actor by Phoebe Seilin Sunday 2nd July 1972 Green Bay Press-Gazette)

Jeremy, Nicola Paget and Alec Guinness in A Voyage round my Father

Traveller Without Luggage 1972 - Thorndyke Theatre Leatherhead

Traveller Without Luggage

Jeremy's next appearance on stage was possibly the most intriguing and the most moving performance of all. He was always a sensitive man and to play the tragic **Gaston** would have touched his heart deeply and profoundly. The true story on which the Jean Anouilh play was based is even more tragic and it is from the records of this tragic case that the playwright has taken the known facts about the returning lost soldier and given him a form, emotions, and a possible history.

Traveller Without Luggage was staged at Thorndyke Theatre, Leatherhead, Surrey in 1972. There is little paper evidence of the performance although a picture of a smiling Jeremy in white open necked shirt does appear with the following article. "Jeremy Brett plays in a new translation by Lucienne Hill of Anouilh's *Traveller Without Luggage* at the Thorndike, Leatherhead from 19th September to 7th October directed by Michael Meacham." (The Stage 14th September 1972) The play was inspired by a series of ten articles by Paul Bringuir which appeared in *L'Intransigeant* in May 1935 which told the true story of a returning soldier from World War I found wandering in a railway station in Lyon on 1st February 1918, suffering from amnesia. He had no identifying marks, papers or possessions and subsequently spent decades in an insane asylum. With no memory of his past, Gaston was a sweet and submissive man who seemed content in his new life and spent his time nurturing plants or constructing models out of wood. The search for his family brought hundreds of claimants attempting to discover if he was their missing son, husband or brother who had failed to return from the front. Gaston experienced a most distressing nervous reaction when faced with so much grief: *"Imagine having four hundred families, all avid to clasp you to their bosom."* When he appears to have found his awful family, Gaston cannot accept the loutish behaviour of his youth, totally at odds with the man he has become, and his sole desire is to be left in peace with his new self. He lashes out at those who have forced him to uncover his past, *"I was so peaceful in the asylum... I was used to myself, I knew myself well. And now you want me to leave myself, to find another self and put him on like an old jacket."* (Traveller Without Luggage)

With the loss of four hundred thousand French soldiers who had disappeared in foreign trenches, leaving no trace beyond the notice of their disappearance in action, Anthelme Mangin became the embodiment of their loved one, and revived hope amongst the grieving families. Litigation continued over almost two decades, as they fought over him. "It was hardly surprising that Jean Anouilh should use Anthelme Mangin to create the hero of his *Traveller without Luggage*, first staged in 1937 – at the very moment the lunatic was surrounded by experts who were trying to decide among the litigating families." Anthelme Mangin was never given his release, although by 1937 the courts had decided his name was Octave Monjoin as everything matched. Tragically, the other families in their fight to claim him launched an appeal which kept him in the asylum as the Second World War conflict began and he died there probably from hunger in 1942. "He was called the last vestige, the last prisoner of the Great War." (Introduction to The Living Unknown Soldier by Jean-Yves Le Naour)

Gaston

Mendelsohn and Elijah - Radio 4

His next appearance would thankfully be less challenging and a little less emotional. He would take the role of **Mendelsohn**, the golden boy of Victorian music on BBC4 Radio in a programme about the composition of *Elijah* charting the nine years of struggle to complete it for the first performance in 1846. Entitled **Mendelsohn and Elijah** and broadcast on 10th April 1973, the programme was written and told by Edward Greenfield starring Jeremy as Mendelsohn with Robin Browne, Godfrey Kenton, Sandra Clarke, Fraser Kerr.

Rosmersholm 1973 - Greenwich Theatre - Company Theatre

Jeremy and Joan in Rosmersholm

Company Theatre remained a very attractive concept for Jeremy, recalling the joys of working with Laurence Oliver at the National Theatre and his time in repertory at the Manchester Library Theatre. With the aim of promoting new plays, Robin Phillips asked him to join as a Director and Founder member of a new company and later, as Joan Plowright showed a willingness to join, it became a company of three who agreed to take only nominal salaries and carefully choose their opening season of six plays beginning on 24th January 1973. Joan would also appear as Rebecca West alongside Jeremy as **Rosmer** in Ibsen's ***Rosmersholm*** which ran for four weeks from 16th May to 9th June at the Greenwich Theatre. It was described as "a remarkable company" with Jeremy Brett, Joan Plowright, Mia Farrow, Elizabeth Bergner, Penelope Keith and Lynn Redgrave, Keith Baxter, Gwen Watford, Patience Collier and Norman Rodway. In an interview with Ronald Hayman for *The Times*

Jeremy explained his aims of working with Robin in this new venture; he said that he wanted to follow his father's example, to display a greater *"sense of responsibility"* towards the theatre, to promote writers as well as actors. *"I consider one of the major jobs of an actor to be the promotion of writers."* (Jeremy Brett: A New Confidence 1973)

Rosmersholm features many of the themes and motifs of Ibsen's greatest and better known plays and typically showed his characters in the way they saw themselves and only gradually revealed their self-indulgence, self-deception and moral decline. The story of how a respected former vicar and landowner, an example of modesty and moral rectitude, with plans to bring reform to the government of the day should be unable to live with his new-found guilt and commit suicide is brought about by a series of immensely painful revelations of his responsibility for his wife's death. As the truth is revealed their inadequacies are highlighted; Rebecca's as a destroyer of the family and Rosmer as the failing husband; they each realise they are unable to live with the guilt and commit suicide, by jumping to their deaths into the mill race from the same spot as Rosmer's wife the year before. "The big climaxes are powerfully played: Rosmer cracked in two by the collapse of his ideals; Rebecca fixing terrified eyes on Rosmer as she makes her verbal concession to Kroll…" (The Times 18th May 1973)

Ian Wardle in *The Guardian* said, "Robin Phillips's production is admirable. Rebecca herself is a vessel for implicit rather than explicit emotion; and Joan Plowright conveys this perfectly by starting outwardly serene; slowly cracking apart with the words coming in a throttled rush, the body losing all coordination; and then finally achieving fulfilment in death. And Jeremy Brett's Rosmer is a revelation; a bookish, ravaged individual with just enough latent sensuality to make you understand his magnetic attraction for Rebecca."

The Company: Joan Plowright, Jeremy, Robin Phillips, Mia Farrow

Design for Living 1973 - Phoenix Theatre

John Stride and Jeremy in Design for Living

The next performance saw Jeremy appearing with one of his favourite actresses, Vanessa Redgrave. Earlier in the year they had performed together in a six part series for television, *A Picture of Katherine Mansfield*, a dramatisation of the writer's story interspersed with scenes from her life. It is no surprise that he should say, *"I see a lot of V (Vanessa Redgrave). I adore V. She's one of the loveliest people on earth and one of the great pre-Raphaelite beauties. Every time I see her, I'm stunned by her."* (Women in my Life) The role of **Otto** in ***Design for Living*** appeared first in Brighton in October and November and then in December 1973 at the Phoenix Theatre, Charing Cross Road in London. Jeremy had first met Noel Coward at the Savoy Theatre in 1960 whilst he was performing in the musical *Marigold* and he received good advice from the master which he would remember for the rest of his life. Noel had died, on 26th March aged 73.

Design for Living was an amusing comedy originally written as a star vehicle for Coward's friends the Lunts. "It is stylish, crisply written and frequently amusing, but Coward never really addresses his chosen subject: the sexual equation between the three leading characters, two young men, probably gay, who feel their lives are incomplete without the presence of the remarkable Gilda." (Michael Blakemore in Stage Blood) The changing seasons of their relationship would see Gilda sharing the apartment of first one and then the other, before the original trio is re-established. Gilda's infidelity lacks any moral judgement and it is even suggested that Gilda should have the right to choose. "In this direction Michael Blakemore has evidently regarded his characters as fully responsible people who behave as they do, not because they are taking part in an artificial comedy, but because they are actually prompted by the selfish and wilful motives that would prompt a real person into such actions. He directs it, in fact, as if it really happened. Well, fortunately, most of what

Coward has invented would have been very funny if it had really happened; but although I very much enjoyed the performances of Vanessa Redgrave, Jeremy Brett and John Stride as Gilda, Otto and Leo, I should probably have enjoyed them better if they had worked less at making us believe in them... Jeremy Brett is a slightly apologetic Otto who doesn't seem to me to radiate quite as much sex-appeal as he would need to enslave both Gilda and Leo in his affections. John Stride, on the other hand, has made Leo a faintly pompous figure on whom horseplay sits uncomfortably." (B.A. Young Financial Times)

"In Jeremy Brett and John Stride she has the perfect partners: the former's Otto is fetchingly tousled, a fatuous tornado of rage when Gilda betrays him and a marvel of patronising idiocy when he thinks he has her cornered; while the latter is cosily sleek, given to paroxysms of bleating laughter at his own wickedness, then relapsing into an understated urbanity that would not disgrace the Master himself. The two of them have a drunk scene at the end of Act Two which, with a present-day audience who are probably expecting them to fall into bed together, treads delicately over every hurdle while effortlessly arousing uproar in the house."
(Sandy Wilson in The Evening Standard)

The Stage called Vanessa "delightful as Gilda, charming to look at, catching the spirit of the woman in lightness and seriousness only failing from time to time in projecting the wit of the part. Jeremy Brett is a most engaging Otto, John Stride attractive though a trifle stolid as Leo... The company are sometimes better at bringing out the serious characterisation and purposeful intentions of the work than pointing the wit and fun, though there is still plenty of Coward hilarity and bright laughter. The love that flourishes between Gilda and Leo and Otto – they do love each other very much – is touching as well as amusing, and the intricacy of their relationship is a delight to behold, in human terms and technically..." (The Stage 29th November 1973)

Design for Living

Television 1970s

The early 1970s would be a time when Jeremy would display a new-found confidence in his ability to create a convincing character in a wider range of roles. His experience remained rooted in the classical but since his return from South America his recent appearance on stage had brought him into the twentieth century with the pleasure of playing comedy opposite the lovely Vanessa Redgrave and being able to laugh always gave him joy.

Country Matters - An Aspidistra in Babylon 1973 - ITV

Captain Archie Blaine in An Aspidistra in Babylon

But first he was to play an Army captain, a man who appears to be the romantic hero but this time with a sinister motive and therefore a very different character to the engaging Otto. The role of Captain Archie Blaine, an officer in the British Army would have been familiar to Jeremy as he had personal experience of living with the irascible army officer Colonel Huggins who had returned from two World Wars.

Jeremy appeared as Archie Blaine in the Independent Television series *Country Matters – An Aspidistra in Babylon* on 25th February 1973, written by H.E. Bates and set in the English countryside during the period following the First World War. The stories were described as "provocative and heart-warming tales" although one reviewer said they were slow and brooding and more reminiscent of Thomas Hardy. In the interview for *TV Times* Jeremy said he was proud of his performance as **Captain Blaine** as he wore his father's old cavalry boots. *"It's the nearest I've come to being a soldier, and I look very much like my father did as a young man. Very spooky. He wouldn't like the part I play – I'm a corrupt character – but I know he would have been totally delighted with me because I've had to have all my hair cut down to the bone. Well – almost. Yes, father would have been pleased."*

The role of an engaging "magnificently band-box" Army Captain would certainly have pleased his father just as much as it arrested the attention of the girls of the seaside town and Christine is a naive inexperienced girl ready for romance who surrenders herself blithely to his charms. His request for accommodation for his seventy year old aunt Bertie for the summer in the respectable boarding house run by Christine's widowed mother brings them together and the subsequent affair will change her life. "A long, blistering summer in Dover and a shy, awkward, 17 year-old girl suddenly finds herself transformed into a passionate mistress of a middle-aged army captain, starring Jeremy as Captain Blaine, Carolyn Courage as Christine, Agnes Lauchlan as Miss Charlesworth, Renee Asherson as Mother." (The Real Jeremy Brett Alive and Well in Exquisite Poverty)

The *LA Times* summed up the seduction as "a dashing officer who arrives to rent a room for his crusty Aunt Bertie… Blaine talks of faraway places and heaven on earth and she drinks in every word so that Christine (Carolyn Courage), an innocent young girl whose mother owns the boarding house, finds herself in love and planning for the future. However, Blaine has thoughts only of the money and the expensive jewels of his Aunt Bertie on his mind. He also expects Christine to help him in his plans to acquire them. Blaine keeps telling Christine that Bertie trusts you… His suggestion is clear. And Christine prepares to commit an act that will change her life for ever." (L.A.Times)

One amusing incident occurred during filming in which Jeremy was the saviour of the day, and of the practicalities of filming. "However cost-conscious you are, actors can sometimes defeat you… On the other hand, they can sometimes save the day. Time is always precious and an incident which occurred during the filming of *An Aspidistra in Babylon* for *Country Matters* (1973) nearly cost us dearly. There was a beach scene near Dover and the leading lady was meant to appear in a 1920s bathing costume but she refused to come out of her caravan because she was ashamed (wrongly) of her shape. Jeremy Brett, the leading man, offered to help. He entered the caravan and five minutes later she came out smiling and as docile as a lamb. I've often wondered what he did." (Prudence with Money by Richard Everitt in Granada Television: The First Generation. By John Finch, Michael Cox)

The Protectors – With a Little Help from My Friends 1973 - ITV

Kahan in The Protectors

Another role of the villain was to follow as Jeremy accepted a part in a popular television series which gained considerable viewer recognition between 1972 and 1973. The British Television series, **The Protectors,** created by Gerry Anderson for ITC was pure escapism and the twenty five minute episodes each presented a challenge for the international private detectives, Harry Rule (Robert Vaughan)... an American lone wolf in London, Contessa Caroline di Conti (Nyree Dawn Porter)... a beautiful British aristo abroad and Paul Buchet (Tony Anholt)... a suave Parisian specialising in gadgetry.

The episode titled **With a Little Help from My Friends**, subtitled "Harry's son Johnny is abducted by his client's rival" was first broadcast on 23rd February 1973. Jeremy as the guest star played the criminal element, **Kahan**, supposedly of Middle Eastern origin, dark-skinned, with a moustache and magnetic eyes. He presented a very attractive and charming villain. The Protectors have been asked to guarantee safety of the visiting Middle Eastern President Ali and Harry is to be persuaded to assassinate him. His wife Laura, played by Hannah Gordon, arrived with the news that their son had been taken hostage to ensure his cooperation. A charade was enacted, the only instruction being "the same as The Conroy Case outside the hotel" so that Rule is able to outwit the terrorists by appearing to carry out the assassination with sleight of hand.

A Picture of Katherine Mansfield 1973 - BBC Television

Jeremy as John Middleton Murry and Vanessa in A Picture of Katherine Mansfield

When Jeremy was asked in interview whether real people were more difficult to play than fictional ones he replied, *"They're both as difficult! But you have to be very careful if you're playing a person who has lived, not to offend the relations if there are any still alive. I'm always aware of that. I remember when I was playing* **John Middleton Murry** *in* **A Picture of Katherine Mansfield***, I had a letter from Murry's widow, saying, 'Please take care how you portray him.' That made me think quite a lot, as you can imagine."* (Secrets 17th Jan 1987)

John Middleton Murry would be a challenge for Jeremy, not only to present a fair and accurate portrait of the man but also because he was a very different character to anything he had played before; a shy scholar and writer who had been blamed for his betrayal of the much loved novelist Katherine. Alongside a dramatisation of Katherine's best short stories, each presenting a painful reality, the series presented their love story from the first sizzling moment of their introduction to their becoming lovers. They lived and worked together for six years until Katherine was free to marry but within six months they discovered she was dying of tuberculosis. The presentation of their time together in "cameos of experience", random moments beginning with Murry (Jeremy) assessing Katherine's life and work over her coffin interspersed with scenes from their early courtship, living in Paris or sharing a cottage with D.H. Lawrence and Frieda living the simple country life together but always working to produce the literary periodicals *Rhythm* and *The Athenaeum* alongside their own writing. As Katherine declines in health, spending more time abroad and becoming more dependent, Murry seems to loose his capacity to cope with her illness alongside his responsibilities to the War Office. It would be an emotional presentation in which we can appreciate the subtlety and depth of their performances.

Jeremy and Vanessa appeared in the first of the Mansfield stories, *Psychology*, which presents two novelist friends discussing psychology, a man and woman in love seething with an undercurrent of emotion but unable to tell the other just how much they want to develop their relationship whilst meticulously following the conventions. "We saw Vanessa Redgrave as Katherine only in an exaggerated form of her character in *Psychology*, in a beautifully overstated performance full of elongated vowels and grand gestures. Jeremy Brett's pinched figure of Middleton Murry and Annette Crosbie's effectively embarrassing, transparently loving L.M. were just right." (The Stage 10th May 1973) Another reviewer was delighted. "The greatest performances are by Redgrave and Brett – two of the finest actors of their generation – who have all six episodes to develop the relationship between Mansfield and Murry… Together, Redgrave and Brett are magical to watch. *A Picture of Katherine Mansfield* also deserves credit for not skirting over the issue of sexuality, especially amongst the English literary circle of the early Twentieth Century." (www.entertainment-focus.com)

Unnamed novelist in Psychology

Thriller: One Deadly Owner 1974 - ATV Television

Peter Tower in One Deadly Owner

In his next appearance for **ATV** Jeremy would play **Peter Tower**, a photographer, in modern dress of open neck shirts and tight flared trousers, in ***One Deadly Owner***, 16th February 1974, a story about a car which strangely chooses its new owner and appears to be haunted.

Peter Tower would be a completely fresh experience for Jeremy as he appears as an enthusiastic commercial photographer and agent for the stars caught up in an intriguing whodunit. He would attempt to dissuade his girlfriend, a photographic model, from buying such an expensive car as a white Rolls but Helen (Donna Mills) is petulant and determined to keep the status symbol, especially as she is wanted for a new magazine deal. The strange events of a three month old broadcast on the car radio, a leak of "blood" from the car boot, the discovery of an earring and then the steering wheel which seems to be locked in one position, all appear inexplicable. Helen is upset but Peter can offer no help, just to tell her to get rid of it.

As Helen investigates the car's previous owner she is provided with some troubling facts about the disappearance of his wife so there is no surprise when she is taken, once more by the car, to the scene of a murder. Peter joins her reluctantly and the real horror is reasonably predictable as the details of murder and the murderer are revealed. "The plot is fast moving, the acting very good and the ending - not quite expected. Good viewing. I couldn't quite get over Jeremy Brett in full blown 70s brown flares, platform shoes, tight tee shirt and incipient love handles... a rare performance as the ambitious stop-at-nothing photographer boyfriend... does not quite mask his shock and disquiet." (IMDb)

Jeremy and Donna Mills

Affairs of the Heart: Grace 1974 - ITV Television

Hon. Captain Clement Yule in Grace

The series **Affairs of the Heart** was based on the stories of Henry James with a Victorian setting and a stellar cast which included Derek Jacobi, Anna Calder Marshall, Ian Ogilvy, Gayle Hunnicutt and Edward Hardwicke, amongst others. **Grace,** based on the James story *Covering End* was broadcast on Independent Television on 13th October 1974, directed by Michael Lindsay-Hogg and the opening credits set the scene for a tale of romance between the elegant and titled Captain and the rich widowed American Mrs Gracedew (Diana Rigg). As the **Hon. Captain Clement Yule**, Jeremy was back in classical dress in the romantic role of an Edwardian gentleman who does not have sufficient funds to buy back the ancestral home which he has recently inherited, but still remains under mortgage to the unpleasant Mr Prodmore.

Jeremy was quiet and watchful but convincing in his role of the disappointed Honourable Captain, however, he cannot match the villainous ambitions of Mr Prodmore who is expecting him to marry his daughter Cora, in settlement of his debts. As a middle class entrepreneur Prodmore had bought up the promissory notes to gain an entry into the aristocracy and to gain political leverage, and the Captain's refusal to change his political allegiance and abandon the Radical Party will make him believe he will not recover his house after all. Only the charming and enthusiastic Mrs Gracedew can outwit the dastardly Mr Prodmore but he still sells the house to her at an extortionate price. When she offers it back to the Captain, encouraging him to take up his responsibilities, he offers her marriage in return bringing the episode to an enchanting conclusion.

"Much of the tale concerns the sparring and flirting between the characters of Yule and Grace, beautifully played here with understanding and humour by Brett and Rigg. They fit their roles perfectly and are hugely enjoyable to watch. So much so, that you really hope that Prodmore's plans don't come to be." (MemorableTV.com) The introduction suggests the romantic fiction of Barbara Cartland but is a delight because its serious tone means the happy ending is not assured, in fact, for most of the play there is little chance of Captain Yule gaining his inheritance. For this reason, the conclusion is especially satisfactory.

Jeremy and Diana Rigg

Jennie: Lady Randolph Churchill 1974 - ITV

Charles Kinsky in Jennie

The next performance would again see Jeremy in his familiar time-zone of the early part of the twentieth century, and this time with an intriguing accent, as **Karl (Charles) Kinsky** the Austro-Hungarian Ambassador to Great Britain and as Jennie Churchill's romantic interest in an authentic historical drama. The only real identifying mark was the rather flamboyant moustache which was strangely attractive and he certainly suited the formal clothes with the intricate neckties and jaunty hats. ***Jennie: Lady Randolph Churchill*** 5th November 1974 was a series which told the biographical story of Jennie Jerome and the Churchill family, set and filmed at Blenheim Palace in Oxfordshire, the family home, which was a royal gift from Queen Anne to the first Duke of Marlborough as reward for his exploits on his country's behalf.

Lee Remick played the part of Jennie, the vivacious American socialite, born of a wealthy Brooklyn family, who was famed for her beauty, her intelligence and her salon; renowned for the brilliant political atmosphere in which the future Prime Minister, Winston Churchill, was encouraged to foster his talents. Winston would forever pay tribute to his mother's energy and dedication to her role as supporter of a government minister. "She shone for me like the evening star."

Count Karl (Charles) Kinsky was once more the romantic role for Jeremy; an Ambassador, a playboy and lover of horses and as Jennie's lover he frequently acted as her escort at her soirees. Kinsky won the Grand National on his own horse, Zoedone, and he enjoyed playing with the young Winston and entertaining Jennie whilst Randolph was absent in the House of Commons or on state visits abroad. He was totally infatuated with her and their affair was the best held open secret, however, their inability to marry would lead to his increasing unhappiness and their eventual estrangement. As a prominent émigré he had considerable position in his own country and expectations from his father for continuing his hereditary line. Count Kinsky would marry the Countess Elisabeth Wolff-Metternich zur Gracht in 1895 and he left Great Britain in 1914 when war between England and Germany was declared. He was keen to do his duty but unwilling to fight the country he regarded as his second home so volunteering to fight on the Russian front.

"The death of Lord Randolph in 1895 would seemingly open the door for Lady Randolph to finally marry her lover, Count Kinsky (Jeremy Brett). However, Jennie's continual putting off of the Count's entreaties along with her numerous infidelities against him convinces the Count to move on to another marriage." (dvdtalk.com)

Jennie

Haunted: The Ferryman 1974 – ITV Television

Sheridan Owen in Haunted – The Ferryman

Originally broadcast on 23rd December 1974, **Haunted: The Ferryman** is described as a modern play of the supernatural based on the story *Who or What Was It* by Kingsley Amis, adapted by Julian Bond and directed by John Irvin, produced by Derek Granger. Jeremy appears as the hero of the story, a young writer in his thirties named **Sheridan Owen** who has finally written a successful novel, top of the best sellers, called *The Ferryman* and is unexpectedly acclaimed by the critics as "a good literate horror story" which acknowledges the fact that ghosts exist. Personally, he doesn't believe it and escapes the unwanted spotlight with his wife into the country for the weekend.

This novel is Owen's first success as a writer and he is challenged by the outcome. Running away from the horror enthusiasts at a book-signing event he thinks he has escaped but instead he runs into his own nightmare. His ghost story becomes a reality as Owen and his wife discover an idyllic hotel in a sudden and violent storm with the same name as his novel's title. As he finds other similarities with his novel in the names of the hotelier, the manager and the waiter, he discovers the gravestone of a drowned ferryman William Grimsditch the bogeyman of his tale. The story becomes a haunting, as the ferryman appears and Owen is faced with the terrifying climax of his own story.

"Magnificently produced... intelligently directed... The acting was first class. Mr Brett and Miss Parry, supported by a hard-working cast which included such dependable actors as Geoffrey Chater, Andrew Bradford and Ray Mort, played the story for all it was worth and held the viewer's respectful attention from start to finish. "But alas, despite their efforts, the tale didn't manage to strike terror to the soul. Finally, the idea of the incubus, the demon in the guise of lover or husband visiting a woman's bed in the night, may have carried frightening conviction at a time when witchcraft had wider acceptance. To the sceptical modern mind however it provokes more hilarity than horror. For me, the incubus was just one too many improbable passengers for the ferryman to carry, and served only to spoil earlier pleasure and tip what had been a fairly good yarn into the depth of absurdity." (The Stage 2nd January 1975) *The Ferryman*, Mr Bond's adaptation of the story, was full of nice irrelevant detail and nervous tension. (Jeremy Brett played the writer) but slow to build and short on scalp-thrills until the scarifying climax itself which left one adequately disturbed...' (Michael Ratcliffe. The Times 24th December 1974)

Jeremy as Sheridan Owen

The Prodigal Daughter 1975 - Anglia Television for ITV

Father Michael Daley with Christine and Father Perfect in The Prodigal Daughter

The Prodigal Daughter, a play written for television by David Turner, would examine the role of the Roman Catholic priest in society and how they should carry out their responsibilities in the church and in the lives of their parishioners. The familiar question of whether a priest should remain unmarried, was also explored through the very different personalities of the three men in the story. In *The Prodigal Daughter* Jeremy was totally believable as **Father Michael Daley**, the sensitive yet troubled man who is questioning his future in the Church.

Jeremy's earnest performance of the caring priest, who becomes disenchanted by the ways of the priesthood becomes the focus for a discussion of celibacy in the modern church. As Father Daley administers the last rites to Sister Annuncia, the person he has known better than any other, he echoes her concerns, *"What has Christ to do with a woman?... A priest needs a woman! A specific woman, otherwise, how can he deal with thousands unless he knows one?"* The new housekeeper Christine has experienced the enormous implications of an unwanted pregnancy, and abortion, for which she expects some judgement, but not one of these men has the necessary experience to help her. The saintly Father Perfect, played by Alistair Sim responds with the compassion demanded by his calling. The unhappy, more devious Father Vernon, (Charles Kay) condemns her, bringing about the breakup of this particular household but not before Christine had unsettled its unity with her presence.

An article in the *TV Times* also described the play as "the story of the love of a woman for a good man - too good... he's a priest" but Jeremy and Alistair refused to comment on the quandary the priest faced. Jeremy said, *"It's one thing for an actor to hold opinions, it's another to air them - as an actor."*

Father Michael Daley in The Prodigal Daughter

The School for Scandal 1975 - BBC Play of the Month

Jeremy as Joseph Surface and Pauline Collins as Lady Teazle in The School for Scandal

The School for Scandal broadcast as part of the BBC Play of the Month on 16th February 1975, was a perfect role for Jeremy, a made-to-measure classic part aimed at an educated audience with expectations of a new interpretation of a classic text. Even those who had little knowledge of Sheridan would be entertained with the satire of pseudo upper class, bewigged, cane-carrying men and women of fashion trying to outwit each other in order to marry well and gain the monetary prize. Jeremy's role as **Joseph Surface** in this play *"is outwardly a paragon of virtue, but inwardly is a miserly fortune hunter."* He always looked good in the breeches roles which showed off his slim, athletic figure to perfection.

Joseph Surface is at the heart of the gossipy fast paced scenes and a man who is a welcome addition to the drawing rooms where intrigue has just one aim – the manipulation and exploitation of those with money. Jeremy presents him with measured style and consideration as a good man, a man of sentiment with a reputation for prudence and restraint whereas in truth he is selfish and malicious, taking delight at the misery of others. His greatest rival is his brother, Charles, recognised as a profligate, facing ruin through his reckless extravagance and a libertine who is in reality kind-hearted. The comedy and the intrigue focuses on the spirited Lady Teazle with a husband old enough to be her father and Sir Peter's ward Maria who has a large fortune which Joseph has his eye on but as Charles emerges as his favoured rival he must mask his pretensions. The situation reaches a farcical climax in Joseph's apartment with the wife behind a screen and her elderly husband hiding in a cupboard before revealing the true nature of the whole affair.

Joseph in The School For Scandal

"This was, in all, a distinguished production with Jeremy Brett and Edward Fox boxing and coxing as the Surface brothers, Constance Chapman a splendid gossipy Mrs Candor and Russell Hunter and Andrew Robertson, contributing to the unexpected but effective dash of Scotch to the mixture of part of Crabtree and his incredible nephew, Sir Benjamin Backbite. It is difficult to present a classic so familiar as this one with any degree of freshness and originality; but Stuart Burge, directing and Cedric Messina, producing managed to do so. All credit to them." (Glasgow Herald 17th February 1975)

The *Radio Time*s advertised the new *Play of the Month: The School for Scandal, Sunday BBC1* as "a marvellous comedy," says director Stuart Burge, "which just happens to have been written in 1777. We've tried to present it as though it were written yesterday, to give viewers a wild slice of life straight from the 18th century, where only the very few, like the landowners and the Indian nabobs were rich, and everyone else who fancied himself in society was dependent on them. It was a world where appearance was all that mattered and intrigue and exotic fantasy was the breath of life. When Benedict Nightingale talked to some of the play's stars, Jeremy spoke "with exhilaration of his days at the National Theatre" and said how much he valued the *"ensemble"* approach where *"everyone knew and trusted each other's abilities."*

The School For Scandal

On playing the role of Joseph Surface, he said he didn't want to appear an obvious villain but would prefer to be seen as a charming, likeable fellow, *"Joe's a brilliant trickster, who gets fun out of manipulating others; a really naughty character."* The article described Jeremy: "as actor, he's both sensitive and intelligent; as man, outgoing, enthusiastic, garrulous; and, as Surfaces go, might seem more Charles than Joseph," a familiar portrait, especially when he was preparing for a performance. His degree of preparation would once more be all consuming and he clearly enjoyed the humour brought by his role. Jeremy still saw himself as a romantic heroic actor and suitable parts were certainly becoming rarer on television, although the theatre would retain its classical focus. *"I was a romantic heroic actor, at a time when there were no romantic or heroic parts! But sweet people like Cedric Messina at the BBC were doing* Play of the Month, *offered me about a play or maybe two a year sometimes. Wonderful roles like Jack Absolute in* The Rivals, *or again* School for Scandal." (Radio Times)

A Legacy 1975 - BBC2

The five part presentation of Sybille Bedford's historical novel set in the Kaiser's Berlin *A Legacy* began its broadcast on BBC2 on 29th March 1975, with Jeremy playing the role of the eldest son **Eduard Merz (Edu)**, married to an admirable wife Sarah (Claire Bloom). Edu was a clubman, a rake and a gambler previously supported by his father and since his marriage, by his elegant heiress wife, but as she grew tired of his infidelities and his debts she cuts off his funds forcing him to go bankrupt, thereby cutting him off from society.

Jeremy's restrained and formal Edu is introduced as the eldest son amongst the eight members of the solid well upholstered Merz family seated at the vast dining table where they meet three times a day for endless meals with the extended family who have attached themselves to the source of wealth. Julius von Felden is seated at the same table as his marriage to Melanie Merz, has brought his aristocratic birthright to fulfil everyone's expectations. "Each family stood confident of being able to go on with what was theirs, while in fact they were playthings, often victims, of the new united Germany and what was brewing therein."

"Sybille Bedford's novel about two German families at the turn of the century is complicated and intricate, and peopled with a bewildering number of characters whose names and relationships are initially difficult to identify. However, by means of a straightforward piece of introductory narrative, read by Flora Robson in her admirably clear and musical voice, the viewer could with a bit of concentration fix the right labels on the right people within 10 minutes or so of the opening sequence round the Merz's dinner table. The major part of episode one was concerned with the trials experienced by two sons of the other family (the von Feldens) when their father, Baron Felden (Hugh Griffith) decrees that Julius (John Fraser) shall go to Bonn to be prepared for the Diplomatic Service and that Johannes (Christopher Guard) shall become an army cadet. Meantime, a third son, Gustavus (Geoffrey Whitehead) is pursuing the saintly Clara (Angela Pleasence) somewhat to his papa's disapproval. It is too early to be sure that this five-part adaptation of the novel is going to be wholly successful: but with Claire Bloom, Irene Handl, and Jeremy Brett to help, the chances seem good." (Alison Downie in the Glasgow Herald April 1975)

The series is based on Sybille Bedford's memories of her childhood growing up in Berlin in the build up to the First World War amongst these passionate people who are rich, self-indulgent and eccentric. "Presented with love and humour they become victims of circumstances and of their own character. This is a star-studded fantasy. Dame Flora Robson does the narrating, and Hugh Griffith, Irene Handl, Angela Pleasence, Richard Hurndall, Jeremy Brett, Robin Bailey, Geoffrey Whitehead, and John Fraser play an assortment of elegant cosmopolitan aristocrats... There is obviously going to be food aplenty in *A Legacy*... this time haute cuisine." (The Times 31st March 1975) One viewer agreed, "... all the cast were terrific. A wonderful piece of television, well worth reviving."

Ten from the Twenties: Motherlove 1975 - BBC2

Willie Edwardes in Motherlove

Jeremy's next appearance was for BBC2 Television on Friday 27th June 1975, in the series ***Ten from the Twenties***; based on short stories written in the 1920s, each play featuring a particular year. ***Motherlove*** was written by J.D. Beresford (from a family of clergymen) the original story entitled *The Indomitable Mrs Garthorne,* was dramatised by Robert Muller and directed by Mark Cullingham. It is set in 1922 and tells how Hugh Garthorne played by Barry Quin, falls "heroically, beautifully" in love but not with Lady Rose, his mother's choice for him and dreads telling her.

Jeremy played **Willie Edwardes**, a stylish middle-aged "poet", and everything about him proclaimed him a character of the Twenties. He was sitting in the hotel lobby in Biarritz where Hugh and his mother were staying for the winter, when he was asked to intervene on behalf of the idle and spoilt Hugh, a fellow Harrovian, in his endeavour to disentangle himself from his mother's dominance over his life. The fact that the very rich Mrs. Garthorne (Isobel Dean) is "an upper-middle-class oh-so-superior dragon of the twenties" makes his decision extraordinary. Jeremy's Willie Edwardes wears a small moustache with smooth short hair parted, a large rose in the buttonhole and personifies elegance. He is affected, histrionic with dramatic hand expressions and pursed lips with occasional lip fingering not seen before.

"There were isolated joys in the dialogue. Mrs Garthorne's 'what a plain child' when first shown a photograph of her grandson; Hugh's 'oh anything – champagne?' when invited to take a drink; the topical hindsight of 'they've finally arrested Mr Gandhi.' But above everything else there was the acting, stylish, elegant, so very much of the period. Isabel Dean as the mother who never cut the umbilical cord, discarding her lovesick son as readily as she once discarded her errant husband, but supremely confident that one day he will return. A performance of forceful elegance, seeking sympathy from none. And Jeremy Brett as Willie Edwardes, author and fellow Harrovian, urging the son to defy the mother and storing it all away in his little notebook. Elegance again, but marked with perfection of timing and the most expressive use of the face. These two helped to hide the improbability of a situation in which a son falls madly in love with a girl who just happens to be the adopted daughter of his own father whom he has never seen since his mother disowned her husband when he went to jail for petty theft in the days when both were poor." (The Stage 3rd July 1975)

Guest Appearance on The Twiggy Show - BBC2 - 15th October 1975

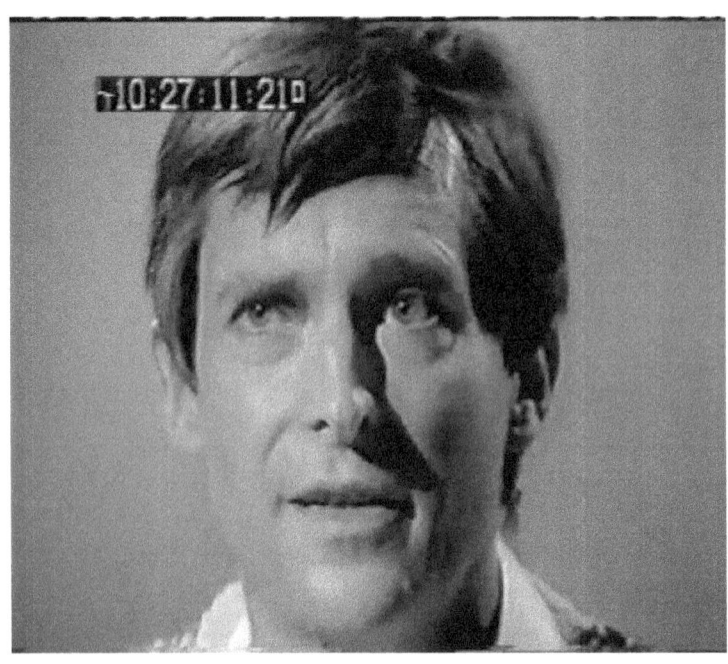

"She moved through the fair"

Twiggy, nicknamed Twigs at school, became a symbol of the Swinging Sixties as a model, an actress and a singer. Her slim shape and elfin looks with her large eyes, long eyelashes and androgynous figure defined the sixties fashion industry and she became the iconic representation of the age. On his appearance with **Twiggy** in 1975, Jeremy, dressed in his own shirt, slacks and sleeveless jumper sang three songs, the first of which was a charming folk song called "She moved through the fair." The second was a romantic duet with Twiggy taken from *The Merry Widow* "Love Unspoken", for which they both changed into evening wear in a fade sequence. The final song, "Two Sleepy People" in a further duet, dressed in white shirts and flannels with draped tennis sweaters around their shoulders. Jeremy also read the Poem *Dancers* by Oliver Bernard to accompany a performance by the Irving Davies Dancers.

Twiggy Lawson – "First I was a fan. I remember being captivated by his Bassanio in *The Merchant of Venice* in the late 60s - the first time I'd seen him on stage. Shortly afterwards we met and became firm friends. In the mid-seventies I was doing my own variety series on the BBC. Jeremy mentioned how he loved to sing and rarely got the chance. So I invited him on as my guest. He was a delight. A big talent and a special man. I miss him..."

Love Unspoken

Two Sleepy People

Love's Labour's Lost 1975 - BBC Play of the Month

Martin Shaw as the King of Navarre and Jeremy as Berowne

On 14th December 1975 Jeremy was to appear once more as **Berowne** in Cedric Messina's adaptation of *Love's Labour's Lost* for the BBC Play of the Month, a part he had played onstage in 1969 at the National Theatre and one of his favourite roles. This would be his fourth appearance, as he had also performed it at the *Library Theatre* and recorded it for Caedmon in 1966. On this occasion he falls in love with Sinead Cusack as his Rosaline and Martin Shaw plays the King of Navarre. An outdoor production set in the gardens at Glyndbourne, it is beautiful to look at with the Medieval costumes of doublet and hose for the men and long flowing costumes for the ladies and only occasionally can one hear the sound of raindrops on the leaves as Messina records how the two week's filming had to be completed dodging the showers. Only the six inch stain at the bottom of Berowne's blue cloak provides the evidence.

The release of the production on the BBC Store enabled a new audience to see an excellent production of this rarely screened play. It also triggered the following review: "A sprightly comedy that was out of favour for a couple of centuries was brought joyfully to television in this fun and funny production. Jeremy Brett, always a highly theatrical player, has a ball as the witty Berowne. Martin Shaw is the King who has the much-too-hasty idea of forsaking women for three years, and the scene where the fellas woo the ladies while in disguise is a hoot." *The Stage* agreed. "Aware that the success of any Shakespearean play in production stands or falls on the twin supports of poetry and understanding, Cedric Messina prefaced his version of *Love's Labour's Lost*... by some meticulous casting. Rarely can there have been a more intelligent interpretation of the often irritating Berowne than Jeremy Brett gave us, nor a better harnessed team of comics than Jonathon Cecil's Holofernes and Tony Haygarth's Sir Nathaniel...." (Redeemed by acting by Patrick Campbell The Stage 18th December 1975)

In 1975 Jeremy commented on the fact that work didn't come easy as he always had to look for his own jobs, *"It certainly wasn't a case of me sitting with four or five scripts and wondering which one to do. I've been lucky in the past if I had one... But thank goodness I had some lucky breaks. Laurence Olivier was incredibly kind and asked me to go to the National for four years. I was allowed to play marvellous parts under him. That was another miracle. I had left to do a film* My Fair Lady. *But I managed to get back, but it's all through the kindness of friends really, that I've been allowed to do all this. Then, of course, the last bit of magic, the ridiculous idea of casting me in this part of* Sherlock Holmes!" (Black Box Interview)

Jackanory 1976 - BBC One

Jeremy's appearance on *Jackanory* shows the different ways radio and television were bringing him into the schedules. His reputation as a classical actor performing principally for an adult audience did not prepare him for the challenge of telling stories especially designed for children. It is true he had appeared as Gerard in **Puss in Boots** in Manchester in 1954 and in the role of **Storyteller** in a recording for EMI Starline of the same play in 1972 for a David Frost presentation of the fairy tale, starring Judi Dench as Puss and accompanied by the Mike Sammes Singers. However, when Jeremy was first asked in 1965 to appear on **Jackanory** he had refused – but on this occasion he accepted. For five days, Monday 19th January to 23rd January 1976, Jeremy appeared on BBC One to read *Zadig* by Josephine Gladstone based on the story by Voltaire in five parts. Voltaire had taken his Zadig, a Philosopher at the Babylonian court from the Persian *Nigaristan* an Eastern fable and this man of "uncommon genius", a man renowned for his superior powers of observation and deduction was used as the model for Edgar Alan Poe's detective Dupin and subsequently, Arthur Conan Doyle's *Sherlock Holmes*.

An article in *The Stage* explained Jeremy's reluctance to accept the invitation to appear on the very first programme of *Jackanory* in 1965 and why he would have found it difficult. "But nowadays most actors are anxious to appear on the programme. It has become the OK thing and agents ring us and offer their artists. When Jeremy Brett was asked to do the first ever *Jackanory,* he turned it down. It transpired afterwards that he was terrified of sitting in a chair and telling a story. He need not have felt guilty about it. Five 15-minute solos in front of the camera isn't that easy." (Telling a Story – The Challenge They All Queue up to Accept in The Stage 18th December 1975) The show was first transmitted on 13th December 1965 and the first story was the fairy-tale "Cap-o'-Rushes" read by Lee Montague.

Night of 100 Stars 1977 - ITV London Weekend Television

Jeremy would appear as himself in the **Night of 100 Stars** filmed for London Weekend Television. It was a gala performance to celebrate the Queen's Silver Jubliee performed in the presence of Princess Alexandra at the Olivier Theatre on 5th June 1977. Hosted by Kenneth Moore and starring Patrick Allen, Wendy Craig, Frank Finlay, Sir John Gielgud, Wendy Hiller, Penelope Keith, John Mills, Denis Quilley, Kenneth Williams, Simon Williams amongst many others.

The Impressarios 1975 - BBC Radio 2

BBC Radio 2 featured a programme entitled **The Impressarios**, which featured stories of the men who create the world of entertainment, broadcast on 1st and 8th July 1975. Presented by Michael Craig it examined some of the greatest impressarios of the theatre: H.M. Tennent, Binkie Beaumont, Donald Albery, Andre Chariot and Joseph Leopold Sacks. Jeremy appeared in both programmes and one comment says, "*Oliver* is the kind of thing that every theatre manager prays will happen to him, and if it happens to you once you're bloody lucky."

Man of Action 1975 - BBC Radio 3

An unusual programme with an unusual title was his next appearance on Radio 3 **Man of Action,** gave him an opportunity to play his personal choice of music. It was in December 1975 that he would *"leap at the chance to play some of my favourite records"* for a listening public on the channel dedicated to classical music and opera. Jeremy always adored opera and it is no surprise that he chose classical extracts, some of which were linked to his appearances on television, such as Lehar: *The Merry Widow*. He chose Elizabeth Schwarzkopf in an excerpt from Lehar's operetta, Harriet Cohen playing Debussy's *La cathedrale engloutie*, Leontyne Price singing Puccini's *Che il bet sogno di Doretta* from *La Rondine* and Nat King Cole with George Shearing relaxing with *I Pick Yourself Up*. Some of these records would be chosen again for his eight favourite pieces of music for his appearance on *Desert Island Discs* in 1991.

The Picture of Dorian Gray 1976 - BBC Play of the Month

Basil Hallward in The Picture of Dorian Gray

This was the second time Jeremy had appeared in Oscar Wilde's ***The Picture of Dorian Gray***, broadcast in the BBC Play of the Month series on 19th September 1976. His first appearance had been as the beautiful young man of the title who sold his soul for the gift of eternal youth, but fifteen years later he would take the role of the artist, **Basil Hallward**. It gave him the opportunity to present an intelligent interpretation and enter the pathos of the situation as the picture's creator and involved narrator.

This adaptation was the closest to Wilde's original story as the screenwriter had steadfastly refused to shield the viewers from the more unpleasant details and John Osborne had added some extra witticisms to bring out the sardonic tone. The revelation of the homosexual sub-text presented an intriguing addition and Hallward's brutal murder is shocking. Jeremy would bring a significant sensitivity to the role of the artist which was remembered in David Stuart Davies's *Bending the Willow*. "Jeremy Brett gives a splendid, naturalistic interpretation of the role, not an easy task when playing a Wilde character and acting, for most of the time, with John Gielgud. Odd as it may seem, Jeremy's performance reminded me what a remarkably fine actor he was; and, I think, I did need reminding... His portrait of Hallward came from the heart, from the soul, without any of the mannerisms and tics that he later developed when playing Holmes." On this occasion the role of Dorian would be played by Peter Firth and Henry Wotton by John Gielgud with the added appearance of Gwen Ffrangcon Davies (the dowager in *The Master Blackmailer*) in the role of Lady Agatha.

In his *Introduction to the Complete Works of Oscar Wilde*, Wilde's son explained how Oscar had visited the studio of the painter Basil Ward and been struck by the exceptional beauty of a young man sitting for his portrait. Afterwards, he had wondered aloud, "What a pity that such a glorious creature should ever grow old." The artist had agreed with Wilde's comment, adding, "How delightful it would be if he could remain exactly as he is, while the portrait aged and withered in his stead!" Oscar had acknowledged the obligation by naming the artist in the story Basil Hallward." (Vyvyan Holland)

Canada and USA 1976 - 1985

Jeremy left England for Canada and Stratford in 1976. *"I decided to leave when I found I'd become a semi-establishment figure. I had a lovely home in Campden Hill Square in Kensington, a nice car, a growing tummy and enough money, although it was all basically bluff and plonk and Polyfilla. I think the moment of acute realisation came when my son by my first marriage did a caricature of me which dwelt on all my worst points, right down to the earring! I felt the time had come for a change in my life... I left England because I was getting too comfortable... I was joining clubs. I'm not really like that. I've always had a wanderlust. Now travelling keeps me frisky, keeps the tummy off. I jog, I ride... I don't believe in being settled into middle-age."* (Faced with Success)

"When I arrived in Canada I discovered that not only did I have agoraphobia. I loathed the strong climate. But I was lucky to do A Young Dan'l Boone... *because Jeremy Kemp had left to return to England and any Jeremy in a storm would do! Then I found myself sitting in the foothills, eating avocados and thinking nice thoughts, waiting for a few more parts to come along."* (Woman and Home 1984) Determined to do something to justify his decision, he found himself on "cattle call" auditions for shows like *Starsky and Hutch* and *M.A.S.H* and not getting cast. He admits there were periods of discouragement balanced by his love of the climate and life in Southern California. But concluded Hollywood was *"a dream place, but just not to work in."* (Arts & Entertainment)

Just as he had left England in order to find new challenges, so Jeremy would sometimes just leave, in order to be free. In October 1975 Fred Myers, an agriculturalist, told the story of a trip to Honolulu to photograph sugar cane equipment, when he was hailed by a fellow traveller, whom he described as a tall, dark-haired man with a distinct British accent, and who introduced himself as Jeremy, an actor. He told Fred he was following an impulse to take the next flight out of Los Angeles, which turned out to be Honolulu and from there he planned to visit Maui. No one knew where he was. *"He had run away and was enjoying every heady moment of it."* Fred invited him along and they both looked forward to the companionship. The next morning they met for breakfast and then hit the highway. Fred said, "Jeremy wasn't cut from ordinary cloth. His observations were flavoured with introspection. He was extremely sensitive to the beauty around him and every comment he made was something of consequence, as if it were coming from deep inside him for the first time. When he saw something particularly interesting, he would stop and have a closer look. On one of these stops, he climbed to the top of a large rock on the beach, turned his face toward the sun, extended his arms upward, closed his eyes and stood motionless." Fred went on to comment that he thought it was a willingness to embrace and connect with the world around him. After a little while Jeremy began to have misgivings and worry about the people who may be concerned about his disappearance. Fred took him to the airport for the next flight to Los Angeles. It was several months later that he saw Jeremy on the television and recognised him as his companion on Maui. His conclusion is that although he had been around many creative people he had never met anyone "who personified creativity as intensely, completely and wonderfully as Jeremy Brett. And that none had exhibited the free spirit as spontaneously or as nobly as he did." Another example of this free spirit can be found in the story he told one newspaper reporter. Whilst living and working in Canada, he wandered naked into his back garden, a shocking revelation maybe but told with his usual panache. He said: *"It was a very warm day and I thought I'd do a spot of sunbathing, but my two puritanical elderly neighbours were horrified and ran inside. I invited them round for a proper English tea – fully clothed of course."*

A more fundamental reason for his move abroad could have been his developing romance with Joan Sullivan the Producer at *PBS* and *Masterpiece Theatre* and a desire to spend more time with her. They would marry the following year. A humorous note sent by Alistair Cooke, who was a friend to both of them at Christmas 1975 suggests they had been together since the interview for *The Rivals* on PBS.

For JEREMY BRETT with sympathetic concern for him

and his new life with Joan (Pankhurst) Sullivan!

Alistair Cooke Xmas '75.

Stratford Shakespeare Festival - Canada

Jeremy moved away from England in 1975/6 and stopped in Canada for *The Stratford Shakespeare Festival* which lasted for six months of the year: there he was reunited with his friend from the Greenwich Theatre Company. Robin Phillips had been appointed the Director of the Stratford Festival and had brought in Jeremy to play alongside Maggie Smith, now divorced from Robert Stephens and married to Beverley Cross. Robin had arrived in 1975, "the unwitting target of nationalist fury" but he had "responded by sweeping away Stratford's precious British affectations and replaced them with a "simple but elegant Shakespeare that was played with a cinematic attention to detail." (The globeandmail.com) Maggie and Jeremy were to have an immediate impact in that the twenty two week season of 338 performances increased the audience numbers enormously. The Shakespeare Festival Theatre in Stratford had been founded in 1953 by Tyrone Guthrie and originally housed in a huge tent. Guthrie's aim was to develop a Canadian National Theatre, to work with a resident ensemble and community artists which would remain true to the spirit of the Elizabethan theatre tradition. The classical heart of the festival was a huge draw and the *New York Times* applauded the "mini-miracle" that Phillips had created - a theatrically and visually exciting production but with the added appeal of preserving the original text of three and a half hours of Congreve's comic masterpiece. The season opened with *Hamlet* in matinee at the Avon Theatre and Jeremy and Maggie in ***The Way of the World*** by William Congreve, at the Festival Theatre. "It was a remarkable day - the simple affirmation of a great theater(re) company... The intrigues—both amorous and mercenary—could have been taking place in New York in 1976."

Jeremy as Mirabell and Maggie as Millamant in The Way of the World

The Way of the World 1976 - Stratford Festival Theatre

Jeremy could always find goodness in any character and create a fully rounded sympathetic individual. In this production he became the discerning, gallant **Mirabell**, who, in spite of himself, is in love with the frank, radiant Millamant who wants to be loved but not enslaved. Together they represent two intelligent people in sharp contrast to the fops and fools in a world where all the characters are hypocritical and "impudence and malice pass for wit". In essence, "the superannuated but insatiably lustful Lady Wishfort (Jessica Tandy) controls a fortune and has an itch for the philanderer Mirabell (Jeremy Brett). He, in turn has fallen in love with her niece Millamant (Maggie Smith) and schemes to blackmail Lady Wishfort in order to secure her consent to his marriage to Millamant. That is just about what happens." (Time Magazine)

Mirabell, the dignified courtier and the level-headed Millamant, are strong-willed, determined individuals yet each show the true depth of their feelings in the *proviso* scene where they discuss the conditions on which they would accept marriage; a true marriage based on mutual respect, consideration and equality. Millamant's insistence on preserving certain freedoms would have been more challenging to the audience in 1700 than it was to the 1976 Canadian one. But rampant materialism is all too familiar with its back-stabbing and exploitation so no one can be seen as good. The *New York Times* commented: "Mr Phillips stresses the play's formality – for Congreve was a mixture of wit, a moralist, a dancing master and a pedant – and yet encourages his players to go beneath the surface superficialities to the realities within that make Congreve not merely a craftsman of his time but also a playwright of lasting delight. The performance was, as it had to be, dominated by Millamant, and here Maggie Smith has a role that is tailored to her merits – those lovely spots of wit, humanity and compassion... was both divinely affected and effective. Jeremy Brett's Mirabell had all the manly virtues and foppish overtones that the role demands. A decent man in a naughty world, Mirabell is a giant of moral compromise, and Mr Brett, smiling, but never smirking, makes him just so." *The Times* said of Robin Phillips, "His presence has attracted a strong company to Stratford this season... the stars are brilliant... We had a wonderful performance of *The Way of the World*, with Maggie Smith once again superb as Millamant and Jeremy Brett understatedly elegant as Mirabell... Maggie Smith in particular gives a performance of such sublime sauciness that it creates a standard by which such acting can be judged." (The Fantastic Mr Phillips. The Times 19th June 1976)

The company had begun to notice a disagreement amongst the critics which was difficult to explain. They had been used to universal acclaim and suddenly there was considerable criticism from the Canadian press. *The Stage* highlighted some of the tensions with its headline, *"Clash of critics – and so-called critics at Stratford, Ontario"*, which went on to call it "trouble in Paradise. Deep rooted trouble. I suspect it goes right back to the days of General Wolfe... It too has a summer Festival of Drama, presided over by Robin Phillips who has attracted to it the shining gifted Maggie Smith, who incidentally plays with a serenity that London, Chichester and Los Angeles have never brought out in her. She is supported by eager and offering Jeremy Brett... 1976, the 24th season, presents ten plays – one of them *Eve*, being a new play by a new Canadian author, Larry Fineberg. The others come from the classics... Why, then, the clash of armies joined in battle? The honours are easy, the Maple Leaf shared, and upheld by Canada and England in a joint cultural effort, one would have thought. There is a sorry answer to the question, however. The expanse is vast though it consists of three words – The Atlantic Ocean. In the teeth of international praise from B.A. Young (*The Financial Times*) Sydney Edwards (The London *Evening Standard*) *Time Magazine* (America) Clive Barnes (*The New York Times*) the ladies and gentlemen of the Toronto press wave racist banners in an irresponsible manner. Anyone English and particularly the Artistic Director of the Festival must go, it seems. Canada for Canadian actors and directors, they insist though it accords ill with the international character of their audiences... One wonders if this brash brotherhood has ever paused to consider the nature and purpose of criticism... One of the local lads wrote that he'd never heard Shakespeare so badly spoken – only, a small detail, no doubt, he said it of "*The Way of the World*, by Congreve." (The Stage 22ⁿᵈ July 1976)

At Stratford, Jeremy was forced to re-examine not only his talent, but himself. "*I used to believe that if you gave of your best, that was enough. But that is not true. The actors were simply hated by the people who lived in the town. They didn't speak to us. We opened, and the local paper gave us the worst review that's ever been written. I thought, 'What is all this?' We got rave reviews from all over the world. Then I heard the story. That was when they opened the theatre, with Tyrone Guthrie, there were two actors who one night took all their furniture out of their digs and burnt it in the street, because they said, it was lousy. And that stuck!... a great actor called Wilfred Lawson who taught many actors to drink to the bottom of the bottle, because they might find a further depth to their performances. That was the excuse. That's the kind of thing that people remember. They remember the ones that splurge. They're the ones that get the press... But there it's different because they believe in actors... First of all they believe in success, which we don't believe in here. We love gentle failure.*" (Jeremy to Stage Struck)

Offstage Jeremy was receiving a good deal of attention from fellow actors. Gale Garnett whose boyfriend was playing Lysander in *A Midsummer Night's Dream* wrote about her memories of meeting Jeremy in the bars after the performance. "As with many of us, of varying ages, sexes, and sexual predispositions, I was thunderstruck by his beauty: his face, voice, hands, hair, classical profile. Aesthetically, when people insisted that someday one's prince would come, Jeremy Brett was surely what they had in mind. For most of that season, a group of us younger actors would sit in the pub of the Queen's Hotel while Jeremy, eyes twinkling, elegant fingers flying, Borsolino hat tilted rakishly atop his movie-star head, held court." (Gale Garnett on Brettish.com)

A Midsummer Night's Dream 1976 - Stratford Shakespeare Festival

A Midsummer Night's Dream is a popular and frequently produced comedy. On a Midsummer's Eve four young lovers, Hermia and Lysander, Demetrius and Helena are lost in an enchanted forest where sprites lurk and fairies rule to ensure that true love does not run smoothly. Close by the feuding Fairy King Oberon and his Queen Titania are at war over possession of 'a changeling' young boy and the King's vengeful spell causes his wife to fall rapturously in love with Bottom, one of the mechanicals, suddenly wearing a ridiculous asses' head. The naive Bottom and Quince with their friends are preparing a play within a play for the wedding of the Duke of Athens, Theseus to his Hippolyta. The chief mischief-maker Puck is responsible for the enchantments and confusions which are all finally removed by Oberon and replaced by fantastical dreams.

The *Calgary Herald* called it "Phillips' most imaginative effort" and identified the producer's intentions which were appreciated and Jeremy's performance was praised, "*A Midsummer Night's Dream* is about many things. It's about love and illusion and hatred and honesty. It's about the truth which can restrict us and the fantasies that can set us free... The production begins and ends with an image – a Queen – who may look rather like the historical Elizabeth, but who in the play is Hipployta, the formidable Queen of the Amazons. Jessica Tandy plays Hippolyta, but she also plays Titania, the Queen's fairyland counterpart. Theseus, the Queen's suitor, is portrayed by Jeremy Brett, who also portrays Oberon, the King of the fairy kingdom. It could be argued that these two pieces of double casting reveals Phillips' indebtedness to Peter Brook's legendary 1970 Royal Shakespeare production. The argument may be valid, but only to the point that Phillips accepts the promise that the play's fairyland events stem from the subconscious of the real-life characters. But even this interpretation seems inadequate in view of the essentially dream-like quality which pervades the evening.... Jessica Tandy plays the Queen as though to the manner born and later nuzzles the donkey's head of Bottom with a girlish abandon. Jeremy Brett is a bold and resourceful King..." (The Calgary Herald 20th August 1976)

As his time in Stratford was coming to a close Jeremy was called upon to give interviews on his plans. He said he would have liked to be recalled to Hollywood as *War and Peace* and *My Fair Lady* were a source of pride, but maybe also of disappointment as he received no new offers. He told the *Ottawa Citizen* that he would like to "*give Hollywood a second chance.*" He was planning to return in the hope that someone had pulled out of their contract and a stand-in was needed, although he went on to say he preferred acting on the stage. "*It boggles my mind to think of the power of movies, especially television, to attract and influence people. If you are going to be a stage actor you can't assume that people will come to see you. You must intrigue them to the point where they will come...*" (Ottawa Citizen) "*I love to work. Being allowed constantly to play charades and be paid for doing what one adores is unbelievable. It's also an escape. It's easy to become a workaholic because when you're working there's a clear focus. Life is much more complicated, but when it's such an honour to be working when only four per cent of actors are employed.*" (Woman and Home 1984)

Piccadilly Circus 1976 – PBS Television

Jeremy as Host on Piccadilly Circus

A regular monthly appearance for Jeremy during 1976 was that of **Host** of ***Piccadilly Circus,*** an anthology programme on Boston's Public Broadcasting Company. The introductory article explained the choice of *Piccadilly Circus* for the title which brought focus onto the centre of London "The place visitors to London gravitate to," with its flashing lights and glitz. Although the "host Jeremy Brett will be taking viewers on a 12-month entertainment tour that roams far from the London neighbourhood. The TV tour offers a smorgasbord of the best of British entertainment – from the 'Goodies' to a drama of a clay miners' strike in Cornwall, England, to the inside story of a carnival family in Italy." (Sarasota Herald Tribune 15th February 1976)

The first personality to appear on this new programme was the comedian Dave Allen with his "unique take on comedy." The comedian was renowned for being a born storyteller, relaxed, assured, with an ability to draw the viewer into his world. "I don't see why I shouldn't joke about God, religion or anything else. There's humour in everything." (Milwaukee Sentinel 19th January 1976) Jeremy commented on the way the Irishman's irreverent humour "*had created a kind of island between*" the two countries when "Bombs were going off in England! Civilians fear for their lives because of the tense situation." He told of his relief at arriving at Kennedy Airport and leaving the "*terrible time at home. I had a bomb go off 100 yards from my house. And a friend of mine's car was blown up.*"

In one article entitled "*Junk on British TV*" Jeremy said that British television was not all excellence and that the programmes on PBS were not typical of British television. *"It is a very strange image that American viewers have been presented. We have much more junk on our screens than you could imagine. No one realizes the fact that the producer of* Classic Theatre, *Joan Sullivan, screened over 100 productions before she came up with 12. The same system was used for our series – these shows are the absolute best we have to offer. You never get to see the rest.*" He went on to underline the differences between the two countries especially as the British viewer was intrigued by the American crime series; "*Back home, it is American programming that is popular, rather than our own. I mean* Kojak *has knocked the whole of our younger generation for six. And then, there's Karl Malden's series,* The Streets of San Francisco. *It's doing fantastically, but then he's just a marvellous actor.* Hawaii Five-O *is also extremely popular; I suppose because we hardly see the sun, it's such a treat.*"

Jeremy brought a unique perspective to some unusual programmes. One such item was a documentary called *The Circus Moves in Calabria* and in one newspaper the Gypsies were described as "performers whose artistry and way of life comes from the most ancient tradition of entertainment. For several months, a film crew lived and worked with a family circus in Italy which still travels to villages, setting up a tent for one or two night stands. The gypsy life revealed in the resulting documentary allows viewers to share in the joys and heartaches of this small isolated family community." And on their origins: "*We all think of the circus, like its name, as originating in the arenas of Rome with chariot races and gladiators. But I like to think the real birth of the circus was the first time a group of people gathered in a circle because a man or a woman dared to display a skill – like a juggling act – creating a moment of magic for those who gathered around. The circus allows us all to be children. Through its grotesqueness, its absurdities, its frantic activity, the preposterous or daring behaviour of the performers, through the miraculous communion with animals – the circus celebrates the joy of being alive.*" (The Virgin Islands Daily News 20th August 1977)

Robert and Elizabeth 1976/7 - Yvonne Arnaud Theatre Guildford

Robert Browning in Robert and Elizabeth

"I think it has some of the best music since My Fair Lady. *And I think it has a better story, because it's more universal. It's a great zonking love story."* The emotional aspects were more difficult to convey to today's audiences, *"You have to play it in the front of your brain. You have to literally remove some of the sugar from it. Sally Ann and I do it on a mental basis, and it's like two very strong personalities meeting. What we've done is try to show the pain underneath. It's a killer to do because it means you have to work on three levels at the same time. It was a testing and I survived it. It was a tremendously valuable experience – one that I didn't really enjoy at the time, but I'm very glad it happened.... I can't think of doing anything better than a positive outgoing character in 1977. It gives the audience a tremendous lift."*
(British Musical is A Zonking Love Story to Audrey M. Ashley)

The stage roles continued to be offered as Jeremy's next appearance was in the musical **Robert and Elizabeth**, at the Yvonne Arnaud Theatre in Guildford between 22nd December 1976 and 29th January 1977. It was based on the Rudolph Bezier play *The Barretts of Wimpole Street,* an authentic presentation of the love story between the equally famous poets Elizabeth Barrett and Robert Browning. Jeremy was universally praised for giving a powerful performance that was both passionate and convincing. "In this version of the famous Barretts of Wimpole Street story, the Oedipal aspect of Moulton Barrett and daughter are

stressed – certainly from the father's angle – together with the whole Victorian view of physical love. Then into Elizabeth's claustrophobic room and life sweeps Robert Browning like a quintessential life-force from the world outside. The play stands or falls by the quality of the two leads, and Jeremy Brett injects Browning with a poetic zest for life, an example of how a musical can benefit from a powerful performance by a dramatic actor who can also sing. Equally effective as Elizabeth, Sally Ann Howes brings an almost operatic quality to her numbers – especially the show stopping *Soliloquy* opening the second half. She too has strong straight acting ability… Verdict: a triumph for Sally Ann Howes and Jeremy Brett."
(The Stage 6th January 1977)

"Jeremy Brett as the dashing and successful poet Robert Browning makes a powerful job of sweeping the invalid Elizabeth onto her feet. I doubt if Browning was quite the swashbuckling character who comes across, but he certainly puts lots of oomph into his role. Again the singing voice does not quite do justice to Ron Grainer's music, but there are few flaws in his acting. And he certainly appears to be enjoying himself despite the rigours of the role. Fortunately, the musical numbers are sufficiently melodious and hummable to overcome any lack of quality in Jeremy's singing voice. Besides this young man's domination is such that he is at all times a convincing Browning with ideas of his own and a worthy suitor for the beautiful Elizabeth." (Adam McKinlay)

With the heading "Lyrics linger in love drama" this critic proclaimed the audience "spellbound" by an "unforgettable experience": "Some of the stars held the opening night's audience spellbound. But they were matched by the considerable chorus members of which were highlights of perfection making *Robert and Elizabeth* an unforgettable experience. Lovely Sally Ann Howes as Elizabeth Barrett had more than Robert Browning metaphorically on bended knee, reeling with anxiety as she swung pendulum fashion between her love for the poet and subservience to her domineering father. Quite overpowering is Jeremy Brett as Browning, his dynamic personality and powerful voice dominating the musical developments of the story." (J.A.M) When Jeremy was approached to do a musical about Robert Browning in 1964 his answer was, "*I think a musical about a poet would be nauseating.*" However, his change of heart in 1977 brought the comment that he "boosts the show with a sincerity that few of the professional drum-beaters could match."

Mr Nightingale 1977 - BBC Television

Mr Nightingale

Mr Nightingale in the *Supernatural* series for **BBC1 Saturday,** 2nd July 1977 was an appearance which showed Jeremy in a totally different light. A series featuring werewolves, vampires and ghosts which haunt the living is an attractive vehicle for an edgy almost neurotic performance. Jeremy is barely recognisable as a grotesque lame old man who tells his chilling story of haunting and possession in order to be welcomed into the Club of the Damned. The prize was membership but those story-tellers who failed to impress the assembly were never seen again. He tells a bizarre tale in which he is lured into offering up his immortal soul in exchange for the precise time and method of his death. The setting is Hamburg where, as the impeccably behaved shy young man, he is visiting an old friend of his father's on business and the nightly reading of *"hideous stories of vampires and werewolves"* leave him terrified. As he gives himself bodily to the evil forces in the form of a sinister doppelganger his behaviour becomes first uncharacteristically disrespectful and gradually more sinister as he becomes all too aware of the two attractive young ladies, one of whom is clearly intended as his future wife. "You killed the daughter and you are entirely responsible for what happened to the unfortunate widow and your unborn child in that institution." The Club of the Damned take a dim view of his story regarding him as no better than "a damned murderer" disposing of him in the approved manner.

The Stage Magazine applauded Jeremy's performance and the mysterious effects, "In his room, Mr Nightingale encountered another version of himself, a sort of instant Hyde, though of his own appearance, to his Jekyll. With the help of some tricky camerawork, gulls screaming outside, drumbeats and a celestial choir he was possessed by this phantom and immediately looked quite evil as a result. Subsequently, his behaviour was very erratic... Jeremy Brett handled the grotesque Mr Nightingale with expertise and did what he could when the demand was to be bloodcurdling. Susan Maudsley as Elyse calculated her neurotic effects nicely, and Lesley-Anne Down, somehow put erotic as well as eerily prophetic undertones into every measured word." (The Stage 7th July 1977)

The writer for *TV.com* thought Jeremy possessed a disturbing quality of his own and for that reason suited those characters that were "repressed and neurotic." "Englishman (Jeremy Brett) becomes obsessed by a mysterious beauty (Lesley-Anne Down). Is she all she seems? Is he? A doppelganger story owing more to Poe's William Wilson than to Stevenson's *Dr Jekyll and Mr Hyde*, this was one of the series' weaker episodes. However, the casting of Jeremy Brett in the title role makes good use of that very disturbing quality which he always seemed to have, even as a young man cast as dashing juveniles, and which he exploited so effectively in his great role as Sherlock Holmes. Handsome as he was, Brett never seemed quite right as a straightforward leading man – he was far better at tormented types, and is both as Mr Nightingale. This is the only episode of the series where the storyteller fails to impress the Club of the Damned's committee – we have, in the closing moments, a hint of the dreadful fate that awaits unsuccessful applicants." (TV.com)

Young Dan'l Boone 1977 - Trail Blazer

Young Daniel Boone

In 1977 the American television network offered Jeremy the familiar role of the villain, **Langford** in the four part series ***Young Dan'l Boone -Trail Blazer*** shown from 12th September to 10th October. Set at the outbreak of the Franco-Indian War of 1754 this series recounted the story of the legendary Trailblazer Daniel Boone of the early American frontier who as a young man takes on the heroic task of crossing the wilderness to Kentucky to open up the territory for settlers and eventually to map and supply the essential safety for the move West.

Trailblazer was the first episode for the adventure series featuring the young Daniel Boone (Rick Moses), welcomed by some reviewers and clearly aimed at a young audience. Boone sets off to explore the forbidden Cumberland Gap, unaware that the French in the person of Monsieur Duvall want him dead, and thereby aiming to halt other settlers who might be eager to move into the territory. As Boone begins his journey, Langford (Jeremy), a smiling professional killer hired by the French and their Shawnee Indian allies, assumes the role of a painter and joins the companions on the trail waiting for the opportunity to kill him. The series aimed at authenticity by basing the plots on actual events and by filming in the Appalachian Mountains near to where Daniel grew up in east Tennessee. Jeremy had reservations when he heard that the producers wanted to make the wilderness the star. "*I knew that was doomed when they said they were going to sell it on the scenery.*" (Jeremy) On a personal level this performance would give Jeremy the opportunity to become a cowboy in the Wild West which had been a childhood dream, a result of all those hours in the cinema on Balsall Common.

Langford in Young Daniel Boone

The Medusa Touch 1978 - ITC Film

Edward Parrish in The Medusa Touch

Jeremy had appeared in films at different times in his career although the stage would continue to be his first choice as the necessary standing around waiting for his scenes was both tiring and for him, demanding. He would always fulfil his commitments with zest, but his role in this film was a minor one as he appears in just one scene and the waiting around would have been challenging. *The Medusa Touch* was a significant film, especially as the star Richard Burton was a favourite amongst movie goers and would draw the audience into the cinemas. This would be the first film of several over the next few years.

The Medusa Touch was released in 1978: filmed in the summer of 1977 with Pinewood Studios as the principal location and Bristol Cathedral for the final climactic scenes. Some of the movie posters used the title TELEKINESIS as the main attraction. In the starring role Richard Burton appeared as John Morlar, once a talented barrister and now a writer, but also a man with a powerful psychotic disorder. "I am the man with the power to create catastrophe." Morlar is shown inflicting death with a single glance upon any one who annoys him. He asks, "How can I will death?" but is forced to acknowledge his capacity for making accidents happen in the loss of a manned spacecraft on a moon mission and a Jumbo plane crash with 300 people on board; for killing his parents, his nurse, a master at school who had victimised him; a disagreeable judge and finally sought help from an analyst. It is to Doctor Zonfield that he identifies the "insane urge to kill."

As one of Morlar's victims, Jeremy had a minor role with around five minutes of screen time but he created a believable and striking character in his one scene. Playing **Edward Parrish,** a film star and Patricia Morlar's lover, he is willing to take her away to safety from her repressive and dangerous husband, *"How did she ever come to choose you?"* and *"You really are just as foul as she says..."* and in so doing, he brings about their almost immediate deaths in a road accident. The fact that the accident happens only in report and without the visual evidence underlines this as a shocking psychological thriller. For this reviewer, Jeremy's short scene was the "highlight". "In *The Medusa Touch* Jeremy Brett plays one of those roles he has essayed so often and so well over the years: a handsome, mocking, sardonic man of the world at whose well-shod feet attractive women tend to queue to tumble. In this particular case it's a 40-ish star actor named Edward Parrish who runs off with Patricia Morlar (Marie-Christine Barrault) the wife of writer John Morlar (Richard Burton). Since Morlar is possessed of an uncanny telekinetic power to cause death and disaster, whenever he fancies he not unnaturally wreaks his revenge upon his erring wife and her smoothie lover by thinking them into a fatal car crash. Brett appears in only one scene in the film with Burton and Miss Barrault, but it's one of the highlight sequences of the picture, with veiled - and not-so-veiled-insults being imperturbably batted from side to the other rather like a lethal ping-pong match. And, even up against the brilliance of Burton and the kittenish cruelty of Miss Barrault, Brett emerges memorably." (Collections at bfi.org.)

Jeremy and Marie-Christine Barrault

The Incredible Hulk 1978 - Universal Television for ITV

James Joslin in The Incredible Hulk

The Incredible Hulk, which premièred on 24th March 1978 was an unlikely guest appearance for Jeremy who still dreamed of restarting his career in Hollywood. *"They needed somebody to play a guy with a deep voice who was in cosmetics in Chicago. I put on my blazer and went along with 18 others to read. After the audition they said 'Welcome to the Colonies.' I had the part and was suddenly afloat in Hollywood. Because I was in Hollywood the people in England began inviting me back. I am very glad I made the move, although there were times it was touch and go."* (Woman and Home 1984) The fifth episode in the hugely popular series entitled *Of Guilt, Models and Murder,* opens with Dr David Banner (Bill Bixby) waking up from one of his transformations into the Incredible Hulk (Lou Ferrigno) with the body of a dead girl in the next room. Banner was a research scientist whose laboratory experiment with gamma radiation had gone wrong. It had changed his body chemistry and resulted in a metamorphosis into a seven feet tall, hugely muscular and powerful creature when he is under extreme stress. He learns that his monstrous alter-ego is being blamed for the murder of the model girlfriend of **James Joslin,** the cosmetics giant played by Jeremy. Although his memories of the event are fuzzy, he doesn't believe he could commit murder and with images of the fateful night playing across his mind, he begins his search for the truth. He takes a job as a valet under the pseudonym David Blaine in order to investigate Joslin whom he suspects was involved in the murder simply because when he was interviewed by the press his grief didn't ring true. "*He picked Terri up in his arms, squeezed her, crushed her.*" Did the Hulk cause it or was he responsible for her death? And who was the other girl he had seen at the window? "We get to see different accounts of the murder in flashback. But which one really happened?" (IMDb)

Incredible Hulk

Rebecca 1979 - BBC Television

Maxim de Winter in Rebecca

Back in England, **Maxim de Winter** in *Rebecca* (1979) was a dream part for Jeremy. Based on the novel by Daphne de Maurier, it was the role of the romantic, heroic actor for which his appearance and training had been waiting. Romeo and Edward Rochester in *Jane Eyre* had not come his way, or Heathcliff. However, the haunted and mysterious Maxim would fit him impeccably and the description in the novel would be given flesh; "His face was arresting, sensitive, medieval in some strange, inexplicable way and I was reminded of a portrait seen in a gallery. I had forgotten where of a certain Gentleman Unknown." (Rebecca) As the *New York Times* reviewer said, "Mr Brett is the matinee-idol type of actor who can make a thoroughly impossible character unexpectedly tolerable. He expertly maintains a layer of intriguing vulnerability just below the surface of Max's arrogance." Jeremy was also thrilled. *"It's very rare I've been able to get into the 20th century. When I turn from 1899 to 1900 I jump for joy. I did in* Rebecca *(1979), I got into the 30's then. I have done some modern stuff but I'm so thrilled I overact like crazy. I've got pockets! I'm so used to wearing tights all the time that when I put my hands in my pockets I nearly fall over. I'm so unused to playing a modern guy. It all started because I was a classical actor, I was trained that way. When I left Drama School, I wanted to do Shakespeare, I loved the words. I really fell in love with them. I loved the sound of them. So, most of my training was classical."*

Manderley

The unnamed naïve nineteen year old girl (Joanna David) of the novel is employed as a travelling companion, or "friend of the bosom", to a wealthy American who is touring Europe. On a stopover in Monte Carlo the recently widowed Maxim de Winter (Jeremy), who is staying at the same hotel is drawn into a relationship with the shy, awkward girl. Their courtship is swiftly advanced when Mrs Van Hopper (Elspeth March) changes her plans to return home so when Max offers marriage, the smitten child accepts. His ancestral home Manderley, located on the Cornish coast is haunted by the ghost of the stunningly beautiful Rebecca who had died in a tragic boating accident and her devoted housekeeper Mrs Danvers, played by Anna Massey, attempts to keep her memory alive. The truth will bring a major change to the lives of each one of the protagonists. But the destruction will last longer.

Jeremy told *Mystery!* that he thought Maxim was a self-centred, *"dark, sad, and angry character"* but he had developed a sympathy for him when his past life with the troubled Rebecca was finally revealed. And although he had initially protested about the moustache he was asked to wear for the production as it reminded him of Laurence Olivier in his 1940 performance, he finally relented. The fact that the Olivier film won a Best Picture Oscar also brought fears of comparison and when Jeremy had phoned to tell his mentor from the National Theatre of his plans to appear in the production he was told, "You might have waited until I was dead." *"He's a great friend of mine. Once I got over the fear and awe – that took about five years. He's a sweetheart – the feeling is all in my head... but he's been my idol for years, ever since I saw* Wuthering Heights." Jeremy had also been asked to be godfather to Larry and Joan's youngest daughter Julie-Kate.

The Washington Post thought it was excellent. "This version of *Rebecca* is handsome, haunting and beautifully paced to capture the subtle psychological suspense that builds slowly and inexorably in Du Maurier's novel... Within its framework of four one hour weekly episodes, it can explore the characters and flesh them out. The suspense builds more slowly, but just as relentlessly... once he has won her love, Maxim takes her back to Manderley... Jeremy Brett, cast in the Olivier role, plays Maxim closer to the novel. He has a darker side; he can be contemptuous and fall into cold rages. Olivier's interpretation was more brooding with a touch of Heathcliff. Of course, in 1940, the Hollywood code did not permit a hero to be a murderer. Joanna David is a brilliant choice for the role of the young woman who is to become the second mistress of Manderley only to find it haunted by the memory of Rebecca, the stunningly beautiful first wife... Mrs Danvers becomes a malevolent character with softened edges in the hands of Anna Massey..." (Jean White Washington Post 11th March 1980)

In this production Anna, Jeremy's first wife, appeared as Mrs Danvers. She said she had been intrigued by the part and decided she would really like to play the obsessive, cruel character, "Even though Jeremy was the lead, my desire to play the part was not weakened... (although) working with Jeremy was not easy." Their son David also appeared as an extra in the part of the young man who was nearly run down by Maxim's sister as she drove to see Gran in the retirement home. David's appearance resulted in a rare occurrence of marital discord when Jeremy bought a motor-bike for his son against Anna's wishes, something she felt very strongly about. "I was utterly furious... So I decided to ignore Jeremy and not speak to him, except in the most formal way." Later David injured himself in an accident, although it was not a serious one, and the bicycle was removed so the topic was not mentioned again and peace was restored. "In fact, when the show was first shown on television Jeremy wrote me a most complimentary letter about my performance, which I found very touching." (Telling

Some Tales) David gave his view of the spat, "At the time I took my father's side, but now my sympathies lie more with my mother. It was the first time they had fallen out openly, and the row pinpointed the fact they were, by nature, opposites." (The Guardian 14th November 2001)

On the second Mrs de Winter, Jeremy thought that she was "Max's whim:" *"We were very lucky in having Joanna David for the role. She's absolutely definitive. Plain? The book is very explicit…she starts out as a little tiny frightened schoolgirl with a damaged past. She's Max's whim. But her life changes. Very slowly Joanna's hair starts to curl. By the end of the film, Joanna's beautiful."*

It was filmed in a nineteenth century Gothic castle in South Cornwall with its setting of "a fabulous garden full of azaleas, camellias, magnolias and many hundred different sorts of rhododendron" the serial was rehearsed for ten days and produced in just three. Everyone involved reported how good it felt. Joanna said that it was "*very good*" and Jeremy as always was enthusiastic, *"I know it's good, but I don't know until I've seen it whether it's brilliant. You know how it is when everything clicks into place and the people are all wonderful. That's how it was. You just knew inside that things were going well."*

Dracula 1979 - San Francisco and Chicago

Dracula was a significant stage show that surpassed all box office records, and Jeremy became *The West Coast Dracula* which catapulted him into the media attention. *Applause Magazine* called 1978 The Year of the Bat: "A bloody bunch of matinee idol vampires have been winging it on stages in New York, London, Boston and Los Angeles."

Jeremy was offered the part of *Dracula* by two of the New York producers Elizabeth McCann and Nelle Nugent, but a delay was necessary as he was filming *Rebecca*. He saw a performance by Frank Langella in New York and replied, *"God! Yes please!"* and agreed to take the show to the West Coast when his commitment was fulfilled. They replied with a request for a week's rehearsal in order to practice the cape. He was surprised but was told that "the cape is a show in itself." As Dracula enters he removes his large luxurious velvet cape, "he swirls it, flutters it, flaps it like giant wings" he twists it "like a giant bat wing" with enormous dexterity so that it lands neatly into the arms of the maid. As the cape was weighted it was quite a feat. *"Well, when Frank did it he brought the house down; I remember the audience applauded for a full minute. The first night I did it, with the adrenalin pumping through my veins, the cloak went straight out of the door and flew like a bat into the night! I lost my cape; it went all over the maid. She was fighting for air under all the velvet. Sheer adrenalin!"* (Scarlet Street 1992 Number 8)

The American audience were terribly enthusiastic about his performance which filled him with characteristic enthusiasm, He was very happy to talk to the reviewers about what he was trying to achieve. He had caught the feline walk by walking on his toes, just as he did with Sherlock Holmes and due to his method of *"becoming,"* this would be another character which he would have to purposefully leave behind at the end of a day or it could have become dangerous for him. Although he was only on stage for around twenty minutes (he said it was 18 minutes) the costume and the props enabled him to become menacing for this performance. He had created a back-story for the character with his imagined response to a love affair and thus become a lonely, old *"man out of control."* Once more he was trying to create a sympathetic character from the traditional evil creature of the horror movies.

Dracula

Jeremy told Jeff Lyon for *Close-Up*, *"I thought I'd play it for the first time as if Count Dracula were in love. He says, 'I'll set my Lucy above all else.' My God, he's fallen in love. So I play this man who's gone out of control, who becomes terribly careless and makes mistakes because he's got this girl under his skin. He's 500 years old and he's a love-sick child. He's a very sad creature, actually... I think he's very lonely and very old. He's deeply corrupted sexually. Sex is obviously his main preoccupation. Also he's hooked on anything, and he's hooked on blood... All that roaring — I roar all through the show, you know — it's bad on the throat. The scene amazes me. Here a man in a black velvet cape comes in the window with a blast of mist blowing it, and he seduces a girl on the bed, and there isn't a laugh or a titter in the place. I think it affects women terribly. To be swept off their feet, to be possessed, is their wildest dream. Men get an enormous fizz from it too."*

Dracula

The critic was surprised to see he was just an ordinary guy dressed in a navy blue suit and not carrying any of the characteristics of the vampire within him, "The last I'd seen him he'd had blazing, magnetic eyes and razor-sharp fangs, and horrible sounds were bubbling from his throat. He was wrapped in a black cape, with a crimson lining and he was busying himself with peoples' necks. Now he looks harmless enough. The fangs were gone, the eyes were normal..." In spite of this Jeremy had admitted to biting the necks of several women over one evening when he was requested to do so and the morning before he had bitten the hostess on *A.M. Chicago*. Once more this Dracula was a charming, attractive creature. *"After all, he really doesn't do any harm. We're living in an age where people do much worse than sip a little blood. All he does is take the blood he needs to live, and meanwhile he gives the girl a great night of love-making. Her only problem in the morning is that she is a little pale and feels a bit weak... he is loving it and so are the audiences."* (American Statesman 26th November 1978) When he was asked what was the scariest thing about him, Jeremy emphasised the menacing effect by acting out the role, *"When I'm crossed, I rear back. I have a dominant nose... and I have enormous nostrils."* His magnificent voice was also used to create fear, *"I have a loud voice and I roar. I lowered my voice four notes for this role."* He explained the core of his interpretation. The three aspects to his Count Dracula lay in first, the count: then the vampire bat in Act II, and finally, the wolf he becomes in Act III. *"The count is a sort of a distressed schizophrenic count"* which tends to build some audience sympathy for Dracula. *"My count comes out to be pitied,"* he said. *"I'm not sure that's right. But he's been doing it – turning women into slave brides and men into jackals – for 500 years, and he's lonely. One person told me, "I was so happy to see him smile, to see him in peace at last at the end."*

One review thought that this Dracula needed even more bite, although it did recognise Jeremy's talents. "Brett comes at the role with his fine English training and a shadowy kind of sensual maturity. He is older than Langella, which makes his relationship to Lucy a more glamorous master domination. He can change concentration with a flicker or glower, sinking his iridescent eyes into their sockets." (Dracula needs more bite by Linda Winer) The personal cost of playing the part was significant; he developed *"Dracula's elbow"* from his swirling of the thirty pound cape and *"a sore throat from all that roaring."* And he also revealed that he had contacted a back injury in Stratford, Ontario the previous year whilst playing *A Midsummer Night's Dream* and *"probably shouldn't be doing this. It's a bit much for me,"* as lifting a body out of a casket was quite a strain.

Jeremy had finally achieved recognition in this performance and it would be linked with his appearance as Holmes. "*Dracula* may symbolise death to many, but to Jeremy Brett the old blood-guzzler, it means life. Brett is playing the title role in the smash play *Dracula* in its Los Angeles run. For the distinguished English actor, the engagement here means that his calculated risk in abandoning his London career is finally paying off." In his obituary notice *The Guardian* critic applauded his interpretation. "Jeremy Brett honed the manner of his later *Sherlock Holmes* – lush melodrama tinged with wicked, knowing humour – in a stateside theatrical tour of the Hamilton Deane/John Bladerston *Dracula* in the early 1980s. Within a lurid black and white setting with jagged slashes of red devised by macabrist Edward Gorey, Brett ripped and tore with abandon, reaching a delicious peak in the scene where he steals upon Van Helsing shaving. As Van Helsing staunches the flow from a careless cut Brett/Dracula's hand flies to his mouth. He wrenches his head aside, his hiss mingled with a moan of pleasure denied. If ever a vampire could have swooned from sheer camp, it was Brett's Dracula at that moment." (The Guardian 20th September 1995)

And there was comedy as the actress Helen Hayes got in on the act. She was the co-director of the Actor's Blood Drive in Hollywood and as a gimmick the person to be drawing the blood would be Dracula, aka Jeremy. Pictures of them both appeared in the press with Jeremy biting her neck whilst she laughed. Both Helen and Jeremy donated their blood for the cause. Another article recorded the lengths the producers were prepared to go for authenticity: the acquisition of soil from Transylvania. The stage coffins of Jeremy's Dracula, and also that of Raul Julia who played the role on Broadway, was to have a handful of dirt imported from the village of Snagov, Romania where Dracula, believed to be Vlad the Impaler, was finally laid to rest. The disappointment came when the parcel arrived opened by US Customs and empty.

Dracula

Hart to Hart: Death in the Slow Lane 1980 - Television

Mason Parks in Hart to Hart

His next appearance would give him another opportunity to perfect the role of "baddie", in this case a dangerous Russian spy. As **Mason Parks** in Season One Episode Five of **Hart to Hart** titled **Death in the Slow Lane**, his suave appearance and cultured British accent were used to great advantage, especially in the Bond Street showroom where the murder of the salesman takes place.

Mason Parks would be a formidable and charming opponent in this episode. But who he was and why he was there is not explained until much later. Jonathan wanted the vintage car for Jennifer's birthday present but he would have to pay an outrageous $80,000 because Parks was just as determined to buy it for his companion Andra Akers. Having lost the auction, they would pursue Jonathan home to America and attempt to persuade them to sell the car for profit and even try to steal it in the most imaginative ways before the F.B.I. finally trap them. Espionage is the final reveal with the discovery of the car's bugging capacity which has been added in a recent trip to Moscow, however, Jonathan and Jennifer are once more victorious in their fight against wrong doing.

The series was a spoof detective show with Robert Wagner and Stefanie Powers appearing as the wealthy amateur sleuths dealing with murder, smuggling, theft and international espionage and the tone was always one of humour as they dabbled in the scariest situations. Jeremy became firm and lasting friends with Robert and Stefanie during the making of this series and he would work again with Stefanie in *Deceptions* in 1985.

Jeremy

One interviewer introduced Jeremy as "one of the London stage's most important actors" and judged his decision to leave Britain for the USA in 1976 a radical one. Jeremy admitted the difficulties he had experienced finding work over that period but highlighted the need for challenge in his personal life. *"I was too settled in London and too content and going to too many cocktail parties. The move upset my family and friends in England and I had to start from scratch here. It hasn't been easy."* By 1984 the benefits of the move were made clear in another interview. He had purchased a very nice home in the California Hills and was enjoying his role as "*a resident alien.*" He told the interviewer on *Desert Island Discs* that he and Joan '*had a garden to build. We were too late for children so we were planning this glorious garden. I wanted L.A. for the climate because I wanted sprinklers. She wanted an older garden, Wisconsin, Warwickshire...*"

This period of his career had been highly productive and he had accomplished some of his most memorable roles for both stage and screen in Dracula, Macbeth and Prospero. In spite of his success he was still humble about his achievements. *"I feel blessed to be working, whatever the part, America has taught that to me. One's career is only there by the grace of God and this carpet! I love to work. Being allowed constantly to play charades and be paid for doing what one adores is unbelievable. It's also an escape. It's easy to become a workaholic because when you're working there's a clear focus. Life is much more complicated, but then it's such an honour to be working when only four per cent of actors in Britain are employed."* "Jeremy radiates a sudden and disarming smile. It seems incredible, looking at this handsome face with its sharply defined features and blue grey (green grey) eyes, to think that Jeremy Brett's career has spanned 30 years. But at the age of 48, it is more than apparent why he has won so many heart-throb – if classic – roles in the theatre, film and television. He rarely gives interviews but it's clear he savours acting back on British soil, having been away in the United States for eight years. Another great joy is that he's brought his American wife of five years back to this country to share his glory. *"I'm so happy now I think I've become a bit of a hazard! I'm simply over the top at having found great, unexpected happiness.'* he enthused." (Woman and Home 1984)

It is true that his move to America had brought a temporary interruption to his secure career path and in order to make a name in a new country he had turned up for some unlikely screen tests. *"It was a salutary experience at first because I had to re-establish myself. But gradually I did a few guest spots on television and played* Dracula *on tour. That was my breakthrough."*

The Crucifer of Blood 1980 – Ahmanson Theatre in Los Angeles Music Centre

Doctor Watson in The Crucifer of Blood

Jeremy needed to work and this need was thankfully fulfilled. He would earn the title of an international star of stage and television in the coming decade. But first he was to take on the role of **Doctor Watson** to provide a much needed preparation for his signature role of the great detective in a stage production of *The Crucifer of Blood* starring Charlton Heston as Sherlock Holmes. The play was loosely based on Conan Doyle's story *The Sign of Four* and appeared at the Ahmanson Theatre in the Los Angeles Music Center from December 1980 to January 1981.

In 1984 the *TV Times* reported his thoughts on playing the role of Watson and how it helped him prepare for the Granada *Sherlock Holmes* series three years later. As always his comments on playing Watson like "*Winnie the Pooh*" or "*Snoopy*" were an attempt at humour as he was consistently noted for his "perfectionist" approach to each new role. His Sherlock was "all saturnine glances, cold command and noble cunning... a natural vehicle for Brett's drawn and enigmatic glamour than the good foursquare doctor was" but Jeremy went on to say how happy he was to have played Watson, *"It was tremendous fun, and it taught me a lot about how to approach Holmes when the series got under way. I learned about the interrelationship of the two men. If you look at it from Watson's side, Holmes emerges as about the loneliest man in literature."* And he pointed out that, *"he needs Watson much more than Watson needs him. But being British, he can't show it. The whole thing is Watson's caring for a man who has no way of reaching out, a man totally incapable of saying 'thank you for your help.'"* (Alex Coleman TV Times 19th May 1984)

In this play Dr Watson was attracted by the charms of a lady in distress, a femme fatale, played by Suzanne Lederer and the villainess of the piece. In the original story *The Sign of Four* Mary Morstan was a tragic heroine, whose father had disappeared ten years before and thereafter she had received a regular gift of a rare and precious pearl from an unknown donor. The heroine Mary Morstan has become Irene St Claire and she is not the innocent victim but "a murderous Jezebel (who) has employed Holmes and Watson for the sole purpose of leading her to the treasure, which she plans to then seize for herself." (Alan Barnes Sherlock On Screen)

One reviewer of the film of the production noted that it was "excessively theatrical and static" and that its shortcomings lay in "the fact that it simply has not been opened out from its stage origins." Jeremy was not given an opportunity to develop his interpretation of character in his usual manner and maybe it was this experience which convinced him of the need to develop the bond between Holmes, Watson and Mrs Hudson which he achieved with David Burke and Rosalie Williams for the Granada series earning such praise. Another critic called Jeremy "a rather junior Watson," and his appearance; tall, attractive, elegantly moustached and active, did not fit the expectations of the role. *"Early in the rehearsals for the play, there was a marvellous moment when Heston, who is ten years my senior, became conscious of the visible age gap between his Holmes and Watson. He asked me, 'Are you too young or am I too old for the part?'"* In spite of his concerns, Charlton Heston called Jeremy, "a superb Watson to my Holmes. Watson has a unique function in that play; he falls in love with the woman who turns out to be the villain. Jeremy handled all this with wit, and exquisite taste. Later on, of course, he had a triumph as the Great Detective in the Granada series in which he starred so memorably..." (Charlton Heston in Scarlet Street 1996)

In the interview with Terry Wogan on BBC television, Jeremy pointed out how much easier it was to play the kind and enthusiastic Watson than *"the cool, dismissive, internal creature"* of Holmes. He went further in another interview: *"Watson is much more my kind of person… Watson is a warm, loving, sunny person who's very enthusiastic… and hurt and slightly upset when his friend is rude to people or him. This is much more like me. Playing Watson was tremendous fun, and it taught me a great deal about the inter-relation between the two men."* And to another: *"I was fortunate being the son of a soldier, I have some military blood in my veins, I suppose. I played him with enormous enthusiasm and devotion to Holmes. With enormous respect although I got quite angry and upset – very upset – when Holmes abused himself. I would kill for him. That's how I played Watson."* (www.zombostloset.com)

The Crucifer of Blood

Battlestar Galactica 1980 - ITC Television

Xavier in Battlestar Galactica

Battlestar Galactica was an American science fiction series produced in 1978 by Glen Larson and starred Lorne Greene, Richard Hatch and Dirk Benedict. It lasted just one season of twenty four episodes and the new series would take up where it left off. The first three episodes of the original *Battlestar Galactica*, with some differences, became the film version, released in 1979 and received an enthusiastic welcome in cinemas. It told the story of the human race involved in a thousand year war with the robotic Cylons. A false armistice allowed the Cylons to launch a surprise attack almost wiping out the twelve colonies of humanity. Only the Galactica survived, led by Commander Adama and, accompanied by a number of civilian ships, they travel across the galaxy in search of earth. However, the Cylons follow them determined to destroy every last human being.

In *Spaceball* Galactica's children are sent to integrate with the children of Earth both for their safety and for teaching purposes; they join a baseball camp for underprivileged children in the care of Jamie Hamilton. The differences of gravity and physiology mean the children display superhuman powers and find it increasingly difficult to remain incognito: their expertise with a television camera drawing unwanted attention from the experts. Their extraordinary skills at baseball are more difficult to explain and they are persuaded to lose the game but that is changed when their safety is at risk.

As the rebel **Xavier**, in the epidermal transformation of Lt. Nash, Jeremy is in pursuit of Jamie and the children firmly believing he has successfully dispensed with Troy and Dillon. Their false mission at the beginning of the episode was his attempt to murder them by the sabotage of their spacecraft and luckily it had failed. He also fails to capture the children due to Jamie's quick thinking and Xavier escapes to fight another day. Jeremy had adopted an accent reminiscent of Eastern European with a little sneer which helped him take on the cloak of the baddie. But there was very little else which required investment and appearing in just one episode meant he was unable to develop Xavier further.

On Approval 1980 – BBC One Play of the Month

George Duke of Bristol in On Approval

Jeremy moved between drama and comedy with ease at this time. He said in interview that he would have liked to play more comedy and admired the work of Frankie Howard and Tommy Cooper. His performance in **On Approval** by Frederick Lonsdale is one of his best in which he played **George the 12th Duke of Bristol**, with his great friend Penelope Keith in the role of Maria Wislack. He said how much he enjoyed making people laugh as the impossible, arrogant George and added the secret was to give a secret smile to the situation and to "*bubble on it,*" and that ability to bubble makes the words a constant smile. The play directed by David Giles was first shown on 27th December 1980 and repeated on 21st June 1982 on BBC television as part of the *Play of the Month* series.

The story is an improbable one but also highly entertaining. A spoilt wealthy widow Maria Wislack played by Penelope Keith has finally challenged her long term friend and would-be husband, Richard (Benjamin Whitrow) to tell her he loves her. To his enormous surprise and delight, she agrees to take him away to her country house in Scotland for one month, "*on approval,*" and if he proves to be as amenable as she thinks he is, she will marry him. Maria's friend Helen, the daughter of a wealthy pickle bottler (Lindsay Duncan) who is hopelessly in love with George, the penniless 12th Duke of Bristol, agrees to come too. The two relationships are tested in the isolation of a Scottish retreat and both are found wanting.

Initially, Helen declares herself "the happiest woman in the world" but as the constant needling between George and Maria threatens to break into violence doubts begin to surface, eventually leading to disappointment as she discovers how impossible he would be as a lifetime partner. Consequently, when George discovers his love for Helen and offers her marriage, her refusal is totally unexpected. The wit can't fail to amuse as George is called "*a brute*" and "*a congenital idiot*" and Richard "*a vulgar little man*" whilst Helen and Richard behave impeccably, attempting to satisfy their partners' every whim. The two of them leave in the hope that a snowstorm could provide the people they love the chance to mend their ways.

"I shall watch tonight's brand new production of Frederick Lonsdale's comedy *On Approval* (BBC1) because (a) it stars Penelope Keith who can never be serious for long and because (b) it also stars Jeremy Brett who has been serious for too long (Maximilian De Winter in *Rebecca*, etc.) and I want to see how he looks when the sun breaks through and the ice cracks. The other reason I shall watch it is that this is a very entertaining play indeed." (The Times 27th December 1980) The *New York Times* thought Jeremy was "a tad too long in the tooth for the part of the Duke, who is supposed to be a 'hideous child', but he brings a flair and an assurance to the role that are eventually disarming."

The Secret of Seagull Island 1981 - RAI/ITC Television

David Malcolm in Secret of Seagull Island

The Secret of Seagull Island appears to be a break from the anti-hero as Jeremy is first seen in swimming trunks in a spa at a luxury hotel. The next moment he is dressed in a white suit which would seem to reinforce the assessment of a good guy, especially as **David Malcolm** is kind, considerate and compassionate to the "blind" Barbara. *"Mysterious"* is the word used by several critics but this production is difficult to place. The conclusion would bring a disturbing revelation and Jeremy surprises us all in the final scenes of this thriller. His role as the mysterious David Malcolm, an archaeologist and anthropologist whose wife and son were both drowned in a tragic accident may, or may not be part of the sinister plot to keep Barbara Carey and her blind sister Mary Ann apart. His role was "perhaps the toughest and the most demanding in the film." Jeremy said it was the first time he had played a father and *"the thought just terrified me."* (Press release for Seagull Island)

Originally entitled, *L'Isola del Gabbiano, Seagull Island* was filmed entirely on location in Italy in 1978 (shown August 1981) as a joint English/Italian production in five parts scheduled for transmission on Italian television. The disappearance of Barbara's sister Mary Ann in Italy where she has been studying music brings the fear she may have been murdered by a maniac obsessed with young sightless women. Under cover of blindness Barbara's attempts to find the killer leads her to David Malcolm the owner of the isolated and mysterious Seagull Island. But what happened to David's wife and son on the island? And why is David's cousin Carol (Pamela Salem) so unhappy to see her? The solution to the mystery in the final scenes is full of shock value and high drama.

Peter Davalle in *The Times* said it was highly recommended; "No point in beating about the bush: this is an altogether superior thriller serial, expensively staged, heavy with menace and almost as suspenseful as a good Hitchcock. We have now reached the final episode. Last week's final shot must have had many viewers starting out of their armchairs as someone leapt out of the Italian shadows and had the sister-hunting Barbara Carey (Prunella Ransome) by the neck. Whence comes the ghostly piano music? Is the smooth David Malcolm (Jeremy Brett) on the side of the angels or the saints – or of the seagulls? Why is the British consul (Nicky Henson) dithering about when he ought to be on the island saving Miss Ransome? And why have you not been watching the serial for the past three weeks?" (Peter Davalle Television. The Times 7th August 1981)

Clive James was just as complimentary. "The Mediterranean mystery series is usually a bad format, but *Seagull Island* has proved an exception, the production values being well above the customary... it is a pleasant surprise to find Jeremy Brett filling most of the close-ups and speaking English with his lips as well as with his voice... Everyone on the island is a head-case except Barbara who pretends to be blind in order to find her missing sister. Jeremy is not fooled but pretends to be. He turns a blind eye..." (Clive James in The Observer 16th August 1981) "Jeremy Brett as the mysterious, respectable Englishman owner of Seagull Island is fantastic, as usual, and does not fail to impress. His acting is very impressive and exciting. His skill, in part, keeps you guessing until the very end – a very exciting end. I must say... he makes for a nice piece of eye-candy for the ladies, as usual." (IMDb review)

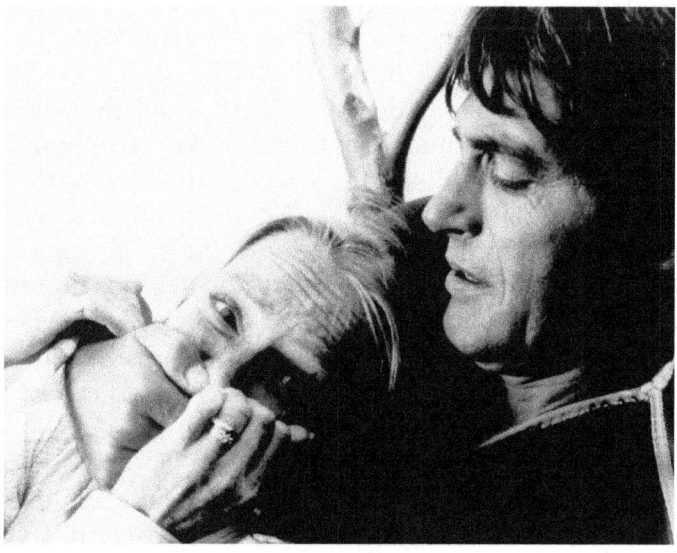

Secret of Seagull Island

Madame X 1981 - Film

Dr. Terrence Keith in Madame X

Jeremy needed to be busy and needed the challenge of a new role to fill his time. Anna has spoken about his inability to be still; to sit and read a novel, or just to be at leisure amongst nature. Working was a necessity for his peace of mind and in fact he said on one occasion that he thought he was at his best doing too many things. In this brief episode he was given the opportunity to get into the twentieth century and explore the modern world.

Jeremy's guest appearance as **Dr. Terrence Keith** in a made for television film ***Madame X*** lasted around five minutes of screentime. It was released on 16th March 1981. In spite of the lack of opportunity to develop his character in relationships with others, he makes an impression, as he has created the Irish cardiologist with conviction. Here he is a hero who saves the life of Holly, the tragic heroine. He is looking for romance but is fated to be disappointed as she is at the centre of a personal and traumatic nightmare and she will simply disappear, leaving him bewildered and lost. One feels that he is in many ways playing himself in the bright, eager, caring individual who can inspire others. He was very proud of his mother's origins as an Irish Quaker and his singing of the Irish verse *"Molly Malone"* feels totally natural and impromptu.

"The nice Danish doctor protector of the 1965 entry becomes a nice Irish ditto, played by Jeremy Brett with the hectoring raillery that would soon fit him to be Sherlock Holmes." (IMDb)

Macbeth 1981 – Film for television

Macbeth

After his brief appearance as a modern Irish doctor, Jeremy returned to his Shakespearean roots with **Macbeth** which was released on DVD in 1981 under *Quantum Leap Productions* with the front cover featuring the soliloquy from Act 5 scene 5: "*Out, out brief candle!*" It was to be an authentic reading of the text with minimum background and especially presented for the student market. Jeremy plays the title character, the loyal Brave Macbeth, who becomes the bewitched Scottish nobleman prepared to murder the King in order to fulfil his ambitions, with Piper Laurie as his equally ambitious wife Lady Macbeth. Simon MacCorkindale plays Macduff.

The relationship between Macbeth and his wife is given prominence particularly in the early scenes where Jeremy and Piper Laurie bring their closeness into focus. His return home from the battlefield to Dunsinane is greeted with passionate abandon, although the strange breathy delivery of Lady Macbeth's lines has been commented on as a distraction. The prospective visit of Duncan to Dunsinane Castle to honour Macbeth for his courageous exploits in Scotland's victory against the Norwegians offers them the opportunity to plan his murder and seize the crown. Unable to hold his moral ground, Macbeth is spurred on by his wife and Jeremy adopts a dangerous quality in his rejection of her as he pursues the murderous path to his downfall. Overall there is an intensity and a suggestion of menace in this performance that mirrors Macbeth's decline from "brave Macbeth" to the "dead butcher" of the final act.

One *IMDb* review commented, "Jeremy Brett gives a great, eccentric performance in this presentation of Shakespeare's classic play. The locations are all on stage, so the sets are not fancy. Still, the acting more than makes up for it and the action scenes are well done, as well. Any fan of the play cannot go wrong with this performance." (IMDb)

Jeremy had played the role of Malcolm several times, including a filmed version for Hallmark in 1960, but this was his first appearance as Macbeth, He said he found Sherlock Holmes much more challenging than either Hamlet or Macbeth. He did, however, show the actor's lore of the theatre where the name of the play must never be mentioned without paying a penalty. "Mr Brett was an animated and quirky interview subject. An actorly superstition holds that it is bad luck to speak of Shakespeare's *Macbeth* in a theatre. Over the course of two evenings Mr Brett took great delight in trying to coax the offending title out of me: '*That was the year,*' he would say, his voice falling to a dark whisper, '*that I toured with... the Scottish play...*' I had spent enough time around theatre people to know if I rose to the bait – '*You mean Macbeth?*' – tradition would require me to run into the hall, turn three times and spit on the floor in order to ward off bad luck. I kept my mouth shut. Later, when I spotted a friend of Mr. Brett's spitting mightily into a fire bucket, I knew the actor had sprung his trap. His laughter echoed through the wings, followed by the peculiar sight of Sherlock Holmes giving Dr Watson a high-five." (Daniel Stashower in The Armchair Detective)

The Good Soldier 1981 - Granada Television

Edward Ashburnham and Leonora in The Good Soldier

Jeremy's appearance as **Edward Ashburnham** in ***The Good Soldier*** on 15th April 1981 for Granada Television is one of his most moving and career defining performances. Teddy may have been impeccably turned out, a dashing and sentimental man, the epitome of "the good soldier", but in reality he is a flagrant philanderer who couldn't help falling in love with a pretty woman. His reputation and financial security has been saved only by the interventions of Leonora, his controlling wife. Tragically, her passionate desire for vengeance will destroy them both.

John Dowell in the role of narrator presents "the saddest story I have ever heard," with an introduction to the gallant Edward Ashburnham and his perfect wife, the elegant and capable Leonora at the centre of two genteel couples who meet annually in the German spa town of Bad Nauheim, a resort favoured by those with heart conditions. The wealthy Americans are filled with admiration for the Ashburnhams, sharing their daily pursuits as in a minuet, but John Dowell will learn that his wife Florence has been conducting an affair with Edward after her death. Edward's life has been notorious for his adulterous and costly affairs but perhaps the most shocking revelation that he shares with John is his love for his wife's ward and his torment at the decision to leave her alone. "At first glance, the two families seem the picture of Edwardian respectability, but as the tale gradually unfolds through flashbacks, the appearances give way to a reality filled with deceit and betrayal, suicide and madness."

In a telephone interview with the *New York Times* Jeremy concluded that, *"Ashburnham is not merely a simple villain or an insensitive cad... he is a basically decent man trapped between societal pressures to be a good soldier – that is, loyal to the woman he married for the wrong reasons – and his own emotional and sexual need. He lives in total agony. He is a man of immense control, with a seething passion hidden behind the veneer, the facade, of proper Edwardian behavio(u)r. He's a pressure cooker with the lid very, very gently being lifted off. You can't blame him, really, for being such a lecherous creature. I feel sorry for him."* (NY Times 9th January 1983)

"Although it is essentially a sad story – the 'soldier' of the title seems at first to be the villain, then turns out to be the victim – Jeremy Brett's performance is such that this scarcely matters, one is more struck by the quality of his portrayal, which far surpasses the undeniable excellence of the other characters. Brett is able, with a minimum of words, and slightest of gesture or fleeting expression, to reveal an entire sea of this character's suffering." (Amazon.com)

BFI's *Sight and Sound* magazine also approved, "This is the saddest story I have ever heard – and so it is... so it was not only a pleasure to see Miss Fleetwood in action, she was also a pleasure to look at striding about in her splendid low-cut dresses. She was the only one who got to run and to shout, and she was impressive. She had the best role, or she made it the best. She and Jeremy Brett were like a god and a goddess painted by Sargent. The two Americans seemed like dwarfs in comparison, and that was right too somehow, though it goes against the stereotype. Jeremy Brett's cracked-mask playing of Captain Ashburnham, in his dressed-for-dinner aspect, merely served to make more plausible the side of the character we scarcely glimpse and which is left by Billington to the imagination: the male animal side with its shaming lusts. He's completely pathetic when he croaks out that he's *'dying for love'* for his ward Nancy, as if that justifies all the horrors it will bring in its train..." (James Ivory in Sight and Sound 1980)

"Beneath the starched decorum, a seething mass of metaphors ensues. The acting of Brett is brilliant, as is that of Fleetwood as the put upon wife who hates him with a passion." (Amazon.co.uk) Granada Television put forward *The Good Soldier* in the drama category for the 1981 International Emmy Awards. Michael Cox, the producer of Granada's *Sherlock Holmes*, cited the performance of Edward Ashburnham as one of those which convinced him that Jeremy would be an ideal choice for the role of Holmes.

The Good Soldier

Noel 1981 – Goodspeed Opera House Connecticut

Jeremy as Noel

Jeremy knew Noel Coward well and would appear to be a suitable choice to play him in a tribute evening. He had first earned a pleasing comment from Noel on his performance as Ron in *Variation on a Theme* and he and his friend Robert Stephens had starred in several of Noel's plays, Jeremy followed on from Robert in the role of Otto in *Design for Living* and Robert and Maggie had played in *Hay Fever, Present Laughter* and in *Private Lives*. The production **Noel** was adapted from an earlier revue called *Cowardy Custard*, directed by Ed Sherrin, which was staged at the Goodspeed Opera House in Connecticut from 8th April to

13th June 1981. It was a glossy revue with silver and black striped panels and Jeremy appeared in the role of Noel, dressed in formal white tie and tails but was listed in the programme as Jeremy.

Jeremy adopted the urbane Coward stance of detached amusement and wandered in and out of performances of the songs and extracts from his plays dressed in evening dress never in the character of Noel, but delivering the writer's witticisms. "His genius lay in the interpretation of an era for a sophisticated audience. And how welcome were his words of acerbic and witty, yet always humane diagnosis of national and class characteristics were." (Noel The Hour 27th May 1981) Accompanied by Millicent Martin playing Coward's close friend Gertrude Lawrence, they hosted an evening of reminiscences which was entertaining and never boring. Coward's most memorable songs were also remembered *Mad Dogs and Englishmen, I'll See You Again, Mad About the Boy*, and *Don't Put Your Daughter on the Stage, Mrs Worthington* so it was a light-hearted entertaining programme. The only omission was Coward's contribution to the war as a spy and his film *In Which We Serve*.

The critics liked the evening and gave praise to both Noel and Jeremy. "Jeremy Brett stars as Coward in this autobiographical work, and he is suitably dapper and wry. As a song-and-dance man, Brett dances well." (The Day, New London, Conn. 22nd April 1981) "But *Noel* itself works, largely thanks to Jeremy Brett and Millicent Martin and the pacing of Ned Sherrin. It isn't a deep evening or an emotionally moving one. It is strictly an evening of amusement by one of the 20th Century's great talent to amuse." (New York Times)

"Brett excels in the frequent monologues. Tall, lean and elegantly tuxedoed, he stands alone, at centre stage, commenting on the incongruous lunacy of his life. Wryly, he embodies Coward as he asserts a belief that a public figure may commit any act save that of boring the multitudes." And yet another reviewer applauded his "excellent Noel Coward." "To its credit, Goodspeed's *Noel* boasts a capable cast, Jeremy Brett, as Coward is appropriately sleek and brittle as Coward. With eyebrow arched, Brett adds spoken whiffs of the playwright's cynical wit between the snatches of his music. Brett's sighing solo rendition of Coward's *World Weary* may be the most compelling moment in the show." (Westport News 6th May 1981)

Jeremy had appeared in another Noel Coward tribute show **A Talent to Amuse** at the Phoenix Theatre in 1969, where an invited audience had enjoyed a performance of around four hours at a midnight matinee with one hundred and twenty actors, singers and musicians, friends and colleagues gathered to celebrate Noel's seventieth birthday. The programme was made up of songs, sketches, monologues and extracts from his life in the order of their happening.

Patricia Hodge said that she and Jeremy had plans for a show together about Coward, "He was also, as it happens, the most enchanting man in real life and, for a short while, we romanced about playing a show together that I had already done, about the life of Noel Coward and Gertrude Lawrence, in New York, where a producer very much wanted to put the two of us. Sadly, Jeremy's illness got in the way and it was never to be, but it was very exciting to do the initial work on it with him, and I am sure he would have been as brilliant at playing the Master as he was at Sherlock Holmes." (Patricia Hodge in Scarlet Street)

The Tempest 1982 – Toronto Workshop

Prospero

"I went to Canada and I did a production of The Tempest, *in 1982. I produced it, directed it, and played Prospero. I hobbled away afterwards. I was exhausted... I played him without a beard, and angry, and nutbrown. After all, he is a Bermudian, and it's quite hot in Bermuda. And I had a Miranda and my two sides of Prospero's spirit, Ariel and Caliban, are played by the same actor. And I like to do that."* (1991 Interview)

This is one Shakespeare play for which Jeremy received discouraging reviews from the critics. The Canadian audience once more showed that they preferred the traditional approach to Shakespeare and Jeremy's image of the vengeful magician Prospero was innovative and therefore disappointing, even disastrous in the eyes of some. "***The Tempest*** is to have a setting by its director and star, the British actor Jeremy Brett (whom we saw doubling Theseus and Oberon at Stratford a few seasons back). Sharon Purdy does the costumes to match Brett's vision and revision of Shakespeare's masque for five speakers. Toronto will see it May 14th at *Toronto Workshop Productions*, before Brett takes it on to launch a new theatre in the Bahamas, and later film it there... Here Brett plays **Prospero** – '*Why should he always be old?*' – with two young Canadians, Peggy Coffey and Geraint-Wyn Davies, as his Miranda and Ferdinand, and the Barbadian actor, Iain Deane doing the remarkable double of Ariel and Caliban."

One reviewer was not at all kind. "Taking anything larger than a paring knife to a Shakespeare play is a barbaric procedure, as Jeremy Brett's vanity production of *The Tempest*... has proved itself empty of magic... in order to realize a 'personal vision' of it... It is perhaps not surprising then that his vision appears little more than an emphasis on Prospero's demented (or so it appears in his performance) craving for revenge at the expense of the object of that revenge – namely, the nobles of Naples and Milan whom he has shipwrecked on his island... Brett presents a Prospero he doubtless hopes will be seen as a severe, stormswept warlock of ambiguous moral quality, something like Merlin as seen by C. S. Lewis. There is some support in the play for this. Prospero certainly treats Caliban, the rightful owner of the island, with hideous contempt, plays games with Ariel's freedom and makes zealous Ferdinand lug great lumps of firewood from place to place. But there is a wistful side to Prospero, the observer of midnight mushrooms and the enchantment of magic that has soothed a lengthy, impotent sojourn while awaiting revenge. And there is the whole matter of his abjuring of magic. The sense of real and imaginative worlds in tension with each other requires a subtler performance than the bombastic, wild-eyed Prospero that Brett presents us..." (Ray Conologue in Globe and Mail (Toronto) 17th May 1982)

The double responsibility of carrying the performance and the production eventually took its toll. "*When you're in charge of the kaleidoscope at the centre of it, it's a bit hard, as you can imagine, to keep a just view of it all... I remember when I was doing The Tempest in school, I hated it. Then I played Prospero and found that all I had learned was actually very useful. Television is its own enemy. It's a monster. It keeps people away from books.*" (Jeremy in The Armchair Detective 1992)

Jeremy had ambitions to make a film of *The Tempest* and if he had been successful, he would probably not have accepted the role of Sherlock Holmes and when he met with Michael Cox and the representatives of the Granada production team in Manchester this point was clearly made. He still had ambitions to follow the "company theatre" model that Olivier had set up at the National and the Bahamas would be an ideal location for such a project especially as it would have fitted into his world at that time. Joan was still committed to her role at *Mystery!* at *PBS* and Jeremy was receiving work on both sides of the Atlantic so as committed workaholics they were both highly productive but not always together.

The Last Visitor 1982 - BBC Television

Vincent Tumulty im The Last Visitor

Jeremy had returned from Hollywood to take the central role in the chilling play **The Last Visitor** which was transmitted on 14th September on BBC2 an adaptation of the novel *Sleeping Beauty* by Elizabeth Taylor. It is set in the seaside town of Seething in the late summer of 1953 with only a few visitors remaining, amongst them is **Vincent Tumulty** played by Jeremy. After his departure from the scene, things will never be quite the same again. The introduction to the novel describes it as a small, exotic, disturbing garden and

Vincent is a quiet, sensible man, yet repressed and at first a "rather creepy figure who derives pleasure from comforting the recently bereaved."

An interview with Jeremy at this time reveals much more about the production which seems to be lost. Vincent in *The Last Visitor* is an insignificant man. He is the hero, a victim and more than just a handsome face. He explained the attraction of playing this complex character; *"When I read the book, I couldn't imagine why I'd been asked to play the part. Then I realised what a Graham Greene kind of character he was, the complexity of the man, the conundrum... I imagined. Vincent is a very thin man with greying hair, a slight stutter under his voice. He has perfect manners, he's an edifice of respectability, then you realise behind him there's a shadow. That's when the creeps start...* The Last Visitor *is set in an out-of-season seaside resort in 1953. The filming was done in Minehead. Five women are caught up, lonely, desolate, in the life of a 'desirable' – a man. I hadn't realised until I read the book just how far away 1953 was, the way women were isolated then, unable to move without a man for an escort."* The women involved include an over-protective mother, a friend who had recently suffered bereavement a beautiful stranger, her sister, and a backward, unstable 14 year old, eventually make him pay a huge price. The ending of Elizabeth Taylor's novel has been changed. *"It is one of emotional violence, absolutely right, but horrendous."*

Jeremy found the part of Vincent one of the most satisfying he had done. *"It was more complex than anything I've had to do before. He's a man who's perfectly controlled but screaming inside. I couldn't do very dramatic things, the part had to grow almost imperceptibly, but I felt I was in the safest hands. Alan Shallcross, the producer, and Rodney Bennett, the director, took the most immaculate care; and the work of Elmer Cossey, the lighting cameraman, is beyond praise. The whole atmosphere, the detail, the period feel, was there. It's something the BBC always gets right; the Americans take it as their standard. I just had to keep bringing my performance down. It was a mass of restraint. What emerged was someone I, as an actor looking at myself, personally didn't know."*

Jeremy had stayed in the apartment of his friend Philip Kingsley and his wife as was customary. At this time he had been crossing and re-crossing the Atlantic at regular intervals to take such important roles as the *"crazed Egyptologist"* David Malcolm in *Seagull Island*, *"the elegant tortured"* Maxim de Winter in *Rebecca* and he was to begin filming shortly as Robert Browning in *The Barretts of Wimpole Street* again for the BBC. He went on to explain why he thought he was so busy; *"My feeling is that if you move on, go abroad, you get away from being an old boot, someone predictable, expected, I like to think I pop up everywhere like a jack-in-the-box. I think I got the part of Max de Winter because I wasn't here, it gave me a kind of lustre."* His preference for moving on and not settling down is also commented on. He was described as *"charming, kind"* and *"quick to praise others"* and Jeremy concluded the interview with, *"I obey the rules of any establishment,"* he says, *"as long as I don't have to belong to it all the time."* (Interview with Ellen Totten in Faced with Success Radio Times 1982 Printed with permission)

The Barretts of Wimpole Street 1982 – BBC Play of the Month

Robert Browning in The Barretts of Wimpole Street

A return to the romantic leading man was the next role with its classic clothes and love interest, similar to so many of those he had played earlier in his career. Jeremy told one interviewer that he preferred to play *"romantic extroverts with long, flowing hair and passion in their souls."* And the casting directors of the television departments clearly agreed. The constant demand for classical love stories resulted in the huge popularity of this particular genre in all areas of the media which encouraged other writers to join in the feast. In **The Barretts of Wimpole Street** in the BBC Play of the Month 30th December 1982, Jeremy was to play **Robert Browning**, the charismatic poet who inspired the invalid Elizabeth Barrett to rise from her bed and elope with him. He was very comfortable in the role as he had appeared in a presentation of the play on BBC4 Radio on 28th October 1972. with Dorothy Tutin in the role of Elizabeth. He had also sung in the musical version *Robert and Elizabeth* both in England and United States.

"Mr Barrett's objection to Robert Browning is not that of a poet but that he's about to steal the girl they both love... TV can cope very well with mental and physical frustration which is what the play is really about, because the cameras can get in very close. You can see what's going on behind the eyes and behind the lines, and although it does remain in one sense a Victorian melodrama, it also becomes a very modern play about sexual suppression and psychological truth." (Radio Times) Jeremy explained how the use of the camera would contribute to his performance. *"My passion now is film. Of course I love the theatre but film is new. I've always squeezed into films sideways because I'm a stage actor. Film and television seem to have bridged the gap. Filming is magic and I find it thrilling to have as many as 15 people working to the same end to get the moment absolutely right on film. It's a true communion."* (Woman and Home 1984)

Number Ten: Bloodline 1983 - ITV Television

William Pitt the Younger in Bloodline

Number 10 with its historical look at the home of political power was one series where its content, its cast list and its authenticity of detail could have been screened on the BBC. Some of the best acting talent had been chosen to represent the Prime Ministers of the last two hundred years. Starring Denis Quilley as Gladstone; Richard Pasco as Disraeli; David Langton as Asquith; John Stride as David Lloyd George and Ian Richardson as Ramsay MacDonald it would be informative and entertaining so that the viewers would be better informed on this crucial topic. It focused on a selection of important details of political and personal events that delineated their lives and personalities in their time as prime minister in the familiar institution of 10 Downing Street. Jeremy's appearance as William Pitt the Younger was the least political and most personal of all the episodes as it explored his battle with mental problems which he kept under control by drinking a huge amount of port. His decision to reject the beautiful Eleanor Eden is heartrending, but ultimately justified in his response to his father's request not to marry or father children.

Jeremy's performance of **William Pitt, the Younger** in *Number 10: Bloodline* 12th February 1983, for ITV is considered to be one of his finest. He has shared the tragedy of Pitt's life as he is forced to put aside the lovely Eleanor and continue in his dedication to the country of England, fulfilling his destiny as the nation's Saviour. Although William is passionately devoted to Eleanor, he finally accepts that marriage is out of the question. Not only is the beleaguered PM in the midst of a national crisis against the formidable opponent Napoleon, but he's also deeply in debt because of his lifestyle, with the added ignominy of being systematically cheated and defrauded by his tradesmen. The City of London had promised to pay off his debts of £45,000, but Pitt knew they would expect too much in return; "he wanted to be completely free, independent and beholden to no one."

"Factual or fictional, *Bloodline* is certainly the most dramatic of the episodes included in *Number 10* with Jeremy Brett giving a stunning performance as a gifted politician tortured by the knowledge that, at times, he won't be in total control of himself. As well, that loss of control robs from him the one true love of his life, Eleanor, and according to Feely, he won't allow himself even the solace of explaining to her why, instead letting her think he's dropping her for political reasons (her young age and the resulting scandal). Langrishe has a marvellous, playful chemistry with Brett, which makes their tragic parting have that much more impact, regardless of whether or not these events are factual." (dvdtalk.com on IMDb)

Jeremy told *Starweek* how he had prepared for the role. First he had dieted and lost a significant amount of weight in order to create a similar picture to Pitt's portrait. He also adopted shoes too large so that he "*slopped around a bit*" in order to emphasise the similarity. "*Pitt was not the most attractive of characters but he was a brilliant statesman… it was very exciting to play this extraordinary, thin, little, worn-out thoroughbred with this brilliant brain.*" (Starweek) "*Pitt was a fascinating person to play. When you read about him you realise just how fascinating he was. He was a very thin man, with kind of albino features, so a lot of dieting had to go into that role.*" (Secrets)

One reviewer found it to be "a truly inspired performance by a truly inspiring man… Brett is spectacularly original as an actor and pours more effort into this one-hour guest appearance than most actors today would bother with on an entire series. William inhabits Brett completely and shines out through his eyes. When a fit of madness seizes him, we get a terrifying glimpse into what is prowling beneath his composed and unruffled demeanour, before this transgression is brushed away as one would a fly and we're left facing a neat and perfectly tranquil man, hands folded, contemplating the mess he has made… His command of facial expression is exquisite: when he fixes his eyes on Eleanor, or reads her letters, you could not imagine a more touching representation of complete contentment and more profoundly of all, fulfilment. When it comes to the possibility of being parted from her his entire face screws up in such a contortion of agony that you want to look away as if you're intruding on something private." (Ladygilraen.wordpress.com)

Morte d'Arthur 1984 - BBC2 Television

Morte d'Arthur entitled The Knight's Tale, was shown on BBC2 on 5th May 1984. Sir Thomas Malory's epic masterpiece was written in 1470 whilst the author was imprisoned in Newgate Jail for "divers crimes" where he wrote about King Arthur, his knights and the legendary Round Table, weaving the different legends together into an intriguing whole. Jeremy headed the sixteen members of the cast as **King Arthur** with his Queen Guinevere and his favourite knight Sir Lancelot at the heart of the action. The Director, Gillian Lynne, explained her vision for the play to the *Radio Times*, "Everyone knows the story of Arthur but we are bringing the nobility of the language back to the story... We make his visions float before our eyes." She also explained why she had chosen Jeremy for the central role, "I thought he had the right kind of nobility in his face for Arthur, and the right kind of gentleness."

Jeremy found working in silence extremely difficult. *"I find, as an actor, being without words is almost impossible to bear, I feel deprived. So I learned all the Arthur speeches to give me some meat to feed on. But Gillian is an event. She encourages you to dare more than you've dared before. I've lived in a tracksuit for weeks, we all do these work-outs beforehand, and so much of the part is physical. She's such an example; she's hardly young herself but she has the body of a girl. It's been complex, it's been dangerous. You hope that the effect of the flood of emotion you show through the brooding look isn't too grotesque. But it's been innovative. If it's a success people will say, 'How brilliant to choose it!'"* (Radio Times May 1984)

John Barton, the co founder of the RSC as Narrator was the kingpin of the production first as an actor then "telling the tale of friendship, cowardice, murder, hate, virtue and sin". "Barton as Malory is seen in his Newgate Prison cell narrating the epic tales with Jeremy Brett playing in a noble manner the cuckolded King Arthur, Barbara Kellerman, a smouldering and sensuous Queen Guinevere, and David Robb out-swashbuckling Errol Flynn as the almost indestructible Sir Lancelot. A splendid adaptation masterfully devised and directed by Gillian Lynne." (Peter Dear. Weekend Choice. The Times (London, England) May 5th 1984)

During this production, Jeremy asked Nickolas Grace who plays his son, Mordred (born of an incestuous relationship with his sister Morgese) to hit him harder over the helmet when he delivered the mortal blow and he encouraged Nickolas to make it look more effective. Unfortunately, the blow dislodged his contact lens at which Jeremy screamed with pain and accused him of blinding him, although he later forgave him. Another incident in this production was his diva-like complaint to Gillian Lynne about the overrun in production time: with other commitments demanding his attention, Jeremy made his feelings very clear. "He ranted and raved at her, shouting that it was her job to ensure that everything was filmed in the allotted time. After this attack, he did a complete volte-face and said in the sweetest of voices, that he had to explode to get the frustration out of his system." (Scarlet Street)

Florence Nightingale 1985 - Film

Mr Nighingale in Florence Nightingale

Filmed at Pinewood Studios and on location at Breamore House, Fordingbridge, Hampshire, ***Florence Nightingale*** released *7th April* 1985 is a faithful record of the calling of Florence to serve, "*God has spoken to me and called me to His service*" and is a very moving film. This movie for television starred Jaclyn Smith as Florence Nightingale, immortalised as the "Lady of the Lamp", and one of the first women nurses serving during the Crimean War. She was born into the aristocratic world of privilege; her father was a banker from a family of mining magnates and Florence was expected to marry well and live in accordance with her position in society. However, she was determined to create a different future for herself and become a nurse. As nurses traditionally came from the lower classes and were viewed as drunkards and prostitutes Florence's parents were not prepared to support her initially, especially as prospective husbands were available and Richard Monckton Milnes (Timothy Dalton) is willing to offer her marriage. In time, **Mr William (Wen) Nightingale**, played by Jeremy, became more supportive and gave her his permission so long as she didn't tell her mother Frances, played by Claire Bloom. Jeremy brought a great deal of personality to a supporting role so that on occasions he almost stole the limelight from his daughter. One could imagine from which parent Florence inherited her spunk.

Her story is well known so this film is particularly effective as a biopic and tear-jerker but remains an accurate record of her inspirational life and never elevates the woman above her calling. Her career in nursing had brought her the position of Superintendent of Nurses in a London Hospital for Gentlewomen in which she was able to demonstrate her administrative and nursing skills whilst cutting the cost of patient care, although she herself received no pay and even paid her own expenses. A year later when the Crimean War began she would be asked to take a group of nurses to the Barracks Hospital in Turkey which she was eager to do. During her first year at Scutari more than two thousand men would die in her arms from infection of their wounds amongst the filthy, overcrowded conditions of the hospital where sanitation and nursing care was non existent. As a woman in a world where army officers expected the men to suffer in silence, she had to fight first for access to the patients, *"no female has ever been allowed to nurse in the British Army"* and her 40 nurses remained unused for a considerable time until she offered to scrub the floors in an attempt to sanitize the wards. Bureaucracy would be against her all the way, however, she personally ensured the basic provision of chloroform for amputations, even for the basic comforts of beds to lie on, sheets or blankets, and that the terrible wounds were kept clean and redressed. Men were no longer brought into the hospital to die. The Crimean War would provide the opportunity to change the methods of nursing which would save lives through knowledge of the cause and effect of deadly infection. Royal approval and recognition of Florence as Head of Nursing meant that the basic standards would remain beyond the Crimea and her selfless devotion towards the men would fundamentally change the profession. Florence would remain faithfully devoted to her profession, never marry and died at the age of ninety.

"This stirring drama is based on the life of Florence Nightingale, an aristocratic woman who defied Victorian society to reform hospital sanitation and to define the nursing profession as it is known today. After volunteering to travel to Scutari to care for the wounded soldiers of the Crimean War, she was scorned by her community and faced great opposition for her new way of thinking. However, through her selfless acts of caring, she quickly became known as The Lady with the Lamp, the caring nurse whose shadow softened those wounded. From Emmy-Award-winning director Daryl Duke (TV's The Thorn Birds) and writers Ivan Moffat and Rose Leiman Goldemberg (TV's The Burning Bed) comes the classic TV movie starring Jaclyn Smith, Claire Bloom, Timothy Dalton and Jeremy Brett, now available for the first time on DVD." (Amazon.co.uk)

In spite of the issue of an American playing a British heroine, Jaclyn Smith has a warmth and sincerity which could convince the hardest of hearts. "And since this particular movie succeeds or fails largely on the efforts of the lead actress (Smith is in every scene of the 140 minute film), it's appropriate to discuss Smith's portrayal right up front. The most literate script, the finest supporting cast, and the most sensitive, imaginative director in the world couldn't make Florence Nightingale work... Sincerity goes a long way in a film like this, and one can see that quality in Smith's performance... Meanwhile, Florence's mother, despite all the efforts of the talented Claire Bloom, is compressed into a cliché who is forced to spend a great deal of time worrying about her daughter's looming spinsterhood. Evidently, the unmarried remain suspect on television entertainment, and the producers must do their best to assure viewers that all is still well with the world..." (New York Times 7th April 1985) "A top-flight cast and crew back up Smith here in Florence Nightingale. Jeremy Brett has the most fun as the observant father who slyly appreciates the change in his wife's acceptance of their daughter's activities… once they make the papers." (DVD Talk)

Florence Nightingale and her father William (Wen)

The Love Boat: Ace's Valet 1984 - ABC Television Network

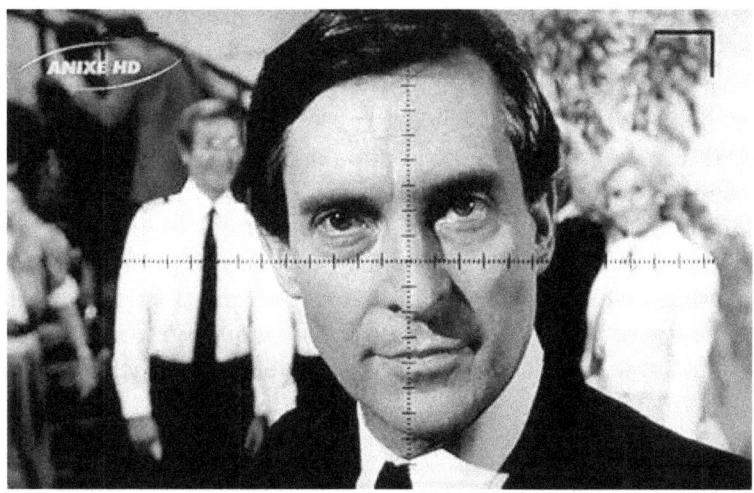

Ernest Finley in Love Boat: Ace's Valet

The Love Boat: Ace's Valet scheduled for 25th February 1984 was number 186 of the episodes where Jeremy appeared as Ernest Finley and one of the few comic performances he gave. His voice and his demeanour were perfect for the part as a valet to a wealthy member of the crew and his comic approach was ideal for the series. *The Love Boat* was an American television series set on a cruise ship which aired on the ABC Television Network from 5th May 1977, until 12th February 1990. The show revolves around the ship's captain played by Gavin MacLeod and a handful of its crew, with several passengers – played by different guest actors for each episode – having romantic and humorous adventures. For its first seven years, *The Love Boat* was very successful in the ratings. During that time, it ranked among the top 20, and even the top 10. The series was built around the voyages of a cruise ship so that the Captain, the Purser and the Ship's doctor remained the same and the passengers changed between the four weeks' cruise. Even the Entertainment Staff was played by familiar faces, and Ace (Ashley Covington Evans) featured Ted McGinley who would appear as the ship's photographer from 1984 until 1986. As a wealthy young man with a valet he is embarrassed when his parents send the butler to care for him; to bring him his milk and to care for his clothes, much as a child. Ace's attempts to distract Finley (Jeremy) and send him home meet only with an embarrassing loyalty and a determination to carry out his tasks to his employer's satisfaction. Slapstick comedy is included, where Jeremy is pushed into the pool and he retaliates by embarrassing his charge further but these are finally resolved when Finley leaves with Miss America: having proposed marriage and been accepted.

Jeremy was one of the guest stars who were pleased to be included in the cast. Other big names included Andy Warhol, Alexis Smith, Jimmie Osmond and the cast of *Charlie's Angels* who appeared in separate episodes. Rita Moreno, Elke Sommer and Jean Marsh had also appeared on board *The Love Boat*, so Jeremy was in good company. "TV: A Special Two-Hour

Star-filled Love Boat ...Realistically speaking, *Love Boat* has always been a little goofy. Each week, the Pacific Princess, a big luxury liner, is sailed by the same crew of five, six if you count Captain Marrill Stubing's daughter. In the regular one-hour episodes, they solve, or at least are party to, three problems, romantic or familial, sometimes both... In truth, there is always sex on *Love Boat* just as there always are young women in bikinis around the shipboard pool. Romance begins immediately: 'Hi there,' and that's pretty much it. A couple may dance together in the Acapulco Lounge (always a fox trot; even the young do not boogie), but a moment later it is morning, and they are having breakfast on the Lido Deck. You know, of course, that they did not pass the night in separate cabins. The effect, at first glance, is to make *Love Boat* seem almost racy. Constant viewers, however, know it isn't that at all. Seldom in the course of fiction have so many couplings been followed by so many engagements. Real promiscuity is frowned on. Doc (Bernie Koppel), the ship's medical officer, is supposed to be a womaniser, but his many marriages and divorces are a running joke. Doc may fool around, but he would just as soon propose. *Love Boat* in fact, upholds all the old virtues, and try as it often does to be 'with it' and modern, the nuclear family always wins..."
(John Corry 4th February New York Times)

Deceptions 1985 – BBC One Television

Bryan Foxworth in Deceptions

Jeremy returned to America after completing the filming of *The Adventures of Sherlock Holmes* and he characteristically needed to be busy. He joyfully accepted a part in a glossy contemporary television movie alongside his friend Stefanie Powers. *Deceptions* was based on the first of Judith Michael's books (the pen name for the married writing team of Judith Barnard and Michael Fain) about the identical Longworth twins who swap places so that they both could escape from the pressures of their lives. Sabrina has a rich and glamorous lifestyle in the midst of European tricksters and Stephanie is a drab New Jersey housewife struggling to save her marriage. On a whim, the two siblings exchange identities, leading to a dizzying series of unexpected complications. The murder of Stephanie in the opening minutes is unexplained and later when Sabrina is injured in a car crash the deception takes on a new sinister twist leaving no opportunity to turn back the clocks to take up their previous lives.

Jeremy with Stefanie Powers in Deceptions

"This week's TV movie **Deceptions** BBC One 21st & 22nd March is a maze of complicated plot twists about identical twin sisters, housewife Stephanie Roberts and jet-setter Sabrina Longworth (both played by Stefanie Powers), who secretly switch identities. "Stephanie has a husband, two children and a suburban home. Sabrina has a country estate, a chauffeur and a rich lover. When identical twins sisters decide to swap lives for a week, no one could possibly guess at their deception. Telling them apart is impossible and leads to murder when a yacht explodes into a fireball, during a jet-set party." (BBC genome site) "There is... barely a moment in *Deceptions* that could claim to being believable. The performers seem understandably eager to get out of their commitments as quickly and as surreptitiously as possible.... *Deceptions* may have some tangential value as a travelogue. The un–location shooting includes a final chase that affords a swell helicopter-eye's view of London. On the whole, though, New Jersey is better." (New York Times 24th May 1985)

Jeremy's contribution was appreciated, "Lending a much-needed twist of lightness to the ensuing melodrama is actor Jeremy Brett, who plays Sabrina's art gallery assistant **Bryan Foxworth**." However, the art business turns out to be far more complicated than expected as Sabrina's partner played by James Faulkner and Jeremy's naughty assistant were using the antiques trade as a cover for a drug-smuggling operation. In his role as Bryan Jeremy appears all "charm", and he himself was charmed. *"Oh, I'm in clover. First, I got to work with my darling Stefanie... I did a* Hart to Hart *in California with her and R.J. (Robert Wagner), and those two turned that show into a class act... In this one... poor darling Stefanie didn't have just twins to play, but with one impersonating the other, she really has four parts. She's also a mistress of comedy. In two or three scenes we have together we have some delightful humour, and the two of us just take off."* He played the great friend of Sabrina, an assistant on whom she totally relies but he is delighted he turns out to be two-faced. *"The audience at first sees me as a friend of Stefanie, but about 20 minutes into the piece they know I'm not as charming as I seem and that I am, in fact, quite dangerous. It's so wonderfully challenging to be saying one thing as my character and mean another."* He enjoyed the challenge of *"a most complex part. Bryan is enormously bright and alive and stylish and happy, and he's also homosexual, which made him harder to play, because the gay community has been so shattered by AIDS. So I took it on with a much greater sense of responsibility. Before, I might have been tempted to camp it up, but instead, I decided to play him with enormous panache and an enormous zest for life. At the same time, the deceptive side of him is thrilling. He is a lethal murderer trafficking in drugs, a monster."* (New York Times 1985) And for a change, he had reached the twentieth century, *"I'm in modern dress, I finally get some pockets. If you know my roles, you know I've never been able to get past the 20s or the 30s."* In fact, his costume is colourful and very individual, ranging from elegant blacks and greys to more interesting choices of casual wear. *Deceptions* was a difficult production that struggled through a series of directors. *"I think in the small time that I was there, which was only four weeks of shooting, I had three – maybe three and a half – directors... Always in these cases, the actors come together and do what they can do. If it works, nothing matters. It only matters if it fails. I was very worried for Stefanie because her neck was on the block... If* Deceptions *comes off, it's largely due to her immense spirit, incredible tenacity and her great joy."*

"The story of the town mouse and the country mouse was dolled up with lipgloss and Carmen rollers in *Deceptions* (BBC1), an American mini-series which translated the fable into terms which undoubtedly found 90 per cent of the female population of the Western world exactly where they lived... *Deceptions* was, by the standards of most of the American mini-series screened in this country, a superior piece of candyfloss, it was shot on location and designed with a modicum of taste. There was a sterling cast of British actors including Jeremy Brett, Judy Parfitt and Joan Simms. Gina Lollobrigida turned up in sequins, doing for the Italian accent what Maurice Chevalier used to do for the French accent. Part II of this confection is to be screened tonight, and we may expect the plot to thicken to the point of no return." (Celia Brayfield The Times 22nd March 1986) "That Ms Powers plays identical twins is, I think, fairly common knowledge. That Gina Lollobrigida gives everything she's got in her supporting role has also been mentioned before. What I don't see anywhere here is anything highlighting the terrific contribution made to proceedings by Jeremy Brett. This film was made in 1985, during the early days of his tenure as THE Television Sherlock Holmes and although this particular role is nowhere near as challenging, it is still a delight to watch him. Apart from anything else, he gets to wear some rather stylish and modern clothes which, for an actor who seemed to spend most of his career wandering through the mists of some other time, must have felt good. He and Stefanie Powers appeared together in an early episode of *Hart To Hart* by the way, years before they made this. They have a wonderful rapport and, to be perfectly honest, I'm not sure who I'm more jealous of..." (Amazon.co.uk)

Deceptions

Song 1985 - New York State Theater

Jeremy's next performance was unusual as it was not on stage or in front of a camera for film or television. He was to appear in a very different role as **Narrator - King Solomon** in *Song*. Martha Graham was in her nineties when her production of *Song* was performed as part of a three week season at the New York State Theater. As Narrator, Jeremy was unseen and delivering his part from backstage. An article in the *New York Times* entitled: Dance: Martha Graham Gives Premiere of Song by Anna Kisselgoff 3rd April 1985 proclaimed it "magic". The use of Solomon's *Song of Songs* from the Bible's Old Testament as the narration was a perfect choice for the sensuous dance presented by Thea Nerissa Barnes as lead dancer in a memorable performance. The opening verse *"I am a rose of Sharon, a lily of the valleys"* set the scene for an evening of sensuous delight and the critics commented that Jeremy's voice speaking the words created an atmosphere totally in keeping with the presentation of an idealised love story. Martha Graham's achievement was to create a total integration of the dance with the words which became "a danced poem, rather than a dance set to poetry... a completeness of form here, an integration of speech, music and dancing, all uniting into one metrical whole" and the audience responded accordingly giving Miss Graham a standing ovation for her vision and "for the theatrical magic created by her dancers."

In another article *The New York Times* challenged its readers with a further explanation of the experience: "If you are not concerned with the essence of dance and prefer its surface, then Martha Graham is not for you. Movement lies at the heart of her work. This obvious fact is easy to overlook, simply because Miss Graham, as theatrical magician, can dazzle us with production values and dramatic imagery. Yet these stage effects and images are a function of the dance movement that Miss Graham sets before us. No choreographer has a firmer knowledge of theatrical rarity, of the integration of dance with all other elements on stage... We have taken so much of Martha Graham for granted nowadays. It is a commonplace to affirm that she knows how to integrate decor... into the fabric of her choreography. We also expect her dancers to be emotionally motivated and frequently forget that they are not acting in the conventional sense. What we should remember is that it is the shape of the movement and its dynamic quality that stir us.... The inspiration is the biblical *Song of Songs*. These are love poems, once attributed to Solomon but generally regarded as fragments from a marriage ritual in which the bridal couple acted out the mime of a king and queen... The lover revealed to the lover - and its eternal values has an apt resonance in the timeless Romanian folk tunes played in recorded form, on a shepherd's pan pipe..." (New York Times 14th April 1985) The two leading dancers of shepherd and his shepherdess carried the presentation of their relationship from the held embrace through to sensuous love, which was "unabashedly erotic at times". The words gave a visual dimension to the action, for example, the verse *"thy breasts to clusters of grapes"* was given reality in the dance, not literally but symbolically. Other aspects of the relationship were presented too in members of their family and friends, the *"little foxes"* were given flesh in the behaviour of the boisterous brothers. However, "Miss Graham is never literal. Instead, she gives the words a visual dimension of their own."

"*The Song of Songs*, sometimes called *The Song of Solomon* is an outright love lyric. And while nothing in Miss Graham's canon can be totally lyrical – it is not her innate style – she has managed to make them of *Song* one long caress. And perhaps this is felt most uncannily in the way Mr Brett's voice seems to actually caress the words. Most television viewers of the moment know Mr Brett as *Sherlock Holmes,* a part he is currently playing on a *Mystery* series. He is, of course, also a Shakespearean actor, and it is a coup, in fact, to have this Shakespearean resonance waft out from the wings. Mr Brett is offstage, but he does not go unheard. Nor can one call his narration a voice-over. Again the success of *Song* lies in the way all its elements fit together. One in particular does not dominate." (Anna Kisselgoff in The New York Times) As the performers took their curtain calls, Jeremy was carrying his script: "The narrator, Jeremy Brett, took a call, carrying his script – an implication that he had just read it live. Since his voice is heard on a recording, he too deserves some cheers – for good acting." In another article he expressed the great joy he experienced in the role of Narrator in this production. "This year in the U.S. Mr Brett has also been the voice of Solomon in Martha Graham's new ballet *Song*. *'It was one of the greatest joys of my life,'* he said, *'I kneel at the altar of Martha Graham. I think she is as important to the United States as the Chrysler Building.'* He added that he plans to do eight live performances of *Song* this September in Paris." (Patrick O'Neill in Happy Home from Holmes!) Unfortunately, this promise could not be fulfilled as Joan would die from cancer just three months later on 4th July and Jeremy returned to England.

Song

In the American press Jeremy was being celebrated for his enormous success on the stage and also on television. He had recently opened on Broadway in *Aren't We All?* with Rex Harrison, Claudette Colbert and Lynn Redgrave, winning unanimous personal rave reviews and the *Times* newspaper in both London and New York were calling his portrayal of Sherlock Holmes "the best Holmes ever." The first series which had been shown on PBS was welcomed with enormous enthusiasm and called "an immense success." Jeremy would comment on the different ways England and America viewed their stars in an interview with Derek Jameson on his late night programme in which he said, *"In this country we're not allowed to say the word star."* Instead he raised a smile when he substituted the term *"star"* with *"a twinkler"*, which is most endearing but highlights a flaw in the system which fails to recognise and reward those who perform in the arts. In another interview he explained in greater detail the difficulties he experienced with his family when he first entered the profession. *"It was hard for my Father and I understand completely. You see the thing is it's not a respectable profession... It is in the States, but it is not here, still. Twenty/thirty years ago, whenever it all came about, it certainly wasn't, and I was a disgrace. I mean it was a shock. I remember no one ever mentioned whether I was going to become an actor, all my parents' friends, it was just not a thing that people did. I still get, you know, quite a lot of pressure when I go back there, saying when am I going to take up a proper job of work and things like that. Because it just wasn't accepted, and it isn't accepted, in this country, still. It's one step away from the gutter. I think even if you talked to Laurence Olivier you'd find we are not accepted into the drawing rooms of England. We might be accepted into the garden to do a little play, but it's still that resistance. It's still, 'Hm, hm.' Not very proper."* (Stage Struck 1990) In spite of the opposition that Jeremy experienced he would relish his achievements and he told *Pebble Mill at One* at the time of *The Secret of Sherlock Holmes* that he was enjoying the *"pink success"* enormously.

Aren't We All? 1985 - Brooks Atkinson Theater

Willie Tatham in Aren't We All?

Aren't We All? opened at the London Haymarket with 77 year old Rex Harrison as the unrepentant old scoundrel, Lord Grenham and Claudette Colbert at 83 as the good natured Lady Frinton who frequently offers him marriage. It transferred to the Brooks Atkinson Theater, New York City from 29th April until 21st July 1985 with Jeremy taking over the role of **William Tatham** and Lynn Redgrave as his wife Margot. After the success in his role as George Duke of Bristol in *On Approval*, Jeremy felt at ease with Frederick Lonsdale's gentle satire and his performance was justifiably praised in this entertaining, if frivolous piece on modern marriage. Willie Tatham may have been angry at his wife's prolonged time away from him in Egypt but her unexpected arrival home to find him kissing an attractive vamp would have been difficult to excuse. Luckily, his father is happy to come to his rescue as he discovers a letter which puts Margot in a similar position in her own wifely indiscretion. "Lonsdale's slight tissue of plot provides the pretext for a genially satiric view of life amid the rich and titled. Principal among them are the wise but cynical Grenham and Lady Frinton, a widow whose cap is firmly set for the old rascal... Mr Brett is a dab hand at the Lonsdale style, combining the nuances of vocal precision with the conviction that is at the heart of all true comedy. The strikingly handsome Miss Redgrave makes a believable transition from the righteous wifely outrage of Act 1 to panic at the threatened exposure of her regretted momentary fling." (Christian Science Monitor) "Mr Brett, in a part played by Leslie Howard on Broadway in 1923, is the most charming specimen of debonair English manhood to come our way since Jeremy Irons skipped town. Miss Redgrave, who looks smashing herself these days, mines all the light wit available in the most humourless role... Mr Harrison's energy level isn't what it was in *Heartbreak House* last season, he's still an impish silver fox who deftly brays his roguish lines while studying *The Times* through a monocle." (New York Times 30th April 1985)

Walter Kerr in *The New York Times* commented on the joy of the production and the pleasure of watching "a whole bunch of charismatic actors come together to employ the charms they have spent lifetimes acquiring. Claudette Colbert, Rex Harrison, Lynn Redgrave, Brenda Forbes, Jeremy Brett and George Rose, jointly delicious – it is worth creating an evening for the sheer pleasure of seeing them work. What felicity, then, to have Claudette Colbert enter to offer Jeremy Brett an enviable social embrace while Mr Brett – presumably speaking Mr Lonsdale's lines – exclaims *'Hello, my dear, you look wonderful! Upon my soul, you become younger every day.'* Inasmuch as Miss Colbert goes around starting rumo(u)rs that she is past 40, and inasmuch as she continues to look the way 20 year olds wish they looked, this calls for a round of applause that is partly a welcome, partly disbelief in the star's continuing and staggering beauty, and partly the beginning of a laugh. The laugh wells up because life and the play have become so happily entwined, one has become a comment on the other. There is a crazy kind of joy in the moment..." (The New York Times 4th May 1985)

Jeremy had some difficulty getting to grips with Willie Tatham but finally he followed his well tried method of creating a background history to plumb the depths of the role. *"The way one works on these things, if you're me, is to try and find the essence of the person, where you came from and where you're going to."* For Jeremy, Willie was a First World War veteran, who had lost most of his friends in the conflict, a situation which was very much like his own father at the end of the war. He told *The Times*, *"I based Willie on my father. He was Henry William Huggins, a famous soldier in World War I. I dedicated my performance to my father. I even have his medals."*

The critics couldn't help referring to his success in *Sherlock Holmes*, "One of the bright lights in the Broadway gloom is Jeremy Brett whose step from 221b Baker Street, to West 47th Street, New York, was one of the smartest moves of his career. For the second year running, a tall debonair English charmer has become the toast of Broadway. Last year it was Jeremy Irons. This year it is Jeremy Brett. He's light years away from the gloomy Victorian sleuth Sherlock Holmes – currently bringing him fame and fortune on TV screens on both sides of the Atlantic – co-starring with Rex Harrison and Lynn Redgrave in a revival of Frederick Lonsdale's classic comedy about the very rich, *Aren't We All*? While American producers on Broadway have been facing crisis, the Englishmen abroad are playing to packed houses. *"I am being feted as the oldest juvenile on Broadway. I love it,"* said 6ft.2in. 49 year-old Mr Brett. *"With Sherlock Holmes and this play I have become a successful British export. And on Broadway where careers can be axed by the critics, success is the important thing... I don't want to play toffee-nosed Englishmen all my life, but this has been a holiday for me. I am learning a lot from Rex Harrison who is the imp of Broadway. They are crazy about him. Lynn Redgrave first worked with me in 1961 at the Royal Court where she fussed around me. She doesn't any more, she's frightfully bossy and marvellous to work with. I think the Americans like this play because it is joyful, not just because it is English..."* (But for a buoyant Jeremy Brett, it's a Happy Home from Holmes! By Patrick O'Neill)

Aren't We All?

Sherlock Holmes

"One document which is going to remain a secret for a few more years is my original list of possible actors to play Holmes in the Eighties. There are forty names on the list, and they are not in alphabetical order but Jeremy Brett's name is at the top. He seemed to me then to be the best-equipped actor of his generation to challenge the great portrayals of the past. I had first read the stories in bound volumes of The Strand and grown up with Sidney Paget's evocative illustrations – they were the benchmark. And I wanted a Holmes with a splendid voice, a commanding presence and the richly varied temperament which Conan Doyle had given him."
(Michael Cox in The Sherlock Holmes Journal Winter 1995)

Writing in the *Sherlock Holmes Gazette*, Michael gave further details of a very wet night in August 1981 in which he and Jeremy had discussed the role of Holmes. David Huggins had accompanied his father to the meeting with Michael and the head of casting for dinner at a restaurant in Charlotte Street and Jeremy would no doubt have felt the contrast with the warmth he had left behind at his home in Los Angeles. Granada had plans to construct a semi-permanent set for a future *Coronation Street Tour,* and Michael had a £5 million budget to create a quality production. The strict control of the character's television representations imposed by the Conan Doyle estate was about to end as the books came into the public domain, and Michael saw an opportunity to return to Conan Doyle's original work and provide the first authentic presentation of Holmes. The decision to use 35mm for the films, the size preferred by the U.S. networks brought the hope of investment from WGBH which was willing to share the financial risk of production in exchange for the right to show it first in the U.S. To ensure advance sales the actor needed to be acceptable to the American market and although Joan Wilson Huggins' position and influence was not mentioned, Jeremy was extremely sensitive about the possibility that he might have been chosen at his wife's request. Above all they needed "a classical actor with a marvellous voice and the appearance of a Sidney Paget illustration from *The Strand Magazine*". Jeremy satisfied all the preferred criteria, but he may not have accepted the role as many actors do not relish the thought of tying themselves too much to a part and Sherlock Holmes had a reputation of being a signature part. Basil Rathbone had been strongly identified with the role long after he had left it. Jeremy Brett knew it could have meant the end of his career so the decision was a difficult one.

Crucially, was the need to be faithful to the Conan Doyle stories plus the determination to achieve the same high standard for which Granada was noted in their drama programming. "He was interested, enthusiastic even, but of course, unprepared to commit himself irrevocably until there were dates and fixtures on paper." (Michael Cox) In the meantime Jeremy was producing, directing and playing Prospero in *The Tempest* in Canada, *"I was acting Prospero in* The Tempest *and trying to raise money to film the play in Barbados – because it was Shakespeare I couldn't find a penny – and then I did Robert Browning in* The Barretts of Wimpole Street, *I thought, oh phooey, Holmes is old hat, been done to death. He didn't intrigue me at the time."* (Jeremy in Brett Noir)

If he had been successful in bringing *The Tempest* to the screen it is unlikely that he would have accepted. However, Jeremy's attempts to explore the world famous detective were not without some surprises. *"When I tried to buy* The Strand Magazine, *I couldn't find one. I couldn't find Doyle's complete works. I did, eventually find one in Foyles, in London, and it was an American edition, which had been sent over and not been collected, and that's how I got one. Now, Doyle is everywhere..."* The red leather bound *Illustrated Sherlock Holmes Treasury* with his many underlinings and annotations would become his Bible and he would carry it with him over the ten years of filming the series. Jeremy had been reintroduced to the Conan Doyle stories by a friend in the Bahamas where he was on holiday following *The Tempest*. Sherlock Holmes was very different from the romantic heroic figures he had portrayed in his career, yet he was intrigued: *"It was there that I became fascinated with Doyle's tales. I thought, Oh yes, there are things I can do with this fellow! They held me entranced; the late Victorian era, full of gaslit, fogbound streets, the scent of shag tobacco. Then the details began to pop up at me from the page. Holmes chuckled and wriggled in his chair as was his habit when in high spirits... Lighting his long cherrywood pipe which he was wont to replace his clay when he was in a disputatious, rather than a meditative mood... Holmes hunted about among the grass and leaves like a retriever after a wounded bird... Images that I had not seen before. The actor in me was on the hunt. The more I delved, the more I realised there was room for me to be someone else, to do something different... I discovered all sorts of things that I could do if I had the opportunity to do so. So I say 'yes!' with enormous temerity, and a certain amount of fear, and an element of excitement."* (Taken from Armchair Detective and Foreword to Television Sherlock Holmes)

A time of total immersion in Holmes followed which was Jeremy's familiar approach and his search for the character would begin. *"I was talking about becoming. What I mean by that is an inner life. Watson describes you-know-who as a mind without a heart; that's hard to play, hard to become. So what I did was to invent an inner life. I mean, I know what his nanny looked like; for example; she was covered in starch. She probably scrubbed him, but never kissed him. I don't think he probably saw his mother until he was about eight... (she) was just a lady moving through a passageway... Maybe caught a touch of her scent and the rustle of her dress. Probably he didn't actually see his father until he was twelve. I guess college days were fairly complicated because he was quite isolated. He probably saw a girl across the quadrangle and fell in love, but she never looked at him... so he closed that door. And he became a brilliant fencer... and a master at boxing... and many more tiny little details which I have to kind of make up to fill this kind of well... that Doyle so brilliantly left out. To bring it off the printed page for myself, I invented little stories about... the loneliness of his university days, of his brilliance at sports, and his total removal from any kind of social activity... everything to bring a bit more illumination."* (Gunner54.wordpress.com & NPR Interview 1991)

Jeremy was a classically trained Shakespearean actor with a love of words and the rhythm they created. His approach to character would be a personal one, a combination of the training he received at the National under Olivier and the Stanislavsky Method. "You study it from the point of view of the epoch, the time, the country, condition of life, background, literature, psychology, the soul, way of living, social position, and external appearance; moreover, you study character, such as custom, manner, movements, voice, intonations." (An Actor Prepares) Sherlock Holmes lived in the Victorian era. *"What you do as an actor, for me anyway, you become a sponge... What you do is squeeze the sponge out. And you learn and assimilate. You read and read and read about the Victorian era. Who was in government? What was the social status of the country? Why was Holmes a bohemian? Then you start to read Doyle and you sort of sniff it through. After a great deal of study, things begin to happen. Like hands. What does he do with his hands? How would he move? And you whisper, whisper, whisper because you have to find the voice. You keep whispering so the imagination keeps going. When you think you've got him – or he's enough in you – you speak. It's an enormously exciting process."* (To Luaine Lee in Scripps Howard News Service)

When filming began for *The Solitary Cyclist* Jeremy had lost a significant amount of weight, around 24 pounds, mostly by swimming, and immersing himself in the part. He reported the effects of his screen tests and described them as a disaster with the choice of white make-up which made his teeth look yellow and his eyes red. *"I started hilariously because I was so embarrassed by feeling miscast and totally inadequate that I did a kind of gargoyle makeup, I put white on my forehead and I put white down my nose and dark violet under here* (his chin). *Trying to look like a hungry eagle, I looked… dreadful. So they said, 'No, we can't do that, that's awful!'"* (SH Behind the Scenes on ITV This Morning) *"Everyone said, 'Jeremy, do you need all that? Where are you under there? Why the funny walk?' I had a painted face, this walk and a ghastly voice. They all went, of course."* (TV Times 19th May 1984) Michael Cox said, "Jeremy is very much an extrovert. He enjoys life, is great fun to be with, is very amusing and has a great way with words. And he saw Holmes as very dark… a rather waspish sarcastic kind of character. I believe the director of one of the first episodes said to him, 'Could you just put a little bit of yourself into this, because the man can't have been quite as black as you're painting him or no one would have ever come to consult him. They'd be frightened away at his doorstep.' Jeremy was persuaded to loosen up a bit and I think his performance improved as a result. He was able to find the moments of humour, moments of warmth, moments when you can see his concern for clients and for Watson in the stories. I think the characterisation has got more interest, has got more flash and fire to it." (Michael in Armchair Detective)

In interview for *Pebble Mill at One* Jeremy said, "*I remember when Sir Alastair Cooke said to me… before we started, he said that the three most memorable people in the last hundred years are Churchill, Hitler and Sherlock Holmes. Now this was meant to encourage me – I was terrified! Well, that's really done it now. I mean, I didn't want to play the part in the first place because I thought I would fail! 'Cause there had been so many people playing it before. But to think that one of those three people never existed at all is extraordinary!" (BBC One)* He was now committed to the role and would make his interpretation of Holmes the very best. Michael said, "From the beginning Jeremy plunged himself into every aspect of production. The scripts had been written during the long layoff, but he had his copy of the original stories, annotated and underlined after hours of reading and rereading and he made a careful comparison."

Jeremy was determined to speak Conan Doyle's original words in a definitive Sherlock Holmes, the vision Michael Cox had set out to achieve. No one had ever allowed the characters to speak the original words before and the prospect excited and challenged Jeremy. *"(When) we approached the scripts, I said, 'But you've asked me to do Sir Arthur Conan Doyle's Sherlock Holmes. These aren't Sherlock Holmes – Doyle's stories.' I mean, the adaptors had gone so far away. And the script editor said, 'Jeremy, you're here to act. Just get on with it.' And I tipped the table over, and my Dover sole landed in his lap. And that was the beginning of the tussle. I used to take the whole canon with me… (at) the beginning of each film, and fight for Doyle. After about a year and a half I said, 'Listen, if you don't start taking care of me, I may lose interest,' because it was such a tussle. But then Granada Studios stepped in and were so remarkable and wonderful and gave me two weeks rehearsal instead of one. So the first week I could fight for Doyle and the second week I could work with my fellow actors. And that's basically how it's been ever since." (NPR Interview 1991)*

The Solitary Cyclist - The Adventures of Sherlock Holmes

"I've looked for the cracks in the veneer to allow me to say more about the character. In The Solitary Cyclist when I'm holding Violet Smith's hand making deductions about spatulate finger ends, I tried to portray the fact that Holmes found the touch sensuous." (Jeremy)

Jeremy and David in The Solitary Cyclist

The thirteen episodes of *The Adventures of Sherlock Holmes* were to be filmed as one complete sequence and Granada would make the decision whether to continue based on the public response. The first episode recorded **The Solitary Cyclist (Dramatised by Alan Plater: Directed by Paul Annett fb: 15th May 1984)** was filmed at Delamere Forest near Chester for the forest scenes of Doyle's story. The Baker Street set had been constructed on the facia of the Bonded Warehouse facing the historical railway at the Museum of Science and Industry in Manchester. *"It was daunting because they'd only just finished the set and it had cost millions and it was all squeaky clean... my clothes were still bristling new, and how do you wear the deerstalker without looking a twit? ... How do I smoke a pipe when I'm left-handed?"* Violet Smith, the sensible, bright and determined young music teacher was seeking help as her safety had been put at risk by the predatory unpleasant Woodley, a friend of her employer who upset her with his unwanted attentions. She was followed each week as she travelled to the railway station on her bicycle to visit her mother and the man on the bicycle behind her wore a beard and glasses. This brought her to 221b Baker Street in fear of her life and seeking help from Sherlock Holmes.

The opening of the story began in the sitting room of the first floor apartment that Holmes and Watson shared in Baker Street. The reading public was first introduced to Sherlock Holmes and Doctor John Watson in the novel *A Study in Scarlet* where Watson was looking for comfortable rooms at a reasonable price and Holmes, having found a suite of rooms, needed someone to share the expense. The friendship which developed from this arrangement was to be one of the great male friendships in all literature. *"To me, the Sherlock Holmes stories are about a great friendship. Without Watson, Holmes might well have burnt out on cocaine long ago. I hope the series shows how important friendship is."* (Jeremy) *"And then the relationship with Watson began to intrigue. What keeps Watson there? They have perhaps the greatest friendship in literature, and it must be something in Holmes."* (Jeremy in Brett becomes Holmes in the Bryan Times) "These men, totally different, Mr Chalk and Mr Cheese as I once called them, do manage to share a life together because they are complementary to each other. They don't have the same faults or the same strengths. We always looked for the moment at which Holmes and Watson could exchange a glance acknowledging that one had understood what the other was thinking." (Michael Cox in The Armchair Detective 1982) His willingness to investigate her situation put the young lady's mind at rest and the adventure that followed was full of excitement and confrontation. Holmes's assurance, *"Miss Smith, I never guess"* is comforting yet his eyes flash at this seemingly low opinion of his abilities.

Jeremy said that he used his physicality as a way to demonstrate Holmes's intelligence. *"He's much faster than any other human being. His brain, when he is working is so fast, that it's blinding to the observer – including Watson. That takes a lot of steam to get up to."* (Sherlock Holmes Review, Interview with Jeremy Brett 16th March 1987) Perhaps it is the elegant, faintly humorous boxing scene in the local hostelry which becomes the centrepiece of the episode. It is a compelling dramatisation of Doyle's description of the confrontation made remarkable by Jeremy's balletic movement around the scene; "The dancing footwork at the start of the fight was his; the ripple of applause from the bystanders when the bully is disposed of was the director's contribution." (A Study in Celluloid) Watching the drunken clergyman staggering from the public house, Holmes deduces that Woodley would also be present and through his questioning of the landlord he lures the blackguard to the bar where he confronts him. Woodley throws a backhanded first punch but as Holmes is a semi-professional boxer he returns to teach him a lesson and defend Miss Smith's honour. The one to one combat will see him defeated but not before Jeremy's intricate footwork with fists upheld in the manner of a gentleman, will make his opponent look a fool and the knockout blow sends him reeling across a table. The cut above Holmes's eye will represent a badge of honour. The impromptu applause from the Pub's regulars gives Holmes a moment of gratification and as he later relates to Watson, *"It was absolutely delicious."*

The final act is pure melodrama with the introduction of an unfrocked clergyman who carries out a forced marriage at gunpoint; the distress of the lovesick employer, Carruthers, who attempts to kill the villainous Woodley and the rescue of the distraught would-be victim Miss Violet Smith who has fainted in her distress. Followed closely by the final explanation by Jeremy Brett's Holmes who is in full possession of the facts of the case long before Watson can even guess at what he has been a part of, all contribute to an accurate and visually stunning representation of the Doyle text.

The chemical experiment which results in so much smoke that the fire brigade is called denotes this Holmes as an impossible housemate with the final image of Holmes and Watson at the open window seeking air. Jeremy said, *"Holmes is an impossible man to share rooms with! I think that what I found in what I call the under-bedding of the part is that somehow Watson sees this man's need... He scrapes on his violin, not very well. He does chemistry – nearly blows people to pieces if he's not very careful, or as happens in* The Solitary Cyclist, *nearly sets fire to 221b Baker Street. So he's obviously a problem child."* (Jeremy Brett: The Real Sherlock Holmes by Rosemary Herbert) "Whatever else he achieved in these stories, Conan Doyle gave us one of the greatest portraits of friendship in English Literature and we were determined to put that on the screen more faithfully than it had ever been seen before." (Michael Cox in A Study in Celluloid)

The *New York Times* reported, "Jeremy Brett makes a truly splendid Sherlock: vain, arrogant, imperious, rude." *Sherlock Holmes On Screen* applauded Granada for its faithful interpretation of the Conan Doyle originals, especially the copying of the Sidney Paget drawings, shown at the commercial breaks, or the end of the episode, to become "a fan's dream". Alan Barnes commented on how the interpretation of Doyle created a new, exciting approach to the text. Some of the "finest moments" occur when the writers read between the lines. "The stand-out scene in the first episode recorded, *The Solitary Cyclist*, being a case in point," where Holmes confronts the repulsive Jack Woodley. "The 'delicious' encounter is only fleetingly reported in Doyle; its mechanics here are entirely invented... In just one minor sequence, Peter Cushing's arch superman, John Neville's self-righteous physicality and Basil Rathbone's sharp superiority are fused into a fascinating whole." (Alan Barnes in Sherlock Holmes Onscreen)

"The momentum had begun and I had begun to find things – the cracks in the marble – such as his delicacy with women, his failures, the little human elements... But he's a very isolated, private man; he's removed emotion from his life and that's what makes him so hard to play." (Jeremy to Hilary DeVries in Christian Science Monitor 1988)

Teaching the blackguard Woodley a lesson

The Speckled Band - The Adventures of Sherlock Holmes

Rosalyn Landor as Miss Helen Stoner in The Speckled Band

***The Speckled Band* (Dramatised by Jeremy Paul: Directed by John Bruce fb: 29th May 1984)** was the second of the series to be filmed, and the sixth to be aired. Arlington Hall, a stately home in Cheshire, became Stoke Moran of the story. The sudden arrival of another young lady in distress to 221b Baker Street means that Mrs Hudson woke Holmes at 7.15 a.m. who then woke Watson, so that Miss Helen Stoner (Rosalyn Landor) may be greeted by a fully prepared household with a fire and an offer of breakfast. Holmes shows a sympathetic concern as he recognises her urgent need for advice. He deduces this by the stains on her clothing from a long journey by pony and trap and then by train. She is trembling, filled with terror at the actions of a violent stepfather who doesn't hesitate to put her in danger and the unexplained horror that surrounds her. She tells Holmes of the loss of her sister, who died in strange and unexplained circumstances. The sound of a whistle and her sister's last words *"The band, a speckled band"* tells of an unsolved mystery which intrigues Holmes and the lack of precise details of Julia's death or a satisfactory explanation alerts him to the seriousness of the situation, *"These are very deep waters"*. The physical evidence of her injuries will convince him that this case requires his expert attention. Holmes immediately recognises the extent of Miss Stoner's danger and the misery she is living with as the bruises he uncovers provide evidence of her stepfather's abuse.

Of Conan Doyle's villains, Doctor Grimesby Roylott is certainly one of the worst. The portrait that the author presents is a villain who has a vulnerable, innocent and dependent stepdaughter at his mercy. He is a formidable opponent for Sherlock Holmes, has bad relations with his neighbours, and a liking for wild animals from India. Gypsies are invited to camp on his land, a leopard and a baboon roam freely around the grounds suggesting Grimesby Roylott is a king of his own jungle. In Doyle's story, Holmes tells Watson, *"When a doctor goes wrong he is the first of criminals. He has nerve and he has knowledge... This man strikes even deeper, but I think Watson, that we shall be able to strike deeper still. But we shall have horrors enough before the night is over..."* (The Speckled Band)

The investigation at Stoke Moran, first from the outside and then from within, reveals that there is no possibility of intruders gaining access which suggests the danger is from within the walls. Inside, there is a ventilator between two interior rooms; a locked safe and a saucer of milk where there is no cat; a bed anchored to the floor and a bell cord that doesn't work, all contributing to a mystery that only a detective of Holmes's calibre can solve. Waiting in Helen's room for the opportunity to intervene and save her from her own father, the tension shows visibly in Jeremy's shaking hands and on his face. *"I put his fear into* The Adventure of the Speckled Band. *Holmes is quaking, but he's got his back to Watson."* (Jeremy Brett: The Real Sherlock Holmes by Rosemary Herbert) Here the Granada team again showed a faithful interpretation of one of the best loved of Conan Doyle's stories

David Burke had discovered why so many actors, from Nigel Bruce on, had made Watson a buffoon. "They had to take refuge in comedy to give them something to do and going for a few giggles was the obvious," he said, "in the story, *The Speckled Band,* I counted the number of words Watson actually spoke. It was 43." By changing Watson's role from Narrator to Friend the dynamic had been changed and some more of the dialogue would be given to David as the series progressed. And Jeremy commented on their relationship, *"We make a very good odd couple, because we found we got on so well. David is also debonair with an attractiveness about him that is unusual and appealing in a Watson. That is a bonus and helps to break the traditional mould."* (The New Tenant at 221b Baker Street)

"The character of Holmes... I have never thought I was right for that... I couldn't understand... why Granada Television were interested. In truth, I was very daunted by it. But, I thought, well I could only fail. But, I didn't want to fail. There comes a time in your life, where you don't want to fail, anymore. It's too painful. Then a miracle happened, people started to like it and the show has been bought and sold abroad, shown in 60 countries. They are asking for re-runs, not one showing or two, but three times. So, it has all happened and it's terribly exciting. But, it has never been easy. I don't suppose I would have liked it, if it had been really." (NPR Interview 1991)

The Naval Treaty - The Adventures of Sherlock Holmes

The Naval Treaty

***The Naval Treaty* (Dramatised by Jeremy Paul: Directed by Alan Grint fb: 8th May 1984)** was also filmed before the official series opener in order to give the actors, the camera men, and the whole team confidence. However, the Granada's standard of excellence was established from our first view of Jeremy Brett staring into the fireplace in *A Scandal in Bohemia*. Jeremy and David created a wonderful camaraderie between Holmes and Watson. With Rosalie Williams as Mrs Hudson given a bigger role daily life in number 221b Baker Street ran smoothly. Rosalie highlighted one moment from the final scene, "Jeremy wanted to give me a flower. He gave me a little marigold, just as a little gesture. It was very sweet. It wasn't Conan Doyle; it was just something that happened when we were playing (the scene)." She called it "embroidery", a fleeting gesture between them both which would authenticate their relationship and enrich the performance.

The episode begins with Holmes "working hard over a chemical investigation" in order to prove a man's guilt, and Watson's arrival shows his astonishment at the chaos in their rooms and his friend's indoor gun practice on the wall in the V.R. sign in bullet holes replacing the picture over the mantelpiece. He arrives with a request from Percy Phelps, a friend from Watson's schooldays, who has written to ask if Holmes might help solve the mystery of the disappearance of a vital government document. Understandably the highly strung Percy became ill and suffered from brain fever for nine weeks, due to the stress of the situation, nursed by his fiancée and nurse Annie Harrison. Holmes is only too happy to help a friend of Watson's in a fascinating inexplicable case: "*It would be absurd to deny that the case is a very abstruse and complicated one.*" He examines everyone who may have had an interest in the Treaty or who may have profited from it, but his challenge is that the trail will be cold as the theft had happened so long ago. Any evidence would have been lost during that time. As he tests every avenue and everyone with scientific precision one is reminded of the aphorism contained in *The Sign of Four* where all the possible clues are investigated and whatever remains, however improbable, must be the truth.

As Holmes enters the sick room he observes it is full of flowers, with the scent of summer wafting through the open window and unexpectedly he presents a philosophical view of a rose. "*What a lovely thing a rose is! There is nothing in which deduction is so necessary as in religion. It can be built up as an exact science by the reasoner. Our highest assurance of Providence seems to me to rest in the flowers. It is only goodness which gives extras, and so I say we have much to hope for from the flowers.*" (The Naval Treaty) When Annie Harrison urges him to return to London to continue his investigation there Jeremy said "*I was aware of the disturbance felt by Miss Harrison when I talk about the rose.*" Michael thought it was "a charming speech although it does not make particularly good sense and it's hard to understand why Holmes indulges in this sudden flight of fancy." (A Study in Celluloid) Michael also records the discussions, some of them heated, about the adaptation of the speech as Jeremy became the champion for Doyle.

Filmed in a hot August in 1983, at Pott Hall in Pott Shrigley, the private home which was chosen to replace the large detached house in Woking in a rural setting allowed Holmes to pass the day in pleasant surroundings whilst waiting for his dangerous confrontation with the thief. And with Miss Harrison's inestimable help the safe recovery of the Treaty. The story's conclusion remains exactly as the author told it and the effect is that we can hear Jeremy's voice quoting Doyle, the first time a Sherlock Holmes production had ever achieved that. "*I managed to persuade Alan Grint to keep Percy's reaction to the recovered treaty much as it was in the script, but it was hard work. I wanted this version to be as faithful as possible.*"
(Nicholas Utechin, Jeremy Brett: Television's Newest Holmes in The Sherlock Holmes Journal vol 17 1985)

His impression that Holmes didn't laugh was gradually being overturned and Jeremy loved to laugh. Jeremy said that this particular episode was his favourite, "*On a difficult case he may build up considerable tension within himself, which explodes in a genial bit of theatricality when the problem is solved. I've tried to get some of that in my Holmes. Of all the stories I've done The Naval Treaty is my favourite, it was the first time in which I felt I could be a bit of me as well as Holmes. I wore a beige suit and a straw hat during that glorious summer. I was allowed to laugh, and at the end, when Holmes knew he'd cracked the problem, I made him do a little skip and dance. Some viewers may not have approved, but for me it was a breakthrough.*"

The Adventures of Sherlock Holmes

The Rose Speech in The Naval Treaty

Jeremy acknowledged his close study of Conan Doyle's stories in an interview: *"I have had this book beside me since we began, because... I wanted to keep Doyle's stories as close to the originals as possible. Now adaptors do have a way of changing things, and so I needed this with me to refer to. When I found something I didn't like I would flip open the book and say, 'Isn't the original better?' I became a bit of a pain in the neck at times, I guess, but it was worth it to get the stories as close to the books as possible."* (Jeremy to Peter Haining) *"I can hear them saying, 'Oh God, Jeremy's brought the book out again."* David Burke explained; "He was a great perfectionist. I mean, he carried his book of Sherlock Holmes stories around with him, almost like a Bible, and woe betide anybody who tried to alter the stories, unless it was absolutely necessary for translation from the page into film. Not merely did he keep a close eye on the dialogue remaining faithful, but also, when we were actually filming, he would concern himself, in the nicest possible way, with making sure everybody was dressed correctly and that the action mirrored what it said in the book." (Scarlet Street)

When struggling with some aspect of a scene, Jeremy said, *"I would walk about all over Manchester wrestling with the problem. Sometimes I would discuss it with others or else read the lines over and over again. But in the end I realized the best thing was to go back to the original text by Conan Doyle. So I would pick up my annotated copy, read it, and sure enough there would be the answer staring me in the face."* (The Television Sherlock Holmes)

The Bonded Warehouse

Jeremy's appearance relied on the deliberate picturing of the Sidney Paget drawings from the original Strand Magazine in which Holmes was pictured wearing a formal black frockcoat with the customary top hat. *"I am quite broad-shouldered and I wear an amazing frockcoat, it's cut two inches in on the shoulder, so I look long and thin. It doesn't fit me, in other words; it's cut so it's snug, right on the bone, so that it gives a length. The waistcoat is pinched very tight to hide my chest, so that I look even more pencil thin. The shoes again giving greater length... Physically, I am much bigger, broader, bigger chested than he is. So, the costume of the black, long, lean look is what I lean on tremendously."* (The Black Box Club)

Paul Annett said he would have the illustrations at his side when they were lining up the shots in order to match the originals. More stills were inserted at the end of the episode, or either side of the commercial breaks so the Sherlock Holmes aficionados would recognise the reverence of Doyle. "We all agreed that if we were going to do this series properly, we wanted it so that people who watched it could actually do a PhD on Conan Doyle if necessary because it was so true to the originals." (David Stuart Davies in Bending the Willow)

We love the romance of Victorian London yet, the reality of the industrial age city was sometimes at odds with its yellow fogs from burning coal; its streets became an overflowing cesspool from the horse traffic and lack of any effective way to clean them. Granada's realistic reconstruction of Baker Street was alive with the noise and constant activity of horse drawn traffic or street workers. "Even Baker Street the elegant desirable residences of Holmes and Watson smelled more like a farmyard than London's fashionable West End yesterday. I keep shouting 'Give me more horse manure,' said Mr Cox who has masterminded the rebuilding of Baker Street on a disused railway just a stride from the Coronation Street set." (Elements of Holmes in Daily Mail 27th September 1983)

Another downside to this authenticity lay in the need to show Holmes using drugs. Conan Doyle had described him injecting a seven percent solution of cocaine intravenously at the beginning of his novel *The Sign of Four. Holmes* justifies his actions to an astonished Watson in *"My mind rebels at stagnation..."* And Watson's reaction is at odds with the rest of the medical profession who recommended cocaine as a cure for everything, even baby's colic. This scene was used in *A Scandal in Bohemia* as a means of introducing the audience to this new portrayal of Sherlock Holmes. It included everything Conan Doyle said about his character. Here he was a musician wearing a dressing gown, thin, languid, an aesthetic with eccentricities and bad habits: the first time as a complete person. But drug taking was no longer as socially acceptable as it was to the Victorian public and this element had not been shown quite so graphically in previous adaptations. Jeremy said, *"They're pre-Freud, pre-psychology, and much wilder. You realise they're much more destructive and dangerous than you could have imagined. Holmes is his own Special Branch. He's a man who flirts with crime all the time and I always think this rubs off."* (TV Times 19th May 1984) *"I have to admit I've become very like him in certain ways. I even started smoking a pipe, though I draw the line at snorting cocaine..."*

His career had centred on the classics so he was used to playing characters who *"never stopped talking"* and he found Doyle very difficult in comparison with Shakespeare which has a rhyme and rhythm to aid memory. So he resorted to intensive learning, to know it inside out so he could *"bounce"* on it. *"When we first started I was getting up at 3 am to prepare. It takes a lot of effort to go deeper into a story so that it's not simply a parody. I was bouncing a scene like a trampoline. I'd be polishing my magnifying glass, eating breakfast and making up all while doing twenty-six pages of dialogue. I seemed to have more lines than I'd had hot dinners. By 4 pm when the director wanted fire, my fire was out."* (The Television Sherlock Holmes)

The drunken groom

A Scandal in Bohemia - The Adventures of Sherlock Holmes

Gayle Hunnicutt as Irene Adler - The Woman

The fourth story filmed was to be the first shown as the series launch. ***A Scandal In Bohemia, (Dramatised by Alexander Baron: Directed by Paul Annett fb: 24th April 1984),*** This began with the two most iconic moments in *Sherlock Holmes*: the introduction to Holmes in the opening speech taken from *The Sign of Four* which identifies the detective as a man and the introduction of Irene Adler as *The* Woman. She changed his view of all women. The intelligence, beauty, operatic voice, and bohemian ways showed him a woman who broke the stereotypical Victorian mould with grace and style.

The episode begins with Watson's return to Baker Street after a few days in the country, unsure what Holmes's mood will be and the viewer shares his first impressions. Watson's discovery of the hypodermic syringe and the accusation that Holmes is under the influence of drugs brings the information that it is *"a seven per cent solution"*. In a brilliant use of the fourth wall, Holmes to Watson and the audience and asks, *"Would you like to try it?"* This is a memorable moment as the first view of Sherlock Holmes is that of a very real and exceptional gentleman. *"My mind rebels at stagnation. Give me problems, give me work, give me the most abstruse cryptogram, or the most intricate analysis, and I am in my own proper atmosphere. I can dispense then with artificial stimulants. But, I abhor the dull routine of existence. I crave mental exaltation. That is why I have chosen my own profession, rather created it, for I am the only one in the world... the only, unofficial, consulting detective."* (A Scandal in Bohemia) The delay in which we see only the back of his head before Holmes turned to camera adds a frisson of excitement to a long awaited moment. The image of the great detective with his slicked back hair, his long gaunt face with expressive eyebrows is Jeremy's face transformed into another being, one which is new and intriguing.

Jeremy and David with Paul Annett

The case begins with the introduction of a masked King Wilhelm of Bavaria who requests the great detective's help in recovering an incriminating photograph of himself with Miss Irene Adler. The acceptance of the case sends Holmes on a mission for information, dressed as a groom. The use of disguise is a triumph for the make-up department under Esther Dean. The drunken groom is a close recreation of the Sidney Paget drawing and Jeremy was thrilled to be unrecognisable even to his producer, who when he asked where Jeremy was, found he was standing next to him. "He bounced with joy." (Michael Cox)

As he works to outwit this resourceful lady, Holmes becomes a witness to her wedding and later that evening he hires a group of unemployed actors to create a near riot outside Irene Adler's secluded home. Jeremy explained how his own reaction to Irene's perfume could be used in his characterisation. *"I was absolutely overwhelmed by it"* and her femininity, *"There was a great shock to him... Holmes has never been so close to a female breast before. She is a beautiful woman with all the sweet essences of her sex. Gayle Hunnicutt wears a scent called 'Bluebell' by Penhaligon. Holmes is affected by this – his senses are acute – and he becomes disoriented. What is going on in his head at the moment? Uncertainty? Is this onslaught of femininity the reason he refers to her as The Woman?... This is the lovemaking of a shy man.*

He would like to remove Irene, too from his life because he can't waste his precious energies on emotion. But Irene sings divinely, and that means a very great deal to him because he loves music... Holmes changed his whole code of ethics about women after meeting her, but he does this at a cost. The question is, is it worth the cost?" (Taken from Scarlet Street, The Armchair Detective and The Real Sherlock Holmes)

A Sidney Paget illustration

Gayle Hunnicutt was a perfect and even inspired casting choice for the lovely Irene Adler, charming and intriguing in her dealings with Holmes so it is no surprise that he is enchanted by her. Her intelligence would be fascinating to his clinical mind. Unlike everyone else, she recognises Holmes under his disguise, but only because she has revealed the photograph's hiding place and had been warned he might be engaged in the affair. *"He fails to get the compromising picture. Holmes covers his error. He says he'll go back. But she has cheated him and gone away. She's a very remarkable woman."* Her decision to forego any revenge on the King and destroy her insurance policy, the photograph, is another reason for Holmes to admire her. The portrait of her is his reward and it will remain in his locked drawer to be looked at and cherished over the coming years.

Jeremy was finding out new things about the character of Holmes as he dug deeper into the part. "The Scandal in Bohemia *was when I discovered that Holmes laughed and I went right over the top and never stopped laughing in that one. I was so excited. Before then I had only dared a flicker of a smile."* (Jeremy in Video Today) He was bringing a new exciting interpretation of the detective and his friend Watson before the public. *"Watson sees that Holmes can't say*

'Thank you.' He can't say, 'Good night.' Can't say, 'Help!' But what Holmes does occasionally is rather sweet little things like in A Scandal in Bohemia *he tells Watson, 'You see, I did remember you were coming; here are your cigars.' And it's the little things that mean a lot. I tried to show how much Holmes does actually need Watson without actually saying it. I think that Holmes would be dead… if Watson weren't there."* (Jeremy Brett: The Real Sherlock Holmes by Rosemary Herbert) David also had his view of the relationship, "Watson always seemed to me to be a very innocent man, really bordering on the naive. Nigel Bruce had played the part mainly for comedy. I thought it was a very nice characterisation but perhaps went a little too far towards the comic. I tried to bring a balance to it: to be able to play the comic aspect of it; to accentuate the contrast between the rather intolerant, driven Holmes and the laid-back, gentle character of Watson." (David to Daniel Smith in The Sherlock Holmes Companion)

The Guardian gave their full approval, "*The Adventures of Sherlock Holmes* – a seven part series with another to come – is a very posh job indeed. So polished that, if you rub your hand over it, you would leave greasy finger marks, so don't. I can recommend it: as a luxurious, even luscious, way of passing the time. It is the best butter that I can't think why that is not what Sherlock Holmes needs." (Nancy Banks-Smith in The Guardian 25th April 1984)

"Jeremy Brett as Holmes is superb from the word 'Go'. His magnificent performance in this episode engaged me instantly, and prepared me for the 40 adventures to follow… during which time, I would come to embrace his Holmes as THE definitive screen characterisation of the world's greatest detective… his presence alone made each and every episode a delight to watch." (IMDb) "Brett portrays a Holmes of a type not seen before; bordering on the arrogant, he will not suffer fools light, be they clients or villains. But his sympathies for those who have real need of him and his abilities are genuine, however brusque he appears on the surface. He is not a social worker, and he presses his clients for the hard facts he needs to do his work properly. It is the solution of a mystery for which they have come to him, not hand-holding. There are many subtle indications at his great trust and affection for Watson. The doctor is not a clown figure, he is Everyman to the remoter Holmes." (Kate Karlson Redmond in The Baker Street Journal)

Baker Street File – Scandal in Bohemia

93 - Had immense faculties and powers of observation

94 - Had a Bohemian soul – but did not miss company

95 - He was the most perfect reasoning and observing machine that the world has seen

109 - Pacing room; head sunk upon chest, hands clasped behind him

110 - Rubbed his long, nervous hands together

111 - Laughed – sometimes heartily and for some time; sometimes till limp and helpless

The Dancing Men - The Adventures of Sherlock Holmes

Tenniel Evans as Hilton Cubitt in The Dancing Men

***The Dancing Men* (Dramatised by Anthony Skene: Directed by John Bruce fb: 1st May 1984)** would be close to the top of anyone's list of favourite episodes, including Michael Cox who thought it worked particularly well. It was third on Conan Doyle's list of twelve best stories. It was very effective, firstly due to the chosen picturesque setting in Leighton Hall, Lancashire, but also due to the puzzle of the dancing men *"absurd little figures dancing across the paper"* in the notes strewn around the gardens of the stately home which for some unexplained reason brings great distress to the mistress of the house. The mystery lies in who has sent the notes and why they bring such unhappiness. The arrival of Mr Hilton Cubitt at Baker Street with the tale of his three-year marriage which has been spoiled by the strange appearance of indecipherable messages around his home offers intrigue. A letter from Chicago thrown unopened onto the fire may be puzzling, however, it is the fact that Cubitt had refused to ask his wife for an explanation which most concerns Holmes.

"By the time of *The Dancing Men* Jeremy and David had established a very good working rapport and they contributed quite a lot of fun about the solving of the code. I suspect they also contributed the moment where Watson is secretly reading Holmes's monograph on cyphers. That was the kind of thing they enjoyed." (Michael Cox to David Stuart Davies in Bending the Willow) The blackboard set up in the Baker Street rooms was used to show the progress of the notes' translation, meticulously drawn by Holmes and as more messages arrive, the text is gradually revealed. These scenes represent an illustration of both Holmes's methods and his relationship with Watson as Holmes asks his friend to leave him alone whilst he attempts to solve the puzzle but the demonstration of the end of word flags would offer some relief to an all consuming task.

Jeremy was naturally left-handed and he found it difficult to use his right hand on anything they gave him to write, so it has been said that a hand double was used. However, Michael Cox in *A Study in Celluloid* says he persevered with his right hand for this particular episode and with persistence was successful. This determination is one of Jeremy's great strengths as an actor and can be seen on several occasions in the series. It enabled him to maintain the authenticity of Holmes even when he was struggling to achieve it. The deerstalker hat which accompanies the light grey suit is a pleasing addition in this episode and a sign that Holmes is visiting the country, as no gentleman would wear a deerstalker about town. It was a decision the team had made to remove some of the trappings which were not part of Conan Doyle's stories, yet others had been added as signature aspects of Holmes's character.

On his arrival at Cubitt's home the news of Hilton Cubitt's death and of his wife's injuries was a complete surprise to Holmes. Inspector Martin's theory was that Elsie has killed her husband and then attempted to take her own life. This is one of only two instances in the Conan Doyle tales when Holmes has delayed too long and lost his client. He was too late to prevent the tragedy but he was anxious to ensure that justice is done. The investigation and the solution is a masterpiece of sleuthing. Holmes has already explored his theories, reached tentative conclusions and through questioning the household staff, confirmed his expectations. The smell of gunpowder from downstairs, the discovery of the bullet in the window jamb, and the search amongst the gravel outside the window, with the precision and grace of a ballet dancer, show him using many of the modern methods of policing and show him as a celebrated master of his trade.

Jeremy remained committed to presenting the authentic Doyle wherever possible and was eager to include the opening exchange in this episode, although it had not been included in the script. He prepared and learnt it over his lunch break and was justifiably proud to record it in one take, putting every single line of Doyle into the mouths of Holmes and Watson. *"I lifted the whole of the first page and a half of* The Dancing Men *straight from the page, and there it was, thanks to John Bruce, my director, who allowed me to do it. I said, 'If I can learn it and bounce on it, can I do it?' And he said, 'Try it.'"* (Armchair Detective) This scene helps define the relationship with the comment from Holmes concerning his friend's investment in South African Securities with the demand that Watson should not say everything is "*so absurdly simple*" when it was explained to him. The humour of Watson saying these very words when it "*was*" finally explained to him brings a sign of contrition and a triumphal response from Holmes. But as Watson retaliates with his own jibe about Holmes being unemployed and the inevitable black moods or an escape into the cocaine bottle, he reaches the inevitable conclusion, "Sherlock Holmes is cheerful, therefore Sherlock Holmes must have a case!" Moments like these would bring further insight into the way the two men dealt with the other and to Watson's tolerance and depth of understanding.

When asked to choose between his different Dr Watsons, David Burke and Edward Hardwicke, Jeremy said, *"I couldn't possibly choose. They were both splendid in their own individual way. There are moments I'm fond of. I loved the way David stood up for me in* The Dancing Men, *when the local police didn't know who I was. He stepped forward, 'This is Sherlock Holmes.' I was very touched by his performance in* The Final Problem. *Ted's faint and obvious relief at his friend's return in* The Empty House *was also very touching. He showed such vulnerability. He was so very good in* The Musgrave Ritual, *which is one of the best we ever did. Ted really didn't want to play Watson; he was a reluctant hero."* (Scarlet Street)

The Dancing Men

The Crooked Man - The Adventures of Sherlock Holmes

The Crooked Man

***The Crooked Man* (Dramatised by Alfred Shaughnessy: Directed by Alan Grint fb: 22nd May 1984)** filmed at Sandhurst Training College, is a military tale and Jeremy's attitude in the barracks at Aldershot, where Holmes has been called in to investigate the sudden death of the Colonel is rude and overbearing. Jeremy's close connection with the army through his father, Colonel William Huggins, is unlikely to have coloured his responses to this tale, as he always showed immense pride in his father's achievements, but his stalking across the parade ground in his long black coat and topper with cane swinging as in a military parade, and his hostile approach to Major Murphy suggests that Holmes was antagonistic towards the military. Jeremy seemed to go several steps further and show contempt although the suggestion of a scandal may offer some justification alongside his demand to be told the facts which is necessary if he is going to solve this case.

This episode begins with the "murder" of Colonel Barclay of the Royal Mallows, one of the most famous Irish regiments of the British Army. Their achievements in the Crimea and the Indian Mutiny were significant and James Barclay was rewarded with a commissioned rank and since his marriage to the "charming, vivacious, and spirited" Miss Nancy Devoy, his career had flourished and he had been appointed Commanding Officer. In spite of his success,

Colonel Barclay suffered from black moods, sometimes displaying a violent turn of mind, and even depression which could last for days. The details of a quarrel with his wife, Nancy, behind a locked door, became serious when there was a crash, a piercing scream, followed by silence. On entry to the locked room through the window, the Colonel was found dead with a severe cut to the back of his head and Mrs Barclay was found lying insensible on the couch.

There is an opportunity to view a different Holmes in the scenes that follow as he responds sharply to Watson's comments in the carriage; *"mild adultery has always been commonplace among officers and their wives serving in hot climates"* with the tetchy comment that he didn't need education in *"military morality."* In contrast, the seductive manner of his interrogation of the housemaid is an example of Holmes at his most charming and persuasive as he suggests that marital upset was a regular feature of the Colonel and Mrs Barclay's relationship.

The interview with Miss Morrison led to the solution and the discovery of Henry Wood, accompanied by his mongoose. "I cannot betray a friend, please don't ask me to!" may have been a heartfelt plea but the cause was too great to ignore "I must break my promise of friendship" and true friendship required the sacrifice. The tale told by Wood was one of love and betrayal and one which was to bring about the death of the Colonel. "It is a heart-wrenching love story which has stood the test of time. The tragic events are brought about by jealousy and misuse of power which allows Barclay to send his rival for the hand of Nancy to his certain death. When we are told the background it is no surprise that Barclay is the unhappy, haunted man who dies of apoplexy." (Lynne Truss) The shout of "David", from Mrs Barclay, heard through the locked door was explained by reference to the Old Testament story of David and Bathsheba where the King of Israel had put Bathsheba's husband, Uriah the Hittite at the front of the advancing troops so that he would be killed and she would be free to marry him. "We are avoiding the clichés and what has been added through the years both by writers and actors. There is no 'Elementary, my dear Watson,' because Holmes never said those four words together. But at the end of the episode we turn that cliché on its head when Holmes and Watson replies, 'Elementary, my dear Holmes'". (Michael Cox in A New Tenant at 221b Baker Street)

There was considerable disquiet over the changes to the story which had been turned upside down, due to the inability of the cameras to record the details as Doyle had presented them. One scene that was changed had upset both Jeremy and David who commented on the lost moment of pathos when Henry Wood had first seen his Nancy under a street light and had called out in recognition of his long lost love, but did not know of her marriage to the man who was responsible for his suffering. It was replaced by the more mundane mission scene and both David and Jeremy were dismayed: "Blood was almost spilt and tears were shed. I'm afraid we lost the battle." (David Burke) Jeremy was so upset that he went further. *"By the time we got to* The Crooked Man *we were so far away from the story that I despaired. Adaptors would dread me pulling them up on things. I went to them and said that I would lose interest in the project if they didn't stick closer to Doyle's original. I was committed to the first thirteen so I could not have left but my heart nearly broke."* (The Sherlock Holmes Gazette)

This may have been a difficult episode to produce and Michael Cox needed a significant amount of persuasion to include it in *The Adventures* but for the critics this was a very successful episode. "The central part of the investigation, devised by Shaughnessy as a typical

Holmesian inquiry, is enthralling and superbly performed. Brett, with his velvet voice, his persuasive tone and his charming smile, conveys the seductive power Holmes can display to draw the truth from a close-mouthed witness. And striding across the lawn like a foxhound, he expresses perfectly the animal passion for hunting which spurs on Holmes. As for David Burke, he plays with conviction and brisk energy the active part Shaughnessy has granted Watson. Thanks to the work of the whole crew, this episode, getting the most out of Conan Doyle's short story, retains the fundamental elements of a Holmesian investigation, while its pathos and its exoticism enthral the viewer's sensitivity and imagination." (sirarthur-conan-doyle.com) "If you are going to buy one Conan Doyle DVD let it be this. If you're going to watch as single episode, let it be *The Crooked Man*. For this is as good as it gets. We have a glorious incarnation of Holmes and Watson here. Brett's Holmes – cantankerous, affected, whimsical, rude, arrogant, precipitous, charming – can only have been drawn from the deepest possible understanding of the text. There have been similar efforts along the same lines, though none so successful. No other Holmes has come close to Brett's portrayal of the brilliant but obsessed mind, teetering on the knife edge dividing madness and genius." (IMDb)

Norman Jones as Henry Wood in The Crooked Man

The Blue Carbuncle - The Adventures of Sherlock Holmes

"Chance has put in our way a most singular and whimsical problem, and its solution is its own reward."

The Blue Carbuncle

The Blue Carbuncle (Dramatised by Paul Finney: Directed by David Carson fb: 5th June 1984) was a Christmas story shown in June and unfortunately not part of the Christmas schedules. This lack of forethought on behalf of Granada was a lost opportunity to enjoy the Victorian seasonal delights of a goose, holly and the presents bought already wrapped from the Gamages Department Store. The opening credits provide a history of the blue carbuncle, a precious blue gem discovered twenty years before and then lost, stolen from the cold and remote and widowed Duchess of Morcar whose screams of outrage are strangely unmoving. The sympathy in the story has been transferred to the man arrested for the theft, the innocent tradesman John Horner, clearly hired for a menial job to take the blame. Thus the setting of a crime is explained with the need of the only unofficial consulting detective to investigate the events.

Watson is the man who is up from his bed and out early to purchase his gifts whilst Holmes is still asleep, only to be awakened by Mrs Hudson as they have a client. It is a unique occurrence to see Holmes being shaken awake when he is usually the one waking his friend which is humorously followed by a frantic search for a match to light his first essential cigarette, an instance surely inspired by Jeremy's addiction to nicotine. His reaction to Peterson, the commissionaire, standing in his living room clutching a goose and a stiff felt bowler hat is full of finely created detail and humour; a Paget illustration faithfully recreated.

Conan Doyle's story of the investigation of the theft of the Blue Carbuncle began with Watson arriving at Baker Street the second day after Christmas to find Holmes lounging on the sofa in his purple dressing gown, with his magnifying glass and pipe rack within reach, surveying a "*very seedy, and disreputable hard felt hat, much the worse for wear, and cracked in several places.*" Granada had decided to bring it forward to a couple of days before Christmas and Holmes's perceptive and detailed analysis of the hat and its prospective owner is full of assurance on his part and playful questioning from Watson. The conclusions that the owner is a "*highly intellectual*" man who has "*fallen on hard times*" and that "*his wife no longer loves him*" is confirmed by his observations at which Watson responds with a mixture of disbelief and delight. This beautiful back and forth exchange is one of the cornerstones of this friendship.

When Jeremy was asked which episode he found the most difficult he said it was *The Blue Carbuncle* because of the Sidney Paget drawing, "*so marvellous, with Holmes lying sideways on the sofa. I had to actually be in the position for about a day and a half, so I could very nearly not stand up straight at the end of shooting the scene. It was an undiluted piece of brilliant deduction. And one so invariably gets it wrong... a particularly tough film.*" (zombostcloset.com) The tracing of the thief is a masterful gathering of evidence and of personal experience as Mr. Henry Baker comes to the Baker Street rooms and confirms much of Holmes's sympathetic analyses of the owner of the hat. Henry Baker is clearly not the thief as the knowledge that the bird has been eaten causes him enormous distress but once in possession of a replacement goose he leaves, a contented man.

Holmes and Watson will finally meet with James Ryder as he tries to locate his missing goose. This section of the episode follows the original story closely and the confidence aligned with the panache with which Jeremy presents Holmes provides added pleasure. Watson also enjoys his moment of triumph as he claims his £5 reward for his wager on the difference in taste between town and country bred geese. The luring of the thief James Ryder to Baker Street changes the tone entirely as Holmes becomes a predator pursuing his prey: catches him and hears the rest of the sad tale from the beaten man. Freeing the innocent man Horner languishing in custody at the local police station awaiting conviction and "*seven years penal servitude*" is Holmes's focus. This is the first instance in the series that we see Holmes acting outside the law and "*commuting a felony*" in the name of justice.

The examination of Henry Baker's hat in The Blue Carbuncle

Jeremy was a technician as much as he was an actor creating a character. He understood the mechanics of filming and watched the rushes whenever he was given the opportunity. In behind the scenes photographs he can often be seen peering through the camera lens to check how the scene was lit, what was in the shot, where his edges were. *"Filming is magic and I find it thrilling to have as many as 15 people working to the same end to get the moment absolutely right on film. It's true communication."* (Elementary)

The communication would continue offscreen too. "A film crew would do anything for Jeremy and there were two reasons for this. First, because he was absolutely professional in his work, and second, because he knew them all personally. Not only had he memorised everyone's name by the end of the first day's shooting but he also knew whose car had been broken into or whose baby was ill. And it wasn't a trick to curry favour, he genuinely wanted to know." (Michael Cox in Sherlock Holmes Gazette)

Later on in the series Jeremy invited Edward Hardwicke to view the daily rushes with him, and was surprised by his refusal but the justification was a personal one. "When I'm in the process of working I find it personally very destructive to see the rushes. Jeremy would say, 'Yeah, but you're not just looking at you. All the other people – the lighting man, the sound man – they all want a pat on the back. And if you watch it, you can go up the next day and say, 'Terrific!'" (The Armchair Detective) In his speech at Granada Television in 1992 Jeremy would pay tribute to each of the experts in their field, not only to the crew and the electricians but also to the film editors, composers, the set designers, system directors, production managers, the researchers, the script editors and paid particular tribute to Sue Milton *"my brilliant makeup artist"* and Esther Dean as *"this country's finest costume designer"*. (Charles Allen Granada Television)

The casting of David Burke as Watson was just as important as the choice for Holmes. Michael said, "Very determinedly, I went for someone who could restore the image of Watson to the rather dashing, good-looking, military man who was a believable friend for Sherlock Holmes, who must be one of the most demanding people in choosing his friends, as you can imagine. It seemed to all of us that there was no way in which one could give Holmes as a friend and colleague someone who was a buffoon. So we went for that rather more believable man who also, I think, represents people like you and me in the stories. He is a reasonably intelligent, moderately skilled fellow. Not, of course, anywhere in the same league as the superman Holmes, but he is someone that you and I can identify with." (The Television Sherlock Holmes and Armchair Detective)

In spite of his determination to create a happy working atmosphere Jeremy found Holmes a very difficult part to play as his own character was so unlike that of the detective: *"He's chilling... If I saw him walking down the street, I'd say, 'Poor soul... what a tortured creature. He's not a happy man.' Who could be happy who falls apart when he's not working or has to be drugged in order to go to sleep?"* The dark, brooding side of the character worried him and his way of coming to terms with such a superman was to *"look for the cracks in the marble"*. *"When I was doing the first five films I used to go back to my hotel room in Manchester and say 'Damn it! I can't play this black figure with a white face all day! I must have a celebration in the evening.' So I would order a half-bottle of champagne. But, of course, I'd wash my hair, and put on something bright and cheerful. Two years go by. That half-bottle has turned into a bottle. Another year goes by. Now it's a bottle and wine at dinner. I realised it wasn't to take me out to celebrate. It's to make me sleep. And that's why Holmes shoots up. To knock himself out... Someone asked me if I dream about him. I said 'No, and I'm very lucky because otherwise I'd have him all day and all night as well.'"*

The Adventures of Sherlock Holmes

Baker Street

The thirteen episodes of *The Adventures of Sherlock Holmes* were recorded without a break in production, although there was a thirteen month gap between the broadcast of the first seven and the next six on television. This meant there was no feedback from the public to gauge how effective it was, or to give them guidance about the prospects for a new series. The excellence was in evidence from the very beginning, however, the next six episodes seemed to have an added confidence. Jeremy was sharing his interpretation with the press, "*I will never get to the bottom of the barrel. When I get stuck I put my hand in further into the sawdust. Holmes is the most complex, isolated creature – a complete eccentric... He's a man with a brilliant instinct who can be a demented nightbird, driving around the streets of London in the dead of night. He's very gracious to women, but a man with a fear of women - a man who doesn't believe in society or in trivia.*" (The Hunt for Holmes Daredevils November 1984) "Jeremy Brett and David Burke are the best Holmes and Watson I've ever seen. For once we can see why Holmes's only passion is detection. The first hint of an assignment galvanises him into a fury of excitement. He takes an inordinate pleasure in dressing up as a labourer and an aged clergyman in order to spy on Irene Adler, and he takes a mischievous delight in the little deductive feats to astound Watson." (Philip French in The Sunday Times) Another article called him, "one of nature's most engaging extroverts playing the part of the manic depressive detective - a role which nearly destroyed him. Except that he has too much spunk. A more brazenly charming chap you could not hope to meet than Mr Brett, who returns tomorrow as the famous Baker Street sleuth on a new series of *The Adventures of Sherlock Holmes*. Hailed on both sides of the Atlantic as the best ever Holmes, the masterly art of Mr Brett's caustic drawl and cadaverous make-up has even managed to eclipse the memory of the great Basil Rathbone in the role." (Margaret Paton) Jeremy received a letter from his 82 year old grandmother saying, *"Now suddenly this burst of stardom. It's almost frightening! Do you feel the same way? What she was saying is, Are you still humble?"*

The Copper Beeches - The Adventures of Sherlock Holmes

Natasha Richardson as Miss Violet Hunter in The Copper Beeches

The Copper Beeches (Writer: Bill Craig, Director: Paul Annett fb: 25th August 1985) had an audience of 11.23 million which clearly suggested the studios had a hit after all. Initially, Holmes dismisses the request of the young lady who arrives at Baker Street, seeking his advice regarding the strange requirements of a job as governess as he is unable to find any challenge in the case. He greets her with bad humour but quickly thaws as he hears that Miss Violet Hunter, played by a very young Natasha Richardson, is an orphan. She is poorly treated at Miss Stoper's *Westaways Agency* (Miss Stoper is played by Patience Collier, Jeremy's frequent bridge companion). Also, of the unusual demands of Mr. Jephro Rucastle, who is presented with appropriate menace by Joss Ackland. Holmes becomes intrigued. It was a mystery why this man should wish to pay her a three figure salary, with an advance of thirty pounds for her expenses, and then ask her "*to obey any little commands*" and to have her luxurious hair cut short. As she describes her experiences, Holmes calls it "*a strange fad*", and can't resist touching her hair himself.

Jeremy talked about the need to preserve the personal integrity of his clients: "*People in distress – I found them much more emotional when you start putting flesh and blood onto them, when you get actors to play those people, when for example you have a young girl coming in deep distress because she's been told that she's going to have all her hair cut off; otherwise, she won't get the job…"* (Nicholas Utechin in Jeremy Brett: Television's Newest Holmes in The Sherlock Holmes Journal Vol 17, Number 2 1985) *The Copper Beaches* has many of the elements of the Gothic genre in the setting of a remote house holding a dark secret. The house, Storrs Hall, near Carnforth, is Gothic in design with a locked turret and as sinister as Miss Hunter's new employer also reflected in her unpleasant charge Edward, the boy who enjoys killing cockroaches. The presence of a vicious mastiff dog, kept hungry specifically to keep strangers away, all strike fear in the vulnerable new governess.

Violet's call for Holmes's assistance is one of urgency. In a nearby hostelry she tells him of the demands surrounding the wearing of the blue dress and Rucastle's strange antics whilst she sat in front of a window in full view of a man watching from the street. This was followed by her investigation of the turret room with his violent threats to throw her to the mastiff if she ever returned. The sinister story becomes a tale of terror when Holmes and Watson arrive at the Beeches with the house surrounded by mist and the padlocked but unlocked gates suggesting something momentous had occurred. Jeremy and David are athletic and urgent in pursuit, running swiftly after Rucastle but things become much more dangerous when the guard dog deprived of food for two days is released and serious injury becomes inevitable. The revelation of the strange events surrounding Rucastle's daughter Alice, a story of subterfuge and imprisonment, brings light into the mystery. Fortunately, Holmes is able to offer protection to the vulnerable Violet, who has been unwittingly caught up in the events. As Rucastle gets his just deserts it is certain that without the intervention of Holmes and Watson the ending would have been very different.

Some of Holmes's more difficult moods are revealed in this episode, his demand for *"Data! Data! I can't make bricks without clay"*. His statement about scattered houses reminding him of what evil may lurk in the countryside. His criticism of Watson's writings in the introduction where he complains about the misrepresentation of his cases which have brought a decline in the nature of his enquiries, *"It seems to be degenerating into an agency for recovering lost lead pencils and giving advice to young ladies from boarding schools."* Watson may have been hurt at the outburst but he understands his friend's distress and the reasons he feels aggrieved. Furthermore, the companionable humour is reinstated at the close when Holmes says with good grace, *"My dear fellow, I leave all these things to your excellent literary judgement."* (The Copper Beeches)

Michael Cox explained the nature of some of the negotiations that took place during filming, "Jeremy would sometimes say to me or to the director, 'My goodness, this is a huge mouthful of words. Do I really have to say this?' I can remember in *The Copper Beeches*, he says something about the great public who couldn't tell a weaver by his tooth or a compositor by his left thumb. He cut that out originally, but I said, 'Oh, it's wonderful, a marvellous illustration of Holmes's observations.' So that went back. It was give and take. I must admit I respected Jeremy when he did defend the stories, and we hammered it out between us." (Michael Cox in Armchair Detective) Michael also commented on the response to the Granada series in United States when it was first aired on PBS Television. "It was tremendous to walk down the street in New York and see posters on all the bus stops. People would say hello to him in the street and everywhere we went they would congratulate him. They were very forthcoming about what they thought of the series. Usually it was complimentary, and he enjoyed that enormously." (Scarlet Street Number 21)

The Greek Interpreter - The Adventures of Sherlock Holmes

The Greek Interpreter

***The Greek Interpreter* (Writer: Derek Marlowe, Director: Alan Grint fb: 1st September 1985)** begins as usual in Baker Street with a domestic scene which provides more personal information about Holmes to his friend, Watson. The fact that he has a brother, named Mycroft, with an important job dealing with government finances was totally unexpected. Watson had come to think of Holmes "as an isolated phenomenon, a brain without a heart" and that his pre-eminent intelligence accompanied by his lack of sympathy and aversion to women, originated in a lack of relatives.

The meeting with Mycroft took place in the private gentleman's club, the Diogenes Club, which *"contains the most unsociable and unclubbable men in town,"* filmed at Tatton Park, Knutsford. Sherlock has described his elder brother as superior to him in observation and deduction *"but he has no ambition and no energy"* and their skills are put to the test as the audience are invited to share Watson's experience, to see the two brothers either side of a window, listening to them as they compete with each other to provide a detailed analysis of two people in the street below each offering proof for their brilliant deductions. As the visitor Mr Melas is brought into the room to share his story, we are able to appreciate the stylishly framed moment, choreographed and managed by Jeremy, of the younger, slender Holmes stepping out from behind his "much larger and stouter" screen-stealing brother, Mycroft, played by Charles Gray. We also hear of Sherlock's fame due to Watson's publications in "I hear of Sherlock everywhere."

The strange tale of Mr Melas, the Greek Interpreter, is a direct contrast with the domesticity of the early scenes and contains sadistic elements of the Gothic. He recounts his story of accepting the job of Interpreter unwittingly and being forced under some duress to wear a blindfold on the journey to a secret location where he was required to question a man who is clearly a prisoner and a victim of torture. As only his interviewee and himself could understand Greek, he was proud of his ability to gain more information about Paul Kratides with his extra questions but when the victim's sister entered the room, he was ushered from the room and taken home with the same precautions of secrecy.

An advertisement appealing for information about Paul and Sophia Katrides, which Mycroft had placed in the newspapers brings more details and provides a link to the house in Beckenham. Tension is created by the need for a search warrant and the difficulties in finding a magistrate who could sign it bring a significant delay but Holmes must wait. When they eventually arrive at the house, an upper room reveals a disaster beyond their imagination; a scene of suffering and death from sulphur poisoning and Holmes once more takes charge, prepared to risk his own safety by dashing once more into the room to rescue Mr Melas and carry him outside. Paul Katrides was found dead and Watson's medical skills were essential once more.

Kemp is a soft spoken sinister villain wearing thick lensed glasses, not in the same mould of Grimesby Roylott or Jephro Rucastle but all the more dangerous as he is prepared to use knives as weapons in a vicious and mocking manner. The death of Paul Katrides in the sulphur attack is murder and moral justice required them to pay for their crime. Conan Doyle's version had allowed Latimer, Kemp and Sophia to escape but they had all died on the Continent, recorded in a newspaper account of two Englishmen travelling with a woman who *"had met a tragic end. They had each been stabbed, it seems, and the Hungarian police were of the opinion that they had quarrelled and had inflicted mortal injuries upon each other."* (The Greek Interpreter) Holmes believed that the girl had taken her revenge on her brother's attackers.

However, Granada chose to continue the story beyond where Doyle finishes. The result is an entertaining conclusion which merges seamlessly into the original story and provides a convincing bringing together of the different threads. With the aid of a *Bradshaw Railway Guide*, Holmes, Mycroft and Watson followed the escaping villains onto the train to the continent and confronted them. The scene in the railway carriage where Latimer is told that he is sitting face to face with Sherlock Holmes and Doctor Watson is both tense and ironic as he realises he is trapped. Jeremy's Holmes emerges as the brave and courageous hero who reacts instinctively to the crisis by grabbing hold of Sophia to save her from certain death as Latimer jumps from the carriage into the path of an approaching train. The picture of an inscrutable Holmes holding both Watson and the girl is a heroic one as they seem to be looking into the face of hell. Sophie had been promised marriage in exchange for her involvement in the plot to steal from her brother, and as she is taken away by the police, Holmes cynically observes, as one would expect from a misogynist, *"It is not a crime to have a cold heart and not a single shred of compassion."*

The episode was filmed at the Bluebell Line at Sheffield Park, Sussex, chosen because it was a, "fine period station, but also because the rolling-stock, impeccably maintained by the Bluebell Railway Preservation Society, includes the London, Brighton and South Coast Railway's directors' saloon where the meal was set up between Mycroft and Wilson Kemp and where he takes the small pistol away from him." (A Study in Celluloid) The final image of Jeremy's Holmes walking elegantly and energetically down the platform (in the wrong direction) into the mist is a memorable highlight. Jeremy fought for the reinstatement of Holmes's speech about the virtue of modesty; *"To the logician all things should be seen exactly as they are, and to underestimate one's self is as much a departure from truth as to exaggerate one's own powers."* His justification lay in his desire to show more about the man that was Holmes which was *"not just his brilliance but the vulnerability and the... human being that is inside him; lonely, brilliant."* (Jeremy)

The *New York Times* commented on the Holmes brothers, "With eccentricity clearly being a pronounced family trait... Mycroft, played deliciously by the veteran actor Charles Gray, has attained a state of blessed distraction that approaches otherworldliness. Mr. Melas finds himself involved with the Holmes brothers in a scenario involving murder, fraud and a heartless woman, who reinforces Sherlock's low opinion of women in general. It's not a very absorbing case but, directed by Alan Grint, Derek Marlowe's adaptation does give Sherlock an opportunity or two to berate the police while flashing his own inimitable powers of deduction. Mr. Brett is by now perfectly haughty and irresistible in the role, while Mr. Burke's Watson has developed into a splendid partner and foil. Meanwhile, Mycroft, rousing himself from periodic fits of dozing, is only too happy to admit that Sherlock has all the energy in the family." (New York Times 8th February 1986)

During an interview for the Morning show *TVam* on ITV in 1990 in which Jeremy was celebrating his winning of the Pipesmoker of the Year award, Jeremy smiled as he told the presenter Mike Morris of how he had lost one of his valuable pipes during the filming of this episode. Whilst showing the two that he had brought with him, the long thin cherrywood with a curved stem, smoked when Holmes was in one of his disputatious moods and then the long clay pipe which he smoked in his more meditative moods, just like Popeye! *"I was robbed whilst I was doing* The Greek Interpreter. *We had some VIPs round and they stole my pipe. It was either the* Young Conservatives *or the* Royal Ballet. *I bet it was the* Young Conservatives."

The Norwood Builder - The Adventures of Sherlock Holmes

The Norwood Builder

***The Norwood Builder* (Writer: Richard Harris, Director: Ken Grieve fb: 8th September 1985)** captures the imagination by so many intriguing elements: an incomprehensible villain with a desire for revenge; a client who seems to be beyond help and a daunted Holmes without the essential facts for so much of the story. The scene of Holmes sitting in his nightshirt and dressing gown, in despair, rejecting food because he *"cannot afford energy and nerve force for digestion"* or his client will go to the gallows, is distressing but the presence of his friend who will persuade him to have some breakfast and "go out and see what we can do" together brings further evidence for their dependence on each other. *"I feel I will need your company and moral support today."* (Holmes) Jeremy presents the active and athletic Holmes as he investigates the scene of the fire; the disguise of a tramp with a blackened face and loose floppy hair which is clearly Jeremy in *mufti*, and the dramatic conclusion make this one of the more entertaining episodes.

The drama begins with the introduction of John Hector McFarlane, "a wide-eyed and frantic young man, pale, dishevelled, and palpitating," who bursts into the Baker Street rooms with the assumption that he was already known to Holmes and Watson. Holmes's conclusions that he was "*a bachelor, a solicitor, a Freemason and an asthmatic,*" give evidence once more to his deductive skills. McFarlane reveals the startling fact that he expects to be arrested for the murder of Jonas Oldacre of Lower Norwood and shows him the newspaper story in the paper Watson has just purchased. The precipitous arrival of Inspector Lestrade, played by Colin Jeavons, prepared to arrest McFarlane for murder brings the threat of danger; Watson facetiously calls him "our old friend," but in this case he becomes a rival for the life of their client. The story told by McFarlane is a strange and incredible one in which he is promised a legacy but is then accused of arson and murder. Although Lestrade is prepared to listen to his account he still takes the accused away in handcuffs with the purpose of having him hanged.

Holmes has some possible theories, beginning at Blackheath, which puzzles Lestrade, but which provides a useful introduction to the builder Oldacre to whom McFarlane's mother was once engaged, and she describes him as a cruel and vindictive man. As the villain of the piece, Jonas Oldacre appears to be the victim of murder as human remains have been detected in the remnants of the fire at the timber yard; indeed there is no evidence to disprove the theory until the final scenes where his Machiavellian plot is revealed. There is no opportunity for Holmes to examine him or test the evidence and in this case the dead tell no tales. One of Mr Oldacre's trouser buttons also found in the ashes of the burnt out building, is presented as further evidence against McFarlane.

The stand out scene in this episode concerns the fatal error, which brings the bewildering case to a satisfactory conclusion. The gathering of three police constables, with buckets of water standing by, whilst the group shout "*Fire*" has the desired effect. Holmes becomes the great magician who reveals the perpetrator with a deadly desire for revenge. It is a scenic highlight as the group are encouraged to shout louder and together, with Jeremy providing the example in his stentorian tones. The positioning of Holmes, Watson and Lestrade is one of those perfectly staged moments as they peer at the panelling to see the "murderer" emerge from his hiding place.

The changes made in the Granada version centred on the murder of a tramp dressed in Oldacre's clothes, designed to provide evidence for McFarlane's guilt; however, Holmes's disguise helped to reveal the missing information and he spots something the police had missed in his inspection of the fire: a shark's tooth and the signs the people of the road leave for each other when they receive a kindly welcome. Jeremy's physicality is a positive asset in this episode which requires Holmes to investigate the fire in the grounds of a large Victorian house in Bowdon to represent Deep Dene House.

Jeremy said he found the character tougher to play than any other in his distinguished career, "*Holmes is terribly difficult to play because he's so private and so much cleverer than anyone else. He's what all men want to be, what all women want to seduce.*" (TV Times) "*He keeps me fit. Every time I think I get somewhere, he's a field ahead of me. Can't ever relax, can't pin him down.*" He thought he was getting somewhere when he learned how he walked. "*That's largely the result of the shoes, the boots with the pointed toes that are pictured in the books. Then came the hands.*" "*I tried to become him, to sort of find out how it would be if you were a minimalist, an isolationist, not much interest in anything except work. I mean, he should be like a stone, and I tick and twitch all over, I get so depressed when I'm watching myself. I think I'm being still. An eyebrow goes, a nostril goes and the mouth. The thing is; he doesn't."* (Sherlock Holmes Behind the Scenes interview ITV This Morning) "Brett still is a bit of a glamour boy which originally made him surprising casting as Holmes. But he has captured the fastidious theatricality of the master criminologist and given him a neurotic vulnerability that forever eclipses the memory of Basil Rathbone playing him straight. You care about his lonely Holmes like no other incarnation. And he makes you laugh frequently at his answers to everything, delivered with wonderfully dry timing. This is a Holmes with humour and unexpected heart." (Maureen Paton in The Daily Express) Jeremy told *The Calgary Herald* of a moment in a New York taxi; "*And the driver spoke to me out of the side of his mouth, 'When you stood on that burning log and walked across it with your cane and looked down, you looked like a cat.' So I said, 'Are you talking about...?' 'Yes, Mr Brett,' he said. 'I'm talking about* The Norwood Builder (an episode in the PBS series).' *That was a moment! It was terribly exciting that someone, a cab driver in New York has watched the show and picked a moment. I think that's thrilling.*" (The Calgary Herald 5th November 1991)

The Norwood Builder

The Resident Patient - The Adventures of Sherlock Holmes

The Resident Patient

***The Resident Patient* (Writer: Derek Marlowe, Director: David Carson fb 15th September 1985)** was another dramatic episode but with a criminal element in the mystery. The opening credits show "Sutton" (Blessington) in the middle of a terrifying nightmare with himself in a coffin surrounded by gold coins. More information is given with the arrival of Doctor Percy Trevelyan to Baker Street who is known to Watson as the author of a renowned monograph on "obscure nervous lesions." Although he was university trained he was grateful when a philanthropist, Mr Blessington, offered to set him up in a West End establishment in exchange for a proportion of the doctor's income and a place in the house for himself as a *"resident patient."* In two years Trevelyan had made him a rich man and Blessington locked it away in a strong box in his own room. Inexplicably, a sudden fear of break-ins caused Mr Blessington to panic; he insisted that locks and bars should be installed and he remained in his rooms in "a state of mortal dread." Two men seeking the doctor's help for a case of catalepsy added to his concern and when they suddenly disappeared there was evidence they had invaded his sanctum at which Blessington demanded Doctor Trevelyan call on Holmes to ask for his help. Holmes recognises there is a mystery at the heart of the case, especially as he is greeted at gunpoint by a terrified Blessington. However, he senses deep distrust and lack of honesty in this proposed client, without which he refuses to help and leaves.

The detailed analysis of the different types of cigar and footprints in the hallway show he has recorded every detail from the moment he has entered the house. Michael Cox said, "Jeremy Brett always showed great enthusiasm for sequences in which Holmes investigated the scene of a crime. If there was a floor to throw himself on, or a mantelpiece to climb, Jeremy would flare his nostrils in anticipation. He was very fond of the scrutiny of Blessington's room in this film, not because it presented a physical challenge but because it was carried out in absolute silence. He called it the Rififi sequence in honour of Jules Dassin's famous gangster movie in which a burglary lasting twenty five minutes is conducted without a sound. Our sequence lasts only two minutes… based on a short paragraph in the story, which is acted out in detail as Holmes collects fibres, dust and ash from different surfaces in the room. This enables him to describe the crime…" *(A Study in Celluloid)* "That seems to me so very Sherlock. It was also very brave because one of the rules of television is that you don't leave the soundtrack blank for long or you get people ringing up and saying, 'What's gone wrong?'" (Michael Cox in The Sherlock Holmes Detective Magazine) Holmes's monograph on different tobaccos and cigars enable him to see that there were three people in the room and to reach well-informed conclusions about what had taken place just a few hours before. He had even methodically measured the footprints on the stairs on his first visit to enable him to construct a picture of the men. But it is the clean, clinical precision of his examination of the room where the man has died that lifts the whole episode into a new realm for detective television. Conan Doyle's account is not only brought to life by Jeremy's well choreographed physical interpretation but it is given an elevation to a new sphere of performance.

Back in Baker Street, when Holmes goes in search of a newspaper cutting which will eventually provide evidence for the case, he sifts through all his papers and notebooks scattering paper is pure abandonment and leaving total chaos in his wake. So much mess is created, that Watson leaves the door to their room closed so that Mrs Hudson, who had just completed her spring cleaning, cannot see the results has been turned into until they are safely away from the house.

The villains are not apprehended but when Holmes discovers Blessington is one of a gang of murderous bank thieves involved in the Worthington Bank affair he can provide the rest of the details. The picture accompanying the article shows Blessington was in reality Worthington (also known as Sutton) and the worst of the gang who had turned Queen's Counsel and double-crossed his partners in crime prompting them to seek him out and avenge themselves by hanging him from a hook on the ceiling in the enactment of a trial and execution. In fact, real justice is done when the three criminals go down in a shipwreck during their attempt to escape overseas.

The friendship between the two men is given further detail in the opening scene in the barber shop where Conan Doyle's short story *How Watson Learned the Trick* was included to demonstrate how he had learned Holmes's methods of deduction only to be told every single one of them were incorrect. In "Nevertheless" he does concede that there was an element of truth in Watson's comment, much to his friend's great delight. The final scene where the choice of title for the narrative is in dispute where comedy is used again to change it from "The Brook Street Mystery" to Holmes's choice of "The Resident Patient".

"The adventure of *The Resident Patient* is hardly an exhilarating one but scriptwriter Derek Marlowe's humour brightens, warms and livens up the episode. In the delightful opening scene at the barber's and in the final one, when Watson, at first doubtful, ends up appropriating enthusiastically the title Holmes has suggested, of course, but also when Mrs Hudson congratulating the Doctor on the progress of his model ship, he slips away like a guilty kid before she discovers the living room she just cleaned up has been turned into an appalling dumping ground. The upright, likeable and entertaining Baker Street trio act as an antidote against the criminals' loathsome wickedness." (arthur-conan-doyle.com) "Much of the well-deserved praise this series has received is due to the truly inspired casting of Jeremy Brett as Holmes. There have been other fine interpretations of the role... The fact remains that Jeremy Brett is the definitive screen Holmes and his performances are unlikely ever to be surpassed. This is a brilliant and mercurial Holmes but he is also unstable and neurotic. Playing Holmes in this manner could easily have been disastrous but Brett is in complete control and he does not make the mistake of overly emphasising the great detective's darker side..." (cult-tv-lounge.blogspot.com)

Patrick Newell as Blessington in The Resident Patient

The Red Headed League – The Adventures of Sherlock Holmes

The Red Headed League

***The Red Headed League* (Writer: John Hawkesworth, Director: John Bruce fb: 22nd September 1985)** introduces the arch criminal Professor James Moriarty played with fitting menace by the superb Eric Porter who in the original stories appears only in *The Final Problem*. Michael Cox said he had never thought of any one else for the part of the master criminal, the man chosen by Doyle to kill off Sherlock Holmes. *The Red-Headed League* is understandably one of the favourite episodes of many, and the story was rated as second in Conan Doyle's "twelve best" list of his short stories. The beginning of the episode features a graceful and athletic leap over the sofa by Jeremy's Holmes in his eagerness to prevent Watson leaving the room as he wants his biographer present at the interview with such an intriguing client. Jeremy said, *"The dashing about is rather me. I loved in* The Red-Headed League *when I was allowed to jump the sofa. My son rang me after that and said, 'Dad, you're obviously feeling better.'"*

The case itself centres on a farcical instance of a Red-Headed League with a bemused and angry red-headed man, Jabez Wilson, engaged to write out a fair copy of the *Encyclopaedia Britannica* in exchange for a respectable salary. The opening scene is full of interest and humour. What began as an elegant leap over the sofa becomes an expert analysis of Wilson's background, as Holmes gives a stunning display of his observation skills indicating that he has done manual labour, takes snuff, has visited China and has *"done a considerable amount of writing lately."* This is what we have come to expect of Holmes but the manner in which the red-headed man dismisses his explanation leaves Holmes quite offended, *"I begin to think that my reputation such as it is will suffer shipwreck if I am so candid."* (The Red Headed League) The exchange of giggles and then howls of laughter between Holmes and Watson at the *"bizarre"* situation Jabez Wilson describes is deliciously ironic as the man feels he has been made to look a fool. However, Holmes is intrigued, *"I wouldn't miss this case for the world. It is most refreshingly unusual."* (ibid) *"It is so joyously comic; this mean pompous chap with ginger hair, the bizarre copying up the encyclopaedia and then the bank robbery, well it has all the elements of a Ben Travers farce. Conan Doyle could be a very comic writer."* (David Stuart Davies in Bending the Willow)

Holmes is the genius of investigation, always making sense of the mysterious, and he has picked up on the possibilities of the man who had come as assistant in Wilson's pawnbroking business on half wages and then encouraged his employer to apply for the position offered by the strangely named League, itself a source of mystery as the organisation was willing to pay a generous amount of money for what seems to be trivial work. The description of the assistant, Spaulding, sounded familiar too, so that he was prepared to investigate the area surrounding Saxe-Coburg Square, to see what reasons lay behind the removal of Jabez Wilson from his shop. *"You see, Watson... it was perfectly obvious from the first that the only possible effect of this rather fantastic business of the advertisement of the League, and the copying of the Encyclopaedia must be to get this not over-bright pawnbroker out of the way for a number of hours every day, It was a curious way of managing it, but really it would be difficult to suggest a better."* (The Red-Headed League)

The bringing together of the police agent Jones with the Bank Manager Merryweather to test the veracity of Holmes's theories is a tense situation and Watson is forced to defend his friend as the "only private consulting detective who is unique in the annals of crime" and thus worthy of listening to and, more importantly, of respect. Throughout these scenes in the bank vaults, Jeremy is grim-faced and intense as we watch him listening for signs of the audacious bank robbers. The large consignment of 60,000 gold napoleons recently borrowed from the Bank of France, means there is a much larger amount of bullion than is usual in the vault, confirming the idea that it was John Clay whom they were expecting and who emerges through the cellar floor. Once more Holmes has outwitted the criminals and in so doing brought himself to the attention of Moriarty; the central power behind all that is evil in the city and the mastermind of the Red Headed League. The inclusion of Moriarty was Granada's adaptation to the story as they wished to give him greater substance and danger for the next story, *The Final Problem*.

Baker Street File – The Red-Headed League

96 - Had a dual nature: swung from extreme languor to devouring energy

112 - Curls up in chair with his knees drawn up to his hawk-like nose. His eyes closed and with his black clay pipe thrust out like some strange bird (while pondering a problem)

The Final Problem - The Adventures of Sherlock Holmes

The Final Problem

The Final Problem was an attempt by Sir Arthur Conan Doyle to kill off Sherlock Holmes. He was finding the demands of the public too great, especially when he wanted to spend more time with his greater interest, writing historical novels like Sir Walter Scott, a great influence on Doyle. He felt this was his chance at immortality. Writing to his mother about the last Sherlock Holmes story he intended to produce (the twelfth), Conan Doyle said: "I think of slaying Holmes... and winding him up for good and for all." In spite of her protests, he did so two years later when his wife Louisa was diagnosed with tuberculosis and he felt the need to spend more time with her. Fandom which had previously only been seen in sports had been created overnight for the death of Sherlock Holmes. The fans wore black crepe and accosted Doyle's carriage in London. They wrote thousands of letters daily to both *The Strand* and to Doyle, they formed Keep Holmes Alive Clubs (the precursors of today's Sherlock Holmes Societies) and they immediately cancelled 20,000 subscriptions to *The Strand*

Magazine. It almost folded under the onslaught. "You brute" was the beginning of remonstrance which one lady sent me." (Doyle) "Waiting from month to month for the next adventure of Sherlock Holmes was agony!" exclaimed the poet laureate John Masefield. Nine years later when *The Hound of the Baskervilles* was published as an early Holmes story, the subscriptions immediately returned to *The Strand*. The next year, in 1903, Doyle responded to an offer from an American publisher that he couldn't refuse, of $5,000 for a new Sherlock Holmes story that would bring him back (he wrote 32 more stories) and queues of people stood outside *The Strand* Office to purchase their first copy of his return, to avoid disappointment in the shops.

John Hawkesworth has created an emotional and memorable episode in the Granada version of **The Final Problem (Writer: John Hawkesworth, Director: Alan Grint fb: 29th September 1985)** so that many viewers have said they need to watch *The Empty House* immediately afterwards in order to feel less depressed at the loss of Holmes. "I suspect Conan Doyle knew it would take no ordinary man to kill off Sherlock Holmes. And even though he created a super-criminal to carry out what he hoped would be the execution, he had not bargained for the incredible reaction of the British public." (Eric Porter in Scarlet Street) The episode was filmed on location in Switzerland, for the very first time at the Reichenbach Falls, "a fearful place" tumbling down to "a tremendous abyss", so that the full horror of the situation was given reality. The one to one struggle brought real danger to both Eric and Jeremy with the necessary six takes due to the specially built slippery ledge above the mist and spray of the 400 foot fall of tumbling water which consisted of three falls with several thundering cascades plunging into a pool of great depth and magnitude. The real heroes of this episode were the two stunt men Alf Joint and Marc Boyle attached to a steel cable and harnesses to ensure they returned alive from the boiling "immense chasm." They were each paid around £2,000 but as they pointed out, if the wire snapped or the platform collapsed there would have been no chance of survival. *"The event quite unnerved me. Eric and I had to film our part of the struggle about eight feet from the edge of the falls – and that was bad enough because every time I looked down I felt quite sick. How those two men went over the edge, I'll never know. You should have seen their bruises the next day. It took six takes to get the fight with Moriarty on the edge of the precipice right... I remember thinking as we slithered around in the mud and grass soaked to the skin that, if we're not careful, we might actually fall over the edge and Conan Doyle would have got his wish after all. There really would have been no return for Sherlock Holmes."* (Jeremy in Television Sherlock Holmes) Jeremy suffered from a fear of heights and when the stuntmen returned safely he immediately opened the bottle of champagne he had brought with him to celebrate their courage.

The drama opened with the arrival of Holmes at Baker Street by a backroom window, in personal disarray and covered in dust. For the first time he told Watson of the challenging situations he had experienced as Moriarty's men had pursued him, physically attacked him, tried to run him down in the street so that he was fearful for his life, and he had returned home only at night and in unconventional ways. These scenes of combat were filmed at the University of Manchester, Chetams School of Music.

The open hostilities with Moriarty would begin in Paris with the theft of the famous painting, the Mona Lisa, from the Louvre, which would spur Moriarty to take revenge for his loss of huge profits from the French gold case in an art copying scam. The story was based on the real theft of 1912 when the picture was missing from the Louvre walls for two years and which John Hawkesworth had added to this episode to develop the scenes for Eric Porter as Moriarty. Jeremy had fought a prolonged battle to maintain the Conan Doyle original story intact and had failed. "Jeremy Brett hated it. The read-through of this episode was not a happy one. Jeremy adopted his fundamentalist attitude to Conan Doyle's work; John was an evil revisionist, I was the devil's advocate. David Burke and Eric Porter wisely kept their own counsel. I tried to explain why it was necessary to add to the original but Jeremy would have none of it. Lunch on the first day of rehearsal was usually convivial but on this occasion I think we all went our separate ways." (Michael Cox in A Study in Celluloid)

The Final Problem

In the story the declaration of open warfare took place in the confrontation in Baker Street where Holmes met Moriarty face to face and openly shared their mutual enmity. Jeremy's Holmes was armed and ready with an unblinking stare of coiled intensity whilst Moriarty's menacing whisper and reptilian appearance promised a monumental tussle. Both of the antagonists reflected what was at stake by their palpable hatred of the other. The list of complaints against Holmes was a long one, headed by the "affair of the French gold" and the *The Red-Headed League,* which Holmes judged *"a very ingenious and well-contrived idea"*. But the list continued, "You crossed my path on the 4th January. By the middle of February

I was seriously inconvenienced by you and at the end of March, I was absolutely hampered in my plans; and now, with this last business in France, you have placed me in such a position by your continual persecution that I am in positive danger of losing my liberty. The situation is becoming an impossible one." (The Final Problem) As Holmes refused to "drop it" and step out of Moriarty's way, a fight to the finish was inevitable. "The verbal exchange between Brett and Porter in Baker Street has EVERYTHING – great dialogue, fantastic diction, beautiful timing, fantastic silences and glances. Any aspiring actor should watch this. It is an acting masterclass." (Amazon.co.uk) In his description of his enemy to Watson, Holmes named Moriarty the Napoleon of Crime and the organiser of half of all the evil in the city, so a holiday in Switzerland appears to be a suitable escape. However, the intricate instructions for the safe arrival at the railway station and the disguise of an Italian priest for Holmes to avoid identification are still insufficient to cover their getaway. Moriarty's hiring of a train to follow them showed the dogged determination and the cunning intellect of this very dangerous enemy.

Michael Cox records how a peaceful Victorian champagne picnic by the glacier was filmed, although it ended up on the cutting room floor due to time constraints. Only a couple of pictures survive, one with Jeremy arms outstretched in "acknowledgement of the camera" reproduced in *A Study in Celluloid*. The arrival at the Englischer Hof, kept by Peter Steiler the Elder, introduced the climax of the story as the inevitable meeting between the two adversaries, clearly managed by Moriarty, with the merest of reasons to split the two friends, but successfully achieved. The letter of farewell from Holmes and the Last Will and Testament are moving enough, especially when it was anticipated. Only Watson was unaware of the true situation and his final words contain all the feelings of loss as he shares his eulogy for the man with whom he has shared so much and "Whom I shall ever regard as the best and the wisest man whom I have ever known," and the Granada Studios team created an excellent record of the story. Jeremy explained, "Moriarty represents the final element of evil. Holmes is to be erased... you see Holmes facing death... Holmes knows that Moriarty's network will get him. So very sweetly he says, 'Listen, Watson, I'm going to leave the country because I don't want to endanger you.' But then he turns around and says, 'Do you want to come with me?' So the answer is, yes, he's scared. And then he uses the Reichenbach Falls as one of the greatest coups of all times." (Jeremy Brett: The Real Sherlock Holmes by Rosemary Herbert)

There was a gathering feeling of confidence and even a bravura atmosphere in the studios as Granada had received a wealth of positive feedback from both the critics and the general public, all of which praised the production and the interpretation. Unsurprisingly, Jeremy's Holmes was the focus of much of this attention. By this stage of production, his understanding and commitment to Holmes was so thorough that Eric Porter told *Scarlet Street*, "I found acting with Jeremy Brett a splendid challenge, too, for he was so deeply involved with Holmes that he understood every nerve and fibre of the man. I like to think I gave a good account of Moriarty – though like Jeremy I could hardly dare to watch the two stunt men going over the cliffs.

Whilst in Switzerland the Granada team filmed some scenes for *The Return* in *The Empty House*. Michael Cox issued a press statement, "Just as Conan Doyle was forced by public pressure to bring back Holmes after his disappearance at Reichenbach, so we have decided to go ahead and make seven more stories for the viewers." The critics were pleased, "Jeremy Brett's Holmes has been a striking portrait of an actor: the undulating velvet of the voice, the finger laid like an exclamation mark against the lips and the broad-brimmed hat, turned up a little to one side as though from leaning too long against the waiting room at Crewe." (Every Holmes should have one) Jeremy had accepted the need to wear the iconic deerstalker in this episode, *"I've always thought of the deerstalker as a kind of schoolboy cap that can be scrunched up and put in your pocket... I always wanted to avoid the clichés when playing Holmes and I didn't like the image... I did do the meerschaum pipe for a brief moment in* The Final Problem *because he could have bought it out in Switzerland."* (Jeremy in Scarlet Street) And David's performance had been superb as always. "David Burke's Watson has been most endearing throughout." Michael Cox had succeeded in his aim to create a viable companion for Holmes. "It is unfair to Watson to make him a buffoon and to Holmes who wouldn't have shared an apartment and a friendship with a man who was an idiot. So I decided to do justice to Dr Watson, because if you diminish him, you also diminish Holmes. Without Holmes, Watson's life would be very dull; without Watson, Holmes's life would be disastrous." (The new tenant at 221b Baker Street)

Jeremy with Eric Porter above the Reichenbach Falls

Jeremy and Joan

Joan with Vincent Price

"We had a once-in-a-lifetime love. She was an incredible person, the best wife a man could have. This was the kind of love where I would start a sentence and she would finish it. Sometimes you can see behind somebody's eyes and feel as if you have known them all your life. That's how it was." (Jeremy to Shaun Usher) *"We were born on the same day. If ever I picked up the phone to ring her, it would be engaged – it would be her trying to ring me. I can't ever imagine having that closeness again."* He says his self-confidence died when he lost his "Joanie," a perfect wife. She had seen him on stage in the Noel Coward play *Design for Living* in New York and decided she would like to marry him. Unsurprisingly, Jeremy points out his dependence on the lady to choose him, rather than the other way round: *"I think she will pick me, just as Joan did, although I'll never know – I'll think I've done it... Women are much cleverer than men; they have this brilliant intellect as well as intuition. They are wiser than men and much shrewder. They can organise a man and make him feel terrific. At least that was true of my wife."* Jeremy and Joan met early in 1975 when PBS Television was showing *The Rivals*, and it was an instant attraction. He was interviewed for the introductory programme on the plays of Sheridan, *"I guess she was keen at organising it because I wasn't the only star in* The Rivals; *there were several others and I was the one that was picked; and*

we met on camera and she wanted four minutes, and we talked for two and a half hours... and when we got married in 1977 (22ⁿᵈ November) our best man gave us the bits that were cut out as a wedding present. Luckily we saw them in the dark because we both went bright pink."

Joan, a former actress, was part Cherokee, four years older than Jeremy and, although she was proud of her candour, refused to admit her age. She had an enormous capacity for work, up to seventy hours a week, and her career was very important to her, especially as she had been the artistic director behind *Masterpiece Theatre* since 1973 and the creator of *Mystery! the* home of British Mysteries for Boston PBS station WGBH. "She was *Masterpiece Theatre,* she chose the dishes with ruthless care and taste. She supervised their service. I was simply the headwaiter." (LA Times 9ᵗʰ July 1985)

Joan was in love with this "debonair, exuberant Englishman, Jeremy Brett about whom she gushed but whom she would not publicly name as her spouse." They both loved dancing and often talked into the early hours of the morning, "she loved to flirt, gloried in marriage and motherhood, yet liked to claim that she placed her career first." They were both workaholics so that when the work was offered, he was often separated from her. In an interview with *Woman and Home* he told the magazine he was pretty demanding of his personal relationships and needed tolerance from a partner. *"I'm not a comfortable person to live with. I tend not to do things by halves. I burst into song at the drop of a hat, or go out disco dancing all night and sometimes I get up at 4 a.m. When I work hard, I'm certifiable."* (Woman and Home 1984)

Whilst making *The Adventures of Sherlock Holmes*, Jeremy and his wife and two stepchildren borrowed the top flat of a friend's home in Mayfair, although during the week he was living in the Midland Hotel close to the studio. "But for now, being so happy makes up for no permanent address. The Bretts' LA house is up for sale. There's a distinct 'devil may care' look in Jeremy's eye and a glowing confidence for the future." (ibid) The same year they purchased the penthouse flat of 47, Clapham Common Northside, the distinctive gatehouse in the French Renaissance style. Joan loved the history with its association to Edvard Grieg, and its placement overlooking Clapham Common which lifted Jeremy's heart too. Unfortunately, they were not to live in it as she became ill before they could move in. The packing cases remained unopened until he finally returned home at the end of July 1985 after her death. He spoke about his children with pride and considered Joan's children his own. *"I have three children, David by my first marriage and two stepchildren, Caleb and Rebekah, by my second. They are all absolutely magnificent. David's a painter. Caleb's a lawyer and Rebekah is a brilliant housewife and also a beauty and very intuitive. Only the other Sunday we had a family party, for the older ones."*(ibid)

With a break in filming for the *Sherlock Holmes* series at the Granada Studios, Jeremy flew out to America to be with Joan. She had been diagnosed with cancer of the pancreas so that he needed to be with her. He had been told the devastating news whilst filming *The Final Problem* in Switzerland. His explanation to the media was that, *"I wanted a holiday... and it was also to be near my wife... I knew at the end of* The Final Problem *in '84 that she had cancer, and the lights really went out in my life... I didn't want to do it anymore."* However, he was not really able to face the trauma that illness brought: *"I felt so frustrated that I couldn't be with Joan, although actually she didn't really want me around while she was having chemotherapy. She said, 'You're not up to this.' I walked into the treatment room and saw the equipment pointing up at her. I just fell apart. But what really threw me was a two-year-old girl who'd lost all her hair because of the chemotherapy. Seeing Joan and that child together was just too much for me. And I fainted. I was such a dead loss. Joan said, 'You mustn't do any more of this, it doesn't do you any good.' I apologised, and in fact I did go again and it was better. It's taken so much time and energy to come through the grief of losing Joan. After she'd gone, I went into a series of bad states of mind. I kept thinking, Damn it! Why bother?"* (At last I'm free from the shadow of Holmes by Jo Weedon)

Jeremy took the part in *Aren't We All?* on Broadway so that he could be near her as she continued with her treatment. They celebrated the success of the play together on Joan's last good day before her death on 4th July in one of their favourite activities, dancing: "*The producers had taken the Rainbow Room on opening night. It was April, and the room was full of peach blossoms. Joan looked absolutely radiant, wearing silver and scarlet, and a glorious wig, a facsimile of her hair. And, we danced as the notices flooded by. There was Lynn Redgrave, looking wonderfully Twenties, and darling little Claudette, looking like a girl of 83… and the critics fell at our feet! Frank Rich mentioned me eleven times, I couldn't believe it!*" When Joan died Jeremy opened his heart to the press: "*I lost her on July 4th 1985. And I went back to England when the play finished, it didn't finish until the 23rd – I don't know how I did those performances… I staggered on and finished the play, but the lights were out.*" He told *The Star*, "*I still get very angry about Joan dying. Then I get into self-pity, but I know that's not good. I suppose I always thought a miracle would happen and that she would recover. But it was not to be…. I miss Joan terribly.*'" (The Sorrow of Sherlock by Carole Malone The Star 9th January 1986) "*Joan gave me the most enormous confidence – she loved me for being exactly the way I am. The last thing she said to me was, 'Are you going to be all right?' Under the circumstances, that was a pretty stunning question. She was 54 and she had such wonderful things ahead of her.*" (Television Sherlock Holmes)

Jeremy and Joan in Stratford Ontario 1976 – By Courtesy of N.S. Johnson

The Return of Sherlock Holmes

Michael Cox called *The Return of Sherlock Holmes*, "The best of times and the worst of times." The confidence which comes with the knowledge that things are good and coming together to create excellence was positively inspiring. At the same time the situation with the star, Jeremy's Holmes was on a knife edge. He had heard that his beloved wife Joan was ill whilst filming the conclusion of *The Adventures*. The diagnosis of cancer was devastating and as many do in these circumstances, they hoped that Joan would survive until the very last minute, but it was 4th July 1985 when she died and Jeremy was grieving. *"Well, it was such a shock. She died in '85 on July the Fourth – quite a day to go, being American... and I was absolutely lost. And I couldn't see the point really in anything, least of all S.H."* When his commitment on Broadway was over, he returned to Clapham Common to the home he had bought with Joan where his possessions were stored in unopened packing cases.

In September, at the Midland Hotel in Manchester where he lived whilst filming the Granada series, *"I became a recluse. I began to have meals in my room and stare at the hotel walls... when you play Holmes you leave out love and affection. He's a very dark person to play and one of the most uncomfortable parts to wear on a daily basis. Several actors before me in the role have had nervous breakdowns. In television you must live inside your character. Holmes is a very uncomfortable person to live in..."* "He became the dark side of the moon because he is moody and solitary where I am gregarious. Holmes is so still and I'm like Jiminy Cricket. I had to wash the part out of me as well as the grease out of my hair." *"When Joanie died, all the lights went out in my life. You see, she was my confidence. I didn't want to play Holmes any more. There was no point. But I was committed contractually and started filming two months later, in September. I played the role differently in the second series, but it quite seemed to suit the part."* (Taken from Happy Home from Holmes; The More Elementary Mr Jeremy Brett; A new tenant at 221b Baker Street)

The Empty House - The Return of Sherlock Holmes

The old bookseller

Footage for *The Empty House* (**Dramatised by John Hawkesworth: Directed by Howard Baker fb: 9th July 1986**) had been recorded in Meiringen Switzerland, exactly where Conan Doyle set the dreadful battle between Holmes and Professor Moriarty.

The team's anticipation of the return meant that they were well-prepared. However, the loss of David Burke as Dr Watson meant that further filming was needed to provide a complete story, and as the funding for a return to Switzerland was no longer available, the Welsh mountains became the substitute setting. David had responded to an offer from the *RSC* to appear with his wife Anna Calder-Marshall, who with a five year old son named Tom to consider, was leaving the Granada production. "We were filming virtually solidly for eighteen months in Manchester and I never saw my home and family. I had the chance to join the *Royal Shakespeare Company* at Stratford-on-Avon to appear with Anna, so I took it. It was marvellous fun to work with her and I had the added bonus of playing a real bastard in Maxim Gorky's *The Philistines* – something completely different from Watson." (The Television Sherlock Holmes) Michael recognised the impact this would have. "It was a blow. Jeremy had found aspects of Holmes which no other actor had presented and gradually measured up to his illustrious predecessors. David, on the other hand had completely altered the public perception of Watson. He had given us the Watson that Conan Doyle created and now we had to replace him."

Anna was responsible for the suggestion of Edward Hardwicke as David's replacement, as she and Edward had been working together on the Shakespeare play *Titus Andronicus* for radio and she recognised his talents. When Jeremy and Edward were interviewed by Richard Madeley and Judy Finnegan on *This Morning* a few years later, Jeremy was asked if he had been concerned about the change of personality in his co-star and he replied, "*Yes. Truthfully! But then this miracle occurred. Edward is a very gentle person, and very sensitive, and tried very hard not to upset the boat in any way, and succeeded. What could have been a disaster for the series turned into a bonus... David and I had been together for about a year and a half and had built up a great rapport.*" He added that he had lost "*my bestest friend*" too.

Edward commented, "One's main concern is not to rock the boat because, as I've discovered, it's such a marvellous atmosphere which is very largely due to Jeremy and all the people working on it. But it inevitably varies a bit because we're different. All actors are limited to some extent by who they are and what they are and how they look." Edward was also given a couple of episodes to create his own version of Dr John Watson before *The Empty House* was filmed. Yet, beginning with *The Abbey Grange,* he proved right from the start that this role would be in a pair of very capable hands. And then *The Musgrave Ritual* would delight the viewers with a relationship tinged with comedy and through twenty-seven films and one delightful play.

"It is now three long years since my dear friend plunged to his death, there deep down under the swirling water, the infamous Professor Moriarty and the foremost champion of law of his generation will lie together for all time. Even now, there is hardly a corner of London that does not remind me of my old friend... the loss of one I shall ever regard as the best and wisest men I have ever known." (The Empty House) Watson would be the focus of the first fifteen minutes of *The Empty House* and for the first time in the series we see him without Holmes as a local doctor, a police surgeon and medical scientist, making intelligent deductions at a crime scene. Edward accomplished the transition seamlessly and with his impeccable focus on Watson's relationship with Holmes he would succeed in satisfying even the most dedicated audience. As his friend returns Watson is tested significantly in both the depth of his friendship and in his response to the drama that unfolds before his eyes. However, his grief is soon to be replaced by excitement and the anticipation of new adventures.

The revelation of the living Holmes and the shock of the unmasking is melodramatic notably for Watson's fainting "the first and last time in my life". And the detective's comment accompanied by his loving touch, *"A thousand apologies, my dear Watson. I had no idea that you would be so affected".* The hunched up figure of the old bookseller is a masterpiece and Jeremy remained unrecognisable and unnoticed as he crept into the back of the courtroom for the inquest on Adair's death and even sat incognito on the steps as Watson walked down them before making his appearance in the Doctor's consulting room. As he removed the black costume he succeeded in translating Doyle's words, *"It is no joke when a tall man has to take a foot off his stature for several hours on end,"* by elegantly stretching out of his tall frame in front of the window.

The footage filmed at Meiringen of a distressed Watson, of David shouting *"Holmes,"* whilst being watched from a safe vantage point was used here. The moment when Holmes is trying not to call out to his friend, emphasises the bond between them. Jeremy told David Stuart Davies that although the moment was unscripted this was a deliberate choice to show that Holmes's deep affection for Watson went beyond "his practical mind" and almost got the better of him. "There is a favourite moment for me when Holmes is tempted to shout to his friend but stifles the impulse and makes his escape into three years of oblivion." (Michael Cox)

Watson would be amazed yet delighted to hear how Holmes had defeated Moriarty in their battle over the spray of the Falls with the rare Japanese sport of Baritsu. How he spent the following three years of oblivion reveals more about the man as he indulges his love of culture. He travelled undercover as the Norwegian explorer Sigerson through Florence to Tibet where he visits Lhasa and the religious leader the Dalai Lama. He travelled on to Persia and Khartoum to meet with the Khalifa. And latterly, he has been pursuing research into the coal tar derivatives another of his interests. Jeremy presents Holmes's ever changing moods under the surface as he moves from the troubled memories of the struggle with Moriarty, Through his escape from the most dangerous of terrains to pride in his exploits, achievements and challenges in new lands with new experiences. Three long years had been explained in just a few sentences but his command of the past and of what is to come has been established as the reincarnation. The detective has a new aura of confidence and a new serenity.

Holmes had miraculously escaped with his life but he is still very much at risk as Moriarty's deputy had been there to witness that escape. A touching reunion with Mrs. Hudson reflected in the mirror in one of the director Howard Baker's signature moments and the picture of the Reichenbach Falls above the mantelpiece now shrouded in black drapes to commemorate the tragic death of Sherlock Holmes remind us of what had been achieved in his Herculean climb out of *"that awful chasm"*.

Colonel Sebastian Moran is considered to be Moriarty's deputy and the sniper who had dogged Holmes's footsteps at the Reichenbach Falls. It is he who had used the powerful air-gun which could fire a soft-nosed revolver bullet of sufficient calibre to kill the Honourable

Ronald Adair, a fact that had remained undiscovered, and now Holmes himself was in his sights, informed by the sentinel who is watching and waiting under the lamp post.

Humour is in evidence too in the midst of the drama as Mrs Hudson is pictured crouched behind the wax figure of Holmes, smilingly changing its position every fifteen minutes and when Holmes and Watson return safely, it is she who has found the bullet and placed it on Holmes's palm; thus providing the proof that will convict Colonel Moran of Adair's murder. The celebratory champagne is a fitting end to the drama. Conan Doyle had successfully resurrected his hero and the public were thrilled.

The twentieth century public were also ready to celebrate. "*The Return of Sherlock Holmes* – For this new series of seven Jeremy Brett again plays Holmes – and it's hard to imagine a better one… Brett has also played Dr Watson on stage. *'They're two halves of the same person'* he said." (Sherlock arises from a fall. The Mail 6th July 1986) "Granada Television, the makers of *The Return of Sherlock Holmes* are, I think, entitled to expect that the television audience that will tonight welcome back the great sleuth after his supposed death at the Reichenbach Falls in last year's episode, will be as glad to do so as were those readers of the Holmes stories in *Strand* magazine who were told in 1903 that the detective managed to survive his Falls fall in 1892 and that he would, in fact be returning in *The Empty House*. The simple truth is that Granada's adaptations of Conan Doyle have been the best to date. The more I see of Jeremy Brett's Holmes, the less fondly I remember Basil Rathbone. The more I see of Granada's successive Doctor Watsons (originally David Burke and now Edward Hardwicke), the more ludicrous Nigel Bruce's Hollywood Watson becomes in the memory…" (Today's Television and Radio. The Times 9th July 1986) "Cocksure exuberance underlines all the first seven instalments following *The Adventures of Sherlock Holmes* (1984-5), whereas those episodes were manufactured in the dark, without praise or plaudits, the next set would be produced by a team assured of their own brilliance. And it shows…" (Sherlock Holmes on Screen) "Jeremy was wonderful to work with, such a large talent, the consummate Holmes for me." (Patrick Allen in Scarlet Street 1996)

Baker Street File – The Empty House

90 – Work is the best antidote to sorrow, my dear Watson

103 – I am not a fanciful man

120 – Again in the utter silence I heard that thin, sibilant note which spoke of intense, suppressed excitement

121 – Moran calls Holmes, "You clever, clever fiend!" and "You cunning, cunning fiend!"

Jeremy and Edward in The Empty House

The Priory School - The Return of Sherlock Holmes

The Priory School – Chatsworth House Derbyshire

The Priory School (Dramatised by T.R.Bowen: Directed by John Madden fb: 16th July 1986) is a favourite episode of many. The location of Haddon Hall for the Priory School and the imposing Chatsworth House as the seat of the sixth Duke of Holdernesse is in itself an attractive and commanding backdrop for the story of a missing pupil from his prestigious preparatory school. The opening scenes are workmanlike and driven by the perception and commanding presence of Holmes, here imperturbable and cold. The client on this occasion may not be a King but he is a Duke, who had been a cabinet minister, with money, power and influence. With the exception of the concluding scene, the episode remains faithful to the Doyle original and opens in Baker Street with the humorous moment of a card placed in the sleeping Holmes's pocket by Watson with the simultaneous, very dramatic arrival of a man, "so large, so pompous, and so dignified that he was the very embodiment of self-possession and solidity." (The Priory School) Dr. Thorneycroft Huxtable M.A. Ph.D., who promptly faints on the "bearskin" hearthrug and then on his recovery urges them to return with him to the Priory School, where he is principal, to investigate the "abduction" of one of its most important students, Lord Saltire. The unhappy childhood of the only son of the Duke of Holdernesse may explain the nine year old boy's disappearance and Holmes is pressed into finding him. A reward of six thousand pounds for discovering both the boy and the person responsible for his disappearance is part of the attraction of the case which will become a prestige one for Holmes. His query about a ransom demand is revealing as there has been none and the suspicion of the part played by the German master with the discovery of a bicycle shows Holmes at his incisive best. It also provides sufficient spur to accompany Huxtable to Derbyshire to begin his investigation where Holmes, as always, dispassionately challenges the Duke regarding the reasons for the disappearance of his son in the hope of finding some clues. The opening scenes are accompanied by the choirboys' refrain of *Libera me*, a fitting choice of music which seems to suggest a link with the missing boy.

As Holmes flings himself into the case with characteristic eagerness he is soon able to trace the events by which the German master followed the young Lord Saltire from the school and onto the moor. Bicycle tyres and horses' hooves are the means by which the mystery is solved; one bicycle for two escaping people is insufficient and horses with new shoes will be significant. Out on the moor as they search for tracks, humour is brought into the relationship in the mention of Watson's hunger, as it is something Holmes hardly ever experiences. *"They are a great essay in male friendship, which has gone now. Men's friendship has been debased. One of the lovely things about Holmes and Watson is that they do have this great platonic relationship."* About that "disgusting" lunch, "it was a nice comic moment that we shared." (Edward Hardwicke)

The hiring of two horses first to visit the Hall and then to follow the trail left by the runaways allowed Jeremy to show his skills as an accomplished horseman and to enjoy his favourite pastime. There is one moment when Jeremy's leap from his horse resulted in a poor landing but it is scarcely noticeable as he effortlessly untangled himself from the reins. This skill also enabled Holmes to expertly examine the hired horses with the discovery of, *"old shoes, new nails"*, which remains unexplained until the Duke mentions the fact that they were unable to winter cattle outdoors in the district when the significance of the cattle tracks brings enlightenment. *"I have been as blind as a beetle!"* says Holmes. What they find is the body of the dead German master Herr Heidegger who was strangled and left behind for the vultures. Confessions reveal the knowledge that Wilder is the Duke's son from a previous relationship with the reluctant admission that he has been instrumental in his father's broken marriage, and that he enjoys exerting power over the Duke.

The music of Patrick Gowers and the choristers of Westminster Abbey under Choirmaster Simon Preston are particularly effective in this episode. "One of my favourite films was *The Priory School* directed by John Madden… the final sequence filmed in a cavern was very dramatic and I thought improved on the original story. Jeremy was wonderful. It was a bit like playing tennis with a great tennis player. If you manage to stick the racket in the right place he is going to hit it hard enough for the ball to just go back." (Edward Hardwicke in Elementary My Dear Watson for ITV) *"The Priory School*, this week's ration of Holmes and Watson, is even better than Conan Doyle's original which has an uncharacteristically lame ending. The adapters, John Hawkesworth and T.E. Bowen have risked being lynched by purists by setting the finale in a cavern, with the villain cornered in classic fashion, in all other respects, though this is Conan Doyle's scrupulously respected tale... Although it has become a commonplace to praise Jeremy Brett's and Edward Hardwicke's definitive Holmes and Watson, potential first-time viewers still ought to have the right to be told what a treat is in store for them tonight." (Choice by Peter Davelle in The Times 16th July 1986). *"Another thing I have found about doing this series has been the people working on it with me. It is very seldom that you get an entire studio of people that have actually read the script before they come to the first shoot. That does help... We need brilliant artistry, great lighting, and pure sound to get the maximum effect."* (The Television Sherlock Holmes)

The Priory School

The Second Stain - The Return of Sherlock Holmes

Lady Trelawney Hope with Holmes and Watson in The Second Stain

The Second Stain (Dramatised by John Hawkesworth: Directed by John Bruce fb: 23rd July 1986) was the third film in the sequence designed to help Edward settle into his role as Watson before his appearance in *The Empty House,* and this is notable for his visit to see Holmes in his retirement, beekeeping in Kent, to request permission to publish the story. These scenes complete with the beekeeper's costume and beehives, ended up on the cutting room floor, probably because of editing and timing issues with the programme. However, some photographs still exist of the missing scenes.

The filming was done around Whitehall and Westminster and although 10, Downing Street was off-limits, the location of the seat of Government is totally authentic. Godolphin Street was also located and used for the Eduardo Lucas scenes. "I can remember at one point we got into a street and Jeremy Brett and I were sitting in a Hansom cab... in which there's a window behind us. The camera was there, and... I can see the yellow lines in the road... And immediately the props department came out with a roll of tape... and you just thought that's fantastic, somebody's actually sat down and thought there may be yellow lines on the road." (Edward Hardwicke in Theatre Archive)

The "*bookends*" introduce the case of a missing document with the arrival of two very distinguished personages in their private capacity at 8.30 in the morning, which requires a rapid clear-up of the breakfast things in the Baker Street rooms. Lord Bellinger, the "illustrious" Prime Minister and his Secretary for European Affairs, Rt. Hon. Trelawney Hope, arrive with a most pressing request for help in finding, "a letter from a foreign potentate and one of immense importance," which had disappeared from a locked government dispatch box. There is no evidence of security issues at home or personal carelessness to indicate how it might have disappeared and only the Cabinet knew of its existence. Both men stress that they are sharing a state secret and that any investigations must be carried out in the utmost secrecy as the discovery and publication of the letter could bring a European catastrophe – and war. Holmes is reluctant to take the case without full confidence in him and his methods and his steely smile and dismissive actions challenge the men of power to fully confide in him or find someone else.

Their departure is immediately followed by another arrival, of Lady Hilda Trelawney Hope enquiring about her husband. Holmes appears intrigued by her, especially as her coming has no purpose other than obtaining information, which he is unable to give her due to his vow of professional secrecy. He is intrigued by her appearance of beauty and charm but is forced to answer, "*Madam, what you ask me is really impossible.*" He has also characteristically noted her demeanour, her "*suppressed excitement, her restlessness, her tenacity*" and wonders what her true motive was. This is one of those moments when Holmes shows some interest in a woman and although he tells Watson that "*the fair sex*" is his department, followed by a tirade against women's inscrutability, "*their most trivial action may mean volumes,*" one can't help feeling he is protesting a trifle too much. In fact, Jeremy felt this was the case when he said as much to an interviewer, "*Holmes appears to be this rather cold and distant figure who holds the rest of humanity at arm's length. But deep down I believe – much deeper down – he is a man of tremendous sensitivity and feeling.*" (The Bryan Times 8th September 1988)

The three names Holmes suggests as the only possible receivers with sufficient money to purchase the stolen document are Oberstein, La Rothiere and Eduardo Lucas, two of whom will appear in *The Bruce Partington Plans* and just as Holmes is leaving Baker Street to investigate their whereabouts he is stopped in his tracks by the news of the murder of one of them and thereafter he follows the connection. The stand-out scene in this episode takes place at the home of Eduardo Lucas of Godolphin Street, one of the eighteenth century houses near Westminster Abbey. Inspector Lestrade is hopeful that Holmes might help to explain the worrying detail of a second stain on the floor of the living room which did not match the one on the bloodstained carpet but neither he nor Holmes is prepared to share what they know, especially as the law is as dangerous to Holmes's investigation as the criminals. The investigation of the scene whilst the constable and Lestrade are purposefully distracted outside is full of humour and tension, as with furious energy Jeremy throws himself onto the floor "clawing at each of the squares of wood," pulling himself along as he seeks some hiding place for the missing document with Edward anxiously looking on, whilst maintaining a watchful eye on the Inspector and his constable. Jeremy was once more copying the Sidney Paget drawings from *The Strand Magazine* as he examined every inch of the wood blocked floor until he finally lifted one piece with a snort, "a bitter snarl of anger and disappointment as it was empty". (The Second Stain) Jeremy explained, "*And it is fascinating when he takes to the ground – you can read about this and not think it funny at all. But, when you actually do it, actually see him swoop down and hoover the carpet with his nose, searching for a clue, it is hysterical. The speed of the man is my pathetic attempt to show his mental agility.*" (Jeremy in Holmes Rule - Video Today) "The whole mechanism of the rotated rug – Lestrade's finest hour –

is beautifully handled and Holmes's feverish examination of the wood-block floor has tremendous tension." (A Study in Celluloid)

When Lestrade returned he was nonchalantly sitting on his chair and the original position of the rug restored. The constable's report revealed that a young woman had visited the rooms on the night of the murder providing Holmes with the link to Lady Hilda. The lady herself is persuaded to tell her story which is one of blackmail and vicious murder, finally revealing that she did it and still holds the document. All that was needed now was to return it to its rightful place in the dispatch box, which remains in full view, yet the illusionist Holmes achieves the impossible by a masterly sleight of hand off camera. This scene displays the bravado that the Granada team had developed as the deed is not shown and no explanation is needed. His almost careless lighting of his cigarette as he once more came into view showed the supreme confidence that Jeremy was feeling in the character in this episode.

The final leap of triumph from the steps with the shout of "*Wa-haay*!" was a fitting conclusion which Michael Cox said was very much a Jeremy flourish but unfortunately, he landed in an ungainly fashion and the scene was cut at the crucial moment. It does, however, recall the earlier comment when he was at a loss on how to proceed with the case, "*Should I bring this case to a successful conclusion, it will certainly represent the crowning glory of my career*" with Jeremy gloating over his puffing pipe. Almost immediately, he accidentally set fire to his newspaper giving evidence for Jeremy's description of Holmes as "*a problem child.*" "*First of all, Holmes falls apart when he's not working. Well, that's easy to play because actors do that – we all fall apart really, when we're suddenly made redundant. But what does Holmes do? He actually shoots up, straight to the vein, the seven-percent solution. He smokes too much. He scrapes on his violin, not very well.*" (Jeremy Brett. The Real Sherlock Holmes by Rosemary Herbert)

"I consider it one of the great privileges of my career to have worked with Jeremy Brett and most particularly in his portrayal of Sherlock Holmes, which was his crowning glory and a definitive interpretation of such a great character. I shall never forget his complete absorption in the role, his meticulous attention to detail, his knowledge of every prop and artefact on set. He also had a stunning concentration on camera." (Patricia Hodge in Scarlet Street)

The bee-keeping scene from The Second Stain

The Musgrave Ritual - The Return of Sherlock Holmes

"The butler of Hurlstone is always a thing that is remembered by all who visit us."

"My friend and colleague, Doctor Watson" The Musgrave Ritual

The Musgrave Ritual (Dramatised by Jeremy Paul: Directed by David Carson fb: 30th July 1986) was the second in the sequence of filming in this series. Holmes is very much centre stage with Watson in the supporting role, and it has been described as a vehicle for Jeremy to mould more closely with the character of Holmes. In this fifty four minute episode he displays a wider range of moods, often changing as on a pin head, with a unique opportunity to explore the effects of cocaine. Holmes's first appearance in the opening scene is on the back of a wagon as he and Watson journey towards Hurlstone Manor in Warwickshire; he is displaying signs of "bad grace", accompanied by complaints about the coldness of the Manor and the grim prospect of hours of boredom in the company of his old friend, the grey Reginald Musgrave. It is no surprise that Holmes finds an escape into cocaine. His uproarious laughter at the expense of his host and his butler is an unusual and daring picture of Sherlock Holmes as no one has ever shown him high on cocaine before. Jeremy Brett's laughter is contagious and the viewer inevitably finds himself laughing along as does Watson. The butler Brunton was a schoolmaster with some significant gifts and somehow out of place at the Manor, a paragon and "a bit of a Don Juan" over whose attentions two local girls Rachel and Janet were quarrelling thus "unsettling the household". Jeremy told Peter Haining, *"I was not sure to begin with because Holmes suppresses so many of the emotions in himself. But once I began to find the cracks in his armoury I realized there were moments when he laughed. I was also anxious to let a little of my humour into the part."*

Brunton would be at the heart of the story as he had the education and the curiosity to investigate the Musgrave Ritual. He had evidently understood much more than his employer and Holmes will find that at each step of the way the butler has been there before him. His disappearance with the strange actions of Rachel Howells and her own subsequent disappearance will only be solved when the secret of the ritual is forcibly ripped out. Baddesley Clinton in Warwickshire was the location for the medieval, manor house with its own moat which is a feature of the Musgrave Ritual. Holmes is intrigued enough to ask for the ritual to be read and explores the details. He points out "*a patriarch among oaks*", and there is a memorable scene of the three principals with umbrellas shown in silhouette against the darkening sky as they are forced to reject it. The strange behaviour of Rachel as she throws a rotting bag of metal into the lake and her own disappearance will cause Holmes to get to grips with the riddle.

The great detective is in his element as he throws himself into an enthusiastic treasure hunt and with the discovery of the weather vane with an oak on top, the original position of the elm with the length of its shadow, remembered by Reginald, precise measurements can be made and the hunt begins. The search for the treasure is carried out with humour and military precision with the counting out of steps led by Holmes, his baton pointing the direction or tucked under his arm, in his most energetic manner, first one way and then another. And finally, when the ground runs out the three explorers can be seen in a rowing boat crossing the moat with Holmes stood at the prow appearing to walk on water. The discovery of the treasure trove, the Charles I coin, plus the ancient crown that "*once circled the brows of the royal Stuarts*", which emerges from the twisted pieces of metal and provides the opportunity for a Jeremy flourish of pleasure at his success.

The scriptwriter Jeremy Paul had achieved an effective turnaround of the original story allowing him to explore Brunton's tangled love life and to interact with Holmes and Watson. Justifiably, he won the prestigious Edgar Allan Poe Award from Mystery Writers of America. "We were lucky in our choice of location for Hurlstone – a magnificent moated house in Warwickshire – but we had trouble in remaining faithful to the stepping out of the ritual. A truthful and exact rendering would have deposited our heroes in a bank of thistles. There was also an 'oak and sun' problem, solved, as if by an act of God, by the fortuitous presence of a weather vane with an ornamental oak on its top. We had fun with the notion that Holmes's steps led him to the edge of the moat, forcing him to cross to the house by rowing boat... Two early scenes depict Holmes clearly under the influence of drugs, to Watson's evident dismay. This is not emphasised in the existing text, but we saw the chance to lay the ground for the moment in a later episode when Holmes is seen to discard the cocaine and clear the matter (contentious in these present times) for good." Edward commented on their experience solving the riddle, "We actually did it and went around in a complete circle, ending up where we started! Doyle is full of little things like that. But it doesn't really matter because he's managed to convince you, which is what really good writing is about." (Introduction to The Musgrave Ritual script)

The Abbey Grange - The Return of Sherlock Holmes

Holmes's appeal to Lady Mary Brackenstall to trust him

***The Abbey Grange* (Dramatised by T.R. Bowen: Directed by Peter Hammond fb: 6th August 1986)** was Edward Hardwicke's first film as Watson and as he has very little to say, it is a perfect vehicle for adapting to his role. The opening scene of Holmes waking Watson with a lit candle is a familiar opening to a dramatic episode. Doyle has quoted from Shakespeare's *Henry V Henry VI* in *"Come, Watson, come! The game is afoot."* And within ten minutes they were both in a cab and travelling to Charing Cross Station for the Kentish train with a letter from the young Inspector Stanley Hopkins of the local police urgently requesting their assistance. The train journey also allows time for Holmes to criticise Watson's method of writing about his exploits which has made them into stories rather than scientific exercises which had ruined what might have been. At Watson's bitter remark that he should write his own, Holmes replies *"I will, my dear Watson, I will in my declining years."* Edward was discovering the difficulties of playing a character with so little to say; who just needed to react to the more dominant Holmes. "I remember saying to Jeremy, 'I feel I'm disappearing inside my costume. 'I just felt everything was too overwhelming..." (Elementary Mr Dear Watson Interview with Edward Hardwicke)

An investigation of the murderers is not needed as Lady Brackenstall has given an excellent description of the Lewisham gang, the three Randalls, and also the fact that they had killed her husband, "one of the richest men in Kent," with a blow to the head with his own poker. She is a beautiful young lady, who had travelled from Australia, with her maid, Theresa, to marry the violent Lord Eustace, and she freely admits their marriage was not a happy one, as he was a drunkard. However, Holmes is not convinced by the lady and the clues which he identifies: the three glasses of port with their crusting (bees-wing) at the rim on just two of them; the cut bell rope three inches below the clasp and the use of a candle from the candelabra need explanation.

This episode is notable for Jeremy's physicality and accelerated movement around the scene. He jumps from and into carriages whilst they are moving in order to show the speed of his decision-making and the journey back to the Grange from the station reflects how his reassessment of the evidence changes his views on the criminals. Most impressive is his energetic climbing of the massive overhanging oak mantelpiece of a large deep fireplace which is a dangerous escapade but a necessity when it is so graphically described by Doyle; Jeremy doesn't show any hesitancy and climbs confidently with some style to explore the top of the mantelpiece, even stretching across to examine the cut bell rope, but he was well aware of the hazards in a situation like this, *"The athletic stuff can be extremely dangerous especially when you have to climb up a fireplace and along curtain rails."* (Jeremy in Holmes Rule - Video Today)

Jeremy's Holmes is very much the driving force in the investigation as his honed observation skills identify the position of the stolen silver in the lake, crucial evidence that will unlock the case. He also recovers the buried twice-broken memorial for the Lady's pet dog Fudge by thrusting his arm deep into the mud and bringing up the collar and tag too. By this discovery Sir Eustace will be exposed as a *"sadistic ruffian"* and the Randall gang were not involved on this occasion. Lady Brackenstall has lied to him.

With the identification of the chivalrous hero Captain Crocker, Holmes will use all his powers to bring the good Captain on side and with a detailed analysis of the murder of Sir Eustace, he persuades him to tell the full story. The confession will put him at Holmes's mercy but once again the investigator turns from the letter of the law in the cause of justice. *"I'd rather play tricks with the law than with my conscience."* The concluding scene with Watson as a representative of a good British jury brings the expected verdict. Jeremy adjusted the request, *"Now, gentleman of the jury"* to *"gentle man"* to emphasise the compliment to his friend and to show his approval for Captain Crocker. *"Not guilty, my lord,"* is confirmed in *"Vox pupuli, vox Dei. (The voice of the people is the voice of God) You are acquitted Captain*

Crocker", who may initially have been reluctant to accept the method but is finally persuaded to accept the verdict.

Edward had done a superb job with his portrayal of Watson. *"Well, Edward's a very, very remarkable man. One – probably the nicest... I've ever met in my life. And... he wanted to fit in. So he watched the previous thirteen films... Decided to try and look a little like David Burke, as much as he could, bless him. So he put on a rug, I mean a toupee, and... put lifts in his heels. And the first film we shot together was The Abbey Grange. And we were running across a field, and... these heels were too high so he was slipping and sliding. And I said, 'Oh, Edward, take them out! I'll bend my knees for the rest of the film!'"* (Jeremy in Radio Interview 1991)

Baker Street File – The Abbey Grange

92 - I have learnt caution now, and I had rather play tricks with the laws of England than with my own conscience

Abbey Grange

The Man with the Twisted Lip – The Return of Sherlock Holmes

Jeremy and Edward in The Man With The Twisted Lip

The Man with the Twisted Lip (Dramatised by Alan Plater: Directed by Patrick Lau fb: 13th August 1986) *"I confess that I cannot recall any case within my experience which looked at the first glance so simple, and yet, which presented such difficulties."* The episode which features two missing husbands, one found by Watson and the other by Holmes, focuses on the picture of a beggar who quotes Shakespeare, Wordsworth and Chaucer, entertaining businessmen in the city centre. In the opening at Baker Street only Watson is at home as Holmes has "disappeared without trace" and a visit from Kate Whitney brings him the task of finding her husband Isa Whitney, who has also "disappeared without trace", presumably indulging his addiction in the opium den, the Bar of Gold on Upper Swand(h)am Lane where as an addict he would escape amongst the other ruffians. It is there that Watson finds Isa in a catatonic state, but unexpectedly he finds Holmes as well in another of his disguises as an addict, "a tall, thin old man" carrying out his own investigations.

Watson sends Whitney home in a waiting cab, and Jeremy's Holmes, once more convincing in his disguise of a poppy addict with long hair and shambling gait joins him soon afterwards.

He suggests they visit a villa in Lee, Kent, where his investigation had began with the unexplained disappearance of Neville St Clair who had been missing for several days. A young man of 37 years, "a man of temperate habits, a good husband, a very affectionate father" with no debts there is no valid reason for his disappearance. It is assumed that he has been murdered, however, his wife shows Holmes a newly arrived letter from her husband and gives a strange account of having seen him at an upper room window in one of the buildings on Upper Swand(h)am Lane. She had been forcibly removed by the Lascar manager but when she returned with Inspector Bradstreet of the police, they found only "the sinister cripple" Boone, the professional beggar with a hideous face still quoting Shakespeare and Wordsworth. The evidence of her husband's presence in the room was a box of building bricks, which Neville had promised to buy for his little girl that morning as he left home for the office; her husband's clothes behind a curtain; a bloodstain on the window sill and an overcoat found at low tide on the beach beneath the window with a considerable amount of money in the pocket so that Boone the beggar is taken into police custody still protesting that he is "an honest trader."

Jeremy's Holmes is surprisingly still through much of this episode although his body language and facial expression remain a clear reflection of his moods. The moment of enlightenment for Holmes is very dramatic as he views his own face in the mirror during the morning wash, thus revealing the truth. "*I have been as blind as a mole.*" Consequently, Watson is woken at dawn by a tickle to his foot simply because the detective has a theory he wishes to test. "*Downstairs in five minutes*" shows little consideration for how Watson might feel after only a few hours' sleep. Now Holmes is in his own atmosphere and confident he can complete his theories. He has the key to the mystery in his Gladstone bag and there is humour mixed with drama in the scene where Neville St Clair is finally revealed under his disguise as a black encrusted beggar. The enormous sponge in the Gladstone bag is the first assault but as more water is poured over his head, each element of St Clair's disguise is removed. "What am I charged with?" His story of how he made a living from begging and "fell among thieves but found honour of a sort" makes an interesting tale and one to evoke sympathy from his listeners. However, the Inspector is prepared to free him with, "one condition: there must be no more Hugh Boone."

Jeremy and Edward had become a close team in this episode working separately on their own investigations and then coming together to share what they know and how these details might bring them to a solution. As Holmes finally has a revelation which will find the missing man he pays his friend a compliment when he tells him he has an invaluable gift of silence. Moments like these underline the valuable contributions Watson makes to his friend's investigations, first by being at his side in the moments of danger as a doctor and as advisor but also in the times when a fresh examination of the evidence can open his mind to the solutions. Edward told Peter Haining how much he had appreciated Jeremy's help: "Jeremy has been absolutely marvellous in helping me into the part. Right from the beginning he was always thinking of new ways of developing the relationship between Holmes and Watson – pushing it into new directions. This I have found immensely stimulating. He also generates such a feeling of team spirit on the set that everyone – not only the actors, but also those working behind the cameras – want to do their best for him." (Edward to Peter Haining in The Television Sherlock Holmes)

The pictures of Sidney Paget feature in this episode much as they do in all the episodes wherever they are available. One newspaper critic pointed out the "uncanny likeness in the vision of the great detective, as imagined by the author. Then he has given the character the tense, nervy, melodramatic fizz which has made the series take off." The creation of these poses was a deliberate choice by the Granada production team to show they were determined to be faithful to the Conan Doyle stories. Jeremy told the reporter, *"I tried very hard to look like the original drawings... I was so nervous of failure that at first I put far too much make-up on, then, I took most of it off again. In the end I got confident and really enjoyed the series."* (The Shaping of Sherlock)

Baker Street File – The Man with the Twisted Lip

97 - Very persuasive manner

The Man With The Twisted Lip

The Six Napoleons - The Return of Sherlock Holmes

Colin Jeavons as Inspector Lestrade and Eric Sykes as Horace Harker in The Six Napoleons

The Six Napoleons (Dramatised by John Kane: Directed by David Carson fb: 20th August 1986) is a story of passion and murder told throughout with humour. The scene in Baker Street begins with the three companions around the fire, Holmes, Watson and Lestrade; the two friends sit waiting for the Inspector to explain the reason for his visit. He tells of an unusual series of thefts of Napoleon busts, first from the shop of Morse Hudson in Kennington Road and one from a Doctor Barnicot at Lower Brixton Road and another from his surgery. The fact that nothing was taken other than the busts, later found smashed into pieces, causes Holmes to proclaim it "*singular*" and "*grotesque.*" Watson suggests a mania or idée fixe concerning the Emperor Napoleon as the possible reason, but Holmes shows some doubt and his "*My dear Watson, it won't do!*" is wonderfully delivered by Jeremy, showing all the arrogance mixed with tolerant amusement that describe their friendship in this episode. The moment when Holmes is told "two minutes" as he interrupts the lifting of the teacup to his lips brings sweet revenge for all those times when his friend had got him from his bed to catch the early morning train.

The villain of the piece at first appears to be more mad than evil and scarcely suitable for a Sherlock Holmes investigation. Beppo is part of the Italian community and speaks no English so the early scenes are rather difficult to follow. The sustained and passionately fought battle, cheered on by a partisan crowd, is a dangerous affair with flailing knives and swiftly weaving bodies, which will have tragic consequences. With the stabbing of his opponent and the arrival of the police, Beppo's wild behaviour is reminiscent of the madhouse as he escapes into the factory hurling ornaments at the police and leaving carnage in his wake. Thus the backdrop to the Conan Doyle story becomes a violent yet exciting opening for a tale concerning the Mafia.

As they approach the case from their respective viewpoints the competition between Holmes and Lestrade escalates and it will offer an opportunity for Holmes to show the advantage that theorising can bring. Holmes is always one step ahead and shows a sense of achievement as things fit in with his theories. *"You must have a twinkle in your eye, a naughtiness – and the audience must realise your mind in working faster than your words."* (Jeremy) Holmes will lead the trio in a series of discoveries about the busts and Jeremy is good natured and supremely confident that they are the source of the strange and as yet unexplained events whilst Lestrade continues to view them as a mere distraction.

Holmes would finally reveal what he had discovered, with the coming of a visitor to Baker Street. From the moment of Mr. Sandeford's arrival Jeremy had taken control of the space with the use of what Edward called his Victorian signalling much in the manner of a master showman delivering a great performance. His movement about the room was carefully choreographed with Watson and Lestrade moving apart to allow him to carve a passage between them to take the final Napoleon from the mantelpiece. They both looked on in bewilderment as the red tablecloth from a fully laid table was swept away with a theatrical flourish, before being laid as appropriate covering for a side table with whip and bust in readiness. All this was conducted without dialogue or explanation and it must have taken much practice and skill to perfect the feat but it was one of those moments which Jeremy's Holmes achieved with his customary eye on perfection. He appears very much the magician as he miraculously reveals the famous black pearl of the Borgias from the remnants of the smashed Napoleon.

The uncovering of the blackboard with its detailed account of the stolen black pearl reveals a model record of the investigation with all the main offenders clearly linked together. As Lestrade congratulates Holmes for his supreme management of the case Jeremy's reaction is remarkable. "We're not jealous of you at Scotland Yard. No, sir, we are very proud of you, and if you were to come down tomorrow there's not a man from oldest inspector to the youngest constable, who wouldn't be glad to shake you by the hand." (The Six Napoleons) The way in which Jeremy showed the overwhelming emotion was so effective that the assessment of Holmes was to change as a result of moments like this. He had proved that his Holmes was not the automaton that Conan Doyle described but was in reality a thinking, feeling man who kept his deeper emotions tightly in check. His work and the satisfaction that it brought him came at a greater price than he would care to admit. The offer of his hand to Lestrade as he left the Baker Street rooms is a rare and significant gesture which sealed the relationship and reflected a closer understanding based on mutual respect.

"I used to come in to work on days I wasn't scheduled so that I could watch them at work. He was the greatest of old school actors, and a big proponent of the "less is more" technique of acting. His loss was a tragedy for everyone, and for the profession. Losing Jeremy was the end of an era." (Marina Sirtis, Lucrezia in The Six Napoleons) The critics and the audience agreed with Marina. "Once again it is superbly made, evocative in atmosphere and meticulous in detail. The music is hauntingly beautiful, and the writing is droll and intelligent. Jeremy Brett, Edward Hardwicke and Colin Jeavons couldn't have been more perfect as Holmes, Watson and Lestrade. Brett is commanding, Hardwicke is composed and quietly intelligent and Jeavons is a comic joy… Overall such a fun episode." (IMDb) "To me and clearly a great many others, Jeremy Brett was the man born to play Holmes. No-one else can or will ever come close. The point that struck me about this particular episode above all others is perhaps the most "singular" moment of the entire Granada series… Holmes's tears goes way beyond the "softer human emotions" mentioned by the author. It seemed to come straight from

Brett's heart. That he allowed this definitive portrayal of Holmes to be so very human (and caused me to shed a tear in the process) was quite simply extraordinary…" (IMDb)

"Jeremy Brett's portrayal of Holmes on ITV's *The Return of Sherlock Holmes* is nothing short of brilliant: his facial expressions, abruptness, and the tension shown as he perches on a chair, for instance, are faultless. Now, no other portrayal of Sherlock Holmes in films or series will do. All seem a poor shadow by comparison." (Superb Holmes: Berkshire) "Edward Hardwicke seems more than an adequate replacement for the excellent actor David Burke, who played Dr Watson in the previous series. Hardwicke provides an intelligent foil for Holmes, and the shades of Nigel Bruce, the cinema's best known Dr. Watson are at last laid to rest." (Petersfield) "I deem a critic derelict of duty if he does not express an opinion he has seen fit to change… and I have come to relish that Sunday hour on ITV as perhaps the week's regular best. Jeremy Brett's possessed, capricious, volatile, dangerous but above all convincingly brilliant Holmes wipes the memory clean of all previous portrayals. It is not easy to portray genius. Maybe he has to be one." (Alan Coren in The Mail on Sunday)

A *Daily Mail* article in 1986 recorded the end of filming for series and Jeremy's personal investment in the role with the headline *Why Jeremy's happy to leave Holmes*. Shooting on the third and last Granada series on the Baker Street detective ended at the weekend, and after 20 episodes in the title role… Jeremy Brett is delighted. At last he can abandon the pipe, the deerstalker and the constant dieting that a Sherlock Holmes's physique demands. *"I'm longing to do something different,"* he says, *"Each episode of Sherlock Holmes has been like a little polished diamond and each one has demanded its own infusion of adrenalin. I think it makes a great deal of sense to stop while I'm ahead."* (Daily Mail 10th June 1986) Jeremy also told Peter Haining how much he appreciated the new actors coming into the series and how much it had helped him. *"I have enjoyed new directors this time around, new actors in guest roles, even a new lighting cameraman or technician joining the team. On a long series you become terribly aware of new faces, but if you are trying to continue being creative then you need them, for each new face brings in new ideas. All the time the format is changing ever so slightly and that is terribly important, I think."* (The Television Sherlock Holmes)

The Six Napoleans

The Return of Sherlock Holmes

Promotion photograph for The Return of Sherlock Holmes

After filming ended on *The Return*, Jeremy was leaving Manchester for a year's break from playing Holmes. His comments on the demands of the part emphasised the cost of acting in a long-running series but also the unexpected discovery of how popular Sherlock Holmes was in the U.S. as a super hero. The Americans considered they more or less invented Holmes since the early appearance in the Lippincott Magazine – "which makes the Stateside accolades ringing in Mr Brett's handsome ears all the sweeter." But the personal cost was enormous. *"It was like being on the brink of a breakdown. They put in millions – and there was no room for failure. The strain was enormous. It was so nerve-wracking that I was smoking 60 cigarettes a day... Making the series wound me up to such a pitch that I was trembling like a greyhound before a race. It took me two weeks after filming stopped to sleep at night again."* (A case of nerves for Mr Holmes) *"I was on the verge of cracking up several times. I had been living with the part for three years. I saw myself in some rushes one morning, manic, obsessed – a perfect portrait of Holmes, but far too real for comfort. I knew that to play a man who lives on the dark side of the moon was dangerous, but I hadn't realised just how much the part had got to me... I was getting up at three in the morning to go through the script and I started to dream about the part... One weekend I stayed in my hotel room and didn't go out at all. I had my meals sent in to me, and remained totally detached."* (The grim curse of Sherlock Holmes by Brian Whittle in Today 4th December 1986) The complexity of the man, his genius and his isolation could be overwhelming, *"I've played Macbeth, and that's a tricky one to play, psychologically. I've played Hamlet too. But there's nothing as tricky as Sherlock Holmes. Of all the parts I've ever played, it's the most complex. We are in a never-ending maze. You never get to the bottom of it."* (Jeremy)

In spite of the pressures of carrying the show whilst learning to live with his grief at Joan's death, Jeremy was also masterminding the 1987 publication A Centenary Celebration for Sir Arthur Conan Doyle with the release of the *Granada Companion: A Sherlock Holmes Album*. It is a colourful, detailed view of the series to date with an introduction to the first two-hour production, *The Sign of Four* and a collector's piece. The introduction by Vincent Price contains an interesting comment: "Inevitably all productions stand or fail on the casting and playing of Sherlock Holmes. I do not envy the producer who has to choose his Holmes, or the actor who decides to play the part… Michael Cox's choice of Jeremy Brett to play Holmes in this series was inspired. Mr Brett brings just that degree of novelty and differentness to his portrait of Holmes – but not too much – to give the character yet another incandescent lease of life."

Jeremy's own contribution to the illustrated slim volume contains some clues to his interpretation, *"It's difficult for me to say what I may have given to the image of Holmes. Faith to Conan Doyle's text, certainly! I've worked very hard at that, encouraged by Mike Cox, and by Peter Hammond, the director. I carry my annotated volume around with me. Also, I've tried to bring out the emotion that there is in Holmes. On the surface he seems a cold, sometimes dark, rather off-putting figure. But deeper down, I think, he is a man of feeling. He is complex. He loves music – he plays the violin very well – he enjoys a joke, he is vain, maybe a little conceited. He likes to be praised. He can be bitchy when he assesses other great detectives. He can be a bit of a drama queen; he shows off sometimes, he's something of an exhibitionist, especially when he has pulled off a coup. On a difficult case he may build up considerable tension within himself, which explodes in a genial bit of theatricality when the problem is solved. I've tried to get some of that into my Holmes… The things I hate about my performance are when I suddenly see a flare of a nostril or the twist of a lip and I didn't mean that. He's exciting to play because he's such an adventure. I never know where he's going to take me next."* (Granada Companion: A Sherlock Holmes Album) *"My outlook changed. I became a vegetarian and felt better for it. I learned that I'm much stronger than I thought. I must be strong to have survived and that knowledge gave me confidence. Now I'm much more relaxed. I still miss my wife, of course. The worst thing about not being part of a couple any more is that you've got no one to share things with, but at least now I can go forward. I no longer feel the weight of those other Sherlock Holmeses. I'm no longer up half the night worrying about learning my lines."* (Tragedy leads to a new Holmes in TV Times 19th December 87)

The Sign of Four - The Return of Sherlock Holmes

The latest set of episodes to complete *The Return of Sherlock Holmes* began with *The Sign of Four*, a two hour special, the format of which was to be repeated another four times. An article in *The Times* indicated that it had been made to celebrate the centenary of Sir Arthur Conan Doyle but the two hour detective programme was becoming a popular feature on ITV with *The Inspector Morse* series (began 1st February 1987) where there was time to develop character and details that were often lost in the one hour format. And after all, Sherlock Holmes was the first great detective so it seemed a good decision to follow the trend.

The River Thames in Sign of Four

The Sign of Four (Dramatised by John Hawkesworth: Directed by Peter Hammond fb: 29th Dec 1987) is a very classy and faithful adaptation of the Conan Doyle story. Unfortunately, the first scene of the novel in which Holmes justifies his use of the seven percent solution of cocaine had been used as an introduction to the characters in *A Scandal* *in Bohemia* and was thus unavailable here. The revelations about Watson's family with the examination of the watch as the means of deduction had also been used in *The Man with the Twisted Lip*. It remains notable, however, for one of the memorable axioms that Holmes works by: "*How often have I said to you that when you have eliminated the impossible, whatever remains, however improbable, must be the truth?*" (The Sign of Four)

The epic story begins with the arrival of the beautiful Mary Morstan played by Jenny Seagrove, who comes to Baker Street with two puzzles for Holmes: the disappearance of her father ten years before in unexplained circumstances and an annual gift of a priceless pearl together create sufficient intrigue for Holmes to be interested. Her presence brings very different responses from Holmes and Watson: the former remains unmoved by her grief, in fact he is quite dismissive, offering no sympathy; instead brushing his clothes and complaining at the state of their rooms. On the other hand, Watson is clearly attracted by her beauty and shows her the personal support she is seeking. He will go on to marry Mary at the end of the original tale, but not in the Granada stories where Watson remains a bachelor as Holmes's companion in the Baker Street rooms.

On Westminster Steps

The choice of Ronald Lacey in the dual roles of the Sholto brothers, Thaddeus and Bartholomew, is inspired. His appearance is extraordinary, and he captures the poor health and neuroses of Thaddeus, who describes himself as "a valetudinarian", a hypochondriac. It is interesting to see Holmes in the secondary role, listening, watching, and never interrupting the story of the father Major Sholto's return from India with a vast treasure, and his irrational unexplained fear of a one-legged man. The story is intriguing enough, especially as the son tells of his father's greed, the threat from the two strangers and the notes containing the Sign of Four hieroglyph, which appear from time to time. The account of the involvement of Captain Morstan and his death brings Mary grief even though she had been prepared for his loss. Jeremy commented about his desire for stillness in his interpretation which we can see here: *"trying to stay as still as I possibly can when listening, thinking; trying to let it all go through my face without moving, every thought I've had. And then huge physical activity. ... you suddenly jump off the sofa, or you fly down the stairs with Watson running after you, or leap onto a moving cab or whatever. In other words, his mind is made up."*

The party's eventual, long-awaited departure for Pondicherry Lodge is the strangest section in the story with an atmospheric setting providing evidence for the Sholto brothers' search for the treasure in Watson's reaction, "It looks as if all the moles in England had been at work." Holmes cannot wait to meet Brother Bartholomew, to pursue the mystery and Jeremy dominates these scenes as he gains entrance to the house and runs up the stairs swiftly and almost eagerly to view the death scene. The manner of Bartholomew's death is indeed terrible and at first incomprehensible but Holmes's seeking gaze forensically interprets how the roof space was entered and identifies effects of the poison on the rigid body creating *"rictus sardonicus"*. Oblivious to the effects on his clothing Jeremy is on his knees crawling through the office desk to examine the floor for any hint of a clue to the murder and the theft of the treasure. It becomes a masterpiece of sleuthing with every detail given relevance.

The arrival of the police in the person of Athelney Jones, brings another policeman who needs lessons from Holmes as he bumbles around the attic room, making preposterous theories "weaving a web" until the expert Holmes directs him to the poisoned tip of the arrow, the Sign of Four hieroglyph and the stump of the *"timbertoe"* alongside the creature footprint etched in the spilt creosote, all of which will provide the evidence for his theories. Considering that Jeremy was not in the best of health at this time, his energetic exploration of the large medieval building by clambering over the roof area is extremely hazardous and heart stopping especially when he almost slipped on the descent of the water pipe down the side of the building only to be relieved by his sympathetic quick smile to Watson.

The chase on the Thames was difficult to film, carried out at night, very dramatic and full of incident, with Holmes balancing on the prow of the boat or clinging to the funnel as they gradually catch up with the *Aurora* and the escaping murderers. The Granada team maintained the authenticity of the episode by using an 1874 steel-hulled launch in the pursuit from the Westminster Pier. The death of the islander, Tonga, whose final gesture was to aim a poisoned arrow at Holmes and the capture of Jonathan Small bring a dramatic turn of events and prepares for the disturbing story of the Great Agra Treasure. One of greed and betrayal with Small the honourable man who had attempted to return the precious gems to their rightful owners: the Sign of Four. Mary Morstan did not receive her inheritance as it disappeared into the depths of the Thames along with Tonga's body, and Small would spend the rest of his life on the chain gang on Dartmoor.

Jeremy said, *"The programme I'm most proud of? Again, personal: The Sign of Four. It was very demanding because it's a full-length film with a good number of varied scenes – tremendous action. I wasn't in normal health at the time, and in particular, I had to do a lot of walking about on roofs, and I've no head for heights. I was pleased with myself when I got through that film in one piece."* (A Centenary Celebration of Sherlock Holmes) The Mail on Sunday recorded the details of his illness in the article *Holmes is where his heart is*. "The agony of bringing to life one of fiction's darkest and most complex characters whilst grappling with the loss of his wife, eventually took a terrifying toll on Brett. Last October he was admitted to a mental hospital in London suffering from manic depression. Ironically it was Holmes that rescued him. He recovered at the end of last year, just in time to return to work at Granada Television's Manchester studios in January to make a two-hour Holmes special, *The Sign of Four*, with Edward Hardwicke, John Thaw and Jenny Seagrove. It will be shown on ITV at Christmas to celebrate the 100th anniversary of the creation of Holmes. '*I felt that if I could get on that train to Manchester again, I would be all right.*' Brett says now, '*That is what pulled me through. When I got on to the set I thought: My God, I've cracked it. I am better...*'"

John Thaw said: "I think Jeremy's better than Rathbone now, because he's more; more human. He brings a humanity to the guy that Rathbone didn't." (ibid) R. Dixon Smith in his monograph *An Adventure in Canonical Fidelity* went further when he concluded, "Basil Rathbone *was* Sherlock Holmes, Jeremy Brett *is* Sherlock Holmes." Alan Barnes agreed. "Jeremy Brett's Holmes is the centrepiece, the piercing eyes, brilliantined hair, bat ears and death-mask pallor creating an indelible image of 'true cold reason' personified. Whether clambering around the upper reaches of Pondicherry Lodge (filmed at a Gothic Pile in Harrogate, rather than Norwood) or crinkling in amused fellow-feeling as Thaddeus explains his addiction to the hookah, he is riveting to watch from start to finish." (Alan Barnes in Sherlock Holmes Onscreen)

The vindication of his approach to Holmes came with reference to Conan Doyle. "Jeremy Brett would, I am sure, have warmed the cockles of Conan Doyle's heart... Played with the shrewd neurosis which the character suggests, his manner is as taut as one of his fiddle strings, and at times he resembles a bird of prey, concentrating, twitching, then pouncing, but always with subtlety and eloquence." (Ann Mann in Television Today) "Granada's slightly belated contribution to the centenary celebration is a typically polished production of a little produced Holmes adventure, *The Sign of Four*. Indeed, to get the best possible visible quality, the film unusually for television, shot in 35mm. There has been so much Holmes in the cinema and on TV that there must be a great temptation to find a new approach, or even to send the whole thing up. John Hawksworth's adaptation, directed by Peter Hammond, eschews frills and plays it straight down the line. This also applies to the principal actors – Jeremy Brett who plays Holmes, Edward Hardwicke as Watson – who give notably unmannered, almost self-effacing performances. Brett, of course, is no stranger to the role having made an excellent Holmes in Granada's previous forays into Conan Doyle. Emrys James as the hapless Inspector Jones seems, by contrast, almost to be hamming... once the story proper gets into its stride, there is more opportunity for visual impact, not least in the riverboat chase, that finally nails the thieves of the priceless Indian treasure." (Peter Waymark in The Times 29th December 1987) In another review the critic Antonia Swinson wrote: "*The Sign of Four* was simply magnificent... For two hours, I sat transfixed... But it was, as usual, Jeremy Brett's performance as Sherlock Holmes himself that held me spellbound.... For me, he simply is Holmes. That one flaring nostril, those well-trained eyebrows; who could resist his ice-cold logic and charisma? And yet in this production, I felt there was a new quality; a humour."

In spite of the accolades Jeremy told the *TV Times*, *"I found him cold, chilling a walking brain without emotion... I didn't like the man but, worse still, I was aware of all the actors who have played Holmes... that knowledge was like a great weight. I was so afraid of doing it badly... but now all that's changed."* Suddenly Brett has thrown away the ghostly make-up, cut his hair and sees Holmes now in a new light. For the first time he feels some sympathy for the man, and for the first time he feels he's got his interpretation absolutely right." (TV Times December 1987)

Rosalie Williams gave some clues as to the creation of the relationship between Holmes and his landlady, "At 7.00am on recording day I would walk into the make-up room. Jeremy would be sitting in his chair with Sue Milton gently transforming his early morning face into Sherlock. Script in hand and a twinkle in his eye, he'd say, *'I've thought of a lovely moment between us,'* and there and then we'd rehearse a new little piece of action and reaction between Mrs H. and Mr Holmes... Jeremy had spent the previous night after a long day's work going through today's script." (Scarlet Street) Jeremy told David Stuart Davies about his delight at having Rosalie with him at this time, *"I invented the relationship with Mrs Hudson because I really find it so difficult to have no woman to play opposite. That's a very important little relationship which has come through the films... Rosalie and I love each other so much."* (Dancing in the Moonlight)

Baker Street File – The Sign of Four

59 - He whipped out his lens and a tape-measure and hurried about the room on his knees

60 - He took out his revolver... and having loaded two of the chambers, he put it back into the right-hand pocket of his jacket.

101 - There are in me the makings of a very fine loafer, and also of a pretty spry sort of a fellow

117 - Are you going to bed, Holmes? No, I am not tired. I never remember feeling tired through work. Though idleness exhausts me completely...

127 - Mr Sherlock Holmes, I began; but the word had a magical effect

The Sign of Four

Jenny Seagrove as Mary Morstan in The Sign of Four

The Devil's Foot – The Return of Sherlock Holmes

The Devil's Foot

The Devil's Foot **(Dramatised by Gary Hopkins: Directed by Ken Hannan fb: 6th April 1988).** In the episode, *The Devil's Foot* we were able to admire Holmes's new puckish haircut or reject it as a bad decision. Jeremy had cut it himself in an attempt to avoid the use of gel which made his hair into a hard, immovable cap. It was also necessary sometimes to renew the greasing during the day and altogether it was an unpleasant business that he was pleased to be freed from. It was not popular with Michael Cox, however, who had to wait until it grew back to its original length, which was the end of the series. The ever critical Nancy Banks-Smith in *The Guardian* judged it as a savage cut with the "decimated remains standing in protest." She also commented on his scarf-wearing fashion statements, "sometimes under his hat and sometimes over". Whatever the purpose of her words, Jeremy explained the personal cost of playing the part of a genius. *"He was invented in a very dark time you see... Dark people tend to play him best, sardonic, saturnine people. Lee? Cushing? Marvellous actors! Rathbone I imagine could just get in front of the camera and be the man. I can't do that. I have to glue up my eyebrows, slick back and darken my hair, do my face white. It's hard trying to look like a genius."* (Jeremy to Max Bell in 'Brett Noir' Music and Video Insight 1989) In another interview he would explain more: *"But it's the loneliness of the man that one has to find, the isolation of the man, the man who is not alone, but is perfectly happy to be on his own. The privacy of the man; he's private, utterly private. And, therefore, you have to let the camera come in and see you. You mustn't reach out for it, it must come to you. And they – the director, cameraman, and production people – must choose the moments when he's seen and when he's not. Was that the flicker of a smile, was that a moment of sadness, what was he thinking at that moment? He's frightfully difficult to play."* (Arts & Entertainment 1992)

At the opening of this episode, Jeremy presents an exhausted, ill and out of sorts Holmes, his costume an unusual combination of blankets and scarves to keep himself warm. He is protesting at the prescription of complete rest and change of scene in order to avoid a complete breakdown of his health. Holmes's state of health may have been shaken, but it is still a shock to see his use of cocaine, injected intravenously, as the first thing he does on their arrival at the cottage in Cornwall. The following scene is full of unexpected moments of humour due to the influence of the drug, as he makes his observations about the Reverend Roundhay followed by his great shout of laughter and applause at the response to his explanation.

The arrival of Roundhay and Mortimer Tregennis with a sorry tale of insanity and murder in "a convulsion of terror," brings a halt to any further opportunity for recuperation as Holmes is revitalised in the hunt for a solution. The murder investigation brought Holmes into his true atmosphere as he threw off his outer clothes and with his customary energy examined every detail of the Tregennis living room. Watson had warned their visitors that he was unwell and not to be troubled, but seeing Holmes in charge of a case shows the concern to be unwarranted. Just one occasion on the cliff-top where they had been sitting to discuss the details brought a shout of pain to remind us that all was not entirely well. With the second murder Holmes is brought once more to the Tregennis home where Jeremy moved around the living room like a ballet dancer before throwing himself onto the ground outside in search of anything that might reveal what happened to Mortimer Tregennis. On this occasion he would leave with two vital pieces of information.

The relationship between Holmes and Watson is developed further in this episode where Holmes is vulnerable and in need of the Doctor's care due to his poor state of health. The signs of that dependence are touching, but it also shows the lengths to which Watson will go to help his friend with the investigation. The experiment with the lamp, using the crystals taken from the light in the Tregennis house was lunacy. Holmes explained the hazards of what he was planning to his friend, as always, giving him the option not to take part in the experiment *"I thought I knew my Watson,"* and without him there could have been a tragic conclusion. "I broke through that cloud of despair, and had a glimpse of Holmes's face, white, rigid and drawn with horror –the very look which I had seen upon the features of the dead. It was that vision which gave me an instant of sanity and of strength. I dashed from my chair, threw my arms round Holmes, and together we lurched through the door, and an instant afterwards had thrown ourselves down upon the grass plot and were lying side by side conscious only of the glorious sunshine..." (The Adventure of the Devil's Foot) The hallucinatory effects of the poison proved very real in the nightmare visions that Holmes experienced, "all images of death which had obsessed Holmes throughout the episode – Cain, Oedipus, Nebuchadnezzar and Moriarty, orchestrated by the director into a disturbing series of images... When with Watson's help, Holmes recovers, he uses Watson's first name for the only time in the series." (A Study in Celluloid) *"I slipped it in to show that, underneath it all, there was something more than – well what they say, Holmes is all mind and no heart... I tried to bring a little trickle of blood into the marble."* (Jeremy to Scarlet Street)

Holmes now has the method of the two murders in mind and he sincerely apologises to his friend for involving him in the deadly experiment. The murderer on this occasion is pursuing a personal revenge against his own family and in so doing has killed his own sister for which he would have received the death sentence in a court of law. He has also lied to Holmes throughout the investigation and his own murder becomes a just and fitting outcome for the strange and sad tale. Holmes has settled on Sterndale as the guilty party but this time guilty of revenge against the real murderer with the accompanying responsibility of being a keeper of the law. Jeremy said in interview, *"I think he's a very modern person. He's interested in the poor, the street, law and justice."*

The Times critic welcomed the new series. "'Mr. Holmes,' says the vicar, "in all England, you are the one man we truly need." To which Dr. Watson, as a good PR man, replies that the great detective "likes nothing better than to sink his teeth into a problem of this sort." Which indeed, embarking on his fourth and final series for Granada, with this episode entitled *The Devil's Foot* Sherlock does with his usual aplomb and uncanny reasoning. Looking not unlike an undertaker, Holmes has departed for Cornwall for the good of his health and finds that the disentanglement of local dark deeds is as good a restorative as he could wish. He even buries his hypodermic on the beach. It's good to encounter once again ringing phrases like "My soul cried out for revenge!" And the investigation itself is vintage Conan Doyle, who wrote his first Sherlock Holmes story more than a century ago. The Cornish locale, the farthest the Manchester crew had travelled, is somewhat falsely embellished with Stonehenge-like emblems, but these only add to some satisfying melodrama...The story is a fine old piece of nonsense which involves a young woman frightened to death and two grown men being scared so witless that they go off, rolling-eyed and foaming mouthed, to the local asylum..." (The Times 6th April 1988)

The dramatist Gary Hopkins told *The Black Box Club*, "I was already familiar with most of the Sherlock Holmes stories, having read and reread them as a teenager.... *The Devil's Foot* was one I'd come back to a couple of times because, as with a lot of the best Holmes, it was dark and scary. If I was going to adapt one that would be the one... Cornwall was predictably cold and wet in November, and there were times when thick fog added to the problems. But producer June was determined to film *The Devil's Foot* where Sir Arthur Conan Doyle had set it... *The Devil's Foot* has a brooding, sinister and yet romantic atmosphere all its own... The whole thing... works beautifully. And, though I adapted other Sherlock Holmes stories later on, I can't deny that *The Devil's Foot* was – and still is – very special." He won the second of the two Edgars for the series from the Mystery Writers of America.

Jeremy revealed he had sought permission from Dame Jean Conan Doyle for his disposal of the hypodermic syringe in the Cornish sands. *"I wanted to make a little statement to this century that even the great man buries the needle. It doesn't mean to say that Holmes might not pick up the habit again."* The number of messages he received from children thanking him for his interpretation of Holmes had made him aware that he could be a force for good. He commented on his own view of the habit, *"I've never taken drugs. You can't do a good job of acting if you're high on some awful substance. I relieve the pressure of my profession with yoga or meditation. I used to fall over drug addicts in the street outside the theatre on Broadway. I got to know them so well that they started waving to me."* (Private sadness of a super sleuth in The Daily Express 24th March 1985)

At Jeremy's Memorial Service Denis Quilley shared some memories of filming in Cornwall, "After a day's shooting, we sat in this small private hotel in Cornwall singing our way through the score of *A Most Happy Fella*. '*Joe-ey! Joe-ey!*' we crooned into each other's eyes. The other diners, who tended towards the elderly and respectable, stopped in mid-mouthful. June Wyndham Davies was sitting at the same table trying pathetically to pretend she wasn't with us. When we finished, instead of receiving rapturous applause as we would have done in a black-and-white Frank Capra movie, there was a stunned silence. Jeremy whispered in my ear, '*I think we've just lost the contract.*'" (Denis Quilley) Both Denis and Jeremy were very competent singers and had both starred in the role of Robert Browning in the stage production of the musical *Robert and Elizabeth* in the 1970s so the concert would have been a professional one. Maybe the audience were stunned by the intimacy of the performance. Denis also commented on Jeremy's response to his wife's death, "he was in a very fragile mental and physical state... despite all this he managed not only to soldier on but give that extraordinary, electrifying performance of Sherlock Holmes under the most intense physical and emotional pressure. He could easily have packed it in... Far from doing that, it even, it seems to me, deepened his interpretation of Holmes." (Scarlet Street)

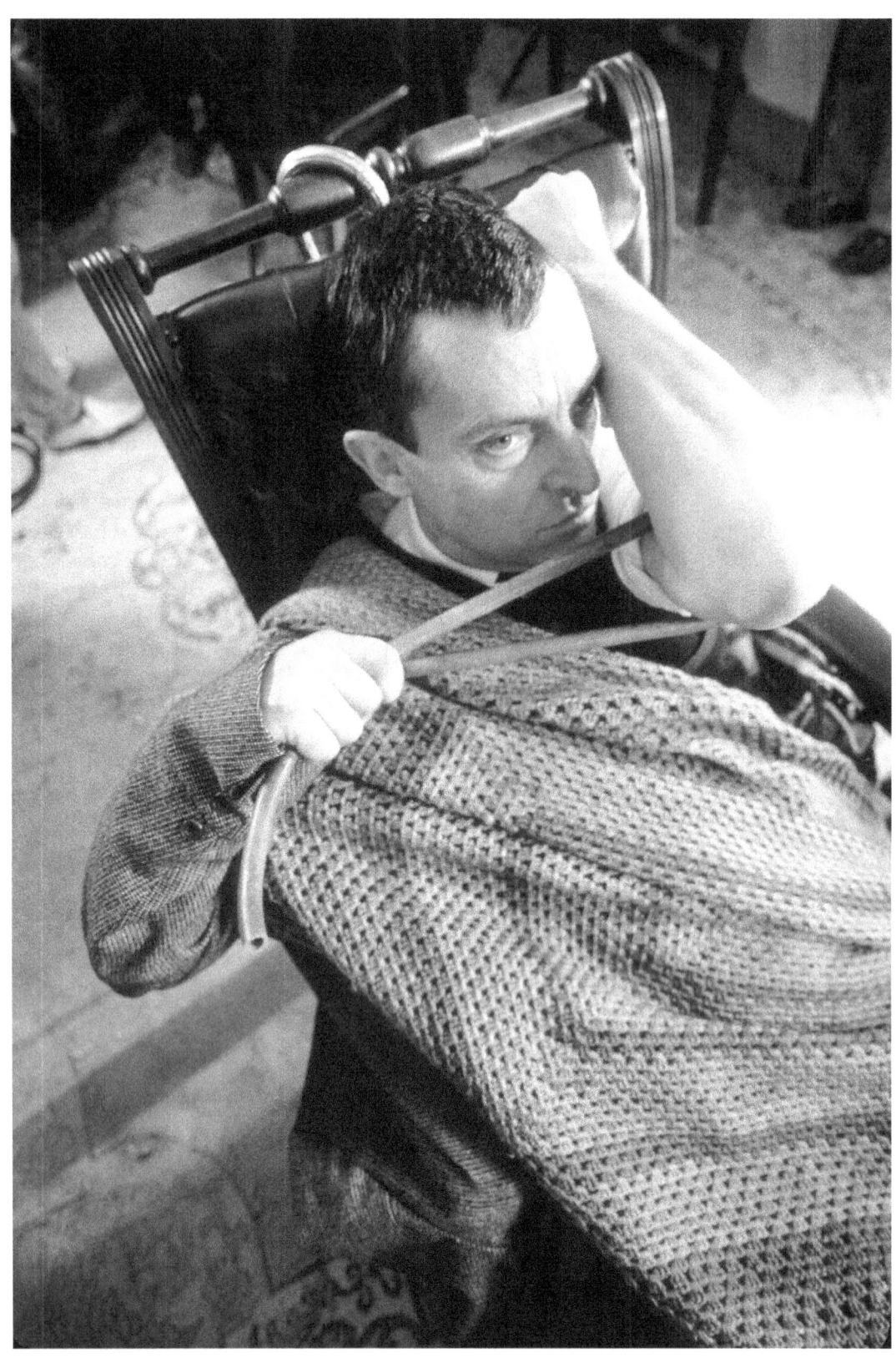

The intravenous injection of 7% cocaine in The Devil's Foot

Silver Blaze - The Return of Sherlock Holmes

Holmes and Colonel Ross in Silver Blaze

Silver Blaze (Dramatised by John Hawkesworth: Directed by Brian Mills fb: 13th April 1988) Jeremy's Holmes had been undergoing a transition from the cold, repressed man who was incredibly difficult to play, to gradually let more of his own personality flow into the performance so that every move, every expression appears totally natural. It is also interesting to realise that he has been building the jigsaw piece by piece and each piece seems to fit more securely into place. *Silver Blaze* is an episode in which Holmes and Watson visit the Kings Pyland Stable on Dartmoor to investigate the disappearance of the famous racehorse, Silver Blaze, the odds-on favourite to win the upcoming Wessex Cup. The brutal murder of the trainer John Straker brings a challenge for Holmes to piece together the events of that night, find the missing racehorse and the murderer. Watson's reading of the sporting paper provides more details about Silver Blaze, of Isonomy stock in his fifth year of racing with an excellent record. Baring-Gould notes in the *Annotated Sherlock Holmes* that Isonomy was a real horse with a remarkable record which won the Manchester Plate and the Ascot Gold Cup in 1879 and again in 1880 and went to stud in 1881. He also gives evidence that Silver Blaze was in fact, Compass, another successful horse.

Jeremy's Holmes takes on the role of interviewer as he first speaks to the principal witnesses, Edith Baxter, the maid; and Ned Hunter, the stable boy and with Watson's help soon identifies a series of important clues to what happened on the fateful night: the unexpected visitor seeking information about the horses, the stable boy who was drugged with powdered opium and the dog which didn't bark in the night time.

Holmes complains that Inspector Gregory has no imagination and is therefore restricted in his success. In contrast, Holmes displays his ability to use his imagination and reach inspired conclusions. Just as in *The Musgrave Ritual* where he constructs the events that led to the death of the butler Brunton, he can see what has happened to the horse. He examines the scene of the crime to recover every last detail of the events of that night. Holmes's close scrutiny of the murder scene was made more dramatic by Jeremy's throwing himself onto the mud, by his "stretching himself upon his face" as he made "a careful study of the trampled mud in front of him" and seemingly oblivious to the effects of the mud on his long, light grey hooded coat, he reveals a couple of items hidden in the soil; a half burnt wax vesta and a piece of candle that the police had missed or failed to trample on. He had found the items because he was *"looking for them."*

His imaginative powers will lead him to follow the missing horse across the moor towards Mapleton and Lord Backwater's stable. Taking one of Silver Blaze's shoes with them he can justify his theory, so it is with confidence that he seeks and finds Silas Brown, the sneaking bully of a trainer, who is quickly outmanoeuvred by Holmes's commanding tone and the missing horse is recovered. But instead of taking it home to Kings Pyland he decides to have a little fun at the Colonel's expense to pay him back for his earlier *"cavalier"* attitude. Although all of the filming took place in the North of England, possibly the Peak District, the *Wessex Cup* was filmed at the Bangor-on-Dee racecourse and it was only there that Holmes revealed Silver Blaze to Ross, *"This, Colonel, is your horse! Found in the hands of a faker"* and taken to the course as he was.

There are two criminals in this episode: first, the trainer who is prepared to injure his own horse in order to make money from those who would pay for such information and secondly, the trainer Silas Brown who is ready to take the opportunity of a wandering stray horse and conceal its identity by painting out its distinguishing marks. Ellery Queen wrote in his anthology *Sporting Blood*, "Silver Blaze belongs prominently to any list of the five leading Sherlockian short stories. It represents the great Holmes at his incisive, dynamic best; despite its author's biographical apology, it reveals no obvious turf errors at least to the lay reader; and we could find no finer yarn to head our parade of The Great Sports Detective Stories." (Quoted in The Annotated Sherlock Holmes by William Baring-Gould)

The Granada team had decided to have Holmes reveal all the details of the case at dinner at the Colonel's house and not on the train journey back to London as in the original story. The dinner presented the opportunity for sharing out details of the investigation between both Holmes and Watson and as such was more effective; it is interesting to note that Holmes remains abstemious and rejects most of the food he is offered whilst Watson is happy to enjoy all the pleasures of the occasion. The amusing manner in which Jeremy suggested the role of the sheep in the story and his request for an amnesty for the nearby stables is sensitively achieved so that Colonel Ross has no alternative but to thank them for a successful solution and drink to his new friends, "Sherlock Holmes and Doctor Watson."

There are several moments in this episode which show Jeremy's flair and flourishes suggesting that he was once more enjoying himself in the role of Holmes. As the two friends leave for London, he calls Mrs Hudson in a singing voice; he waltzes back into his room and the music of Patrick Gowers is particularly effective here. The long grey coat enables him to move about the moor as if around a dance floor, and helps him to dominate the scene, which

Jeremy's Holmes cannot fail to do. He also thanks Mrs Hudson for bringing his telegrams with the whispered endearment, *"Thank you, my dear,"* which surely doesn't appear in the original tale. His show of concern for the distressed maid as she tells of finding Straker's body is a sensitive gesture which reflects Jeremy's own personality. This series would provide instances where he allows more of himself to creep into his interpretation of Sherlock Holmes.

His love of horses can be seen again, especially in the scene with Silver Blaze where he seems to whisper that the sponge and water will not hurt him, but merely restore his beautiful appearance and understandably the horse was reluctant to be dismissed. "The solution to it all is satisfying as well. Jeremy Brett reminds us yet again as to why he is the perfect actor to play Arthur Conan Doyle's legendary sleuth and Edward Hardwicke makes for a Doctor Watson of equal perfection." (IMDb) The *New York Times* commented on Jeremy's performance, "When not flinging himself on the dank moors to search for overlooked evidence, Holmes is delivering tidy lectures on the necessity for imagination. Pointing out the difference between himself and the well-meaning but unimaginative inspector, he says: *'We imagined what might have happened and acted on our supposition and find ourselves justified.'* Holmes has his tricks for keeping others off balance. While they might be walking away from a site, Holmes will hesitate for one last, clearly significant look. Or, conversely, while they dawdle, Holmes stalks out impatiently. It's an ingeniously clever act. Little wonder that the initially sceptical Colonel Ross eventually gasps, 'Good heavens, you take my breath away, Mr. Holmes.' Mr. Brett has developed his impersonation of the character to the point where it is capable of doing just that." (New York Times 18th November 1988)

The Baker Street File – Silver Blaze

118 - Holmes cocked his eye at me... like a connoisseur who had just taken his first sip of a comet vintage

Silver Blaze

Wisteria Lodge – The Return of Sherlock Holmes

Inspector Baynes in Wisteria Lodge

The *TV Times* listing asks, "What is the secret of *Wisteria Lodge*? Holmes and Watson enter into one of the most baffling and intriguing cases of their career. A foreign tyrant, an English governess and an unorthodox police inspector lead them on a wild goose chase which starts with murder." (TV Times 16-22 April 1988) **Wisteria Lodge (Dramatised by Jeremy Paul: Directed by Peter Hammond fb: 20th April 1988)** is a *"grotesque"* story which is brought to Holmes by Mr Scott Eccles. The telegram sent by Scott Eccles read,

HAVE JUST HAD MOST INCREDIBLE AND GROTESQUE EXPERIENCE. MAY I CONSULT YOU?
SCOTT ECCLES, POST-OFFICE, CHARING CROSS (Wisteria Lodge)

The first chapter of the story is entitled, "The singular experience of Mr John Scott Eccles" and it explains what has actually happened but with little information of why he was chosen for this experience. The flourish with which Holmes welcomes the flustered and distressed Mr Scott Eccles suggests he is missing the heady days of adventure and would welcome some distraction from his boredom. It might also be an indication that he had been indulging in the 7% cocaine.

When Scott Eccles was able to organise his tale into an intelligible order, it was indeed a "singular and unpleasant" tale of a night spent at Wisteria Lodge in the company of Garcia, a brief acquaintance who had invited him to stay for a few days. The dinner itself had been a strange affair and not what he had expected, notable for the nervousness of his host and the gloomy servant; the lack of good food and wine served by foreign staff with a sudden unexplained disturbance caused by the delivery of a note which was crumpled up and thrown onto the fire by Garcia. "He gave up all pretence at conversation and sat smoking endless cigarettes, lost in his own thoughts..." He remembers being awakened by his host at one o'clock in the morning, asking if he had rung for something, but in the morning the house was empty: "Foreign host, foreign footman, foreign cook all vanished in the night." The explanation of how Scott Eccles came to accept such an invitation is also rather strange, especially as he didn't know Garcia before this event took place, so one can't help feeling he had been rather foolish or simply too trusting.

Freddie Jones as Baynes enjoys showing off before Holmes with his analysis of the note that Scott Eccles had said was thrown into the fire the evening before: he had "overpitched it" and the Inspector relishes sharing every last detail as a personal challenge to Holmes who looks on bored by the performance and the competition. In spite of this show of bravado the real detective, Holmes, finds a few more *"trifling points"*. As he examines very area of the room, Jeremy amusingly examines the fireplace with more vigour than usual and carelessly covers his elegant black coat in ashes, proving that no further evidence would escape notice before he finds the gun case for two pistols one of which is missing. It is interesting that Watson is the one who sees and chases the mulatto who has been looking through the window, leaving the two detectives still in personal competition with the other. Michael Cox described Freddie's interpretation as "smug": "He certainly gives us the vain, ambitious character described by Conan Doyle. He embroiders it with a few actor's tricks – the mittens, the outrageous hat and the boiled sweets – and sits up and begs for words like rich and ripe to be applied to it. I would describe it as smug. It is certainly such a big performance that it nearly throws the picture out of balance." (A Study in Celluloid)

By using his usual method of his investigation Holmes has discovered information about the local residents and has identified the suspect, Henderson at High Gables. Watson on his own instincts has accidentally discovered the person who can provide the backstory of events and tie them together. Don Juan Murillo, the Tiger of San Pedro, under the alias of Henderson is an extremely dangerous villain, a savage dictator responsible for endless crimes of murder and torture who had escaped from justice. It is assumed by Sherlockians that he was Dom Pedro II, the last emperor of Brazil deposed in 1889, he spent his final years in Europe. It is even more surprising when both Holmes and Baynes independently identify him as the murderer. The story of the once dictator of San Pedro, Central America *"A lewd and blood-thirsty tyrant"* is finally revealed along with the plot for revenge *"for the rivers of blood,"* on behalf of the families of his victims, led by Garcia and Miss Burnet, which had ended in tragedy.

The *TV Times* provided an assessment of the success of the series to date with the headline, *Detecting a good series,* "Thanks to ITV's Sherlock Holmes dramas... a new generation of fans has discovered the pipe-smoking violin-playing sleuth. And enthusiasts for Sir Arthur Conan Doyle's detective stories have praised the TV series for its authenticity. The Swedish Academy of Detection which encourages higher standards of crime literature, recently gave the series a special award for faithfully rendering the text and successfully capturing the period atmosphere and distinctive nature of the classical stories." Jeremy Brett who plays Holmes, tries to explain the character's appeal – to readers and viewers. *"He shows you can live your life according to your own code of ethics. And he combines the logical thinking men are supposed to have with the intuition of women."* (TV Times 23-29 April 1988)

Wisteria Lodge

The Bruce Partington Plans - The Return of Sherlock Holmes

Holmes and Violet Westbury in The Bruce Partington Plans

The Bruce Partington Plans **(Dramatised John Hawkesworth: Directed by John Gorrie fb: 27th April 1988)** is based amongst the backstreets of London and Holmes solves the case of the murder of Cadogan West and the missing submarine plans by his detailed knowledge of the city's railway system. The "*bookend*" of this episode shows Holmes in a state of boredom with no cases needing his attention and fog and the dull London criminal is to blame. The piece we hear him singing is *Palestrina's Psalm 42 "Sicut cervus desiderat ad* *fontes aquarum, ita desiderat anima mea ad te, Deus*" (translated as "As the deer longs for running waters, so my soul longs for you...") Rosalie as Mrs Hudson would bring more "embroidery" to their relationship, as she says she must have a word with him, but his reply, "*I apologise for the state of my room,*" feels like a Jeremy led addition. The telegram announcing Mycroft's visit to Baker Street brings some relief and is of particular interest as it is such a rare occurrence, "*Once and only once he has been here... But that Mycroft should break out in this erratic fashion. A planet might as well leave its orbit.. Jupiter himself is descending upon us today.*" The death of a Government employee, Cadogan West explains Mycroft's presence.

The appearance of Charles Grey as the benign Mycroft Holmes is always a pleasant addition to an episode. The brotherly relationship created by Charles and Jeremy is a close one, no rivalry here, as one would expect from two men of equal intelligence. As a government official, on this occasion accompanied by Inspector Bradstreet, Mycroft brings his concerns about the Bruce Partington submarine plans (probably the British built E-class submarine) found on the brutally murdered body of Cadogan West, left lying beside the railway track. Holmes's observation of the murder scene can be seen in Jeremy sitting cross-legged on the side of the railway track, in full Holmes attire with top hat and scarf, oblivious to the effects of the dirt upon his pristine clean black coat. "*Points and a curve*" in the railway track is of interest to Holmes and he goes away laughing loudly, as he can see "*possibilities*" where the others cannot.

This is a workmanlike, almost textbook investigation with the keepers of the keys at the Royal Naval Patents Office at the Woolwich Arsenal being the initial focus beginning with Sir James Walter, the official guardian. In the Granada version there were two people in possession of a complete set of keys; Sir James and Sidney Johnson, the senior clerk which provided an opportunity to create other suspects for the robbery. On arrival at his home, they are informed Sir James has just died from suicide which brings more questions than answers, and interest too, as Holmes and Watson, dressed in their usual formal attire are mistaken for the undertakers, an amusing addition by Granada. Watson is also given another opportunity to introduce his friend Holmes to a stranger with immense pride.

With no crime scene to search for missing clues Holmes follows the traditional approach of making Cadogan West the focus for investigation and Miss Violet Westbury, his fiancée provides a picture of a loyal "patriotic man." The street on which West left her on the night of his disappearance faces the office at the Woolwich Arsenal where the plans are kept, and his visit gives Holmes an opportunity to learn more about the security, the keys necessary to enter and the window shutters that don't meet in the middle, all of which raises questions about what West had seen and his involvement in the theft. We can also see Holmes's need to understand the plans of the submarine and the full implications of the drawings that show the double valves with the automatic self-adjusting slots one of those found on West's body. No one had noticed the implications of the double valves so far in this case and it will prove helpful in trapping the criminals. Holmes has discovered enough evidence to question West's guilt and he is building a picture of the night's events. The station master at the Woolwich Arsenal, played by Robert Fyfe, Howard from *Last of the Summer Wine*, remembers the frantic hurry of West to catch the London train on the day of his disappearance but can give no explanation for the cause of his hurry or of the loss of his ticket.

This is an international crime and the names of foreign spies who might trade in the submarine plans are the same as those mentioned in *The Second Stain* and with the death of Eduardo Lucas there are only two remaining. Hugo Oberstein lives at Caulfield Gardens, an address which Holmes knows backs onto the Underground where two other lines meet and trains are frequently held motionless. Seeking further information, Holmes cannot resist suggesting "*A spot of amateur burglary*" and the request for Watson to accompany him on his criminal exploits brings confirmation of the theory on how West's body ended up on the railway line. The relationship between Holmes and Watson appears particularly strong on this case where they work as a team and each show their dependence on the other. It was Watson who found the messages from Pierrot in the agony column of the *Daily Telegraph* and this same method of communication would be used to capture one and convict both criminals. The unsuspecting visitor, Colonel Walter, is not the person Holmes expected but, nevertheless, he was coerced into writing the letter which would entrap his foreign collaborator as reparation for his wrong doing. The final scene is a well orchestrated drama with the three protagonists sitting nonchalantly at a restaurant table in the lobby of the Charing Cross Hotel, whilst the police and the spies move purposely in front of the observers, every move noted and responded to, so that Oberstein is taken into custody and although Walter had slipped away unnoticed, Bradstreet promises to "keep him on a long lead". One feels that Sherlock and Mycroft Holmes with the indispensible John Watson make a perfect team of investigators.

Jeremy was a master in front of the camera. Edward said of him, "He was a genius. Sometimes the director would say, 'Would you do so and so?' And I would think, How can you do that? And Jeremy would do it in a gesture!" A current reviewer thought his performance encompassed all the qualities of Holmes. "Sly, camp, exuberant, melancholy, savage, trite, pompous, sensitive, manic and loyal – all the qualities that defined Holmes seemed to run across Brett's face in a flickering slideshow, his muscles twitching and jerking, as if he could not bear to suffer any one emotion for more than an instant." The writer thought that Jeremy was "too good. His understatedly intense Sherlock Holmes brought the Victorian menace of the stories to life on screen" and he concluded "Brett outshone every actor who had ever portrayed the Great Detective." (Christopher Stevens in Daily Mail 10th March 2015)

The Hound of the Baskervilles - The Return of Sherlock Holmes

Sir Henry Baskerville in The Hound of The Baskervilles

***The Hound of the Baskervilles* (Dramatised by T.R. Bowen: Directed by Brian Mills fb: 31st August 1988)** is Conan Doyle's best known work, probably because it has been filmed the most over the years. The mystery set on the wasteland of Dartmoor concerning a mystical hound brings intrigue and death, perpetuating the legend of "Sir Richard Cabell, Lord of the Manor of Brooke, in the parish of Buckfastleigh. A gentleman of ill repute and on the night of his death, black hounds breathing fire and smoke raced over Dartmoor and howled around his manor house." (The Annotated Sherlock Holmes) In Conan Doyle's story Sir Hugo Baskerville abducts a young girl "who escaped across the moor at night, cursing. He unkennelled the pack of hounds and hunted her down like a wild animal": the girl was found dead from exhaustion and Sir Hugo's throat was torn out by *"a huge demonic hound."* He would dedicate his story to his friend Fletcher Robinson who brought the original idea to Doyle. "Robinson and I are exploring the Moor over our Sherlock Holmes book. I think it will work out splendidly indeed I have already done nearly half of it. Holmes is at his very best..." (Conan Doyle)

It should be noted that *The Hound of the Baskervilles* appeared in *The Strand* and other magazines nine years after Holmes's death in *The Adventure of the Final Problem*. Holmes fans around the world had waited during that time for the next Sherlock Holmes story from Arthur Conan Doyle.

Jeremy told the TV Times: "I remember how I felt as a child. We would drive across the Moor on the way to family holidays in Cornwall, and to this day I can remember the fear coming from it, the fear of the legends, the bleakness, the prison, and obviously of the Hound. There is danger here. That's what the story draws on so brilliantly. There is the very smell of the supernatural. Then add in the lamb to the slaughter, in the shape of young Baskerville returning to his inheritance. The threat to him runs right through the story, so that you have no idea what is coming at him – whether it's human, animal, metaphysical or supernatural. Is the Hound real?" (TV Times 27th August 1988) Whilst standing on the scene of the Grimpen Mire where the story reaches its climax, Jeremy shuddered and said, *"How brilliant Conan Doyle was to keep – at every moment – the Hound bounding through the story, gleaming and salivating."* But this hound was not scary and the Great Dane, the size of a donkey nuzzled up to him, recognising his love of animals. *"If you can't get the Hound right, it's better you don't see him. We didn't get it right."* (Jeremy)

A story where "the powers of evil are exalted" and detection attempts to investigate the supernatural begins in the Baker Street rooms with Holmes observing Watson who is seated behind him, in his examination of the silver-topped cane left in their rooms the night before. Jeremy explained how difficult he found this simple detail, however, after a great deal of thought and rereading of Doyle, he found that by lifting the lid on his *"well-polished, silver-plated coffee pot"* he was able to view his friend. The arrival of Dr James Mortimer will confirm Holmes's deductions of a young doctor in Hospital medicine with his walking stick, a gift from Charing Cross Hospital and the possessor of a dog. Jeremy's unique humour is in evidence when the enthusiastic scientist asks, "Would you have any objection to my running my finger along your parietal fissure?" and Holmes replies with a twirl of his chair amidst uproarious laughter, *"Behave and sit down."*

Further mystery is brought into the case with the recent arrival of the next of kin, Sir Henry Baskerville the last of the Baskervilles from America and Holmes will need all his skills to unravel the tangle. It becomes clear that he has been followed by someone who knows who he is when he complains of two *"inexplicable"* thefts of shoes from his hotel room and then a worrying note, unsigned and put together from newspaper cuttings taken from *The Times* which reads:

AS YOU VALUE YOUR LIFE OR YOUR REASON KEEP AWAY FROM THE MOOR

Breakfast with Sir Henry at the hotel provides an expert, detailed analysis of the writer of the note which Holmes delivers in his usual methodical and assiduous manner with the conclusion that this was a friendly warning.

The tension of the action slackens as Watson is sent to Dartmoor and the moor itself looks bright and attractive in daylight hours, with no hint of mystery or threat of a raging sinister hound. His role is to protect Sir Henry Baskerville and to be the eyes and ears of his friend, to observe behaviour amongst the country folk and *"to report facts to me in the fullest manner possible"*, but above all, he has instructions to *"avoid the moor where... the powers of evil are exalted"*. Watson is no detective but he is a reliable narrator who responds to events as any normal person would and he concentrates on the people and the realities of country living rather than on the need for detection. However, he is swiftly tested as Watson's first concern becomes the news of an escaped convict, Selden "the Notting Hill Murderer" deemed "insane" and roaming the mist covered moors. The dreadful Grimpen Mire brings further danger with its risk of perishing in the deadly bog. A series of further concerns unsettle Watson: Beryl Stapleton, assuming he is Sir Henry, advises him to leave for his own safety; the suspicious behaviour of the butler Barrymore and afterwards the revelation of Selden's relationship with his wife causes Watson to cry, "I wish to God Holmes was here. Why does he not come!"

There is the possible hiccough of the relationship as Holmes finally returns and Watson realises that he has sent letters when they were not required, but Holmes provides the much needed assurance that they were *"well thumbed"*. There is humour in the *"meagre refreshment"* he serves Watson, a "quite disgusting" stew for which the local boy had provided the ingredients and then drama as he tells Watson that Beryl Stapleton is in fact Stapleton's wife and not his sister. Stapleton will emerge as the villain of the story when he is recognised as a Baskerville; Holmes identifies the relationship in the portrait of Sir Hugo Baskerville hanging in the Hall and concludes that he may have ambitions to inherit the estate. When a trap is laid with their proposed visit to London, we are not surprised to see Holmes and Watson entering, then immediately leaving the train to return to Grimpen. In the final scenes Holmes shows an unexpected concern for an upset Laura Lyons, who is forced to accept that Stapleton's offer of marriage was only a fairy tale. We see him cradle Beryl Stapleton sympathetically in a dramatic rescue from her brutal imprisonment and his concern for Sir Henry is just as caring as he receives a savage mauling from the phosphorous coated hound before it is killed with Holmes's revolver.

The enthusiast might also notice that there are two scenes within this episode which have been taken from *The Greek Interpreter,* one where Holmes takes a carriage to *The Royal Observatory* and another when he can be seen walking down a deserted railway platform swinging his cane and disappearing into the mist, which points to serious cost cutting resulting from an overspend on the earlier four episodes of *The Return*. It could also be attributed to Jeremy's poor health, which required previous footage from earlier episodes to be used. He had told David Stuart Davies that he was *"terribly unwell"* whilst filming this episode and his performance does not have the energetic *joie de vivre* which we have seen in the earlier series of *The Return*.

The critics gave a mixed response to the episode and it may have been anticipation which could be blamed for some of the complaints. Jeremy's interpretation of Holmes had been a triumph and there was enormous expectation on the Granada team to present the very best version of Conan Doyle's most famous story. Overall it was welcomed. "Though many mystery fans think that this is not the definitive version of HOUND, it does have Jeremy Brett, which makes it good enough for me. It also has a superb performance by Hardwicke, who actually has more screen time on this particular outing than Brett." (Sean Farrell in Scarlet Street Winter 1996) "Brett's Holmes is by now justifiably celebrated. The actor brings a calculated touch of 19th century melodrama to the role. If Brett had a moustache, he would be twirling it shamelessly. His Holmes is cold, arrogant, smug and infuriatingly brilliant..." (New York Times)

Nick Smurthwaite in *The Stage* found the pace "predictable and plodding" but was full of praise for the "ravishing camera work" and especially for Jeremy's "outrageously mannered performance, alive with ticks and grimaces". "There is one extraordinary scene, in a hotel coffee lounge, where Holmes applies his scientific mind to dissecting an anonymous letter, while Brett applies every piece of ammunition in his actor's armoury to make the scene appear as riveting and sexy on screen as it must have appeared dull and dry on the page. How can you help but admire the resource of such an actor? Brett does not have the advantage of Basil Rathbone's traditional Holmesian looks... but he compensates with a look of crazed intensity and an actorish charisma. It might not have been what Conan Doyle had in mind, but works a treat nevertheless... Its biggest let down is the hound an 11 stone Great Dane...which looks more silly than menacing..." (Nick Smurthwaite Barking up the wrong tree in The Stage and Television Today 1st September 1988)

The Times praised the episode for its style and polish, "Style is the keynote of *The Hound of the Baskervilles*, the climax of Granada's polished series of Sherlock Holmes adaptations. Deciding, perhaps, that the story is not one of the strongest of the Conan Doyle canon and that it will be familiar to many viewers, the makers have decided to go all out for production value. This means strong locations (with Yorkshire and Staffordshire doubling convincingly for Dartmoor) supplemented by a spooky, studio-created Grimpen Mire, and a standard of camerawork in which no opportunity is lost to squeeze the maximum effect out of lighting and composition. Happily, this attention to form does not mean a smothering of content and my only complaint is that, after steadily pacing for most of the time, the denouement is wrapped up all too quickly. Having enjoyed the bulk of a leisurely and satisfying meal, it is a pity to have to wolf the cheese and gulp the coffee." (Peter Waymark 'The dogged detective' in The Times 31st August 1988)

When he was asked about the effects of living with the character for so long and whether he thought Holmes was taking over his life Jeremy replied, "*I used to think he was. I can't bear to look at old photographs of me looking strained and ill on location. But I no longer feel threatened by him and for the first time I'm really enjoying playing him.*" (TV Times 27th August 1988) "*I began to feel better with Holmes, and I wasn't quite so cross with him... 'cause I blamed him a little... I was working, you see, so far away from Joan, and it had taken up so much of our last – what we – I discovered to be our last few years.*" However, it wasn't quite as simple as that. "*I have to be sure to get rid of him. It's rather like washing. I mean if you really wash. I had to really shower, because the thing about Holmes is it's like walking a magnesium tightrope of blazing brilliance. You're up. You have to reach for him.*" (ibid)

The fan letters he received also helped him make the decision to carry on, "*...the fan letters I have received – about 200 a week from all over the world – have moved me so much I have decided to carry on... I've changed my make-up now so I don't look quite so bloodless and in the current series I play him more of a heroic figure than a neurotic. I think he is still quite an isolated figure but I've warmed him up a bit.*" He felt so confident about Holmes that he said, "*I have this feeling that* The Return of Sherlock Holmes *is better even than the first 13 series. I can't quite tell you why that is – it is to do with some shift of emphasis, some confidence, some chemistry between Edward and me. But there is definitely something.*" (The Television Sherlock Holmes) When he was told by a taxi driver: "*Sherlock Holmes is our hero, you know*" he was amazed because "*I'd never thought of Holmes as a hero before. But as I thought about it I realised that Holmes works for the poor and can't be bothered with the rich, and so he really is a sort of hero.*" (TV Times 19th December 1987)

Baker Street File – The Hound of the Baskervilles

108 - My simple wants: a loaf of bread and a clean collar

125 - Never have I seen a man run as Holmes ran that night. I am reckoned fleet of foot, but he outpaced me...

The Case of the Abbey Treasure 1988

A short feature was made in 1988 to coincide with Jeremy's unveiling of a bronze plaque at Abbey House in Baker Street. At the ceremony Jeremy stated that Sherlock Holmes lived at that address and it would become the Abbey National Building Society. The short film was produced by the Granada team and filmed at the conclusion of *The Hound of the Baskervilles*, in which Jeremy and Edward humorously discussed the need to invest in the Building Society and subsequently in the future.

The Hound of The Baskervilles

The Secret of Sherlock Holmes 1988 - Wyndham's Theatre

Jeremy By courtesy of Marcus Tylor

When asked whether the stage or film was preferable for his interpretation of Holmes, Jeremy said, *"The thing about working on the stage that makes it harder is that film is so instantly near it can see right into the person's soul. With someone so unbelievably isolated and closed, as Holmes is, it's sometimes easier to see the internal workings of the private man across on camera. He is such a private creature... and with the camera you can slide in and see the flicker of things across his face... little disappointments, little angers, little changes of mind. Of course, the other things you can get across on camera are his brilliant deductions and observations, but also his amazing intuition. And that's easier to do on film. On stage I try not to look at them for the first fifteen minutes... I don't even look at Watson very much either... I kind of gradually open up to them. That was the hardest part of moving into the theatre. But my director, Patrick Garland, helped me with that. He said, 'put a pane of glass down between you and the audience and don't look at them, ignore them, and then after about fifteen minutes warm through let them in...'"* (sherlockbrett.blogspot.com)

The Secret of Sherlock Holmes was on stage at Wyndham's Theatre from 22nd September 1988 and ran for more than 300 performances as a two man show with Jeremy in the role of Sherlock Holmes accompanied by Edward Hardwicke as Watson. Jeremy had personally commissioned Jeremy Paul to write the play in 1987 as a response to the centenary memorial for Arthur Conan Doyle. He recorded more than eight hours of material from his study of the character, including his background inventions which he had come to rely on in his interpretation of the role. *"I sent him eight hours of tape. I just rattled off my ideas, and so when it comes to moments of leaving the canon... Jeremy (Paul) has taken them directly from the tapes. The thing I love about the play is that it gives Watson much more to say than the Canon does, because naturally, it was in the first person. I remember David Burke, when we finished* The Speckled Band, *saying, 'I had only thirty-six words to say in the entire film!' And this play does give Watson a platform to speak. Which I think is vital."* (sherlockbrett.blogspot.com) Jeremy wanted to concentrate on the friendship which existed between the two men in the course of their adventures and to develop the character of Holmes both through the tales of Doyle and beyond. None of the stories were done in whole, just mentioned in pastiche, but faithful to Conan Doyle's dialogue *"taken and fashioned into an original mystery which I hope will intrigue Conan Doyle himself if he is looking in."* (Jeremy Paul) The ending was a *coup de Theatre*, a surprise for the audience, unexpected yet fully justified by the stories.

The play began with a one night performance under the title *A Case for Sherlock Holmes* at the Mayfair Theatre to which family, friends and colleagues from the acting world were invited and also included Dame Jean Conan Doyle. Edward Hardwicke was not available so the part of Watson was played by Sebastian Stride, who appeared as Cadogan West in *The Bruce Partington Plans* and the parts of Conan Doyle and Moriarty were played by Jeremy Paul. In this first performance of the play, a narrator was also included. The evening was a success and with the return of Edward Hardwicke as Watson the two man play opened at the Yvonne Arnaud Theatre in Guildford on 30th August with the new title *The Secret of Sherlock Holmes* under the direction of Patrick Garland. It was booked for a six week run at Wyndham's Theatre in the West End and with its Box Office success the play ran for a year in London before touring the major cities of Bradford, Hull, Cardiff, Birmingham, Aberdeen, Brighton, Manchester and Bath for a further eleven weeks. It also appeared in the Chichester Festival Theatre in November 1989. Consequently, Jeremy and Edward were on stage from 30th August 1988 until the beginning of 1990 for six evenings and two matinees a week. Thankfully there were some welcome breaks because it was a punishing schedule.

The main focus of this play was the relationship between the two men who shared the lodgings in 221b Baker Street. Jeremy's Holmes describes his need of Watson to the audience: *"Without Watson, I would have been dead within two years. A man needs a companion, he cannot sit alone... With his silent reproaches, his hurt look, Watson controlled my addiction. And our walks, our conversations, the sheer breadth and enthusiasm of his mind on any manner of subjects kept me sane... when the black fits were upon me. There was never a better friend. And I treated him abominably."* Jeremy's six year study of Doyle had convinced him that, *"Watson and Holmes are two parts of the same person... It's a brilliant creation, their friendship and it needs both, you can't have one without the other, it's impossible."* Dr Joseph

Bell, the exceptional person on whom Conan Doyle based Holmes, would agree with Jeremy. In a letter to Conan Doyle he said, "*You are yourself Sherlock Holmes and well you know it.*"

"The play is about friendship, which I think is terribly important, because it's a bygone thing. It's a Victorian thing, it's a Greek thing. But in the eighties it has lost its way through the rise of feminism – nothing wrong in that... But, men have lost all dignity in their personal friendships. And therefore, I think it's quite foreign to the young... I mean two gentlemen sharing. It's immediately suspect, or the 'odd couple.' So, that's really what the play is about... it's about love actually. I am so glad that several of the critics have managed to tune into that... not in a jaundiced sense... That's what we were aiming for, to show these two remarkable men." On another occasion he said, *"...But this play is really a thank you to Dr. John Watson, since behind every great man there's either a woman or a Watson, and Holmes finds to his amazement and a certain amount of horror that Watson has become indispensable. Holmes feels lost without his Boswell."* (Brett becomes Holmes by Gregory Jensen)

Jeremy's interpretation of the enigma Sherlock Holmes still fascinated the public and the press. "Jeremy Brett's portrayal of Holmes is equally masterful, as one would expect. He entrances his audience with a projected voice and arm gesticulations worthy of Lord Olivier. His skill at changing Holmes's moods is compelling, as he leads the audience through his mental torment brought about by cocaine, his jovial quips with Watson; through Holmes's own exposition on Moriarty, where he leaves us dangling as he pauses for effect until he chooses to bring the audience down. Brett has the versatility of character to produce Holmes's many guises with the mere change of stance or gesture of hand, and the awesome ability to place an audience on the edge of their seats or roll them in the aisles..." (Review Gazette) It was refreshing to see Watson coming into focus, "Watson... comes across as an interesting personality in his own right, a doctor whose vocation was lost during the Afghan War and who has astute detection powers of his own. But it is to Jeremy Brett's mesmeric portrayal of Holmes, fascinatingly reptilian, to which we are drawn as he looks into his own soul, hinting at an unhappy family background, confessing his inadequacies and finally revealing..." (The Stage 29th September 1988)

Audience reviews commented on the magic that Jeremy created by his stage presence, his voice and the movements which were flamboyant but effective. He could move between the cruel, sardonic egotist to the concerned and friendly companion with a move of the hand or a raised eyebrow and bring about a complete transformation with just an alteration of tone or gesture. Edward was the perfect companion; his dependability conveyed in a low-keyed and naturalistic manner. "Edward Hardwicke... stalwartly genuine... not a touch of falsity in his performance." (The Independent) They made a perfect whole in this unique and unforgettable experience. The critics were full of praise: "Jeremy Brett... a brilliantly sculptured piece of exhibition acting... a spellbinding performance." (Daily Telegraph) "We are more preoccupied with this lonely Holmes than with any other interpretation. And he makes us laugh too, because he has an answer for everything and he strikes out with a marvellously dry sense of reason. It is a Holmes with humour and an unexpected heart." (Daily Express)

"In many ways Jeremy Brett is an old-fashioned, barn-storming sort of actor who appears to revel in strutting and fretting his hour upon the stage. Watching him on TV, you sometimes feel he is unhappily constrained by the smallness and intimacy required of screen acting. On stage he is larger than life, pacing around the elegant Victorian set like a caged animal, yet he knows exactly when to tone down the bravura style in order to invest the merest look or line with significance. You may be able to see the cogs turning in Brett's performance, but it's such a marvellous machine you don't really care." (The Stage 15th September 1988) David Stuart Davies said: "Jeremy's real home was the theatre. It was here where his flame burned its brightest, its warmest, its fiercest, its truest... He had the fine intellect necessary to analyse, dissect and intercept a role truly and definitively..." (Bending the Willow) Michael Cox agreed, "I had never seen Jeremy Brett in the theatre before and hardly expected such a powerful presence. Some film actors disappear on the stage, but Jeremy positively flourished, like a genie released from a bottle. Edward, of course, was the perfect Watson for this situation, giving us the most admirable, ordinary man in literature without being overshadowed by his mentor." (A Study in Celluloid) Initially, Edward was *"a reluctant hero"*. (Jeremy) "I remember that before we started to rehearse *The Secret of Sherlock Holmes* I went to the phone several times with the intention of telling Jeremy that I couldn't do it – I hadn't been on a stage for several years and found the idea of a two-handed play somewhat daunting. In fact I never picked up the phone. I knew Jeremy wouldn't hear of it. Jeremy was always positive, optimistic and so encouraging." (Edward Hardwicke)

Jeremy was still discovering new ways to play Holmes. *"I'm so steeped in playing Holmes now that a new idiom comes every day, without my choosing it, and I suddenly have another illumination. Why, just last night I found a new way of doing Holmes's soliloquies. I looked up toward the balcony, let myself open up, and let the audience flood into the words I was speaking. Suddenly I had found a new vulnerability in Holmes. Another essence. Another clue."* (Brett becomes Holmes) One observer recorded these differences, "I saw the show many times but always relished the matinee performances... as he would always push the envelope with left field acting choices. Once, out of the blue, he strutted around the stage, squawking like a demented rooster, flapping his coat tails like wings... brilliant. Two days later on the Saturday matinee, in the same scene, he simply squatted at the edge of the stage and spoke the same text quietly. Equally affecting. To watch the pair of them was a true master class in acting..." (Anon on jeremybrett.info)

Jeremy said of Edward, *"Ted is the nearest thing to a saint I have met on two feet. If it was not for him, I wouldn't be doing the play and I probably wouldn't do the television either. I haven't been on stage for 15(10) years. But I love the theatre."* The last major stage production of Sherlock Holmes had been *A Crucifer of Blood* in New York and Los Angeles with Charlton Heston in the role of Holmes, with Jeremy playing the role of Watson. This had made him one of the very few actors who had presented both Holmes and Watson in this medium. "I always used to think how sweet Watson was, and then I played him on stage and discovered he was a much better part for me. He's so full of love, and outgoing and reassuring, a loyal friend, so marvellous. If it wasn't for Watson, I think Holmes would be dead."

"The relationship which Edward Hardwicke and Jeremy Brett have built up between Holmes and Watson that has captivated audiences on screen becomes electric on stage. The two actors' scholarly performances produce a rare clarity of character. Hardwicke's dignified Dr Watson becomes a more familiar general practitioner as if in a living room with friends rather than an auditorium with an audience... Watson's true compassion and humility and devotion to Holmes in a delicate, intense manner that is perhaps too intimate for the screen but on stage the gestures and words seem to be more meaningful. There is a closeness with literally, just the two of them, that is lost on television... Watson is the stability that Holmes needs..." (Gazette)

Jeremy was thrilled to discover that there were a lot of children in the audience, *"I used to say to the house manager that there are so many empty seats. He'd say, 'Mr. Brett, just look again. The lights are on, now. Look again.' And, of course – children! Little faces! Absolutely unbelievable! They adored him, and I think I know why... a little boy, called Michael McClure II, age 8, of St. Louis gave me a picture of Holmes killing a dragon and he said, 'Oh, he kills my dragons. I don't have nightmares anymore!'... So, he is a hero to the children. Three-year-old Solomon, is there in Dallas, a little aficionado, has all my films, and knows every word! I couldn't believe it."* They were often invited backstage after the performance to see the reality behind the theatre and Jeremy loved sharing his view of Holmes with these *"little aficionados."* He would also keep in touch with some of them in lengthy correspondences in much the same way as he did with his older fans.

Wyndham's Theatre was an intimate and friendly space ideally suited for a two-handed production like this. However, when the play toured the larger cities with large theatres, such as Manchester and Bradford, with two thousand seats it brought new concerns of projection and filling the theatre with their personalities. It became rather an ordeal with necessary adjustments, but immensely satisfying. One observer said, "Manchester Palace Theatre had a production line around the front, round the side along a passage to the stage door of the theatre where Jeremy and Edward were signing autographs. A grey haired lady commented on her way out 'Good grief, you'd think they were royalty!'" (Rosalie Williams)

During the run Jeremy reconnected with the viewing public and thoroughly enjoyed the experience. Jeremy Paul commented on his performance and on the Green Room: "Holmes was a poseur, full of theatrical gestures, and I think Jeremy's high style of acting, though not terribly fashionable today, is in keeping with the period. There aren't many actors around who move around the stage as he does, he's incredibly light on his feet for such a big man, almost balletic. During the run there was one abiding memory: the star's dressing room door was always left open. Jeremy called it the Green Room – and at any time you could wander in and find people – the mighty and the lowly – completely at their ease. He had time for everyone – to laugh with, to share a glass of champagne or simply to listen to their troubles over a cup of tea." And they came from all over the globe; Australia, Japan, and India. One fan recorded the thrill of the opportunity to meet Jeremy after the performance, "We descended from street level, the stairs were fairly steep…"

Jeremy was sometimes overwhelmed by the dedication of the fans, especially from the ladies. *"It's quite tragic, really. They see wedding bells because I'm a widower. The whole of the front row of the stalls used to be women who had seen the show more than 100 times. At one stage I was getting 3,000 letters a week and my dressing room was like a flower shop. The fans also send me clothing – jackets, jumpers – the only thing I've got on today that's mine is my underpants."* Jane Robbins sent hundreds of red roses to his dressing room every week for 15 months inspired by the "Rose Speech" (here delivered in its entirety) from *The Naval Treaty*. She sat on the front row during the run of the play and was thrilled when Jeremy pointed to the rose he was wearing saying *"this is one of yours, Jane."*

Another view of Jeremy in the play of *The Secret of Sherlock Holmes* can be found in the book of photographs by Marcus Tylor in *A Roll with Jeremy Brett*. They are a very fine example of portrait prints and represented a special photo-shoot executed at Wyndham's Theatre in October 1988. In black and white, the medium Marcus was most comfortable with and in keeping with his exhibition of backstage pictures for which the photos were needed – Jeremy was serious in each of them. Marcus said they represented a special record of "such a beautiful man." At the front of his book, he gives a detailed account of the meeting in which Jeremy was "wearing red socks. And in a buoyant mood to match" and struck him as an outstanding presence of "pure charm… his abundant energy making his television appearances seem tame" and almost like a whirlwind.

"In the theatre, when he appeared in *The Secret of Sherlock Holmes* in 1988 he came into his own in a tour de force for him and Edward Hardwicke as Watson. At the end of a triumphant first night, a friend said to me, 'What an evening! The curtain calls alone were worth the price of admission.'" (Michael Cox)

The Casebook of Sherlock Holmes

The Problem of Thor Place

"Women love Holmes. I was astounded when I realised how attractive he is to them. You'd never suspect it for one moment from the books. Girls long to seduce him. I know from experience that quite simply he is the man who has power over women. They lust after him because he's a challenge. Holmes is unattainable and that acts as an enormous turn-on. He treats women as objects of interest, not as objects of desire, and gets to them. Women throughout the world identify with what's going on and see me as Holmes. I know because it's my body they're after! It's all very flattering and frightening at times. I just have to realise I'm

in the fantasy business, but I do feel responsible and I get very concerned about the power this character wields." (Jeremy to William Hall) *"...you have to risk showing the flesh underneath. If he's going to be flesh, then you've got to take a gamble and bring in a little humour, bring in a little vulnerability, bring in a few faults and pray that doesn't offend people."* (Jeremy. Kate Tyndall posted 29th March 1990)

Whilst on set Jeremy would often take "a one o'clock catnap on a bed adjacent to Holmes's consulting rooms, and wore Holmes's uniform – a black frock coat, waistcoat, fob watch and chain and black lace-up boots even to rehearsals." (Today 4th December 1986) *"Queues stretch right around the block in Manchester. I can't believe it. There on the back lot is Baker Street and we have to pay to get on it. As I dart into 221b I turn into a pizza parlour. Mrs Hudson's Pizza Parlour. It's a huge success but I think it's absolutely ghastly. I haven't done the tour, I must be absolutely honest. Those who have are sometimes startled when they turn into Sherlock's tiny bedroom. I sleep on the bed during the lunch break because I only ever eat an apple and sometimes people come through and see this* dummy *lying on the bed. And they talk as though I were a* dummy. *And I suddenly go 'HUL-lo' and they go 'Aaaaaaaaaah!' and I looove that."* (Sherlock Holmes in America –The Morning Call 10th November 1991)

However, there was a personal price to pay for his appearance as the aesthete Holmes in the series; the need to be on a permanent diet. Several of his colleagues had commented on the occasions when he had lived on "a lettuce leaf and a carrot" and could not join his friends for a good meal at the end of a day's shooting. It is no surprise he would want to eat normally in between but then dieting became a necessity for each new series. Jeremy told one reviewer: *"I love nosh but the trouble is Holmes has to be gaunt because he's supposed to be a workaholic and a junkie. When I'm not acting I gain so much weight I have to book into a health farm for a few weeks just to fit into Holmes's suits."* (Chris Hughes in Brett Binges Junk Food Then Diets to Play TV tec.)

Jeremy was also having a significant effect on some of his viewing public in a beneficial way. *"I have a mountain of mail to cope with, which I do very happily."* One letter from a teacher in Wichita Falls, Texas, thanked him for encouraging her students to read the Holmes stories. And another, an unforgettable one, came from an 11 year old girl in Chicago. Jeremy told one reporter the story of how it came about: *"A friend of mine, an actor rang me at the theatre I was playing and said, 'Can you ring tomorrow this number? Little Louise Ann is your greatest fan. She likes you and Bette Midler.' I love that. So I don't know why I did it, but I picked up the phone then – it was about half an hour before the curtain went up – and spoke to her aunt. The girl was asleep, but her aunt promised to tell her of the call. I sent love, and she woke, received my message and died from leukaemia. I then had a letter written about three weeks before she died. And it was a letter of such unbelievable care and cherishment, saying she was concerned about me... she saw a dangerous light around me and was concerned for my wellbeing. That is part of the amazing side of playing this creature, this man (Holmes). It has unbelievably jettisoned me into a place I wasn't in before. Because romantic heroes weren't really in."* (Calgary Herald 5th November 1991) *"One letter had my name on it, and underneath it simply said, 'Somewhere near Clapham Common. Dear Postman, please help.' And it reached me! I found that very sweet indeed."* (Jeremy)

The Disappearance of Lady Frances Carfax

The Disappearance of Lady Frances Carfax

The Disappearance of Lady Frances Carfax (Dramatised by T.R.Bowen: Directed by John Madden fb: 21st February 1991) picks up the story of Sherlock Holmes after a three year hiatus during which Jeremy and Edward had been on stage electrifying the theatre audiences with their nightly performances of *The Secret of Sherlock Holmes*. An adventure tale set in the Lake District is an attractive prospect with its stunningly beautiful scenery and opportunities for such pursuits as sailing and horse riding which would have delighted Jeremy, but the Granada team had chosen to make some significant changes to the original script and thereby lost some support from the Sherlockian community.

This episode features the story of a daring modern woman who is pursued by a very clever trickster and consequently loses her reason and nearly her life. Her disappearance is the central action and the Lake District is an appealing substitution for the original Switzerland, with the added adaptation that Watson is on holiday at the same picturesque hotel in the shadow of Skiddaw, overlooking the scenic Derwent Water, and therefore on hand to assist the distressed Lady Frances. Holmes receives a letter from his friend with details of his walking activities and also the people staying at the hotel. Watson continues to show his special regard for the ladies and Lady Frances Carfax attracts his attention by her adventurous spirit; sailing her skiff across the lake to church (St. Beda's on the shores of Bassenthwaite Lake), or in heated exchanges with her brother the Earl of Rufton, plus her extreme reactions to the bearded man, who seems to threaten her by his presence. Watson also introduces the missionary, Shlessinger and his nurse and "disciple", Miss Calder, and it is he, the man in the wheelchair who rescues Frances when her sailing skiff overturns and saves her from drowning.

As there is no client requiring his assistance or crime scene requiring investigation, Holmes is not there for the first 15 minutes of the episode and he is missed as Jeremy's relationship with the camera always brings excitement to the action. Instead, there are fleeting glimpses of him examining the details of Watson's letters, visiting Scotland Yard or staring at chess pieces to gain inspiration. He hardly speaks in these scenes and his dynamism is much needed where a crime is unfolding and the lady's life is in danger. Once in the Lake District, he makes an essential visit to her brother the Earl of Rufton, played convincingly by Michael Jayston, and there Holmes is told that she has her own inheritance. Holmes and Watson arrive too late to intercept her at the Oxford and Lombard Maritime Bank in Pall Mall, before she disappears completely, taking her gems with her. The Port of Liverpool Maritime building doubled for the bank in the filming of the scene.

With the arrival of a coffin Holmes and Watson are forced to take action but the lady remains hidden until the very last minute, a situation more suited to a horror film with a rescue from the grave in circumstances too horrible to imagine. Holmes contributes his reliable, caring arms to the trapped young lady, whilst the would-be murderer is disabled by Watson. The ending of the Granada production is darker and more tragic than the original story. Lady Frances never recovers her mind from the *"terrors of the grave"* needing the constant care of the man who wanted to be her husband. It is for this reason that Holmes considers the case to be one of his failures, *"I have to say, I have failed"* and in his estimation he does fail. He saves her life but it is a damaged life. And he cannot accept a reward from Green. *"I refuse to be rewarded for fostering a tragedy. I have never suffered such a complete eclipse of my faculties."* One critic gave his approval of the changes made: "There are times when an original short story can be enhanced when adapted for the screen and, on this occasion, T.R. Bowen has produced a dark and quite powerful adventure…"

An article entitled *Sherlock – The Casebook* put his presentation of Holmes into context, charting his success and the onset of his illness; "In 1984 Jeremy Brett was cast as Holmes, and he brought a passion and determination to the role that frequently had the sides of your television set expanding. Determined to be the best, most accurate screen Holmes ever seen – a notion brought out of obsession rather than arrogance – Brett compiled exhaustive notes on the character and lived the part with a ferocity that was perhaps not altogether healthy. Brett had long been friends with Robert Stephens… with his own experience in *The Private Life of Sherlock Holmes*, Stephens tried to persuade him not to take the part… 'You will have to go into such a pit to get into that man that you will self-destruct.' Brett was diagnosed with manic depression in 1986, and he spent the rest of his life in the role becoming more and more unwell… *'I am bloody well trying to shake him off, but Holmes seems to haunt me these days.'*... that he still managed to excel in the role is testament to his skill... a masterful run of adaptations." (Sherlock – The Casebook)

"Jeremy Brett is a magnificent Sherlock Holmes. Not only does he grasp each "Hah!" as an entirely new vocal challenge, but he has banished forever the notion of Holmes as a brain on a stick. It is, of course, a great help that the Granada writers and producers have given him a refreshingly companionable relationship with his Watson (David Burke originally; now Edward Hardwicke). But what makes Brett's Holmes so special is a quality that is strangely easy to overlook – his superb physical performance, which is graceful and seductive. And the way those little smiles play on his lips – well, I could go on." (Lynne Truss in The Times 23rd February 1991)

The Disappearance of Lady Frances Carfax

The Problem of Thor Bridge - The Casebook of Sherlock Holmes

The Problem of Thor Bridge

***The Problem of Thor Bridge* (Dramatised by Jeremy Paul: Directed by Michael Simpson fb: 28th February 1991)** Michael Cox thought the opening of this story was probably his "favourite in the whole Canon... because it is such a fine example of Conan Doyle's wit and invention in fleshing out Holmes's career." (A Study in Celluloid)

This is a stylish episode with a crucial case of a woman accused of murder but with no one making a real effort to find the truth or to rescue her. One may say it was the lack of understanding and co-operation which causes the two main players, Gibson, the Gold King, and Sherlock Holmes to distrust the other. Daniel Massey, Jeremy's brother-in-law, played the famous millionaire and fits the physical description that Doyle provides, "His tall, gaunt, craggy figure had a suggestion of hunger and rapacity… his face might have been chiselled in granite, hard-set, craggy, remorseless, with deep lines upon it and scars of many a crisis." (The Problem of Thor Bridge) Gibson's arrival at Baker Street in a "new-fangled" motor car announces his importance and the expectation of getting his own way. Money and reputation accompanied by *"Booming"* are the rewards he offers Holmes if he succeeds with the case. His first comment is that Miss Dunbar is innocent and that Holmes must be the one to clear her name, however, the question concerning the *"exact relations"* between Gibson and the governess was deemed too personal and he resorted to threats.

When Gibson doesn't return to Baker Street Holmes realises he has made a serious misjudgement but Watson's practical suggestion that they apply for an official permit to visit Miss Dunbar in the Winchester cells (filmed in Chester) provides an opening. Although the unexpected arrival of Gibson interrupts the fact-gathering exercise, the involvement of his assistant, Ferguson, finally brings Holmes an invitation to Thor Place which enables the detective to make his usual meticulous, detailed investigations. This scene differs from the Doyle original as a chastened man returns to the Baker Street rooms to give his version of the relationship between himself, his wife and Miss Dunbar.

At Thor Place, filmed at Capesthorne Hall in Cheshire, the sight of Holmes and Watson, accompanied by a police sergeant on bicycles riding across the park onto the bridge is novel and further developed by Jeremy's hop onto the bridge parapet, in itself a risky action and reminiscent of the early days where Holmes climbed buildings or jumped from carriages with no regard for his safety. Michael Cox went further, "One of the qualities which made Jeremy so right as Holmes was his particular bearing. He was a public school boy in the choir at Eton with Daniel Massey and an actor in the old theatrical tradition. He brought that theatricality of voice and gesture to the part over and over again. It meant that even the most familiar piece of exposition in the sitting room at Baker Street crackled with danger. In the heat of the chase he would leap over the furniture or jump onto the parapet of a bridge with no regard for his personal safety." (A Study in Celluloid) Then he lies down in the dead woman's position to view the parapet, noticing the scuff under the lip in a noteworthy blemish. He was also able to see the relevant evidence of the empty gun-case which had held two pistols and the Brazilian artefacts in the schoolroom contributed by Miss Dunbar to the children's education showing Holmes more about the relationship between Gibson and the governess. The sparring between Gibson and Holmes continues with an archery contest between the two. Jeremy's skills with the longbow was something he had spent many years practising, although he tried not to beat his partner with too much flair and this scene was specifically written into the script to capitalise on his particular talent.

A return to the bridge and the parapet enables Holmes to try out a theory, with his familiar technique of imagining the circumstances. Miss Dunbar provides confirmation of the details regarding the note, the difficult meeting and the hatred that his wife had felt towards the rival for her husband's affections, so that Holmes feels confident in his solution. The story of the pistol is finally proved with another visit to the bridge accompanied by the police officer and Watson's emptied revolver is the means of providing that proof. Holmes underlines the story of "a passionate creature of the Tropics" vindictive, ill-balanced and anxious to gain her revenge on the woman whom she thinks has wronged her, in reality an innocent victim of her plan. They have helped "*a remarkable woman and a formidable man*" with the assumption that they should soon join forces. Jeremy thought the solution to the problem was excellent, "The Problem of Thor Bridge *is my favourite of this new collection. It's about an American gold-mine millionaire and it's got the best piece of deduction in probably all the stories.*" (Jeremy to Louise Sweeney in Tracking the Master Sleuth Christian Science Monitor)

In interview Dame Jean Conan Doyle gave her opinion of Jeremy's interpretation of Holmes, first in *The Secret of Sherlock Holmes:* "I was consulted very early on. I was asked to a private view... I was sent a script. I heard it on a tape. I kept in very close touch with the author, Jeremy Paul and with the star Jeremy Brett. I could see nothing objectionable in it at all. I thought it was a very elegantly written little play. Fascinating in its way, something that would have amused my father greatly... It has been beautifully handled by people who obviously love Holmes and Watson and the acting is splendid." And she said of *The Casebook*: "Jeremy Brett's been appearing as Holmes in films for the television for a long time now but his performance has changed beyond measure. I didn't really like him in the early series. He was far too arrogant and too mannered, too highly strung altogether, whereas Holmes was a very cool character. It has been wonderful to see the change in him. In the last series instead of being a rather unpleasant man he became an endearing man in spite of his conceit: in spite of this, that and the other, he's somebody who you really care about. I think it is an absolutely great performance; he really holds you.... Edward Hardwicke is a splendid Watson just the sort of Watson my father would have envisaged unlike Nigel Bruce... Holmes would never have shared digs with a fool." (Interview with John Tibbetts)

Problem of Thor Bridge

Shoscombe Old Place – The Casebook of Sherlock Holmes

Shoscombe Old Place

"This week brings a five week run of Holmes stories to a conclusion with *Shoscombe Old Place*... *Shoscombe* is no grand summing up of the Holmes myth – it's just a typical Holmes tale, the story of a chunk of bone found on the estate of a British nobleman (Robin Ellis). Holmes and the perpetually impressed Dr. Watson (Edward Hardwicke) are summoned to figure out who the bone belonged to and how that person died."

Shoscombe Old Place (Dramatised by Gary Hopkins: Directed by Patrick Lau fb: 7th March 1991) is the final story (60th) of the Conan Doyle Canon and features a man who is not a villain but who is attempting to bend the law until the circumstances better suit him. Sir Robert Norberton, played by Robin Ellis, who appeared with Jeremy in the tragic tale of *The Good Soldier*, is a man who is dependent on his horse, Shoscombe Prince, winning the Champion Stakes in order to pay off his debts, which are threatening his security. Debt collectors had already visited in the person of Sam Brewer, a well-known money lender, sent on his way with threats, so that when Brewer is declared missing, enquiries are made by the police. A visit to Baker Street by John Mason, Sir Robert's trainer, informs Holmes that his owner had "gone mad", he is reportedly down at the stables or in the old church crypt "at the dead of night", he is mistreating his sister by giving away her pet spaniel and of another worrying fact, the discovery of a human bone, the upper condyle of a femur, found in the furnace on the estate. Norberton is suspected of foul play.

Watching Jeremy in action in this episode we become aware that this is as much Jeremy as it is Holmes. His movements and mannerisms no longer surprise us but they do amuse as we see him do the simplest things in a singular way. The scene opens with Holmes in his familiar task of searching for a particular piece of paper amongst his vast collection showering them aimlessly in his flamboyant manner, looking for the *Handy Guide to the Turf*, and a letter from Mason as he needs to know about Shoscombe and Sir Robert. Watson is able to provide details of the horse, Shoscombe Prince and the fact that Norberton had horse-whipped Samuel Brewer, the week before at Newmarket. William Baring-Gould in *The Annotated Sherlock Holmes* comments on the fact that Holmes has apparently lost his enthusiasm for the turf, which he had displayed so effectively in *Silver Blaze*, and now relies on Watson for his detailed knowledge of the horse owner and his widowed sister, Lady Beatrice.

Holmes responds immediately to an opportunity for distraction in following the trail of mysterious circumstances, and on this occasion seems to enjoy being in the countryside. He will protest loudly in the episode that follows with the comment that the fresh air will kill him. As he said in the very first Granada episode, *The Solitary Cyclist*, the centre of a community and local gossip is the local pub, thus *The Green Dragon,* becomes a suitable base for Holmes and Watson, to carry out their investigations posing as fishermen. The Lady Beatrice's spaniel, Jaspar, had been housed at the pub and as Jeremy has readily made friends with him, he has the Landlord's permission to take the animal along on their daily walks. With Sir Robert in York lured away by a telegram, they might explore without interruption. The carriage scene is probably the highlight of Holmes's investigation and he shares his theories with Watson, *"Let us consider the data. The brother no longer visits the beloved invalid sister. He gives away her favourite dog. Her dog, Watson! Does that suggest nothing to you?"*

In carrying out his exploration of every possible theory to discover the truth he must take into consideration the possibility that Sir Robert might have murdered his sister. As Holmes visits the cellar to explore the furnace, he finds nothing more than the remnants of an item which could possibly be Brewer's wallet. The solution to the problem is achieved with the break-in to the house whilst Watson has diverted the butler. In Lady Beatrice's room Holmes's finds are fairly small, but his sniffing at the pillow, smelling the lady's scents and powders and finally taking the loose hair from the hairbrush is interrupted by the unexpected return of Her Ladyship accompanied by her maid, who are back early and giving him just enough time to escape through the downstairs window. An examination of one of the hairs under the microscope in their rooms in the inn reveals a resin which suggests a wig and not human hair.

The discovery in the haunted crypt is the stuff of nightmares with Watson unhappy about the thought of *"desecration"* of the grave, although as an army doctor he should have been immune to sights such as these. Holmes shows his mettle as he invades the house and confronts the Lady Beatrice stand-in with determination based on conviction and Jeremy's customary flair; the revelation scene is particularly interesting due to the appearance of Jude

Law in the role of Joe Barnes. Michael Cox says "Robin Ellis, fondly remembered from the BBC series *Poldark* in the 1970s, gives Sir Robert an air of romantic mystery, a man under pressure but not an obvious villain." (A Study in Celluloid)

Jeremy's performance was once more the focus of his fellow actors, and the critics. "I don't know what it was about Jeremy Brett but I fell in love with him immediately and unconditionally and have never reviewed it. He was so very, very special as Sherlock Holmes, a very special human being I think. So it was a beautiful marriage, between who the man was, his acting skills and this particular product." (Denise Black in Elementary my dear Watson ITV Documentary) "But really does anyone watch these things for the twisty plots or the invariably indignant suspects? No, you tune in to see Brett's performance which is a hilarious marvel. It's Brett's achievement to have taken the full measure of Conan Doyle's creation and to refuse to make this hero sympathetic and lovable in the modern manner; Brett plays Holmes as a cold, morose, arrogant man whose overriding genius makes him fascinating... Rathbone was elegantly understated, embodying the icy reserve of Holmes, but Brett has gone the other way — he is fearlessly florid, grandly melodramatic in a style that matches the tone of Conan Doyle's prose." (Holmes Improvement PBS) "I used to watch the series with Brett as Holmes and David Burke playing Dr Watson, but I never read the books, so to suddenly be playing a stable boy was extraordinary."(Jude Law in The Telegraph)

Shoscombe Old Place

Boscombe Valley Mystery

***The Boscombe Valley Mystery* (Dramatised by John Hawkesworth: Directed by June Howson fb: 14th March 1991)** opens with humour as Watson is pictured enjoying a fishing holiday when he is interrupted by his friend who appears unexpectedly at the riverbank initially unrecognised. Holmes has found his whereabouts in order to ask him if he would care to join him on a case, *"The newspapers are calling it* The Boscombe Valley Mystery. *I expect you have read something of it... A farmer, called McCarthy, Australian by birth, met his death by a mere at the bottom of his farm."* There is a *"very serious case"* against his son which is something Holmes would like to investigate and the request to join him is courteously phrased. Watson is pleased to accept with his customary *"well of course"*, but is then alarmed to find they have only thirty five minutes in which to catch the local train.

The gamekeeper who was a witness, believes James McCarthy is the guilty party as there was nobody else there and, on his arrest, James had said he was innocent of murder, but that he "got no more than his deserts." Holmes sees his *"contrition"* as the sign of a healthy mind and therefore dismisses the verdict made by the Coroner's Jury on the death of "wilful murder" as scandalous. The police case will be proven false with Holmes's evidence gathering and the viewer will develop enormous sympathy for the accused and the girl he loves. The arrival of Miss Alice Turner is a breath of fresh air to Holmes and Watson especially as her assessment that Inspector Summerby, replacing Lestrade here, is only a policeman and cannot see the truth which is very much how Holmes himself sees it.

Enthusiasm and vigour is the keynote of Jeremy's inspection of a crime scene as he throws himself to the ground in his search for trifles. His examination at the mere's edge brings evidence for so many people having been there, all traced in the ground surrounding the water. The discovery of tiptoes and a square-toed boot takes Holmes full length onto the muddy scene, "he would have made a rare blood-hound", says the Inspector as the detective crawls forward into the bushes. He identifies the murder weapon and the possible murderer with all the details necessary for identification. Jeremy explained, *"when Holmes hurls himself to the ground and wriggles through the bracken like a golden retriever, I felt a complete fool doing it and I thought the audience might laugh. But they didn't because it was perfectly in character – Holmes was using his animal intuition to find a clue and needless to say, he came up with one."*

John Turner played superbly by Peter Vaughan is both the villain and the most tormented as "a sitting duck for blackmail". The craggy and mortally ill land owner may have begun as a "highway robber" known as Black Jack of Ballarat, Australia, but since his arrival in England, his life had been an attempt to pay back for his wrong doing, to do a little good with his money. His daughter is a credit to him and a token of his redemption, but his nemesis, the scheming member of the same gang, "the devil incarnate" William McCarthy is determined to keep Turner in his power, even using Alice as the means of marrying James into the family. Holmes clearly feels sympathy for him and listens with compassion to his story of bitter vengeance in the face of torment. The human reaction to pain and frustration can be seen passing across Jeremy's face as Holmes once more chooses to exercise his method of acting as judge and jury in this case and the murderer signs a full confession in anticipation of the authorities finding James guilty, but with Holmes prepared to speak up for him at the trial with his expert evidence, that was an unlikely outcome. It can be seen as a better bid for justice than the justice system would allow and both Holmes and Watson appear satisfied at the outcome. Michael Cox said, "He has a genuine sense of natural justice, a sense of honour. People wish that he did exist. They feel somehow that society would be a safer place if he did." (Heroes of Detection)

"When he does speak, Brett's line readings are a hoot – he mumbles whole paragraphs of Conan Doyle's fussy dialogue in a rude rush, as if he can barely deign to speak to the dimwits around him. This Holmes delights in being stubborn and perverse; last week in the *Boscombe Valley Mystery* the long-suffering Watson remarked on how pleased he was that the duo's investigation had taken them out of sooty London and into the bright English countryside. Holmes, however, responded by inhaling so loudly that his nostrils seemed to flap in the breeze, and then groaned, '*Oh Watson, all this fresh air will kill me*'. Whether you're a novice or a dedicated fan, there is enormous pleasure to be taken in watching an actor bring a myth to life the way Brett has done so consistently for so long." (Holmes Improvement)

Baker Street File - Boscombe Valley Mystery

113 - Has a keen questioning glance

114 - Like a dog picking up the scent

The Illustrious Client - The Casebook of Sherlock Holmes

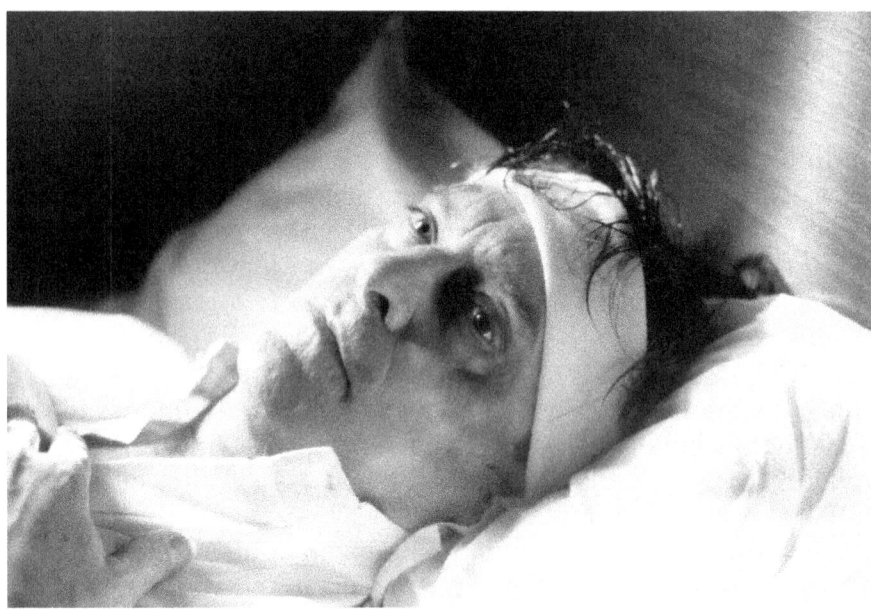

"Murderous Attack on Sherlock Holmes"

In the next episode, *The Illustrious Client*, the relationship between Mrs Hudson and her two charges comes into focus as she cares for the stricken Holmes in the most sympathetic manner and at the same time protects the overworked doctor. Rosalie Williams explained her closeness to Watson, "because they share an affection for Holmes and, in a sense, they manage him together. She's very fond, I feel, and very friendly with the doctor. She has great respect for him. It's a gentler relationship, but the main thing is that together they share this business of looking after Holmes... this man who can be so awful to deal with and at the same time so endearing." (Scarlet Street) **The Illustrious Client (Dramatised by Robin Chapman: Directed by Tim Sullivan fb: 21st March 1991)** features a ruthless and dangerous villain, Baron Gruner, played by Anthony Valentine, who "collects women" and features them in his book which he calls his "commonplace book," a locked diary. The Baron is among the worst of the villains that Holmes faces and the episode opens with a case of murder on the Italian/Swiss border as Gruner pushes his wife down the mountainside in order to be free to lure another wife into his honey trap. The introduction to Holmes and Watson follows the opening of Doyle's story. They are dressed in bathrobes in a Turkish bath, lying side by side on loungers with a hookah pipe between them in a brief moment of relaxation, a place where Watson sees his friend "less reticent and more human than anywhere else." However, their peace has already been broken as Holmes reveals a letter.

The request for Holmes's assistance is brought to Baker Street by Colonel Sir James Damery, in a bid to persuade the daughter of General Merville, Violet Merville, to end her engagement of marriage with Gruner, "the most dangerous man in Europe" and who Holmes recognises as *"The Austrian Murderer."* Violet Merville will hear nothing bad about her intended husband because she is deeply in love. Sir James comes in his own person but he is clearly asking on behalf of a client whose identity he wishes to protect and Holmes is reluctant to work without all the facts at which Jeremy leaps out of his chair in protest, as precipitous as ever.

The meeting between Holmes and Gruner is one of two giants from opposing sides; good versus evil. He is a libertine who uses and abuses women. Holmes's attempt to persuade him to back off is unsuccessful and although the Baron is intrigued by the fact that "they have engaged the very best," he is unwilling to be bullied. "You are clearly out of your depth, Mr Holmes." In return he threatens Holmes with violence unless he 'draws off', and the reply is a witty personal assessment, full of contempt. *"If you aspire to be accepted into English society, you'd do well to remove the band from your Havanna before lighting it – otherwise you'll be put down for a bounder."* Shinwell Johnson locates Kitty Winter, one of Gruner's mistresses and victims, one of a hundred, maybe more, "Women and china they're his twin passions," she says and together she and Holmes visit Violet in a final bid to show her the true nature of her prospective husband. But even the revelation of Kitty's terrible scars, the result of oil of vitriol being thrown at her unprotected body, does not convince Violet of the true nature of her suitor who has been most clever in providing a carefully edited account of his life.

The scene in the carriage is very touching as Holmes comforts Kitty, and in which she provides the details of how Gruner gave her the dreadful scars, although she was less willing to describe the book, with its photographs, names, and details, which she sees as the ultimate humiliation. Gruner is a thug and a villain, a very dangerous man whose method of defeating Holmes is to have him attacked and left for dead. Watson discovers the details in the daily newspaper, in the headline, *"Murderous Attack on Sherlock Holmes,"* and the scenes where he is cared for by Mrs Hudson and Watson are some of the most moving footage of the series.

"Holmes gets severely beaten up by two thugs in a very carefully choreographed sequence. Through all that follows, during which he is in bed with blood-soaked bandages and so on, we have been entirely faithful to the story. And it's a lovely bit for Mrs Hudson too. She is desperately worried about Holmes and Watson is studying the books on Chinese ceramics to prepare for his interview with Gruner. She comes in and says, 'You will remember to turn the lamp out, won't you? Don't stay up too late, Doctor, because we can't have you both ill.' It's all very human." (Michael Cox in The Armchair Detective 1992)

The *New York Times* gave their approval. "But the fun, as usual, is in watching Holmes move into action. In a meeting with the Baron, his contempt is bottomless as he reminds the nasty Austrian that in respectable society to remove the band from a cigar before lighting it... The Holmes plan to entrap the Baron involves a scheme to appeal to his passion for collecting, a scheme that requires Watson to spend 24 hours devouring books that will make him an expert on Chinese pottery. As always, Watson does what he's told with enviable competence. There is a resolution of sorts, and the identity of the 'illustrious client' is revealed with appropriate decorum. Holmes triumphs once again." (New York Times 14th November 1991)

The Creeping Man

The Creeping Man (Dramatised by Robin Chapman: Directed by Tim Sullivan fb: 28th March 1991) appears to be a story of Jekyll and Hyde, which presents a mystery to the reader, but not quite so effectively to the viewer who can recognise the actor if they watch closely. In his introduction for the showing of this episode on *Masterpiece Theatre* for PBS Vincent Price suggested the viewers should suspend their disbelief if they wished to enjoy a story which was more suited to science-fiction than the science of detection. Published in 1924 in *The Casebook* collection of stories it was Holmes's last official case as a consulting detective before his retirement to the Sussex Downs to take up bee-keeping. The case presented to Holmes by the victim's fiancé concerns the daughter of the eminent Professor Presbury who is frightened awake by a figure at her second floor bedroom window and as there are no means of a man climbing to that height it becomes a threatening situation. Her father, a distinguished natural scientist, doesn't believe his daughter and is violently against any investigations but the case becomes more intriguing with the discovery that several monkeys have been stolen from nearby zoos.

"It was one Sunday evening early in September of the year 1903 that I received one of Holmes's laconic messages: *"Come at once if convenient – if inconvenient come all the same. – SH."* On arrival at their Baker Street rooms Watson found him waiting impatiently. This is one occasion when Watson does not show enthusiasm at some diversion and complains that he has left a full surgery but Holmes only sees the protest as evidence of his troublesome war-wound.

"Does Professor Presbury's daughter wake or dream?" is a problem which intrigues Holmes. He would like Watson to be present at an interview with Jack Bennett in order to take notes but also to hear his thoughts on the conundrum. Presbury, a respected man of learning, has been a cause for concern to his friends and family due to his strange behaviour since a holiday to Prague, but as Bennett is the Professor's employee, he feels he should remain loyal, and is understandably reluctant to share his concern with a stranger. The divided loyalties stem from his engagement to his employer's daughter Edith, but eventually he does highlight some strange events worth investigating. In full understanding of his predicament, Holmes challenges him to choose where his true loyalties lie, with his employer or his fiancée.

Presbury's unexpected return home brings a tense meeting with Holmes providing an opportunity for the famous Professor, played with enormous poise and fury by Charles Kay, to show his disdain in the insult, "221-b Baker Street hardly an address to inspire confidence," which receives the expected reply, *"I have no need to inspire confidence in others as I have quite enough of my own."* The Professor seriously underestimates his opponent as Holmes will first explore the problem of Roy, *"Why does Professor Presbury's faithful wolfhound, Roy, endeavour to bite him?"* He considers it curious that the staid, elderly professor should behave in such an erratic manner that it should antagonise his devoted wolfhound.

Watson may suggest that the case is unworthy of Holmes's skills as a detective and he is probably right, however, Holmes does save Presbury's daughter from a terrible attack from the tree-swinging figure. Half way through this case Holmes proclaimed that Edith did not dream but was in serious danger but *"from whom or from what?"* and does he realise that the danger comes from her father? Lynne Truss in *The Times* analysed the reason for Professor Presbury's fall, "The source of this nastiness is arrogance, of course. As Jeremy Brett averred in *The Casebook of Sherlock Holmes*: "When one tries to rise above Nature one is liable to fall below it. The highest type of man may revert to the animal if he leaves the straight road of destiny."...these were wise words, none the less. Incidentally, he also advised Watson, 'Always carry a firearm east of Aldgate,' which may be of no little interest to colleagues on *The Times*." (Lynne Truss The Times 30th March 1991)

"It was not merely that Holmes changed his costume. His expression, his manner, his very soul seemed to vary with every fresh part that he assumed." In fact these words could be applied to Jeremy's performance as each new episode brought a fresh interpretation of the famous detective. Sherlock Holmes had become a real person of flesh and blood in his very capable hands. *"Holmes could be rude, impatient, abrupt, and his intolerance of fools was legendary. I tried to show all this, all of the man's incredible brilliance. But there are some cracks in Holmes's marble, as in an almost perfect Rodin statue. And I tried to show that, too."* (Jeremy) When asked what he enjoyed the most about playing Holmes, his sense of humour was very much in evidence, *"We're all very well-mannered people, aren't we?... It's heaven to*

be rude. I loved that. I loved being able to say, 'Thank you!' dismissively. That was great fun! All that cutting of all the rhubarb! I enjoyed all of those times when Holmes walks away without even saying goodbye. He just hasn't the time to go through all that polite behaviour."
(Jeremy in The Armchair Detective)

A letter from Dame Jean Conan Doyle expressed her appreciation of the *Casebook* series: "What a wonderful success you and all concerned made of *The Casebook*. It was a joy to watch and then to read the acclaim of the critics. As you know, I was worried about *The Creeping Man*, but I was wrong. The changes from the original didn't spoil it. I find that Jeremy gets closer and closer to the Holmes of my childhood and the final episode left me longing to see him in further adventures. Edward Hardwicke is a perfect Watson. Very sincere congratulations and also gratitude in that you have brought my father's works so splendidly before millions of viewers one hundred years after they were written." *(Dame Jean Conan Doyle)*

"If Rathbone was the seminal Holmes, the classic must be Jeremy Brett on UK television (1984-94). Those shows were played without camp or irony. Brett was tall, dark and handsome, but also eccentric and moody. Surely a generation will never get him out of their heads…" (The Guardian, 2nd December 2011)

"With his dry, wind-blown hair, thin gold necklace and diamond stud in one ear, he bore no resemblance to the slicked-down, hawkish detective who has become so familiar to *PBS* watchers. To achieve his mordant Holmes look, Brett said he has to spend an hour in the make-up chair. *'The worst part is the eyebrows. S.H. had arched eyebrows, so they had to glue mine up. Then my hair has to be glued and gelled.'* Whatever humiliations he has to undergo, the results are surely worth it, to judge by the response of viewers. As one critic typically put it, Brett is "the king among all the players who have ever slipped on a deerstalker cap." (John Blades in Chicago Tribune 12th November 1991)

Doctor Who enthusiasts regret that Jeremy never played the role. A recent article records the expectations. *"Jeremy Brett is the Lost Doctor.* At least in our universe which celebrates alternate possibilities and adventures for our favourite Time Lord, his name was oft-cited by fans as potential casting for the role, and in 1994 he was long-listed for the part… imagine a performance infused with more of the actor's warmth and charm that are self evident in interviews – characteristics that he stripped away to deliver a more austere performance as the world's greatest consulting detective. Consider this a tribute of sorts to one of our favourite actors, then, as the quintessential Holmes becomes our latest incarnation of the Doctor." (Dwaitas.wordpress.com)

Larry's Stable 1991 – Old Vic Company

In 1991 Cedric Messina assembled an all-star company to present **Larry's Stable**, an evening of entertainment in support of the Shakespeare's Globe Trust, at the Old Vic on December 15th with Joan Plowright, Jeremy Brett, Anna Carteret, Jane Lapotaire, Edward Petherbridge, Robert Stephens, Tom Stoppard, John Stride, Denis Quilley and Virginia McKenna among those appearing.

Jeremy

On occasions Jeremy had the ability to be philosophical about the loss of his wife as in 1991 he told the Dallas press, *"I'm here for public television. My wife (Wisconsin native Joan Wilson, who died of cancer in 1985) devoted her life to it, and I'm here... in memory of her... My wife was, you see the founder of Mystery!"* In the same interview he watches a hawk which was circling the sky and goes on to say, *"She built a delicate bridge between our two countries. God bless her soul. I'm sure that hawk was her."* But in 1986 he had completely lost that acceptance, *"I was advised that the way to get over it was to get back on my bike, and get back to work. That is what I did, but I think it was wrong. I was worn out, but I went into a kind of overdrive. It wasn't manic depression: more of a manic high. Then when I had finished filming, I was so thrilled to be free and resting, but I couldn't sleep. And then it began to go wrong. I think I probably should have gone on Valium, but as we all know that also has its dangers."* (Jeremy Brett the ultimate Sherlock Holmes looks forward to his last case)

He suffered a major breakdown and entered the Maudesley Hospital where he stayed for ten weeks. Seeing his son at his bedside in tears made him determined he would get better and learn to live again. Jeremy was dismissive about his experiences and not ashamed to talk about his condition. *"One good thing that has come out of it all is that, because I'm well-known, I can say I've been desperately ill and give others some hope... There's a terrible stigma about mental illness. People become isolated, but what they really need is some company."* Loneliness and depression can ambush anyone who has lost a loved one and Jeremy had succumbed to the feelings of loss. However, within two months he was back in front of the cameras and filming the next episodes of *Sherlock Holmes* in *A Sign of Four* and his courage had a positive effect, *"I have been flooded with letters from people in similar circumstances to my own, who tell me that hearing about my own recovery has given them the strength to struggle on."*

Jeremy always loved classical music, especially opera, and told one interviewer, *"I gave myself a tremendous treat – a week at the Salzburg Festival, where I heard some of the most brilliant musicians and the most wonderful singers, like the great Marilyn Horne. I saw the opera* Carmen *and also* Capriccio *by Richard Strauss. My ears were still tingling with all the magnificent music after I came back – I think I had probably too much. I needed to sit in silence for about a week afterwards to absorb all that I'd heard. But it was one of the most exciting, beautiful weeks of my life."* (Secret of Success by Christine Palmer 17th January 1987)

Newspaper articles over the years would centre on his love for Joan and the possibilities of a new relationship. One of these had the heading, *"I had the perfect wife. Five years after her death I can't even decide what age a new girlfriend should be."* In it he said again that he was overwhelmed by grief and his life fell apart when she died. His self-confidence died when he lost his perfect wife and *"to get to know someone that well again is going to be difficult. I can't ever imagine having that closeness again..."*

The Casebook of Sherlock Holmes

"He was a tremendous realist, I'm a romantic. He was an introvert, I'm an extrovert. He was immensely serious, I'm rather a jolly chap. It's difficult for me to say what I may have given to the image of Holmes. Faithful to Conan Doyle's text, certainly. Also, I've tried to bring out the emotion that is there in Holmes. On the surface he seems a cold, sometimes dark, rather off-putting figure. But deeper down, I think, he's a man of feeling." (Jeremy)

The three two hour episodes which follow are under *The Casebook* title but link with the final series of *The Memoirs* especially as the man that Jeremy creates is one who is prepared to show his feelings, where there were only hints in *The Adventures* and *The Return*. He will be shown responding to the charms of the girl, Aggie, in *The Master Blackmailer*, struggling with nightmares in *The Eligible Bachelor* and openly crying at the death of a good man at the close of *The Red Circle;* instinctive responses to these situations but hitherto alien in other interpretations of Holmes.

The *TV Times* listing introduced *The Master Blackmailer* with the following description: "From London's underworld creeps Charles Augustus Milverton, intent on destroying the society wedding of the year unless his blackmail demands are met. Sherlock Holmes who himself is engaged to be married, mounts an investigation." (TV Times 21st December 1991)

Serena Gordon as Lady Eva Blackwell in The Master Blackmailer

The Master Blackmailer - The Casebook of Sherlock Holmes

"It was his search for perfectionism that underlined Jeremy's portrayal of Holmes. His sole intent was being true to Doyle..."

***The Master Blackmailer* (Dramatised by Jeremy Paul: Directed by Peter Hammond fb: 2nd January 1992)** is based on the story *Charles Augustus Milverton* and the script used as much of the original dialogue as was possible. "*Do you feel a creeping, shrinking sensation, Watson, when you stand before the serpents in the Zoo, and see the slithery, gliding, venomous creatures, with their deadly eyes and wicked, flattened faces? Well that's how Milverton impresses me...*" Holmes describes the blackmailer as "*the worst man in London.*" He was based on a real person, rumoured to have blackmailed a friend and patient of Conan Doyle. William Baring-Gould suggests that Charles Augustus Howell, an art dealer who died in suspicious circumstances nine years before the story was written, was the person on whom CAM was based. June Wyndham Davies explained the approach to *The Sherlock Holmes Gazette* "The story is intact and correct. Jeremy Paul has invented some characters and put weight behind those that were already there. I spoke to him beforehand and said we want as much downstairs as upstairs – we need to see the lower and the higher ranks in this. Our story starts twelve years before, in which we show how several people have been affected by Charles Augustus Milverton."

If Milverton is the revolting villain of the episode, feared by everyone, Holmes becomes the hero, the only lifeline in whom the victims are able to trust. This episode opens in Paris with secret love letters being retrieved from the fire by Bertrand (Nickolas Grace) and then handed over in exchange for a great deal of money. The blackmailer had waited for 12 years before demanding an extortionate sum of money and had chosen a time when the stakes were at their highest. Her Ladyship may beg for mercy but there was none. Holmes was informed of the case of the Viscount Croft who was caught "*in flagrante*" in the bed of a prostitute and his brother, Edward, who took a revolver to the footman and left him disfigured for life. The young men were consequently living abroad in disgrace and their grandmother can provide Holmes with a clue to the identity of their oppressor. The monster "lives and breathes, Mr Holmes, with a smiling face and a heart of marble," the signed page of a book of poetry "*CAM Devil*" and the comment "a man who preys upon weakness" is all she can offer. "*And I had a wonderful leading lady in this last film. Dame Gwen Ffrangcon Davies. She's 101, which is intriguing because Doyle, of course, would have seen her... and she said, 'That lady is improperly dressed.' And I said, 'What do you mean, Dame Gwen?' And she said, 'Well I know because I was there. She would have on a Hessian petticoat... very starched petticoat - and she would lift her dress as she walked across the gravel.' Can't knock that, can't question that. She was there. So, that was thrilling. Lovely, lovely, lovely, lady.*" (Jeremy)

Holmes follows his familiar style of investigations when there are no clues to follow; the gossip columns are examined and Watson is assigned the task of reading out possible cases for scandal and blackmail. They are very much a team in this film, with Holmes asking more of his friend than usual. The next victim is shown in a male brothel watching a theatrical performance of a haunting air from Debussy, then refusing to pay a penny to the blackmailer whilst his traitorous boyfriend looks on smirking. The tragedy that follows is reported in the newspaper as "The Hon. Miss Miles calls off her marriage to Colonel Dorking two days before the wedding," with consequences which are "*tantamount to murder.*" Holmes speaks for us all when he says, "*I have had to deal with 50 murderers in my career but the worst of them never gave me this sense of revulsion that I feel at this moment towards Mr Charles Augustus Milverton.*" This tone of indignation is in evidence throughout the episode as Holmes tries to control his feelings.

The Master Blackmailer

Holmes's announcement that he has become engaged to Milverton's housemaid is given credibility by Granada's decision to show the detective in disguise as the plumber Ralph Escott. The romance is certainly a fascinating theory but perhaps one which should have been left for the imagination. Holmes has discovered the identity of the blackmailer's next victim and his approach to her godmother brings rewards as Lady Eva Blackwell's imminent marriage to the Earl of Dovercourt causes her visit Baker Street seeking his help. Holmes may be sensitive to her situation, but the practical concerns of gaining the necessary funds for negotiating with the blackmailer remains his focus. The subsequent confrontation with Milverton at Baker Street is fraught and tentative, almost a game of chess, whilst each explores the lengths to which the other is prepared to go.

The concluding act of burglary and murder presents an excellent opportunity for Holmes to finally take control of the case which hitherto has been out of his range, needing no sleuthing or use of his brain. The working out of justice in this episode is different from similar cases in the Canon in that murder is the means of achieving justice, "as the woman poured bullet after bullet into Milverton's shrinking body I was about to spring out, when I felt Holmes's cold, strong grasp upon my wrist. I understood the whole argument of that firm, restraining grip – that it was no affair of ours: that justice had overtaken a villain; that we had our own duties and our own objects which were not to be lost sight of." (Charles Augustus Milverton). *"When you read something that says, 'Lady Diane empties six shots into Milverton's chest, and rams the heel of her shoe into his mouth and screws it to the ground...' that's fine, but when you do it, it's not pretty."* (Jeremy)

Alas, one change that Granada made to the original story is the omission of the final scene in which Lestrade visited Baker Street to ask Holmes for help in pursuing the two burglars who he believes had murdered Milverton. As Lestrade describes them Holmes makes a humorous comment about one of them, *"That's rather vague!... Why it might be a description of Watson!"* The scene was filmed and then cut from the final version. There is also one guest appearance of interest and that is of David Scase in the role of Art Gallery Owner. He was Jeremy's Director at the Library Theatre in Manchester in 1955 and husband to Rosalie Williams.

Several of Jeremy flourishes remind us of his physicality which is at the heart of his interpretation; his movement around Baker Street which is almost balletic on occasions and his little jig to the music during the ball for Lady Eva which one feels is rather un-Holmesian. We smile at his familiar exclamations of exasperation as he searches through his wardrobe for the necessary disguise for the burglary resulting in chaos as clothes flung onto the floor are left there. The image of the burglars who walk across the night scene with Holmes striding out in front in military fashion with Watson limping behind remains in the memory. Altogether it is a very impressive episode with so many treasured moments.

The Kiss became the most celebrated scene in this episode. And the main thing is Holmes seems to enjoy it. "Ah yes the kiss," chuckled 56 year old Jeremy mischievously, *"If I say it's bending the willow in terms of what Arthur Conan Doyle originally wrote in the story then I only hope it doesn't actually break it... At one point she clasps my face in her hands and says, 'Oh, you poor, poor boy!' and plants this smacking kiss on my mouth. She has glimpsed the lonely man beneath the mask. Of course, Holmes is never the same again."* Jeremy grins. (TV Detective Special) The *TV Times* reported that "the famously chaste sleuth actually falls for a woman! He has been targeted by a hot-blooded housemaid called Aggie, and he seems to enjoy it... *"I went home after shooting to my little bar I go to in London and they said, 'How are you doing today?' I said. 'Fine, I had to kiss Sophie Thompson all day. I'm exhausted.' They were all so jealous. Can you imagine going to work and being kissed by a 22 year old at my age? It was magic."*

"The casting is splendid with Robert Hardy playing rather against type as the repressed Milverton. Brett has rarely been better as Holmes, his distaste for the repellent extortionist being plain in every scene. Daringly, he's given a sort-of-love interest... having inveigled himself into the fortress-like Milverton household in the guise of a plumber, Holmes is required to romance Milverton's flighty maid, Aggie, and his heartfelt reply to her '*Give us a kiss*' – '*I don't know how*' is all too believable. Watson has a big moment too – being moved to strike Milverton in a lengthy 221B scene pregnant with menace." (Sherlock Holmes On Screen) Another review applauded the performance, "Jeremy Brett, as the famed detective, is in his element here, showing off the various aspects of the great mind that is Holmes. Holmes is always driven by the prospect of a challenge, a particularly adept criminal, but in this case, there is nothing to work his mind around. Everyone knows who the criminal is, but there is simply no way to stop him without risking scandal. Holmes is so disturbed by the evil that this man is sowing, that when all seems lost, he decides to stoop to the ways of the petty burglar... the best scenes are the ones in which Brett expresses his indignation and his helplessness." (Parama Chaudhury in Film monthly.com)

The bathing scene as he washes away the grime of the plumber Escott, restoring the real Holmes was memorable for its picture of Holmes naked in a bathtub. Jeremy Paul explained his frustrations with the financiers at Granada who held the purse strings tightly closed, "We were carrying Granada's flag through most of the countries of the world. But each new series had to tough it out against the money... I felt for mood and quality... Right then, could Granada afford a bath for Holmes? And perhaps a samovar with Watson drinking tea? Play it all in a cloud of steam. I like to think it was my shaft of sarcastic wit that came up with this bright idea, but it may have been June. I was not too pleased when several well-meaning friends said later. 'Did you do that one – can't remember the story, but that one with the marvellous scene with Holmes in the bath?'" (Jeremy Paul in Granada Television: First Generation)

This performance would be Dame Gwen Ffrangcon-Davies's last. She was the oldest working British actress who had her first performance backstage at the age of 15 with Ellen Terry and her career had lasted 80 years. "The first take was all over the place. She watched Jeremy Brett's lips and took her cue from that. The second went like a song... The film itself is a gorgeous business. Thickly buttered, not to say jammed with mist and mirrors, greenery and tapestry, reflections of reflections. And a group of girls like a Fragonard on the grass. *The Master Blackmailer*, Charles Augustus Milverton, lives in Hampstead in premises of unparalleled grandeur with his own rain forest, which suggests that business is encouragingly brisk. As Sherlock Holmes remarked there are hundreds in this great city who turn white at his name...." (Nancy Banks-Smith; Holmes and the playful dowager The Guardian 3rd January 1992)

Escott and Aggie

The Last Vampyre - The Casebook of Sherlock Holmes

"It has been a case for intellectual deduction..."

Last Vampyre

***The Last Vampyre* (Dramatised by Jeremy Paul: Directed by Tim Sullivan fb: 27th January 1993)** was filmed at Pitchford Hall in Shropshire and is another glossy two-hour film shot in 35mm based on *The Sussex Vampire*. Conan Doyle wrote to Bram Stoker in August 1897 in congratulation for his book *Dracula*, "I think it is the very best story of diablerie which I have read for many years." They were reputed to be friends and his story of vampires was written in homage to Stoker. June Wyndham Davies would recommend the episode as an intriguing combination of *Holmes* and *Dracula*, two attractive iconic literary figures of the twentieth century. The prologue concerns an event in local history of a hundred years before, in which a young girl was made pregnant by an evil landowner. She was brought to the sanctuary of the church with bite marks on her neck suspected to be those of a vampire and as she lay dying he was burned alive by the villagers in an act of vengeance. The fire was staged in a model mansion built at a cost of more than £30,000 on the footings of a ruined house in Warwickshire.

Holmes has been consulted about a case that appears to involve vampirism and plays a childish trick on Watson as he enters their Baker Street rooms. *"I'm slumped at my desk and*

Watson comes in. I'm wearing a pair of false fangs. I turn with my teeth in and Watson is shocked. I say: 'Your reaction is very interesting, Watson. You believe in these things, then?' Watson is horrified. It's the kid inside Sherlock Holmes that I love." (Jeremy) The appeal to Holmes for help comes not from Bob Ferguson as in the original tale but from the Reverend Merrydew, the vicar of the village of Lamberley, and he is able to provide a narrator's view of the Ferguson family who are at the heart of the matter. Bob has returned from Peru in South America with a new wife and son but problems clearly exist in the relationship with Jack, his fifteen year old son by his first marriage, who had been left disabled in a childhood accident. Peter Cushing was offered the part of Merridew but unfortunately he was unable to accept.

Whether vampires exist is at the heart of the action. The strange paralysis of the family dog and the death of the child, Riccardo, bring fears and accusations to the surface which should have remained unspoken. The report of Bob's wife Carlotta found sucking blood from the neck of her injured maid seems to confirm that the gossip has foundation although the reasons these things happen are understood later, but does anyone want to listen to reason! However, Holmes dismisses the idea of vampires as lunacy. *"What are we to do with the walking corpses that have stakes driven through their hearts to keep them in their graves. Are we to give serious attention to such things?"* and he states categorically, *"This Agency must stand flat-footed upon the ground, and there it is to remain. The world is big enough for us. No ghosts need apply."* (The Sussex Vampire)

The Vampyre in this tale is embodied in John Stockton, a cold pale man dressed in black, played by Roy Marsden and although he proves to be a troubled man with a troubled past, he is not a vampire. The villagers think otherwise as his piercing stares appear to cause the injury of a neighbour and the death of a strong and healthy blacksmith, he never sleeps and haunts the graveyard so they avoid him wherever possible. In this volatile situation we see Holmes explaining away every mystery with common sense and confidence, the voice of reason in a disintegrating community but after speaking to the locals in the public house, admitting that there is *"a dangerous mood in the air,"* although Watson adds, *"but no fresh evidence against Stockton."*

Holmes seeks to discover more about Stockton by accompanying him on a visit to the ruin of his home and thereby to test his theory that the man is innocent. But this atmospheric scene is more suited to horror films and creates questions which remain unanswered, as the man suddenly disappears from Holmes's sight and then is shown in another area of the ruin, sobbing uncontrollably. Holmes will tell Watson, *"I got too close"* and believes he has seen a ghost, but not a vampire. Jeremy had played the role of Dracula and appeared as Watson in Sherlock Holmes before the Granada team chose him to become the new *Sherlock Holmes* which gave him a unique perspective. *"The reason it's called the* Last Vampyre *is because we couldn't shoot it in Sussex... Sussex is so overgrown with people that we had to get away from them. But Cotswold stone is a particular colour and we'd have been the laughing stock of England if we had called it The* Sussex Vampyre." (Jeremy in Scarlet Street 20)

There may have been some reservations about these later two-hour productions, but Jeremy and Edward continued to be applauded for their performances. "The Granada series was beautifully shot and well-acted throughout but kudos must be given to Brett and Hardwicke who make a fantastic Holmes and Watson. Brett in particular is superb, at times arrogant, perhaps distracted and yet always keying in to the most pertinent facts, he is totally believable as the master detective. Purists may baulk at this episode though not at the series as a whole as I'd imagine, because it isn't accurate to the original story but to me the changes were welcome and, despite the fact that there were unanswered aspects, the story telling was superb..." (taliesinttlg.blogspot.co.uk)

"Totally absorbing. Jeremy Brett is the definitive Holmes incomparable as always." *"My relationship with Sherlock Holmes has changed over the ten years... But now I can wear the make-up and the black costume without getting upset. The role doesn't invade me any more. I've found a way of getting into him without screwing up my own existence."* (Alec Lom in Nothing – Holmes haunted me, says Jeremy)

Roy Marsden as Stockton and Holmes in Last Vampyre

The Four Oaks Mystery 1992 - Telethon

The Four Oaks Mystery was filmed immediately following *The Last Vampyre* as part of a *Telethon* in aid of charity and transmitted on 18th July 1992. The Independent Television production gave the viewers a two day presentation of detective dramas in four episodes of ten minutes with a detective murder mystery that the public was invited to unravel. Van der Valk in Amsterdam, Taggart in Glasgow, and Inspector Wexford in Kings Markham would each investigate a murder linked to the Roman treasure which began in Tunlow but it was Holmes and Watson who were the first team on the case. Written by Jeremy Paul, directed by Tim Sullivan and produced by June Wyndham Davies the presentation was enhanced by the gloss and expertise of the Granada series. The filming was carried out at Adlington Hall in Cheshire with the appearance of Phyllis Calvert in the role of Holmes's godmother, Lady Cordelia, with whom they were visiting at Great Tunlow Hall, whilst on a fishing holiday. Two murders in the village will require their expert attention and Holmes will once more be in his true atmosphere. Watson's skills as a Doctor would also be essential here, alongside his role as companion to Holmes.

The initial investigation uncovers information about the murdered coach driver and his passenger Colonel Harrison, a cartographer, supervising the latest ordinance survey of the district who has possibly found the location of a huge hoard of Roman treasure. Holmes is particularly intrigued by the story told by his godmother of a similar murder a hundred years before with the reference to treasure, "a fortune under the Four Oaks by a river." Colonel Harrison's two colleagues appear suspicious and when they are put under scrutiny by Holmes, they leave the inn where they were staying leaving behind an exotic ring which seems to confirm that the Roman hoard was discovered. Further investigations are left for the other detectives as Holmes is called to an urgent case before the fateful journey to the Reichenbach Falls.

Kevin Jackson wrote in *The Independent*: "Mr. Brett's true brilliance is overlooked not because no one says that he is splendid but because everybody does. What Brett offers is a combination of fidelity and audacity. Everything he does can ultimately be justified by chapter and line from Conan Doyle's stories, but he has taken liberties with the myth so confidently that he has also, over the last decade, taken possession of it, and displaced the literary Holmes. Brett's is a richly comic performance. His Holmes is composed of sudden wild stares, dreamy vacancies, hoarse exclamations, dulcet murmurs which wilt into silence..." As he approached the completion of *The Casebook* Jeremy was interviewed by the *TV Times* for an article entitled *It's Holmes and Away* in which he said, "*My Sherlock streaks through the night sky – not naked, you understand, but like a magnesium flare, with all the world trying to keep up with him. A man of utter genius, not a depressant... there is another Holmes: the thinking man's Holmes, who works things through logically – spasmodically puffing on his pipe, as ash tumbles down his waistcoat. That's the one I've never been able to capture."*

The Eligible Bachelor - The Casebook of Sherlock Holmes

The Eligible Bachelor

The Eligible Bachelor (Dramatised by T R Bowen: Directed by Peter Hammond fb: 3rd February 1993) based on *The Noble Bachelor* is a slim tale adapted and expanded to create a totally different story and a glossy production. The eligible bachelor in question is a Lord Robert St. Simon played by Simon Williams and his prospective bride, Henrietta (Hetty) Doran, an American heiress. In the original story Holmes reads the newspaper accounts of the engagement with a comment on the passing of the noble houses of Britain into the hands of "our fair cousins across the Atlantic" with a further note that Hettie is the "fascinating daughter of a Californian millionaire" with a dowry running into "considerably over six figures." The great house of Glarvon, the ancestral home which has been in the family for around 500 years with its wild cats and baboons roaming freely is at the centre of this relationship as much as the bride's money, which is shown in the bridegroom's dealings with money lenders, insistent on the payment of his debts. Some event has taken place during the wedding ceremony, unnoticed by most of the people present, but it has been significant, and as the family gathers for the reception, the bride has disappeared.

The episode opens with a series of unsettling images, references to the mental home, the unruly noise of the London streets and in this version Holmes is not well; he is suffering from nightmares which keep him awake at night and although he wanders nightly amongst the tumultuous streets of London in order to gain some peace, he gains none. A depressed and defeated Holmes suffering from nightmares offers a new insight into his multi-faceted character in Jeremy's hands. There will be a moment in this case when he runs into the street in the pouring rain in his nightclothes in order to make contact with his client and sits in a puddle on the kerbside muttering, "*Damn! Damn!*" Pictures of Holmes in this condition are melodramatic and unsettling. However, it was not going to last long and as the mood changes, he is able to recover himself sufficiently to investigate and solve the mystery of the disappearing bride.

The Noble Bachelor, Lord St Simon in Conan Doyle's original story certainly has his problems but in this story there is no villain. Yet in Granada's radical re-creation of the story he plays both villain and victim. His arrival at Baker Street asking for Holmes to help find his bride has already been prepared for, however, the great detective is in need of sleep so Watson agrees to take the preliminary notes of the case. The delivery of a note: "*What of the Ladies Maude and Helena?*" during the interview brings questions for St Simon who reveals that they were the names of his first wives. Holmes cries in disbelief, "*Married! But you are known, even celebrated, as one of the most eligible bachelors in the country!*" to which there is no satisfactory answer other than signs of personal discomfort. As the veiled lady, played by Anna Calder Marshall, comes again to Baker Street, her terrible story at the hands of St Simon is revealed. Her sister Helena had been his second wife, whom he had committed to an asylum after stealing her fortune. As Agnes had tried to find her at Glarvon she too had been attacked and left for dead. It is her story which brings about the re-energising of Holmes who, now out of his nightshirt and back in his traditional black costume, follows his investigation of Miss Flora Millar. The West End actress has been arrested for the attempted shooting of Lord St Simon and as his discarded mistress she is suspected of involvement in his wife's disappearance.

Holmes may be unwell, suffering from an unexplained malaise yet he manages to find the husband, Frank Moulton, who was thought lost, murdered by Apaches. The extortionate price of a glass of sherry is the one piece of evidence that Holmes thinks worthy of investigation amongst the best hotels and with his success, Hetty's future looks much more secure. She will not remain under the control of the rapacious Lord St Simon but she must survive his attempt on her life first. The concluding scenes are played out with tension and drama at Glarvon as Hetty faces up to a husband not prepared to let her go.

Holmes in his attempt to understand his recurring nightmare refers to Sigmund Freud's *Interpretation of Dreams*, published in 1899, and the possibilities of "prophetic and precognisance". This was added to the story as homage to Conan Doyle. He was an avid proponent of the Spiritualist Religion which included such beliefs, among others. Though he was ridiculed for this belief in his day, it became the precursor to today's New Age Religion.

There is no humour in this episode, only drama in a secret marriage, confinement in horrific and unimaginable circumstances, murder and insanity and each person wanting something from another without receiving any satisfaction. Jeremy was not in good health during this episode but Holmes proves the hero throughout the investigation, once more solving the mysteries and finding the imprisoned Helena. His suffering was shared only by Anna Calder-Marshall, but the viewer catches an occasional glimpse of his lack of energy in a physically demanding episode. And one wonders why the star of the most popular and lucrative series was not allowed another take at another time.

"(Jeremy) was such a very dear friend to my husband, David Burke, they had a very special relationship. There was something like Garbo about him. The face was never blank. So many thoughts would pass over his face, but subtly. It was packed in; it was rich... He was very generous; he wasn't just locked in his own psyche. He was always perceiving things in other people. His generosity, vision, his enthusiasm – he was a star. I was disappointed by the obituary, because it kept on saying what he wasn't. Maybe he didn't have the chances that he should have done, but in every way, in working with him, he was a star." (Anna Calder Marshall in Scarlet Street Winter 1996)

"I made a science of instability, and I succeeded." That line comes near the end of *The Eligible Bachelor*, but it could sum up Jeremy Brett's run nicely: a portrayal of the detective as a man whose genius pushes him to the brink of insanity, though one which doesn't extend to caricature, even when the writers go a bit overboard. The plot device of Holmes's strange dreams is an odd and controversial choice to make; as in *The Last Vampyre*, it pulls Holmes away from one of the things that makes him appealing. That, although Holmes's abilities may appear supernatural, everything he does is comprehensible (even, dare I say, elementary) after it has been explained..." (Jay Seaver efilmcritic.com)

The American critics recognised the fact that he was the "quintessential Holmes". "More than any other actor since Basil Rathbone, Mr. Brett was regarded as the quintessential Holmes: breathtakingly analytical, given to outrageous disguises and the blackest moods and relentless in his enthusiasm for solving the most intricate crimes. The actor regarded the detective as a 'black-and-white figure moving through a world of colour,' as a 'man without a heart,' but within those parameters he performed with a demonic intensity..." (Mel Gussow in The New York Times 14th September 1996)

"Damn! Damn!"

Jeremy and Linda

Jeremy and Linda

Jeremy thought he would never find love again; however, he did find someone else he could care for, and she was to bring the comfort he so badly needed in the last years of his life. The relationship began with his generous response to her request for help with her bid to raise money for Cancer Research by running around the coast of Britain. His surprise phone call with the promise *"Darling, I will do all I can to help,"* was followed by a meeting in his dressing room at Richmond Theatre where he shared with her his sorrow at Joan's death, *"I did not give up hope until the moment she died. There are success stories and there are miracles, and one always thinks you're the one who is going to get away with it, even right up to the very last minute. There are cases, of course, where people do. But I think what is extraordinary is that the human spirit is so strong that one doesn't really give up hope, right up to the end."* (On Wings of Paradise) "That evening Jeremy held a collection at the theatre, which paid for ten pairs of running shoes. This was followed by a photo shoot with the press to initiate interest in the run and get a back-up driver." (The Road is Long) The headline and accompanying picture showed him in Holmes's costume running alongside Wyndham's Theatre, "Holmes goes on the run' Here's Sherlock Holmes, hot on the trail of a missing fortune but without his trusty henchman Watson. Instead the super sleuth – in the person of TV star Jeremy Brett – has sped to the rescue of charity runner Linda Pritchard, who plans to raise £25 million for cancer research by running 5,000 miles round Britain... She has named her marathon 'Keep Hope Alive', but to set off on April 12th, she needs back-up drivers as support. But with Holmes on her side the solution should be, well, elementary." (The Daily Express) Ted, a throat cancer sufferer, responded to the article and volunteered to become Linda's driver on her run.

Jeremy continued to support her and joined her at the launch of her run from the Cutty Sark at Greenwich. "My parents cried, I cried and even Jeremy shed a tear as I set off on this journey of a lifetime..." (Linda in The Road is Long) During her run they would keep in touch by telephone; he was almost telepathic as so many of his phone calls were when she was in need of support. When Linda phoned him to ask for advice about visiting Ireland as her personal safety during the Troubles was an understandable concern, "Jeremy told me it was my run and no one should try to influence me. He said, 'You know why you are doing this run and you know what God wants you to do, so you do what feels right.' He then told me how proud he was of me and that meant a lot." (The Road is Long) Linda would raise £50,000 in her six month run and her relationship with Jeremy would resume when she returned to everyday life.

Jeremy and Linda alongside Wyndham's Theatre

In an interview in 1993 he told of their meeting and how much Linda meant to him. He also explained how she had helped him recover from his latest attack of depression and the contribution he had made to the start of her fund. In 1989 he had been voted *Pipesmoker of the Year*. *"I'd just won a prize of £3,000, so I gave her that."* *"She used to drive a Hoppa bus in Ealing but, bless her heart, she's given that up to help me. When I was desperately ill... this angel, this pixie was sitting at the foot of my bed. She began to question every medicine I'd been on. She saved me. A miracle occurred. I remembered I'd had rheumatic fever when I was 16, which left me with an enlarged heart and a weak valve...."* Will that include marriage? *"I think I am probably married in heaven. I am reborn."* (Radio Times March 1994) In another report he said he had found love with Linda, *"an avid fan."* His help with advertising her run around Britain had brought them together. An unnamed source revealed that, "They are both so happy, it's lovely. Jeremy's life fell apart when his wife died. I don't believe he thought he would ever find happiness again."

Linda explained, "I can never be, nor would ever want to be, a replacement for Joan. She was an amazing lady and they were so in love. Jeremy truly believed she would recover. The anger he felt when she didn't was just immense." Life with Jeremy was never going to be easy. He told one reporter how difficult he was to live with, especially when he was working: *"I'm certifiable."* He was also suffering from a very difficult illness which affected his personality. In her valiant book *On the Wings of Paradise* concerning the last years of Jeremy's life, Linda summed up how bipolar disorder had affected Jeremy; "The real Jeremy... was sensitive and compassionate, full of feeling for others, never saying or doing anything to hurt anyone deliberately. He was jolly and playful, a positive thinker with a marvellous philosophy on life, a joy to be around. His effervescence rubbed off on others and infused them with the same joy and playfulness. People wanted to be around him because he made them feel so good about themselves."

Linda then goes on to describe the other Jeremy that showed itself when the manic depression emerged. Severe mood swings could make him unable to sleep, or even keep still. "No longer the gallant and golden-hearted gentleman he would become edgy, impatient, snappy of tongue, saying hurtful things, crushing things, so out of character for him." In retrospect, he considered this aspect had been affecting his life for as long as he could remember. However, as is typical of these disorders, it had not presented any real problems until his second wife died. The severe shock and grief of this traumatic event in Jeremy's life led to what he called "A good old fashioned nervous breakdown." And it seemed to unleash its power upon his life. "How brave he was... I never heard him moan about his condition once. He never turned round to me and said, 'I can't cope.' Or 'Why me?' He just got on with it." (Linda in Sherlock Holmes: The Detective Magazine) In spite of the miseries that this condition created, Jeremy would show immense courage in his ability to pick himself up and bring comfort to so many others who were suffering. *"My illness has certainly widened my compassion. When I meet people now I can see the stresses and strains they are all under. Life just isn't easy."*

Jeremy and Linda

The Memoirs of Sherlock Holmes

Peter Wyngarde as Langdale Pike and Jeremy as Holmes in The Three Gables

The final six episodes of *The Memoirs* would represent Jeremy's goodbye to the role. They would return to the one hour slot in the schedules as everyone felt a return to Conan Doyle was preferable to the two-hour films. The length of approximately 55 mins of the originals seemed to fit the format better. However, it was clear that Jeremy's health was failing and he was no longer able to fight for authenticity of dialogue and interpretation. Even one or two inaccuracies appeared, for instance, Mycroft's talking to Lord Cantlemere in The Diogenes Club where talking is forbidden in *The Mazarin Stone*, which Jeremy would surely have commented on, if he had appeared in this episode.

The critic in *The Guardian* commented on the first episode and compared the latest incarnation with the previous series, "A few instalments ago Jeremy Brett was the best Holmes ever – a slightly camp drug addict allaying his boredom with the solving of supposedly insoluble crimes. His was an essentially comic interpretation, perfectly suited to Doyle's character. Brett is shouting his lines these days, to no one in particular, and the effect is operatic." (Paul Bailey. Holmes Flares up again. The Guardian 8th March 1994) One memorable comment showed Jeremy had not lost his outrageous sense of humour, "*Holmes has really become a semi-permanent job. But the time is coming when I'm going to have to wash off my mask, show people what I look like and say: 'What do you think?' First though, I've got to think of a way of publicising this series. Perhaps, I could streak naked across Lord's cricket ground with S and H painted on my backside..."* (Why Sherlock Holmes nearly killed JEREMY BRETT by Adam Furness TV Times 1993)

And, after all, he was proud of the success of his interpretation. *"Why should I mind being typecast as a genius?"* Brett laughed. *"It's been hard going at times but I'm very grateful for the opportunity to be recognized for a role that is so close to people's hearts. When I am out in public, people come up and tell me how much they enjoy the series. Many of them tell me they appreciate the fact that we've been so reverent to the original stories. That's a marvellous affirmation for an actor."* (Holmes: Brett Still Essential Sherlock)

The Three Gables - The Memoirs of Sherlock Holmes

***The Three Gables* (Dramatised by Jeremy Paul: Directed by Peter Hammond fb: 7th March 1994)** has remained faithful to the Conan Doyle story with only minor adaptations. It was the third episode to be filmed and would have an impact on Jeremy's health for the rest of the series. It is a very glossy and beautifully filmed drama with rather too many reflective surfaces. As Watson arrives at Baker Street, Holmes is in danger of his life at the hands of the boxer, Steve Dixie who is threatening to push him through the window with the final ultimatum, delivered with significant menace, to stay away from the Harrow case.

It is a strange case for Holmes as there is no crime involved, only a general feeling of something amiss. Mrs Maberley, played memorably by Mary Ellis, has received an over-valued offer on her house which she had accepted until her Solicitor warned her that nothing could be removed, not even her personal possessions. The story of her recently deceased grandson who had been an attaché at the British Embassy in Italy is an important detail although at this stage she does not connect the incident with the offer for her house. The young man had become a moody and "worn-out cynical man" before he died and his possessions remained forgotten in her house. Her story is interrupted as Holmes loudly confronts the maid who has been listening to everything that was said and recognises her as a member of Barney Stockdale's boxing establishment. Her presence confirms Holmes's suspicions, and finding Steve Dixie lurking in the bushes outside confirms his conviction that Mrs Maberley is in danger.

One change the Granada team made to this episode is in the assignment of Watson to remain at the Three Gables to protect her and as Mrs Maberley is burgled in the night Watson is savagely beaten by the thugs. On his arrival the next morning Holmes finds his friend black and blue from the beating and uncharacteristically tells him, *"Physician heal thyself"* which raises the question; where is the more sympathetic and caring Holmes of *The Devil's Foot* and *The Three Garridebs?* The only consolation lies in the final page of a forgotten and incriminating manuscript rescued by the injured Mrs Maberley.

The villain of the episode is revealed as the wealthy Isadora Klein, played by Claudine Auger, a woman who preyed on men. She is exotic, beautiful, of Spanish Gypsy descent and although she was considerably older than he, it is no surprise that Douglas Maberley had been wildly in love with this fascinating creature. His lack of fortune meant she would not accept his offer of marriage, so she would have him severely beaten in a bid to discourage him and these injuries would bring about his death from a ruptured spleen. Her plans to marry the Duke of Lomond, another young man, but this time in possession of a fortune and a title, has put her into Holmes's power and he has accused her of murder. In a dramatic scene of confrontation Holmes will fend her off and preserve his position with the comment, *"You are a destroyer of men. You destroyed Douglas Maberley, and very nearly my friend John Watson."*

One addition made by Granada, was the development of the role of gossip columnist Langdale Pike, played by Peter Wyngarde, whom Holmes approaches for the identity of Douglas Maberley's love interest, and the scenes between Pike and Holmes are full of wit and humour. The midnight masque with revels and fireworks was filmed at Lyme Park in Disley and due to an unseasonable frost Jeremy caught pneumonia and just escaped being hospitalised. *"I thought I was a goner. I should have known better than to stay out there. I was very ill when I was young and I've never fully got over it."* (Why Sherlock Holmes nearly killed JEREMY BRETT by Adrian Furness TV Times 1993) "I knew Jeremy for a long time, but I'd never worked with him until I was asked to in this episode. What I found absolutely fascinating was his hold on the whole production. He'd become Sherlock Holmes – totally and utterly, he'd become this man. It was quite extraordinary. He had this wonderful ability to know what was good for the series and what wasn't, and he always hit the nail on the head." (Scarlet Street 21)

"A lot of sweeping gestures have been made, many a wild shout has rent the air since Jeremy Brett's Sherlock first swept into view. It was a fairly extraordinary characterisation in 1984 and in the new series, a six-parter that began last week with *The Three Gables*, reaches new extremes of extravagant performance: long meaningful glares, much lip-curling, arms outstretched as if summoning spirits from another world. When Ed Siegel of *The Boston Globe* wrote in 1985 that Brett's portrayal lifted "the curse of Basil" from the English speaking world he was putting it mildly: in all the Holmes films he made, including those dire wartime ones, Basil Rathbone never went so recklessly over the top as Brett, never made the great detective's genius seem so akin to madness. It's thoroughly enjoyable, even the make-up goes too far, and Edward Hardwicke is the best Dr Watson yet, even better than Nigel Stock…" (Critics Choice by Richard Bruton)

The Dying Detective – The Memoirs of Sherlock Holmes

The Dying Detective

***The Dying Detective* (Dramatised by T R Bowen: Directed by Sarah Hellings fb: 14th March 1994)** is the fourth episode to be filmed featuring a harrowing case in which Holmes is infected with a deadly tropical disease. "Mrs Hudson... was a long-suffering woman. Not only was her first-floor flat invaded at all hours by throngs of singular and often undesirable characters, but her remarkable lodger showed an eccentricity and irregularity in his life which must have sorely tried her patience. His incredible untidiness, his addiction to music at strange hours, his occasional revolver practice within doors, his weird and often malodorous scientific experiments, and the atmosphere of violence and danger which hung around him made him the very worst tenant in London. On the other hand... the landlady stood in the deepest awe of him, and never dared to interfere with him, however outrageous his proceedings might seem. She was fond of him, too, for he had a remarkable gentleness and courtesy in his dealings with women. He disliked and distrusted the sex, but he was always a chivalrous opponent." (The Adventure of the Dying Detective)

Mrs Hudson tells Dr Watson that Holmes had been working in Rotherhithe. The case may certainly have begun in Rotherhithe amongst the opium dens; however, Granada had chosen to focus on the relationship between Culverton Smith and his cousin, Victor Savage, a director of the Oxford and Lombard Bank with an opium addiction which began when he wanted the kind of inspiration that comes only from a drug-induced state in order to write poetry. By frequenting these dangerous establishments he has put himself into the hands of Culverton Smith, *"the well-known resident of Sumatra,"* the authority on tropical diseases, and strangely enough, the man who will inherit the banker's estate and fortune on his death.

Holmes is called in to help when Savage becomes ill and he and Watson are there as dinner guests as the banker has a fatal collapse from which he subsequently dies. The scene is a tense affair and Holmes points to the different human vices on display, of fever, gluttony, acute irritation and envy, all encapsulated in the different guests. Smith shows his spite and lack of compassion in his pursuit of Savage's wife and children as he has them evicted from the family home under the entailment of the will and watches their suffering from a distance. Watson, who is present in the role of protector, makes a direct appeal on their behalf and even Holmes who appears unexpectedly warns Smith very loudly and publicly that he will pursue him until justice is done. *"It is a singular coincidence, is it not, that you should inherit so much from a man who dies of a disease upon which you are the sole expert. Coincidence, bordering on the unbelievable. Let me tell you, the doors of your profession which have been closed to you, will now be locked and bolted against you. It is my mission."* (Sherlock Holmes in The Dying Detective)

The infection of Holmes represents the dramatic centre of this episode. Mrs Hudson and Watson certainly believe he is mortally ill, and delirious, as does Culverton Smith. Jeremy's acting is convincing and very dramatic and Michael Cox says, "Most actors enjoy nothing more than a part which allows them to die in agony or go mad. Jeremy Brett was no exception and clearly relished the opportunity to don his nightshirt again and succumb to Sumatran River Fever." Baring-Gould wrote, "It is of considerable interest to note that the first account of the isolation of the etiologic agent of oriental plague, *Pastuerella pestis*, was published in 1894..." (The Annotated Sherlock Holmes) It is sufficiently convincing to say the delivered box which held the infection would be an efficient method of infection, had not Holmes been alert to the risk. He had been watching and waiting for such an attack and his perfect presentation of the symptoms is enough for Smith, the only expert in this particular fever. The phrase which Holmes uses as the gas lamps are turned up, could almost be Jeremy's when he says, *"Three days without food and water is one thing. But to be without tobacco I have found most irksome."*

The title of this episode *The Dying Detective* was almost prophetic as Jeremy fainted into the arms of Roy Hudd in his cameo role as Gedgrave during filming. Between scenes he had been confined to a wheelchair and needed to use oxygen to relieve his breathing difficulties so that Linda wanted him to go to hospital to receive treatment. He continued to be unwell on occasions, suffering from "whiteouts" until filming finally ended when he was persuaded to go into hospital again. He was diagnosed with heart failure. (On the Wings of Paradise) *"I thought there was something seriously wrong, but like an idiot I soldiered on. Suddenly I was fainting all over the set. They had laid on a birthday party for me* (his sixtieth) *and I just said, 'I can't go, take me to hospital...' (A heart specialist) realised straight away it was nothing to do with the mind. I had heart failure brought on by rheumatic fever I had as a child. They drained five litres of fluid from my chest cavity just for starters."* (Adam Furness TV Times 1993)

As Jeremy was hospitalised for this new complication he missed the next episode to be filmed, *The Mazarin Stone* for which Charles Gray was brought in to help Edward solve the case. The next two episodes in the *Memoirs* had been filmed earlier so we can see Jeremy at his best in this last series. The absence of Edward in the first of these was mainly due to the lack of go-ahead from Granada and the fact that Dr Watson was committed elsewhere when final decisions were made.

Dying Detective

The Golden Pince-Nez – The Memoirs of Sherlock Holmes

Jeremy with Nigel Planer as Inspector Hopkins in The Golden Pince-Nez

***The Golden Pince-Nez* (Dramatised by Gary Hopkins: Directed by Peter Hammond fb: 21st March 1994)** was the first episode filmed in *The Memoirs* series and follows the original Conan Doyle story with only the occasional adaptation. The timing had been pushed from 1894 into the first decade of the twentieth century to include the origins of the revolution in Russia and the suffragette movement. Unfortunately, Edward Hardwicke was not available to play Dr Watson as he was engaged in filming *Shadowlands* playing the brother of C.S. Lewis. Thus the episode was rewritten to bring back Charles Gray as Mycroft. The appearance of Mycroft here enabled the relationship to be explored in much the same way as the friendship between Holmes and Watson had been developed throughout the series. The opening scene with the shared analysis and clarification on an "original inscription upon a palimpsest", a reused 500 year old manuscript is revealing as the two siblings have a similar intellect. Mrs Hudson is much more in evidence too as she sticks up for Doctor Watson reminding Holmes that he is missing his companion but also putting herself underfoot and inviting more complaints from Holmes for being in the way.

Inspector Hopkins, played by Nigel Planer, is a methodical representative of the law; he explains the Yoxley Case with every relevant detail. It is a murder "without motive" as the inspector can see no reason why anyone should wish to harm Professor Coram's secretary, Willoughby Smith. The secretary was "a quiet, well educated fellow with hardly any weak spot in him at all." The pince-nez found in the victim's hand offers Holmes and Mycroft an opportunity to examine the spectacles for information about the owner. The scene with Holmes wearing the spectacles whilst rubbing the attached cord beneath his fingers is as idiosyncratic as ever. They each contribute to the portrait of a lady of refinement with poor eyesight, almost blind, but it is Mycroft who makes the largest contribution as Charles had been given more of Jeremy's lines. "*I was thrilled to have Mycroft... I asked the powers that be if I could switch my speech about the deduction of the pince-nez and gave it to Charles Gray. And he did it brilliantly. Because after all Mycroft is the brains of the family.*" (Jeremy to Scarlet Street Number 20)

Holmes needed someone to share the investigation with and his elder, equally observant brother was an ideal substitute, especially as Mycroft seems to be one step ahead in his observations and theorising and even leaves the primary clue of the empty snuff case for Sherlock to ponder on. Mycroft will also remind his brother of their father's axiom (taken from *The Sign of Four*) "*after eliminating the impossible whatever remains, however improbable, must be the truth.*"

The reveal of the Professor's wife is dramatic and as she staggers from her hiding place behind the bookcase she tearfully tells her story of the Brotherhood who in 1905 revolted against the Russian authorities in St Petersburg with their own Bloody Sunday and provides a convincing explanation for the accidental murder of Willoughby Smith. The Professor, Sergei is her Russian husband and she has a story of betrayal during their struggles with Czar Nicholas who had quickly put down the insurrection. Her search of the bureau for letters to save her brother Alexis results in the death of Smith but justice was guaranteed as Anna dies at her own hand from poison.

Jeremy shows a mixture of responses in this episode, some of them are familiar and others offer the new impression of Holmes. We hear him shouting at the policeman who was falling asleep on duty as watchman and showing his customary rudeness to the housekeeper, Mrs Marker. But we also see his sensitive and sympathetic treatment of the maid, Susan Tarlton. Willoughby Smith had bled to death in her arms so it is no surprise she is unable to take her eyes from the blood stain on the carpet until Holmes covers it with his scarf and tells her, "*now you can look at me.*" Jeremy's moment of hesitation at accepting the return of his scarf pushed onto him by the weeping girl suggests he has responded to her scent, reminiscent of his responses in *The Adventures,* but a touching moment in these final episodes.

Golden Pince-Nez

The Red Circle - The Memoirs of Sherlock Holmes

Red Circle

***The Red Circle* (Dramatised by Jeremy Paul: Directed by Sarah Hellings fb: 28th March 1994)** the second episode to be filmed remains faithful to the original story and was one of Jeremy's favourites in the final series. Watson introduces the story with the two antagonists, Gennaro and Black Gorgiano, both who loved Emilia. In Baker Street the appeal of Mrs Warren accompanied by Mrs Hudson, who appears in her familiar role as trusted housekeeper but also as a friend, is something Holmes is unable to dismiss even if he would like to, and the mention of Enrico Firmani convinces him he should at least listen. She is persistent, and thereby successful, maybe because she was willing to use flattery; talking about his "kindness," and her faith in his success if he agrees to take the case. The story of a lodger whom the landlady has never seen, yet hears moving around in the room above is frightening, especially as her husband is at work during the day and Mrs Warren is becoming hysterical. However, Holmes can be a magician in circumstances like these, "He had an almost hypnotic power of soothing when he wished." As he lays his fingers on the lady's shoulders her fears eased, "The scared look faded from her eyes," and he requests to hear every detail. Her concerns began when a young man, under thirty, clean shaven and with accented English had offered her more than double the usual rent on a room in exchange for being left alone with no interruptions. He had gone out on the first night and returned much later, but since then he had not been seen. He wanted a copy of *The Daily Chronicle* every morning and left a piece of paper on a chair outside his door when he wanted anything extra. The White Star sticker on the luggage suggests New York as a sailing had arrived ten days before.

Holmes appears to be at the mercy of events here. They come faster than he can deal with them. Initially he pursues the idea that the personal column in *The Daily Chronicle* was used for communication *"what a chorus of cries and groans*!" and very soon the repeated messages with the signature G prove him right.

> "Be patient. Will find some sure means of communication. Meanwhile, this column. – G."

> "Am making successful arrangements. Patience and Prudence. The clouds will pass. – G."

These brief messages help to make the case appear "more intelligible." But then the kidnapping of Mrs Warren's husband, played by the *Carry On* actor Kenneth Connor, appears as the next crisis. He was attacked outside his home as he left for work as a timekeeper, taken into a cab and some time later left on Hampstead Heath which causes Holmes to assume the kidnappers had mistaken Mr Warren for the secretive lodger, especially as they were heard speaking in Italian.

This is a very tight action-packed episode accompanied by high drama as Holmes and Leverton, the American agent, attempt to thwart the attack by Gorgiano but fail to capture him. Jeremy can be seen once more climbing confidently on roofs and crawling through the loft space seemingly without fear or concern about safety. Michael Cox pointed out the anomaly of a watched house with a top-hatted man coming and going through the roof without being noticed, however, he seems to achieve it without interruption.

Jeremy has created a sympathetic Holmes in this episode, a sensitive man beneath the cold exterior, able to express his deep regret for the loss of Firmani, a good man who had represented a point of refuge for the Italian community in London. During the filming of the production of Wagner's *Tristan and Isolde* at the Buxton Opera House he said he was much happier with the one hour productions in which he could stay closer to the original stories. *"We moved so far away from the canon in the last two films that I could not bring my book with me and say 'This is how it should have been.' I lost control. They were interesting but they were not Doyle... The one-hour format is much tighter, I can turn to Doyle and bring a little bit of him in because we are so much closer to the substance of the series - and we can call them by their proper names."* (Jeremy to Elizabeth Wiggins in Sherlock Holmes Gazette) One of the houses in a Moravian settlement in Fairfield, Manchester was used for filming in this episode and the *Manchester Evening News* spoke to Jackie Hammond, 72, who grew up in the settlement with her family. "The team filmed it in my house. I think they were here for about two weeks. Jeremy Brett... loved it, he really got involved with the community. After he left he sent a big bunch of daffodils to the church because he loved it that much."

"In the last series, his Holmes is older, often sad, sometimes moody but he remains the brilliant Holmes we have come to know and love, not only as a genius consulting detective but as a man with all his weaknesses, fears and his inspirational reflections about the meaning of life." (www. jeremybrett.info) After his death a year later Edward highlighted his struggles in the final series. "Jeremy was quite ill in the last series. It was a real test of strength for him, but he battled through. He was an actor who needed to work and was at his happiest on set." (Edward Hardwicke in The Daily Mail 14th September 1995)

Red Circle

The Mazarin Stone - The Memoirs of Sherlock Holmes

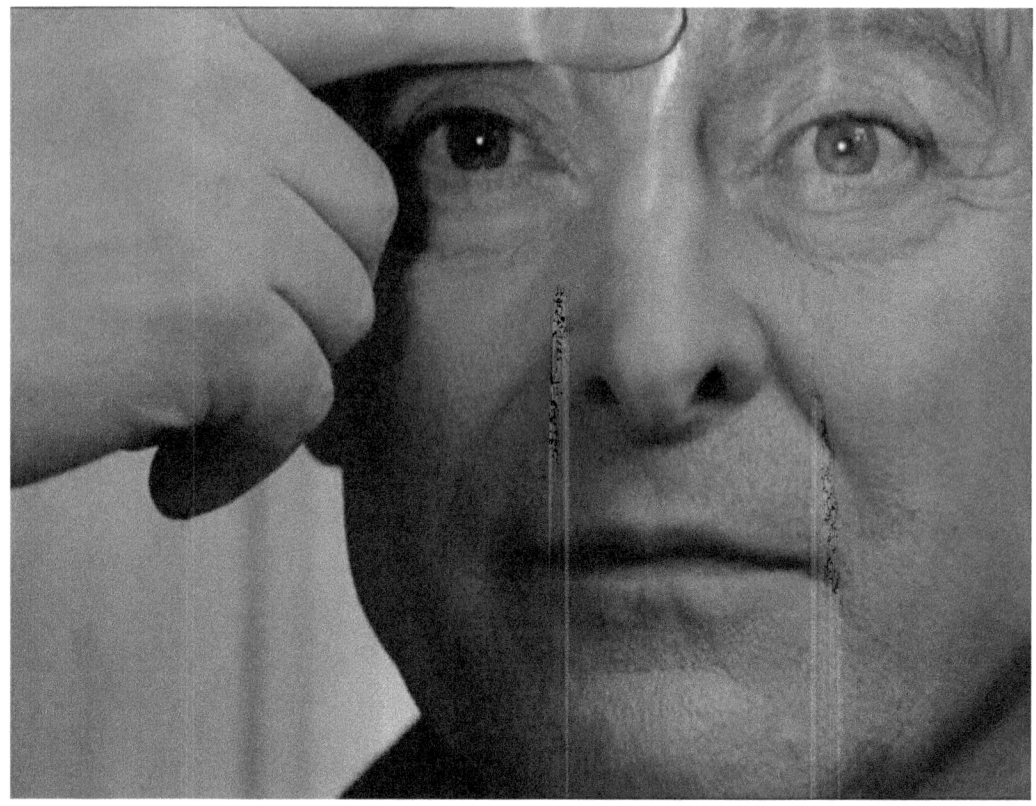

Mazarin Stone

***The Mazarin Stone* (Dramatised by Gary Hopkins: Directed by Peter Hammond fb: 4th May 1994)** incorporates *The Three Garridebs* within the story. The fifth to be filmed in the sequence seriously lacks the presence of Jeremy. He appears at the opening of the story and as a concluding image which reminds us of his genius portrayal of Holmes. Watson also needs him when he is wounded with the splitting tool, which is a missed opportunity for Holmes to finally show him how much his friend and colleague is loved. It has been called the supreme moment when a serious wound had revealed to Watson the depth of Holmes's devotion to him. "'*You're not hurt, Watson? For God's sake, say that you are not hurt!*' It was worth a wound – it was worth many wounds – to know the depth of loyalty and love which lay behind that cold mask. The clear, hard eyes were dimmed for a moment, and the firm lips were shaking. For the one and only time I caught a glimpse of a great heart as well as of a great man." (The Three Garridebs)

Mycroft was chosen as the person to fill in for Jeremy's Holmes who was unwell, so after a brief scene at the beginning in which he demanded that Watson provide "*the medical term for obsession,"* he retired to the High Lands to *"lay to rest the ghost that has haunted me for some time"* and promised to watch him with his *"third eye."*

Sherlock's help is requested by Lord Cantlemere in his meeting with Mycroft at the Diogenes Club, "It is the Prime Minister's personal wish that your brother should employ his detective skills, find the Mazarin Diamond and return it to Whitehall without delay." Mycroft has been accused of letting his younger brother have too long a leash as he was unavailable to investigate the daring theft of the famous Mazarin Stone; which at 110 carats in weight is "bigger even than the Koh-i-Noor." Count Sylvius was the last person to leave the Museum so he becomes the focus of attention. Mycroft will pursue his suspect in disguise, but without the essential skill of hiding himself, Mycroft is identifiable in each appearance. The Count, unsettled by all this attention, becomes threatening and takes a pot shot at his oppressor on several occasions, just missing him, but when challenged, excused his behaviour as "the hair trigger" on his weapon.

Another case for Sherlock Holmes, *The Three Garridebs*, is presented simultaneously to Watson in his consulting rooms by the two elderly, eccentric Garrideb sisters with a story about the promise of immense wealth. Their brother Nathan believes he will inherit five million dollars from Alexander Hamilton Garrideb of Kansas USA if another male called Garrideb can be found, but it is sensibly dismissed by his younger sisters as the bringer of the news, an American called John Garrideb, "doesn't have the bone structure" which identifies a true member of the family. They were unable to persuade their brother that he was chasing moonbeams and sought Watson's help to investigate. Nathan had been one of Watson's university lecturers and persists in calling him Watkins which is amusing and Watson, ever the gentleman, doesn't correct him.

Inspector Bradstreet as Mycroft's assistant, is as ever the efficient representative of the law and provides an update on Presbury, the only jeweller who could cut the diamond, (in the original story he is "The greatest counterfeiter London ever saw") but he was murdered five years ago, for which James Winter (Killer Evans) went to prison. This detail will bring the two investigations together, as James Winter is identified by Watson as the American, John Garrideb, and Holmes has provided further evidence in a letter to Watson where he writes to warn his friend about Presbury's lodger. Mycroft and Watson stake out the Garrideb house and challenge the thief as he breaks into Presbury's workshop in the cellar where his tools remain, looking for a forger's tool to cleave the diamond so it can be transported to Amsterdam. The removal of Nathan Garrideb from his study to Birmingham is also brought into context.

A successful conclusion is achieved by the final confrontation with the Count as Mycroft has pursued him relentlessly until he meets him on the mudflats of the River Thames, identifies the hiding place of the diamond and restores it to its owner, the Princess of Wales. *"Brother mine. Bravo!"* The words of congratulation from a slimmer and more vigorous Holmes reminds us of what might have been if Jeremy had been well enough to appear. As a piece of detection it doesn't disappoint and the scriptwriters had achieved an exciting action packed adventure with all the gloss and expertise the Granada Studios could achieve. But a Sherlock Holmes story without its star couldn't escape being an anticlimax.

Charles Gray in Mazarin Stone

The Cardboard Box

Cardboard Box

***The Cardboard Box* (Dramatised by T R Bowen: Directed by Sarah Hellings fb: 11th May 1994)** is the final appearance of Jeremy as Sherlock Holmes and for many it is the best of *The Memoirs*. Although the original story is set on *"a blazing hot day in August,"* the filming was done in winter so Christmas was chosen which gave the opportunity for Mrs Hudson to put up Christmas decorations and for Holmes, on Mrs Hudson's advice, to buy Watson a Christmas present from Gamages, The People's Emporium. Snow and festivities provide the backdrop for a startling story of a macabre present, two human ears, severed and preserved in salt which the unsuspecting Susan Cushing opens on Christmas Eve. Her little dog is fascinated by the box and has probably smelt the contents, but Susan has no idea and as she discovers the horrors within, she is overcome and faints.

When Susan Cushing arrives at Baker Street seeking Holmes's help to find her missing sister, he is dismissive as usual when dealing with personal affairs for which he feels unqualified. He can only suggest she try the Missing People's Agency. She may be hurt by his lack of sympathetic concern, but she has no idea whether Mary is truly missing or not.

The macabre present of human ears brings Holmes back into the affair as an investigating agent. At the same time he is helping Inspector Hawkins, who is replacing Inspector

Lestrade, to look into a number of grave robberies which have been reported in the press in the Police News as *Grave Robbed Again – Body Snatchers Strike in North London,* "a modern version of Burke and Hare." Holmes wishes Hawkins to continue in his search amongst the records for details of the crimes and, at the same time, to watch Murdoch Gull who could be involved in such things. A possible link with these events is suggested by the dismembered ears, which Hawkins thinks is "a nasty little joke and therefore unrelated" and Watson agrees that medical students can often be unthinkingly callous when involved in post-mortem anatomy, which seems to give evidence for the link.

The relationship between the sisters, especially between Sarah and her married sister Mary reveals the tensions in the household. Holmes's sympathetic and searching questioning persuades Susan to describe the reality of the situation and Jeremy has presented the Doyle original where "Holmes listened attentively to everything" so when Susan mentions Sarah's temper and that "she was always meddlesome and hard to please," his survey of the situation will include this element. Sarah spent far too much time within the Browner household making herself indispensible to her sister but also causing distrust within the marriage. It is Sarah who is the villain and her brooding, malevolent presence seems to dominate the episode; she loves Browner but is piqued by his rejection and in her hatred spits poison into her sister's ear, causing the breakdown of their relationship. The murder can firmly be laid at her door and the two ears, boxed and preserved, were meant as a present for her and not Susan.

The sympathetic and compassionate Holmes is a highlight of this episode and one which would never have appeared in *The Adventures*. Holmes can recognise the truth of how Browner was driven to murder, how emotional outbursts can spill over into violence and love can turn to hatred, *"I believe I wish you had committed this deed in France. They acknowledge the crime of passion there."* He also shows an instinctive understanding for Browner's need of company and the desire never to be left alone with his guilt.

Meanwhile, Holmes has effortlessly solved the body-snatching crimes by pointing out that it is only the graves of pugilists which are disturbed, as boxers often suffer from brain injury. Scarring of the brain creates people who are punch drunk and an examination of such specimens would probably be carried out by Sir Marcus Lanyon, who is reputed to be a ruthless man. The arrival of Murdoch Gull to Baker Street provides Holmes with the evidence about Browner's ship putting into Harwich on the date around Mary's disappearance, and in return he is promised that the involvement with the grave robberies will be halted but a scandal can be avoided.

The final *Sherlock Holmes* episode acknowledged the two people that Holmes lived with, worked with and depended upon. And as always they contained humour, first in Holmes's choice of a Christmas present for his friend, the bicycle cape from Gamages which will go over the handlebars, and then mimed by a delighted Watson. Secondly, Holmes's interchange with his landlady about the aspidistra, *"Mrs Hudson how dare you move my aspidistra?" And her reply, "I do dare!"* an outburst which has been criticised. Rosalie explained Mrs Hudson's response in *Scarlet Street*, "When he throws a tantrum, she can come back at him. She may win or she may lose, but at the end of it, there will be a twinkle between them as if to say, 'Well, you won that time. But I'll get you next time.' It may only be a glance, you know, or a gesture. They're still—not good friends; that's not the right way to put it—but they understand each other and they live together in a sort of harmony." (Rosalie Williams)

The final scene of the whole series was presented by a view of the two dead bodies caught and preserved in the ice, presenting a fitting image for Holmes's lifetime's work. It seemed to sum up his response to the human misery that crime creates, *"What object is served by this cycle of misery and violence and fear? (It must tend to some end, or else our universe is ruled by chance, which is unthinkable. But what end? There is the great standing perennial problem to which human reason is as far from an answer as ever.) That is humanity's great problem to which reason so far has no answer."* Michael said, "Quite properly, Jeremy Brett was allowed to complete his portrait of the great detective with thoughts which are typical of the Canon and its creator." (A Study in Celluloid)

Jeremy's performance in this episode was much improved as he was able to move more freely and swiftly climb the stairs to the Baker Street rooms. *"It was a dark story, but a true story. It happened at the time. I thought June was particularly clever, as was her brilliant director on that one, Sarah Hellings. They set it at Christmas to make it look a little less dark. I was particularly pleased with* The Cardboard Box, *partly because I'd lost a lot of weight and I looked better, and I thought it was very well put together. It was a dark and sinister story and seemed to belong to my attempts at the earlier stories. It did originally come from* The Memoirs *after all."* (Jeremy to David Stuart Davies in The Sherlock Holmes Gazette 1995)

These episodes of the final series underscored Jeremy's professionalism and his courage. It is true that his confidence had been shaken by the decline in his health but this brought another facet of his interpretation to the fore as this reviewer highlighted. "When taken in its entirety Jeremy Brett's *Sherlock Holmes* series stands the test of time as the definitive telling of the stories, the later episodes underscoring Brett's courage as he faced personal tests that shattered his emotional and physical well-being. I would argue that it is that very human element in Brett's portrayal that makes his Holmes so breathtakingly accurate, compelling and poignant. Holmes denied his humanity and in so doing became more vulnerable as a human being, exposing deep character flaws and weaknesses. In Brett, we not only see but feel those shortcomings and something deeper too, each person's ultimate struggle to find his or her place in life..." (Amazon.com) "He certainly included more of the man's moods and manners than any other actor I can remember in the part. He ran the whole gamut from the deepest gloom to the most outrageous laughter." (Study in Celluloid)

Cardboard Box

Jeremy

Sherlock Holmes – By courtesy of Marcus Tylor

As Jeremy was forced to retire from his ten year commitment to Holmes through his recurring ill health, the plaudits came in and they were overwhelming: "Everyone from the scriptwriters, actors and directors, to the production team, the designers, costumers, and make-up people, not forgetting the cameramen, technicians and grips – even the secretaries – all have made a contribution. But if anyone deserves special praise, it has to be Jeremy Brett for being like a father figure to the whole company. He created a family feeling in which everyone wanted to do well. The success was very much theirs." (Michael Cox) "Jeremy had a touch of genius and was a master craftsman in the art of television. I miss him as a dear friend and the theatre has lost one of its finest actors - too soon." (Rosalie Williams)

"Jeremy Brett's Holmes is fundamentally faithful to Doyle's original. The magnetism of his bravura performance attracts a new generation of admirers to the stories. In the years to come it will be his face they see when they read the books, and it will be his voice they hear when the great detective speaks. A part of the monument, that is the legend of Sherlock Holmes, now has Brett's name indelibly carved on it." (Gunner54.wordpress.com) "I have no doubt that few performances in the history of television drama were as perfect, as passionate, exquisitely realised and definitively delivered as that of Jeremy Brett's extraordinary Sherlock Holmes." (Stephen Fry) The critics universally agreed, "Jeremy Brett's Holmes offers a combination of fidelity and audacity. Everything he does can ultimately be justified by chapter and line from Conan Doyle's stories, but he has taken liberties with the myth so confidently that he has also, over the last decade, taken possession of it, and displaced the literary Holmes." (Kevin Jackson. The Independent) Jeremy's visit to America after filming *The Adventures* an admirer paid him the same extravagant compliment that Booth Tarkington paid William Gillette, the first actor to play the part: *"I would rather see you play Sherlock Holmes than be a child again on Christmas morning!"* Praise does not come much bigger than that. Jeremy was always humble in response to the accolades. *"It's utterly thrilling! I mean it is wonderful. I can't tell you how happy it makes me. I'm thrilled to bits. Who would have thought that Jeremy Huggins of Warwickshire, the son of a soldier, would win such an accolade. It's absolutely bizarre!"*

He was often finding explanations for his own success rather than seeing it as a reward for his hard work; in reality a ten year commitment which took away his freedom to live his life as the zestful Jeremy Huggins, the romantic with love his *raison d'etre*. The dark brooding nature of Holmes worried him and he found it a very difficult part to play; the man consumed his very existence at times and the demands were enormous. *"I suppose the only thing that I do have in common with Sherlock Holmes is enthusiasm: mine is for life, his is for work. He's dead when he's not working – in that sense, he is like an actor. But I've had a fascinating time playing him. I said to Dame Jean Conan Doyle: 'I've danced in the moonlight with your father for 10 years.' The moonlight, not the sunlight – Holmes is a very dark character."*

Jeremy admitted that playing the part had made his career. He may have had a long and successful career on the stage and in television, but it was Holmes which had made him a household name. He always responded to the plaudits with sensitivity and grace. *"I've always felt that I could never, ever convey to anyone the thinking man's Holmes. Then this gentleman, who was giving a party, suddenly stood up and said, 'Thank you Mr Brett for giving us the Thinking Man's Holmes'. And I had to step out, to cry. I was so touched. That is what I thought I would never be able to do."*

So many people commented and still comment on the fact that Jeremy never received an award or any official recognition for such a remarkable piece of acting. BAFTA had received the nomination of Jeremy's name year on year from Ellen Dean, the make-up artist throughout the series and herself a member of BAFTA, until finally she had resigned in disgust at the lack of recognition. In spite of the snub, Jeremy was proud of his achievement, *"Now I think it's time to take lots of rest and think about what I actually want to do myself, not about what other people want me to do. But it will be a great comfort to me as I get older to be able to look back and say: 'Oh well, I did Holmes and I managed to do it not completely badly'"*

"Bless your darling hearts. Much love, keep warm and dry and if you see him whisking around the corner – you know who, SH – then wave, because that's all you'll see of him. Bless his darling heart, isn't he wonderful, streets ahead of us – still." (Jeremy Brett 1995)

Mad Dogs and Englishmen 1995 - Film

Mad Dogs and Englishmen

When he had filmed the final episodes of *The Memoirs*, Jeremy's career hadn't quite come to an end. There were just a couple of times more when he was in front of the camera. **Mad Dogs and Englishmen (aka. Shameless)** 1995 in which he played **Tony Vernon-Smith** was a film outing which seems so very different from *Sherlock Holmes* that it is surprising that he considered taking part in such a shocker. He told a reporter it would be an interesting opportunity to make a difference to the way people viewed drugs.

The critics were not kind. "Gorgeous Antonia (Elizabeth Hurley) is on a dangerous downward spiral caused by an addiction to heroin when she meets Mike (C.Thomas Howell), a tough drifter who helps her score more smack. Although they're not attracted to each other initially, Antonia and Mike eventually give in to their growing feelings for each other. But this leads to a dilemma: How does Mike help the woman he now loves kick her addiction. Shrieks in the night will soon disturb the sleep of well-heeled residents accustomed to the quiet life in Knightsbridge's Rutland Gate. It's all in the cause of a new thriller: *Mad Dogs and Englishmen*. The 'shriekers' will be actresses Elizabeth Hurley, devotee of décolletage, and Paula Hamilton while Joss Ackland and Jeremy Brett will be responsible for their distress." (Bloke made good. The Times (London, England) 16th June 1994)

In the role of a drug dealer, Jeremy was able to make the necessary impact and Geoff Brown of *The Times* thought he was most entertaining. "His presence was certainly felt amongst the drug users, laying around waiting for their opportunities to gain the hit." Jeremy would once more get the opportunity to play the death scene and very dramatic it is too. *"I've never played anyone quite so bad as this before... He manipulates other people's feelings... disgraceful. I must admit that playing villains is great fun. I enjoyed playing Dracula some years ago – but that was a different sort of villain. Someone as monstrous as Tony Vernon-Smith deserves to get his comeuppance."* He hoped *"people would feel fairly sick when they see the film. Entertained but nauseated.... it will give people a really good scare."*

Moll Flanders 1996 - Film

Moll Flanders

The final role for Jeremy would be a cameo part as the Artist's father in **Moll Flanders** filmed in 1994 and released 1996. A review of the film in the *LA Times* celebrated the quality of his performance and the director's feelings of loss at his death, "Fans who mourned Brett's passing should make a point of seeing *Moll Flanders*... as it features his final performance. Based on the Daniel Defoe novel, directed by Pen Densham and shot four months prior to Brett's death, the film finds the 61 year old actor cast as an effete aristocrat who opposes his son's marriage to a reformed prostitute. Though he appears in just one scene, Brett is, as always, incandescent. Seeing Brett again in *Moll Flanders*, one is reminded of how much we lost with his passing and how much he left us with his performance as Holmes." (The L.A. Times 1996)

"The Artist is played by Joe Lynch as a fierce, sad young man who drives himself to a higher standard than he can achieve, and is inspired by Moll's own defiant standards. The movie's most amusing scene comes when the Artist proposes marriage. Moll insists on meeting his family, and they drive down to a vast country estate. A friendly man comes running up to greet their carriage. 'Is that your father?' asks Moll. 'You're not going to get off that easy,' the Artist says, as the man opens the gate and doffs his hat... The film's melodramatic ending sorts everything out in the approved style of the genre, but the movie is really better than that, a portrait of a woman who endures, thinks, and survives." (Roger Egbert.com)

In Jeremy's hands the Artist's real father is a much more formidable foe than the one Moll expects and as he wields his authority in matters of money and inheritance there is no hope of any acceptance from the family that Moll would very much like to be part of. As tragedy strikes again she is once more on her own. Jeremy was exhausted by his one scene and a day's work in Ireland and was happy to return home.

The scenes in the family home were filmed in the beautiful Blue Dining Room at Bantry House in southwest Cork overlooking Bantry Bay. Belonging to the Earl of Cork it is a particularly fine example of Georgian elegance with magnificent Italian gardens. Jeremy had stayed at the house during filming and is remembered as a very welcome visitor

More Luverly Than Ever – My Fair Lady

Jeremy as Narrator for More Luverly Than Ever – My Fair Lady

Manic Depression Fellowship 1995 - Charity Appeal - Radio 4

Manic Depression Fellowship

Just a couple of days before he died of heart failure at his home in Clapham on 12th September 1995, Jeremy made a very touching appeal on behalf of the **Manic Depression Fellowship** on Radio 4. The week's appeal was introduced by Myra Fulford for the Fellowship in a celebrity appeal for funds for the charity founded to bring support to sufferers of the disease. Jeremy had spoken to Myra on the telephone and offered his services in his own inimitable fashion, "*Darling, use me!*" in order to have maximum impact.

His surprise admission of his personal suffering from manic depression began in a tentative fashion, "*I have been diagnosed as manic depressive and I need to remind you that I am a successful actor before admitting to having a severe mental illness.*" As he gained in confidence his rich baritone voice became stronger, "*I have coped with these mood swings from the age of 16. But being a member of a profession where being a little mad helps, my moods were tolerated... When I was admitted to the Maudsley Hospital in 1986, I was so depressed I couldn't relate to anything or anyone around me. All I could do was to lie down with my fists clenched to my face.*"

There was little understanding of the illness and that was evident in the way the press dealt with the news. When Jeremy was first hospitalised for the treatment of depression in 1986 the tabloid newspapers had a field day. "They came up with some of the most atrociously insensitive headlines, stories and cartoons that I have ever had the misfortune to see." (Jean Upton in The Gazette) The situation must have been very difficult for Jeremy to deal with when he emerged from hospital to take up the role of Holmes for *A Sign of Four*. However, he would always find the courage and the will to pick himself up and start again: he appeared in another twenty episodes of Holmes and even took his interpretation onto the stage in both London and the provinces.

When he had finally retired from the series he had little chance of receiving the necessary insurance to return to the stage. Due to his ill health he was unable to accept the role of Scrooge at the National Theatre with a script by John Mortimer or a season at Chichester. But he did appear in the documentary *Playing the Dane* about Shakespeare's *Hamlet* and gave an erudite and revealing assessment of his interpretation. He also appeared as Narrator for the relaunch of the remastered film *My Fair Lady,* as the only surviving member of the cast. He was forced to give up alcohol and cigarettes. He told the story of ringing Dame Jean Conan Doyle to tell her the bad news. "You poor boy," she said. "You must come round and we'll open a very good bottle of wine." "*But I'm afraid I'm not allowed alcohol,*" he told her. She chuckled lightly, "*Neither am I,*" she said. His final days were noted for his laughter, the inspirational courage and the dogged determination which he had shown throughout his extraordinary life.

Linda Pritchard - Afterword

Richmond Theatre

Even before reading this book I knew what an extraordinary actor Jeremy Brett was, but having now read the full list of parts, I am more in awe at the diversity of his acting skills. He was truly a star and I am so glad I got to know him and to see him perform live.

The first time I saw Jeremy was in September 1988. He was appearing as Sherlock Holmes opposite Edward Hardwicke as Dr. Watson in the play, *The Secret of Sherlock Holmes* at the Richmond Theatre in Surrey. The theatre, originally known as the Richmond Theatre and Opera House is a beautiful theatre built in 1899, which was most fitting for the play as it was set in Victorian times.

Jeremy oozed confidence on stage. He was the ultimate showman who loved a live audience. He was able to show off his skills that he had honed over many years as a performer. He was quick to ad lib when something went wrong, which is exactly what happened during one stage performance. Jeremy as Sherlock was holding a magnifying glass to inspect a watch Dr Watson had given him to test Holmes's power of deduction. After Holmes deduces a lot of information from the watch, Watson, unable to accept that so much detail could be gathered, becomes annoyed and believes that Holmes is a charlatan and has looked into his background. Holmes hands Watson the magnifying glass and as he does so, the glass falls out. As the glass hits the stage and begins to roll away, the audience holds its collective breath. Edward then promptly puts his foot on it. Jeremy without a second thought said, "Watson, well done, your reactions are quick, but you fail to see the obvious," and then carries on with the next line from the script, which was to explain to Watson how he had uncovered so much evidence. Naturally the audience gave a big round of applause.

The Secret of Sherlock Holmes, ran for a year in London before going on a nationwide tour of the UK, and with each performance, Jeremy would add something extra, either a mannerism or extra dialogue. Edward Hardwicke enjoyed working with Jeremy a lot but said to me once, "You had to have your wits about you when playing opposite Jeremy. When he went off script, I would have to be ready to add words of my own. Sometimes, he would go a little too far and afterwards I would tell him off, but he just gave one of his mischievous smiles and promised not to do it again. But Jeremy being Jeremy always did." Having seen, *The Secret of Sherlock Holmes* many times, I can vouch for everything Edward said. I never got bored of watching the show over and over again as no two shows were exactly the same.

What was most disappointing and unjust about Jeremy's role as Sherlock Holmes was the lack of recognition he received. At the very least he should have won a BAFTA. The only excuse for the lack of any award was best summed up by Kevin Jackson in *The Independent*: "It might seem perverse to suggest that Jeremy Brett's portrayals of Sherlock Holmes are in any way underrated: The Granada series has, after all, proved immensely popular not just in Britain but in more than 70 other countries (it's huge in Japan), and reviewers regularly commend its leading players, its high production values, strong supporting casts, atmospheric scores and so on. Moreover, only die-hard Basil Rathbone fans will resist the proposition that Brett makes a fine Detective, and Edward Hardwicke an engaging Dr Watson. But even the most widespread acclaim can still be insufficient if it does not try to address its object, and popularity is not quite the same thing as recognition. The case of Mr Brett is a little like the case of the purloined letter in the Poe tale which was one of the influences on Conan Doyle. In Poe's yarn, a filched letter was overlooked precisely because the villain had not hidden it at all. Similarly, Mr Brett's true brilliance is overlooked not because no one says that he is splendid but because everybody does."

Of course Jeremy was not only brilliant at playing Sherlock Holmes. I admired his portrayal of William Pitt the Younger, Captain Ashburnham in *The Good Soldier*, Maxim de Winter in *Rebecca*, Bassanio in, *The Merchant of Venice*, D'Artagnan in *The Three Musketeers* and the list goes on and on.

Jeremy had a presence when he acted. One was always drawn to watch him, even when he was not the main speaker in a scene. A look, or a stare would speak volumes and a smile would almost tell you what he was thinking. The fact he is remembered and admired more than 20 years after his death says a lot about Jeremy as an actor and a man.

My own personal memories of Jeremy, was his storytelling. He would tell me moments in his life that had me laughing so much that my sides hurt, or concerned at how he managed to survive an incident. On one such occasion he told me that some poor woman ended up in a ditch in her car when they were both trying to outmanoeuvre each other at speed on a country lane. Before I continue I would like to add that the women was not hurt and they sorted things out amicably thanks to Jeremy's charm. It seems he pulled up alongside the lady at a set of traffic lights. He looked across and thought she looked attractive, but at the same time, his foot pressed heavily on the accelerator. The lady looked across, saw that his was the better car and assumed Jeremy was showing off and was going to speed off when the lights changed. As the lights turned green she took off like a bat out of hell leaving Jeremy still admiring her beauty. He went after her hoping to ask her out for a coffee, but soon realised she had no intention of letting him pass as she moved the car from side to side. He saw this as a challenge and took the next opportunity to overtake. However, the lady lost control and ended up with the car in a ditch. Unhurt, she got out of the car and chastised him for his bad driving. Jeremy pointed out that it was her car in the ditch and not his. Before the lady could further the argument, he explained how her beauty had caused him to hit the accelerator pedal and that he was only chasing her down for a coffee. I asked him if he ever got that coffee. The answer was no, but he did get an apology and a radiant smile.

After listening to this story I was glad Jeremy no longer drove. I was never really sure why he stopped driving. It may have been because of his illnesses but it never bothered him as he enjoyed trips on the bus. His favourite journey was from Clapham into the heart of London. The bus took passengers over the Battersea Bridge and Jeremy would always sit on the top deck so he could see across to the Albert Bridge, which was his favourite bridge in London. For me the bridge is best seen lit up against the night sky.

Another of Jeremy's favourite places was Richmond Park. It is the largest of the capital's eight Royal Parks and is a National Nature Reserve. I would drive there and we would very slowly make our way around the park to see who was quickest to spot the herds of Red and Fallow deer. I remember those days with such happiness. Later we would make our way to a local café for coffee where I reminded Jeremy that it was the nearby Richmond Theatre where we first met. Afterwards, we would buy French loaves from the local bakery and consume them that day with different cheeses we had also bought.

On another day we would do crosswords together and one crossword we did was huge and took days to do. We did not have access to the internet in those days so we relied on our memories. Of course some memories take a while to emerge, hence the reason it took us so long. I made the huge mistake of writing in the final question thus finishing it. I thought Jeremy would be pleased that it was finally complete, but no, he wanted to be the one who answered the last question. I wouldn't say he sulked; it was more him telling me off over the next few hours. From then on I made sure Jeremy always answered the last question.

Living with Jeremy was never dull. He would make a drama out of the smallest incident. One afternoon, I returned to the flat a couple of hours late after visiting a friend. When I walked in, Jeremy was on the phone, pretending to be talking to the police about my disappearance and whereabouts! *"Oh, thank you, officer. You needn't bother with the patrol car and the all-night search. She has just walked through the door. But I do appreciate your willingness to put the entire force on the alert."*

Jeremy was a magical person and incredibly courageous in his battle with bipolar and heart disease. Even in the darkest moments of his illness his strength of character shone through.

He deserved a knighthood for the way he inspired and helped people with the same illnesses. Although he never won any awards, he remains an inspiration to so many people. More than twenty years after his death, he is remembered for his ability to overcome so many obstacles in order to realise his dreams.

Linda Pritchard 2017

Jeremy on Clapham Common

Tributes to Jeremy

"He was a very wonderful man, a giant of the profession and a great friend to those that loved him. Above all, he was quite unique and there will never be anybody like him again, at least for me in my lifetime. He was a best friend perhaps to too many and I shall always miss him..." (Sue Locke)

"Offstage, Brett was a complex and dazzling personality, whose life was troubled with manic depression. His life and work encompassed strange opposites – he seemed to find pride in treachery, freedom in front of the cameras or on stage in a theatre, beauty in ugliness, and saintliness in sin. But he was, above all, a loving, sympathetic and wise man and a true star of British theatre." (Patrick Newley in The Stage)

"In 1988, when I had had no acting work for some time and felt more than adequately rested, I took a job as a day person at Wyndham's Theatre, where the *Secret of Sherlock Holmes* was about to open... Once the first night had passed successfully, it was arranged that the cast would go out for a meal after the show with everyone who was working backstage. At the restaurant, Jeremy was exuberant and flamboyant, but he was the first to leave. When at the end of a thoroughly enjoyable evening, the rest of us asked for our bills, we were told that he had paid for us all. The following night he accompanied all the front of house staff to the same restaurant and paid for their meal. This seemed to me an extraordinary act of generosity, and I will always remember him not only as a very fine actor, but also as a delightful and warm hearted human being." (British Newspaper Archives)

"He was a sweet person, and in some ways a sad person. He switched between great gaiety and moods of depression – but never on the set. This was the extraordinary thing. When he was working, he was bubbling with joy and enthusiasm and drive. And it's funny – I think Sherlock kept him alive in some ways." (Rosalie Williams)

"We were on location somewhere and he serenaded me at a restaurant table in the middle of a very crowded restaurant in the evening... He wasn't taking the mickey, it was absolutely serious as only Jeremy could be serious in a situation like that... suddenly his voice was floating out all over this restaurant, and he improvised this song all about me and my beautiful wife and my beautiful son. I was absolutely crimson with embarrassment. But it didn't make me love him any the less." (David Burke)

"He was charming. He was the only actor who has played Sherlock Holmes who took the trouble to get in touch with me and to come and see me. All along, he would ring me up and ask my opinion. Jeremy was trying to do his very best to be faithful to my father's stories." (Dame Jean Conan Doyle)

"Jeremy's favourite outfit in which one usually found him was a black cashmere sweater and white cotton trousers. One day I was arriving at the studio and Jeremy was getting out of a taxi. As he leant forward to pay the cabby, the waistband of this particular much-laundered pair of white cotton trousers parted company with the legs, which fell to the floor. Jeremy then struggled into Wardrobe where his laughter could have been heard in Liverpool. Whenever I think of him - I think of him laughing. I cannot pay him a greater compliment than that." (Edward Hardwicke)

"Whatever the conversation was about, it would have ended with Jeremy's motto, *'Onwards and upwards!'* It's hard to think of a simpler expression of his attitude to life or a better clarion call to remember." (Michael Cox in Sherlock Holmes Gazette Tribute to Brett)

"The funeral was a moving occasion, and all Jeremy's close friends came, and one realised what a loved person he was. People had found comfort and warmth in his company, even though at times he behaved most strangely, for his manic depression was so severe that there were periods when he went completely out of control. But throughout all his troubles not one friend had deserted him. This must illustrate the magnetic qualities that he possessed... generous, warm, larger than life, and often quite crazy. A light went out in many people's lives when he died, for he was one of life's true originals." (Anna Massey)

'Twenty (five) years on and Jeremy still touches and inspires the lives of many. He is and always will be the special being that made us all realise that our dreams and wishes can be accomplished. I still marvel how he overcame heart disease and Bipolar and had an incredible career. Even in the darkest moments of his illness, his strength of character shone through. His inner strength and spirituality is a shining light that has reached out to us all. God bless you Jeremy.' (Linda Pritchard 2015)

Appendix

Jeremy may not have received a BAFTA for his definitive performance of Sherlock Holmes but he was assured of the highest award from two different sources. His name appeared as a nominee on the New Year's Honours List but at his untimely death was regrettably removed. Another award was the Legion of Honour by the French Government which Jeremy accepted at the 10th anniversary celebration of the Granada series in Manchester.

"Unfortunately, our dear Jeremy died too early. The presentation of a medal requires several steps. After our own request to the French State, it is mandatory that the recipient accepts the decoration. This is what Jeremy did in May 1994, in public, at the closing night of the series in Manchester.

It was then necessary to organize an official ceremony in France (or at the French Embassy in London). Jeremy's state of health and the administrative formalities delayed the event which could not take place before the disappearance of the recipient. The rank would have been that of knight. In a way, the Canon has been respected since Sherlock Holmes, too, receives a letter informing him that France has decided to award him the Legion of Hono(u)r, but, nowhere in Watson's texts, we have an account of the official presentation of the decoration (a scene that we see however in the Granada series).

Having alerted the French State about this aspect of the life of the hero of Conan Doyle, I had the mission, as president of the Sherlock Holmes Society of France, to choose a living person worthy of receiving the detective's medal in our reality. For me, there was only one man: Jeremy Brett, the one who embodies (still today) Sherlock Holmes to perfection. After Jeremy's death, I still had the right to offer this medal to another "living" person, but I chose not to do it in memory of the one who remains unique in his embodiment of the character of Sherlock Holmes." (Thierry Saint-Joanis President of the SSHF, BSI)

Sources and Bibliography

I am most grateful to Linda Pritchard for her invaluable help in so many different ways and especially for the photographs, the majority of which are taken from Jeremy's personal collection. Without her encouragement this book would never have been written. Thanks are also due to Severine Rubin for her valued advice, to Louise Cotulla for her recommendations, to Marcus Tylor for his friendship, to Gretchen Altabef and Bonnie MacBird for their encouragement. Grateful thanks are also due to National Theatre Archives, BBC Written Archives, BFI Archives for access to unpublished films and Manchester Library Archives for access to the Library Theatre Archives. The Times Archive Database and British Newspaper Archives have proved to be invaluable sources. The ProQuest Observer/Guardian source have been used and the BBC genome site. Not all the sources are so clearly marked so in these cases I have given the author the credit. If anyone can provide the missing information to enable full credit, then that would be much appreciated.

Sources for Chapters 1 and 2

(1) Kenneth Passingham in The Real Jeremy Brett... Alive and Well in Exquisite Poverty TV Times 1973

(2) The Black Box Interview Case of the Driven Man

(3) Jeremy in Desert Island Discs

(4) Judith Simons in When I was a Child in Woman's Weekly

(5) Jennifer Selway in Women in my Life in Woman's Weekly

(6) Berkswell Miscellany V

(7) Graham Bridgstock in A simple case of toxophily, Holmes! Daily Mail 1989

(8) To Rosemary Herbert in The Armchair Detective Vol. 18 1985

(9) War Memories BBC News

(10) www,jeremybrett.info

(11) Marion Willison in When the Lights Went Out

(12) Patrick Hill in Nightmares that haunt Holmes star

(13) Younger Brother, Younger Son: A Memoir by Colin Clark

(14) Danny Danziger. 'The Worst of Times: I'd rather my nose had been smashed at school.' The Independent 12th October 1992

(15) Adrian Furness in Why Sherlock Holmes nearly killed Jeremy Brett TV Times 1994

(16) TV Quick

(17) On the Wings of Paradise by Linda Pritchard

(18) The Television Sherlock Holmes by Peter Haining

(19) Interview with Kay Gardella

(20) The Stage 1954

(21) The Holmes Front: The Evening Standard 1991

(22) Jeremy Brett: A New Confidence Hayman The Times 1973

(23) The NPR Interview with Leanne Hanson Youtube

Bibliography

And that's Not All –The Memoirs of Joan Plowright: Weidenfield and Nicolson 2001

A Study in Celluloid: A Producer's Account of Jeremy Brett as Sherlock Holmes by Michael Cox: Rupert Books 1999

Alec Guinness: The Unknown - A Life by Garry O'Connor Sidgewick and Jackson 2002

Anthony Hopkins by Michael Feeney Callan

As Luck Would Have It My Seven Ages by Derek Jacobi: Harper Collins 2013

Bending the Willow by David Stuart Davies

Between Two Worlds by John Middleton Murry: Jonathan Cape 1935

Circulating Genius by Sydney Janet Kaplan: Edinburgh University Press 2010

Chichester 10: Ten Years of Chichester

Confessions of an Actor by Laurence Olivier: Weidenfield & Nicolson 1982

Gielgud's Letters by Richard Mangan: Weidenfield & Nicolson 2004

In Search of John Gielgud A Biographer's Tale by Jonathan Croall: Herbert Adler

John Gielgud Matinee Idol to Movie Star by Jonathan Croall: Methuen Drama

Knight Errant Memoirs of a Vagabond Actor by Robert Stephens: Hodder and Stoughton 1995

Laurence Olivier On Acting pub. Weidenfield & Nicolson London 1986

Letters of Noel Coward edited by Barry Day pub. Methuen/Drama

Letters to Katherine Mansfield by John Middleton Murry: Constable 1983

Maggie Smith A Bright Particular Star by Michael Coveney: Gollancz 1992

Mystery! A Celebration by Ron Miller KQED Books 1996

Number 10 The Private lives of Six Prime Ministers: Sidgewick & Jackson London 1982

Olivier at Work compiled by the Royal National Theatre

Secret Dreams A Biography of Michael Redgrave by Alan Strachen: Weidenfield and Nicolson 2004

Sherlock Holmes On Screen The Complete Film and TV History: Titan Books 2011

Telling Some Tales by Anna Massey: Hutchinson 2006

The Annotated Sherlock Holmes by William S. Baring-Gould 1978

The Central Book by Lolly Susi

The Illustrated Sherlock Holmes Treasury by Arthur Conan Doyle: Avenal

The Jeremy Brett – Linda Pritchard Story by Linda Pritchard: Rupert Books 1998

The Man Who Became Sherlock Holmes The tortured mind of Jeremy Brett by Terry Manners: Virgin 1997

The Motorcycle Diaries Ernesto 'Che' Guevara Harper Perennial 2004

The National Theatre Story by Daniel Rosenthal: Oberon Books 2013

The Road is Long by Linda Pritchard: Amazon Kindle

The Television Sherlock Holmes by Peter Haining 1994

The Living Unknown Soldier by Jean Yves Le Naour 2005

BBC genome site - bbcgenome.co.uk Brettish Empire site - brettish.com

jeremybrett.info.co.uk   Kaleidescope Database

Radio Times TV Times 1955-1995

Scarlet Street Numbers 8, 20, 21, 22

Stage Struck pub. Penguin BFI Sight and Sound Magazine Archives

British Newspaper Archives: The Stage Magazine, lllustrated London News

ProQuest Historical Newspapers: The Observer, The Guardian, New York Times

www.ingramcontent.com/pod-product-compliance
Lightning Source LLC
Chambersburg PA
CBHW080722230426
43665CB00020B/2580